Military Transition

by Angie Papple Johnston

for
dummies

A Wiley Brand

Military Transition For Dummies®

Published by: **John Wiley & Sons, Inc.,** 111 River Street, Hoboken, NJ 07030-5774, www.wiley.com

Copyright © 2021 by John Wiley & Sons, Inc., Hoboken, New Jersey

Published simultaneously in Canada

For general information on our other products and services, please contact our Customer Care Department within the U.S. at 877-762-2974, outside the U.S. at 317-572-3993, or fax 317-572-4002. For technical support, please visit https://hub.wiley.com/community/support/dummies.

Wiley publishes in a variety of print and electronic formats and by print-on-demand. Some material included with standard print versions of this book may not be included in e-books or in print-on-demand. If this book refers to media such as a CD or DVD that is not included in the version you purchased, you may download this material at http://booksupport.wiley.com. For more information about Wiley products, visit www.wiley.com.

Library of Congress Control Number: 2021943089

ISBN 978-1-119-82478-7 (pbk); ISBN 978-1-119-82480-0 (ebk); ISBN 978-1-119-82479-4 (ebk)

SKY10028972_081121

Contents at a Glance

Table of Contents

Introduction

Military transition is inevitable; everybody has to get out sometime. Whether you've served one enlistment contract (or fewer) or you're retiring with 30 years (or more) of service under your web belt, it's probably been a while since you were part of the civilian workforce, got to sleep in past 0530 regularly, and lived your life without a direct line supervisor keeping an eye out for you. You may never have had a civilian job or been to college, paid rent without receiving housing allowance first, or dealt with the U.S. Department of Veterans Affairs or a private health insurance company, either.

The U.S. military discharges around 200,000 people every year, give or take, and if you're reading this book, your number is likely almost up.

I won't sugarcoat it: Leaving the military is hard. I've done it myself. That's true even if you don't like your job, your unit, your branch, or the military in general. But the good news is that you can do it, and you may even be *good* at the whole civilian thing. You're equipped with a unique skill set, body of knowledge, and set of habits that will help you get up to speed in no time.

About This Book

Military transition isn't a one-shot deal. It's a process that starts when you decide to request a release from active duty, to resign your commission, or not to renew your enlistment contract and ends when you finally become accustomed to working or going to school in the civilian sector.

Military Transition For Dummies is the one-stop resource you need to get a handle on your entire transition process. I explain everything from your options to continue military service and the transition programs available to you to finding a job, enrolling in college, getting used to working with civilians every day, and tapping into the benefits you're entitled to receive as a veteran of the U.S. armed forces. I even cover where to go to find help when life starts firing lemons at you on burst.

This book also contains answers to your big questions — including things your branch's transition programs may not cover — such as

>> What if I'm being forced out or involuntarily separated?

>> Are any mental health resources available for transitioning service members?

>> What can I do to prepare a year before I separate from the military? Six months? One month?

>> Are employment programs worth the time?

>> How do I write a resume for a federal job? What about a civilian job?

>> How do civilians get health insurance?

>> How do I negotiate a salary when I'm used to being paid according to my rank?

>> What happens if I want to use my GI Bill?

>> How can I fit into the civilian workforce or assimilate at school?

Now, what this book isn't: It's not full of war stories or complaints about the military, a bunch of stuffy and outdated advice that doesn't apply to your generation of warriors, or a glossed-over guide that tells you the grass really *is* greener outside your installation's perimeter fence. It's not a retention tool for the armed forces, either. None of those things are going to be useful to you — and I like you, so I want to make sure you have a good grasp on what's in store for you when you say goodbye to the military for good. Plenty of books out there focus on how you can write a resume or get a job after you get out of the military, but this book is more than that. It's a well-rounded look at your entire transition from military life to a civilian future so you're prepared for whatever life throws your way. And as a civilian, that's going to be plenty.

Foolish Assumptions

While writing this book, I made a few assumptions about you — namely, who you are and why you picked up this book. I assume the following:

>> You're getting out of the military (or at least weighing your options).

>> You want to find out what the transition process is like.

>> You want to position yourself for success after you have your discharge paperwork in your hot little hands.

Icons Used in This Book

Throughout this book, you find icons that help you pick up what I'm laying down. Here's a rundown of what they mean:

This icon alerts you to helpful hints. Tips can help you save time and avoid frustration before, during, and after your transition out of the military.

This icon reminds you of important information you should read carefully.

This icon flags actions and ideas that may cause you problems. Often, warnings accompany common mistakes or misconceptions people have about the transition process.

This icon points out information that is interesting, enlightening, or in-depth but that isn't necessary for you to read.

This icon points out samples of things like emails you may send or references you may receive.

Beyond the Book

In addition to what you're reading right now, this book comes with a free, access-anywhere Cheat Sheet that includes tips to help you prepare for military transition, including how to apply for federal jobs, advice for assimilating to civilian culture, and resources that can provide additional help when you need it. To get this Cheat Sheet, simply go to www.dummies.com and type "Military Transition For Dummies Cheat Sheet" in the Search box.

Where to Go from Here

You don't have to read this book from cover to cover to successfully transition out of the military. I suggest that you begin with Chapters 1 and 2 to familiarize yourself with the military transition process and the resources your branch has provided for you. Then, you can start exploring the chapters that are most relevant to you. Depending on where you are in the transition process, you can gather intel on how to get a job, how to enroll in school, or how to take advantage of the benefits you're entitled to receive when you complete your term of service in the military.

If you've already decided what your next steps will be, you may want to skip entire chapters. For example, if you already have a college degree and you're only interested in getting a job, skip ahead to Part 2; if you need some guidance on adjusting to civilian life, fast-forward to Part 4. If you're in crisis, call 800-273-8255, text 838255, or visit www.veteranscrisisline.net to connect with someone immediately.

Not sure where to start? Grab your favorite drink, kick back on the sofa, and start at the beginning.

1
Getting Started with Saying So Long

Strategize your exit from the military so you're set up for the best possible outcome.

Explore your options — and what's available to you — with your branch's transition assistance program.

Get all your proverbial ducks in a row by stacking the odds in your favor before Uncle Sam gives you your walking papers.

Take a good look at the processes you're required to complete when you officially want to leave the military.

Figure out how your discharge type will impact your ability to claim benefits and decode your DD-214 or other discharge documents.

IN THIS CHAPTER

» Exploring your options for extending your commitment

» Avoiding common pitfalls servicemembers can make

» Circling around special circumstances that can affect your transition

Chapter **1**

Kicking around the Idea of Moving to Fort Couch

A round 200,000 people leave military service every year. Some choose to pop smoke after one enlistment term, others decide to head for the door after a long and illustrious career, and many are somewhere in between. Veterans of the U.S. Army, Air Force, Navy, Marine Corps, and Coast Guard all go through similar transition processes — and similar adjustment-to-civilian-life processes, too.

Depending on how long you've been in the military, the "outside world" may have undergone some pretty significant changes. You may have been insulated from many of those changes during your time in the military (the military is generally slower to change than society is). But even if the world hasn't changed much since you joined the military, one thing's for sure: *You have.* You're not the same person you were when you shipped out for basic training or joined your branch's officer training program. You've seen more of the world, experienced things that the vast majority of Americans haven't, and probably learned quite a bit about leadership (including how *not* to lead) along the way.

Making the decision to get out is a big deal, and it's not something you can take lightly. Ask yourself the following:

>> Are my family and I prepared for the big changes that come with leaving the military?

>> Do I have enough money stashed away to make it in the civilian world?

>> Does my military job have a civilian counterpart?

>> How hard is it to get a job?

>> Am I ready to start at the bottom rung of the ladder at a new job?

>> Am I eligible for education benefits, and how do I access them?

>> What kind of safety net do I have?

Saying "I'm ready to get out, and I can handle what's on the other side" is easy. But in reality, navigating life with a DD-214 in your hand isn't always that black-and-white.

Looking for Greener Grass on the Other Side of the Perimeter Fence

Making the switch between military life and civilian life can throw you off balance — just like it did when you first joined the military. The difference is that when you joined, you had an instant support network. First-line leaders and higher-up supervisors were there to tell you what to do every second of every day. You didn't have to deal with uncertainty; everything you did was carefully mapped out by your chain of command. Most of the rest of your military career likely followed the same path, even if you made it to the top of the chain. You knew your mission, and you executed it. You had predictable pay, a housing allowance, and all the free healthcare you could handle (and then some).

But the civilian world doesn't have those built-in fail-safes. You're on your own unless you actively seek out help getting from Point A to Point B, and that may be something you're not used to doing. You won't have a first-line leader you can call with personal problems — civilians tend to keep work and home life separate — and you won't have access to many of the resources that the military provides, such as free doctor's visits and prescriptions, housing and subsistence allowances, or extreme predictability on a day-to-day basis. In the military, you had to show up in the right place, at the right time, in the right uniform. In the civilian world, you find many more variables.

Still, for most people, getting out of the military is exciting. It definitely has a honeymoon period, one that can stretch long past your first day of terminal leave. You'll sleep in and probably even take great pleasure in rolling over in bed and thinking about your friends who are stuck doing physical training at 6:30 a.m. (you may as well start getting used to the a.m./p.m. thing now) while you still get to lounge for a while. You may stay in your pajamas all morning, hit the golf course when you'd normally be starting work, or even binge-watch your favorite streaming shows. It's going to feel like a vacation.

But eventually, it *stops* feeling like a vacation. Your final paycheck comes in after you reach your expiration of term of service (ETS) or end of active obligated service (EAS or EAOS). Hopefully by that time, you're working at a job you like, you're enrolled in school, or you're otherwise on the path to your future success.

Mapping the terrain: What it's really like "out there"

The civilian world is a lot different from what you're used to, whether you were in for 3 or 30 years. Although your job may be the biggest culture shock you face, you'll have to account for the following:

>> **Housing:** As a civilian, you're not required to move every two to three years, so you need to find permanent housing and get used to staying put. Civilians consider school zones, job opportunities, cost of living, and a wide range of other issues before making a move.

>> **Finances:** Civilians don't typically get a housing allowance, free health insurance, or a Thrift Savings Plan. Most can quit (or be fired) at any time, so they have very little predictability in pay. They have no emergency relief fund they can tap into for a loan, either. Government assistance programs do exist (I cover those in Chapter 21), but when you're a civilian, you're largely on your own.

>> **Relationships:** If you go back to your home of record, your relationships with the people who have been there the whole time may have changed. Your family dynamics may also change. You don't automatically get military-issue friends, either.

>> **Communication:** Your communication style has almost undoubtedly changed since you joined the military. You most likely use direct, to-the-point, and often blunt communication techniques (sometimes peppered with colorful language) because you *had* to during your time in the service, but that can frustrate civilians and cause you a whole host of problems.

Conducting a risk assessment with facts and statistics

A 2019 Pew Research Center study found that returning to civilian life poses unique challenges that many vets are unprepared for. The study looked at 2,371 veterans who served during a pretty wide range of conflicts, beginning with the Vietnam War and the post-9/11 period. Here are some of the results:

» Among post-9/11 veterans, 16 percent said their reentry to civilian life was "very difficult," and 32 percent said it was "somewhat difficult." Those getting out of the military during the post-9/11 period, which includes you, reported having a harder time readjusting than Vietnam and Korean War-era veterans did.

» If you've served in combat, know that 46 percent of your peers said that readjustment to civilian life is difficult.

» Fifty-three percent of vets who had traumatic experiences had a difficult time, and 66 percent of vets diagnosed with PTSD categorized their experience as difficult, too.

» People have a harder time adjusting to civilian life if they

- Experienced a traumatic event

- Were seriously injured

- Are a post-9/11 veteran

- Served in combat

- Knew someone who was killed or injured

On the other hand, you're more likely to have a smoother transition if you're a college graduate, you understood your mission while you were in the military, you were an officer, or you're extremely religious.

TECHNICAL STUFF

The U.S. Department of Labor keeps tabs on the number of veterans who have jobs based on how many file for unemployment benefits. You can check the current statistics at www.dol.gov/agencies/vets/latest-numbers and keep an eye on trends if you're interested. Likewise, the VA tracks the number of homeless veterans by using the U.S. Department of Housing and Urban Development's Point-in-Time, or PIT, count. If nothing else, the numbers you see there will motivate you to start your job search and line up new housing *long* before you get your DD-214.

I'm not telling you this info to freak you out. I'm telling you so that you don't get out there and crash and burn. If you know what to expect, you can create a battle plan that ensures you're as successful as possible. I know people whose best life choice was to get out of the military — and I know people who should've stayed in and built themselves a better foundation. I want you to use your time in the military as a stepping stone to bigger and better things, whether you were a short-timer or you gave the military several decades of your life.

Deprogramming and reprogramming for civilian life

When you joined the military, your drill instructors chased the "civilian" out of you and instilled military values, traditions, and knowledge in its place. A 2012 study published in the journal *Psychological Science* found that former service-members are less "agreeable" than their civilian counterparts are (including those who never spent time downrange or suffered trauma). The good news? That's probably great for your career, provided that you can harness the personality traits you acquired in the military and use them to your advantage. However, you still need to make a few adjustments to make your transition easier. Table 1-1 shows the major differences between military and civilian life.

TABLE 1-1 **Major Differences between Military and Civilian Life**

	Military	Civilian
Pay	You get basic pay, special pay, and tax-free status when deployed to a combat zone; you don't get overtime pay.	Your pay is often higher than military pay, especially if calculated hourly; you do get overtime benefits.
Housing	The military provides it (either through a physical location or money to pay for rent or a mortgage payment).	You pay for your own housing.
Food	You get a basic allowance for subsistence in your paycheck to offset the cost of food, or free food at military dining facilities; you have commissary shopping privileges.	You pay out of pocket; you may have commissary shopping privileges in some circumstances.
Healthcare	You get free, full coverage for you and your immediate family.	You pay for some or all of your own health insurance, plus copays.
Gym membership	You get free membership, complete with expert fitness trainers.	You pay out of pocket.
Life insurance	You get free life insurance.	Some employers have life insurance plans you can pay for.
Education	Education is free while you're in using Tuition Assistance; certifications and credentials are available free. You're eligible for the GI Bill when you leave the military.	You pay out of pocket (unless you use your GI Bill).
Vacation	You get 30 days of paid leave per year.	Your vacation time varies.
Work hours	You're on call every day.	You generally work 40 hours per week for full-time.
Retirement	You get paid a pension after retirement.	Many companies offer no pension.

You may have to actively try to tone down your military bearing and assimilate yourself back into society. You're used to a high OPTEMPO and a lot of structure, and that just isn't part of everyday civilian life. Some of the most common "reprogramming" challenges veterans face include the following:

>> Relating to people who don't know, or don't understand, what you've experienced in the military

>> Reestablishing a role in the family you left behind when you joined the military

>> Joining or creating a community outside the military, which provided a ready-made community for you and your immediate family

>> Getting used to an environment with less structure than the military provides

>> Providing basic necessities without housing allowance, cost-of-living adjustments, or free health insurance

>> Adjusting to a different pace, both in life and at work

TRANSITION AND YOUR FAMILY: HOW HARD IS IT?

Transitioning out of the military affects your whole family. Your immediate family has its own routines and traditions, and leaving military service disrupts them. Your spouse will have to find a new job (just like after a PCS move), your kids will change schools, and you'll all have to adjust to living in a new location, even if you've been there before. Your spouse has probably heard the phrase "Bloom where you're planted" more often than they care to recall, but it's never more important than when you leave military service. Your family will have to look for or create a new community wherever you land, make new friends, and maybe even develop new hobbies that don't have anything to do with the military in order to stay engaged. Each of you may also have to reestablish your roles with other parts of your family, including parents, siblings, and grandparents. Talking to your family about transition long before you start the process is a good idea. Establish your expectations, including who will take care of household tasks, when you'll get a job or start school, and how your day-to-day lives will change. Many resources are available to spouses and children of family members, including help through Military OneSource and the other sources I describe in Chapter 2, which your family can use for up to a year after transition.

WARNING

Any Veterans Administration rep can tell you that a staggering number of veterans go to the VA because they have no money, no job, and no permanent housing plan. Learning all the skills necessary to thrive outside of the military can be hard — especially if you've been in the military your entire adult life — but it *is* possible. Like the military tells you, proper planning is the key. Take advantage of your branch's transition program, which I cover in Chapter 2, to get yourself ready for the civilian world and position yourself for success.

Extending Your Commitment: Waiting a While Longer to Decide Is Okay

If you're not 100 percent positive that you want to get out of the military, *don't*. Kicking the can down the road is totally fine. Talk to your retention NCO about your options. You may be able to reenlist for a short period, or you may choose to reenlist for another full contract so you have more time to get your affairs in order. (If you're being forced out, see the later section "Involuntary separation: Getting out when you have no choice.")

Often, reenlisting comes with its own benefits. You may be able to choose your next duty station and potentially even get a retention bonus if you're in a critical job that's facing shortages.

You may consider *reclassifying* — changing jobs to see how you like a different version of your branch — or taking another career path, such as becoming a warrant officer or a commissioned officer. Or you can switch branches altogether. That option seems drastic, but if you're not fully prepared to dive back into the civilian world, it may be the best choice for you. You can find out about the jobs available in other branches by visiting their recruitment websites:

>> GoArmy.com

>> AirForce.com

>> Navy.com

>> Marines.com

>> GoCoastGuard.com

If you want to change branches, you need to write a letter explaining your intentions to switch and complete a DD Form 368, Conditional Release, with a recruiter from the branch you want to join. If your branch agrees to release you, the recruiter will help you get into your new branch. You may have to attend a familiarization course (such as when you join the Air Force after being part of another branch) or attend that branch's basic training (such as when you join the Marine Corps). And if you get out and panic, you may still be able to join another branch; it's just a little extra work and a lot of extra anxiety, which you can avoid if you make the choice *before* you ETS. (Go ahead — ask me how I know.)

TIP

In 2021, the Army permanently adopted the *Career Intermission Program*, or CIP. The CIP allows you to take up to a three-year break in service to do whatever you'd like in the Individual Ready Reserves, or IRR. Under the CIP, you earn two-thirtieths of your basic pay, keep your healthcare benefits and commissary privileges, and carry forward up to 60 days of leave when you return to an active status. For every month you spend in the CIP, you incur a two-month obligation to the Army.

WARNING

If you get out of the military and want to get back in later, after a break in service, it may not have room for you — at least not at your previous rank. You may have to take a reduction in rank when you have a break in service, and if it's been too long, you may have to go back to basic training or retake the course that prepared you for your job. You'll also have to reapply for your security clearance, which may expire when your contract with the military does.

Extension programs

The military has explored short-term extension programs, particularly in light of unemployment conditions in the civilian world, in the recent past. Your branch may offer a program that allows you to extend your contract for six months to a year so that you can reevaluate your options. However, some branches restrict these special short-term contracts to people in critical jobs or in certain locations — and you probably won't be eligible for any kind of reenlistment bonus for a short-term extension.

THE ARMY'S INTER-SERVICE TRANSFER PROGRAM

The Army has a special program for servicemembers from other branches. The Inter-Service Transfer program, or IST, allows you to leave one branch to join active duty service in the Army. If you're an E-1 through E-4, you retain your grade and the same date of rank, but if you're an E-5 or above, U.S. Army Recruiting Command evaluates whether you're eligible to keep the same pay grade and DOR. You're subject to the Army's Prior Service Business Rules, which are managed by Human Resources Command, and you must pass a MEPS physical, as well as meet Army height and weight standards. This program is available to enlisted servicemembers, warrant officers, and commissioned officers.

Considering a stint in the Guard or Reserves

When I talked to my retention NCO about ETSing from the Army, he suggested that I join the National Guard or Reserves. I scoffed, thinking that I'd never be a "Weekend Warrior." But he was on to something: The reserve components are still part of the military, and they can help ease your transition into the civilian world.

Like active duty, the reserve components require enlistment contracts. You can negotiate your contract with your retention NCO or a recruiter in the reserve component you choose to join. These are your options:

>> Army National Guard

>> Army Reserve

>> Air National Guard

>> Air Force Reserve

>> Navy Reserve

>> Marine Corps Reserve

>> Coast Guard Reserve

Each of these branches is subordinate to the federal government except the Army National Guard and Air National Guard. If you're in a reserve unit, the department that heads your component (the Army, Air Force, Navy, or Coast Guard) can *activate* you (call you into active service) at any time. It also means that if you move to another state, you don't have to find a recruiter and rejoin the reserves; you can do a lateral transfer instead. On the other hand, both Guard components answer to state governments *and* the federal government, which means that the governor of your state can activate you to respond to local or statewide emergencies, and the president of the United States can activate you to participate in federal missions.

Additionally, when you're part of a reserve component, you may have access to full-time military jobs through Active Guard Reserve (Army), Air Reserve Technician (Air Force), or Full-Time Support (Navy and Marines) employment. Each of these programs has its own requirements, and you must be a member of the reserve component before applying.

YOUR INDIVIDUAL READY RESERVE OBLIGATION

Everyone who joins the military signs an agreement to be part of the Individual Ready Reserve, or IRR, for a term of eight years. If you get out of the military after fulfilling your original contract, you're still technically at the U.S. government's disposal. For example, if you sign a three-year contract, complete your tour, and ETS, you're automatically transferred into the IRR and remain in it for five years. While in the IRR, you're required (you signed a contract, remember?) to provide your branch's human resources command with your current contact information, attend muster duty when ordered to, promptly respond to all official military correspondence, and be ready to be involuntarily mobilized in a time of national crisis. Essentially, you're part of a pre-trained pool of talent that the military can fall back on in an emergency.

TECHNICAL STUFF The reserve components are different from civilian auxiliaries, such as the Civil Air Patrol, Coast Guard Auxiliary, Merchant Marines, and Marine Corps Auxiliary. They're also different from state guard units, although some states' guard units train at the same armories and use the same facilities that reservists and members of the National Guard use.

And in case you were wondering, I *did* join the National Guard after a few months' break in service. It was a good stepping stone, and although it was vastly different from my time on active duty, my prior active Army service opened a lot of doors for me.

Sweeping for Common Landmines That Can Derail Your Plans

When you make the decision to get out of the military — or, if you're like many people, you waffle back and forth about getting out until your retention NCO tells you to do your business or get off the pot — you have to maintain your military bearing and avoid common pitfalls that many about-to-be-free servicemembers fall into. Make sure you don't

>> **Make a decision too hastily:** Unless you've done your homework and you're certain you're prepared, getting out may not be the little slice of heaven you think it will be. Be sure you're completely prepared to find a job, pay for health insurance, secure housing, and take advantage of the benefits available to you before you make a final decision.

>> **Fail to square away your military paperwork:** Listen to the old, salty E-7s in your unit when they tell you to document everything in your medical files, put away some cash, and get all your military awards, decorations, and certifications entered into your records.

>> **Burn any bridges:** Now is not the time (nor is *any* time) to go into your commander's office and tell them just how much you hate your unit. Likewise, be careful not to burn bridges with anyone you come across. In fact, you should use this time to establish and build up your connections, which I cover in Chapters 3 and 9.

>> **Blow all your money:** Save your money before you get out of the military; you're going to need it. There's no such thing as a free lunch in the civilian world. Everything costs money, from paying for rent and doctor's appointments to buying professional work clothes and filling up your tank to sit in traffic. (You think the gates are bad? Wait until you get on the expressway during rush hour.) That may mean swapping out the sports-car you bought after your last deployment for something more sensible, like a gently used sedan, and taking it easy when you're on terminal leave. Unless you've been saving your pennies for a decade to take that Hawaiian vacation, put it on the back-burner for now.

>> **Drop the ball on finding a job and securing housing:** Try to line up a job and place to live before you get your DD-214. These are things you should start doing six months to a year before you get out of the military. Be realistic and realize that a minimum wage job isn't going to get you a penthouse in Manhattan; lack of an MBA and a business plan will probably prevent you from getting a small business loan; and staying with your parents or your in-laws is probably a less-than-ideal housing plan. You have to build your own safety net in the civilian world, and it's not as easy as you may think.

Even if you do make a few mistakes, your proverbial goose isn't cooked. You can rebound, but it's easier to avoid these problems from the start. The better-prepared you are, the smoother your entire transition and readjustment process will be.

Preparing for a Relaxing Retirement

Retiring from the military definitely has its perks. You get BX/PX and commissary privileges for life, you have a great healthcare plan, and you get a steady paycheck until you go toes-up. But before you can claim those well-earned benefits, you have to take on a few additional responsibilities. First, you have to submit your retirement request and wait for your branch to approve it; then, you need to set your sights on retirement-specific transition programs. As a soon-to-be retiree, you get to take advantage of your branch's Transition Assistance Programs up to two years before you get out.

Your branch likely has a wide range of retirement-specific programs available. For example, the Army's Retirement Services (soldierforlife.army.mil/ Retirement) requires you to attend a retirement planning seminar and provides additional retirement planning briefings and guides.

Involuntary Separation: Getting Out When You Have No Choice

Sometimes you have no way around it: Your military career ends without your consent. Regardless of the reason, *don't panic*. You can still prepare for your future and use your remaining time in the military to your advantage. You may even qualify for severance pay or unemployment benefits on your way out the door.

Breaking down the types of involuntary separation

Uncle Sam can show you the door for myriad reasons, whether you're an enlisted servicemember, a warrant officer, or a commissioned officer. Involuntary separation boils down to two main types: administrative and punitive. *Administrative discharges* are for things such as force reduction, violations of the Uniform Code of Military Justice (UCMJ) that don't require a court-martial, and failure to meet standards. *Punitive discharges* are punishments, such as when a servicemember is sentenced to discharge after a criminal conviction.

Here's a short (and incomplete) list of things the military can involuntarily separate you from service for:

>> Failure to adapt to the military

>> Bad conduct, such as a violation of the UCMJ or civilian laws

>> Failure to meet minimum standards, including height and weight, physical fitness, failure of selection of promotion (you know it as *failure to promote*), and other types of performance shortcomings

>> Medical or health (including mental health) reasons

>> Reduction in force (downsizing)

>> Drug or alcohol problems

>> A pattern of misconduct for making multiple mistakes

Your discharge is characterized as honorable, general (under honorable conditions), other than honorable (OTH), dishonorable, or one of a handful of other classifications, which I cover in Chapter 5. OTH discharges are the most "severe" form of administrative discharge. They're sometimes given to servicemembers who have been convicted in civilian courts and those who have brought discredit upon the service.

TECHNICAL STUFF

In some cases, servicemembers can use OTH discharges like civilian plea bargains — they make deals with the military to accept an OTH discharge instead of being subjected to a court-martial.

Each branch has its own terms for involuntary separation. Your branch may call it *being chaptered,* an *admin discharge, show cause,* or *officer elimination,* but no matter what label you put on it, it ends your military career and can affect your future.

TIP

You should contact your Judge Advocate if you're facing involuntary separation to discuss your options — and for Pete's sake, don't just start signing documents because you think you must.

Finding out whether you qualify for severance pay (and how much that is)

Department of Defense Instruction 1332.29 governs who's entitled to severance pay after involuntary separation from the military. In order to qualify, your separation must be classified as honorable or general (under honorable conditions), and you must have completed at least 6 (but fewer than 20) years of service before your involuntary discharge. Head to the preceding section for more on discharge classifications. If you're in a reserve component, you must have served at least six years of continuous active service immediately prior to your separation. Some people get full involuntary separation pay, or ISP, while others get half.

Full ISP

You can get full ISP upon involuntary separation from the military only if one of the following is true:

>> You're fully qualified for retention but are denied reenlistment because of established promotion or high year of tenure policies (this bit goes for officers who decline continuation, too) or because of a reduction in force.

>> You're a commissioned or warrant officer being separated in accordance with Chapter 36 of Title 10, U.S.C. or Section 580, Section 1165, or Section 6383 of Title 10, U.S.C.

You can also qualify if you're a reserve commissioned officer or warrant officer who is separated or transferred to the Retired Reserve in accordance with Chapters 573 or 861 of Title 10, U.S.C. You must also agree to serve in the Ready Reserve of a reserve component for at least three years following your separation.

To receive full ISP, *none* of the following conditions may apply to your separation:

>> You requested the separation.

>> You declined training to qualify for a new skill or rating as a precondition to reenlistment or continuation.

>> You're an officer who has been separated for twice failing to promote, and either or both of those failures were the result of your submitting a request not to be selected for promotion, or you otherwise directly caused your non-selection through written communication to the selection board in accordance with Section 614(b) of Title 10, U.S.C.

>> You're an officer who has been separated for twice failing to promote when you were offered and declined a continuation for a period that's equal to (or greater than) the amount that would be required for you to qualify for retirement.

>> You're released for training.

>> You're eligible for retired or retainer pay.

>> You're released for performance, misconduct, or other disciplinary reasons. This item includes unsatisfactory performance (with very few exceptions, which may qualify you for half ISP) or substandard performance, moral or professional dereliction (which applies to officers), release due to execution of a court-martial sentence, being dropped from the rolls of the military service, or separation under other than honorable conditions. The following section has details on half ISP.

>> You're a warrant officer who elects to enlist after your appointment is terminated.

>> You're separated under a service-specific program established at a no-payment level by the secretary of your branch, or the secretary of your branch determines that you aren't entitled to a separation payment (which only happens in extraordinary cases).

Full ISP is 10 percent of the product of the number of years of active service and 12 times the monthly basic pay you received at the time of discharge or release from active duty or active service. Sound confusing? Math's not my strong suit, but it means that full $\text{ISP} = \big(\text{years of service} \times (\text{your monthly base pay} \times 12)\big) \times 0.1$. Here's what the math looks like if you're an E-5 with seven years of service, which means your monthly pay is about $3,200:

$3,200 \times 12 = \$38,400$

$38,400 \times 7 = \$268,800$

$268,800 \times 0.1 = \$26,880$

In this example, the military will pay you $26,880 in separation pay if you qualify for full ISP. (Check the most recent pay chart on the Defense Finance and Accounting Service's website if you aren't sure exactly how much your monthly salary is. DFAS updates its pay tables each year.)

Half ISP

Half separation pay is authorized only if you meet the time-in-service requirement, your separation is honorable or general (under honorable conditions), and you're being separated *instead of board action* for

>> Weight control failure

>> Purposes of parenting or gaining custody of a minor child

>> Reasons under the military personnel security program

>> A disability that existed before service

>> Mental or physical conditions and circumstances that don't constitute a disability

>> Alcohol or drug abuse rehabilitation failure

>> Failure to meet minimum retention standards

You may also qualify if you're being separated under a service-specific program or you accept an earlier-than-retirement separation.

Half ISP is 50 percent of the full ISP amount (see the preceding section). So if your full ISP amount would be $26,880, the military will pay you $13,440 half ISP.

Dueling with ETS as a Dual-Military Couple

If your spouse is also military, one or both of you may be due to ETS. When you both get out at or near the same time, your challenges are a little different than most people's. That's mainly because you're losing two incomes (and two housing allowances) and both have to strike out in the civilian world to make your own fortunes.

When your other half is staying in, one of the first things you need to do is go to the DEERS (formally, the Defense Enrollment Eligibility Reporting System) office with your spouse — or a power of attorney — and get a dependent ID card. When you ETS, you turn in your common access card, so your dependent ID is your ticket to getting on post and using the benefits conveyed to you through your spouse's continued service.

TIP

If you're ETSing from overseas, your spouse must fill out and file command sponsorship paperwork if you want to stick around. And if you have children or other dependents that *you* (rather than your spouse) sponsored, your spouse will have to get command sponsorship for them, too. Otherwise, the military won't pay your overseas housing allowance and you may be restricted from on-post amenities.

Making the Most out of Terminal or Separation Leave

Terminal or separation leave is like the icing on the cake. You're still being paid for your military service, but you're on leave — and when your leave is up, you're a civilian. Sleep in the first few days; you certainly earned it! But don't rest on your laurels for too long, because this time is a golden opportunity. You have *paid time off* to look for another job, find a place to live, and square away all the tasks I outline for you in this book.

TIP

If you're retiring or being involuntarily separated — provided that your discharge is honorable — you may be authorized up to 30 days of leave to find a job and a place to live. You may be eligible for transition PTDY, which lasts up to 10 days, if you can't take 30 days of leave. That's in addition to whatever other leave you have saved.

TIP

Your spouse, if you're a retiree or an eligible involuntary separatee, is authorized to take one round trip on a military aircraft without you, using space-available (Space-A) travel for house- and job-hunting. Talk to your finance office and the personnel at the flight terminal for more information on claiming this benefit.

You may be able to sell back your leave for cash if you'd rather do that than take paid time off. This option may make sense if you already have a job lined up and you're starting immediately, particularly if you don't want to wait for your normal paycheck to come in. You can only sell back leave if you're being honorably discharged or if you're an officer separating under honorable conditions. The military will only buy back up to 60 days, though, and that's a cumulative total. So if you've ever sold back leave in the past, it counts toward what you can sell back at the end of your career.

When you sell back your leave, the military pays you your base pay only. You don't get entitlements, such as BAH or BAS, in your lump-sum payment. For most people, selling back leave doesn't make sense; they make more money if they take terminal or separation leave.

TIP

You earn 2.5 days of leave every month that you're on the military's payroll. If you have 60 days of leave saved up, taking terminal leave rather than selling back what you already have may make sense. Why? Because after two months, you'll have earned five more days of terminal leave. That translates into five paid days you didn't have before, which puts extra cash in your pocket.

Considering Special Circumstances That May Affect Your Transition

Military transition is different for everyone, and you may have special circumstances that change your plans (or your outcome). Aside from the type of discharge received, some of the most common issues servicemembers encounter when leaving the military involve citizenship, divorce, owing the military money, or involvement in legal issues.

Swearing in as a citizen

I went to Basic Combat Training with a woman from Jamaica who was interested in gaining U.S. citizenship through the Army. It makes sense; people who take this route have shorter residency requirements, no state-of-residence requirement, and waived application fees. You need only one year of honorable service before you file your Form N-400, Application for Naturalization, with the U.S. government, so many people gain citizenship before their first contract expires.

If you haven't gotten around to filing your Form N-400 by the time you ETS, now is the time. Many military installations have a designated U.S. Citizenship and Immigration Services liaison (usually in the JAG office, the community service center, the Department of State family liaison service, or a similar office) who can help you through the process. You need your chain of command to fill out Form N-426, Request for Certification of Military or Naval Service, to show that you have at least a year of honorable service under your belt.

You can still apply for naturalization after you get out of the military by using an uncertified copy of Form N-426 and your DD-214. However, if your I-551 Permanent Residence Card expires shortly after you ETS, renewing it needs to be on your radar. You *must* renew your lawful permanent resident status, or you may be unable to get a job (even with military service under your belt!), buy a house, or even renew your driver's license.

Heading for Splitsville: Divorce and transition

Divorce isn't easy under any circumstances, but when it coincides with military transition, things can become a little tougher. If you divorce while you're in the military, your spouse may be entitled to some benefits, including a monthly stipend; if you divorce while you're on the way out the door, things become a little more complicated. Your best bet is to consult with an attorney in the state that has jurisdiction over your divorce. You can talk to attorneys at JAG, but they can't represent you in any civil legal proceedings; they can only give you advice.

Although you and your soon-to-be ex will lose some of the benefits associated with active duty service, your spouse may be entitled to retain some of them. Generally, an unremarried former spouse can keep their ID card and privileges if the 20/20/20 rule is satisfied. The rule requires at least 20 years of marriage, 20 years of military service, and 20 years of overlap of the marriage and the military service. Additionally, if you're a retiree, your spouse may well be entitled to some of your pension.

WARNING

Don't fall for the myth about having been married for at least ten years, either — your spouse may be entitled to part of your pension even if you were married only a short period of time. (The ten-year myth probably comes from the 10/10 rule, which says that if you were married for at least ten years and have ten years of overlap between the marriage and military service, your spouse's pension payments will come directly from DFAS. If your situation doesn't satisfy the 10/10 rule, you'll be the one responsible for making payments.)

WARNING

You can't tell your spouse to give up their military ID card or take it away yourself. Only the U.S. government has that authority. Likewise, you can't prevent your spouse from accessing military benefits available to all other spouses, including base or post access, even if you're in the middle of a divorce, and even if you know that your spouse will lose those benefits in the future. Your spouse's dependent status is between them and the government, so don't get in the middle of it.

Child custody is another matter, and you should certainly talk to your attorney about your options. Your custody arrangement will be subject to the laws of the state that has jurisdiction over your case. And no matter what else you do, *don't take advice from barracks lawyers.*

Making good on military debt

Whether you borrowed money from your branch's community service organization or you owe the Central Issue Facility several hundred dollars for a Kevlar helmet that someone jacked (I talk about the only thief in the military in Chapter 4), having an outstanding balance may hold up your ETS process. You have to pay what you owe before you can clear.

If you owe DFAS because you were overpaid at any point during your career, you need to know that the Pentagon can send your debts to collection (and put your credit score at risk). DFAS is in charge of other types of debt as well, although not those related to your branch, such as clothing and tactical gear issuance. You may be able to ask DFAS to waive your debt by filing DD Form 2789, but it can't clear debts you owe to

>> Army and Air Force Exchange Service

>> Defense Intelligence Agency

>> Department of Veterans Affairs

- » Department of Defense Education Activity
- » Environmental Protection Agency
- » Health and Human Services
- » U.S. Coast Guard

For the most part, you must pay *all* your military debt before you can ETS. That's why each branch makes you go around your installation and collect signatures from every organization you could possibly owe money to — even the library, where they'll cross-check your ID card and dependents' names for late fees on books and video games. However, in some situations, you can negotiate payment plans with individual organizations.

WARNING

If you're currently signed for anything in the military, whether it's a set of night-vision goggles, a cage full of M-50/M-51 pro-masks, a truck, or an entire arms room, get someone else to sign for it as soon as you start the ETS process. Get copies of the transfer paperwork, too. If nobody will sign for it, go up your chain of command until the issue is resolved. Regulations in all the branches address "command supply discipline" and require someone to maintain responsibility for all military equipment.

Being part of a military investigation

Being part of a military investigation can change your ETS plans. Naturally, if you're not the *subject* of the investigation, you can simply participate in it when asked and go about the business of outprocessing. Normally, the military can't extend your contract without your consent, but during an active investigation in which the military suspects you of a crime or violation of the UCMJ and has an "eye toward prosecution," it can keep you under its umbrella to follow through (and, if applicable, punish you). If the investigation centers on you, you probably aren't going anywhere until it's resolved. That's true whether you're subject to non-judicial punishment for a UCMJ violation or you're court-martialed.

If you're convicted in court-martial proceedings, your term of service may even be extended while you serve your sentence. The military uses three types of court-martial, and each has the ability to extend your contract for the duration of your trial and punishment:

- » A *summary court-martial* can put you behind bars for 30 days, reduce you in pay grade to E-1, reduce your monthly wage to one-third, and put you on 45 days of unconfined hard labor.

>> A *special court-martial* can send you to jail for up to a year, reduce you in pay grade to E-1, reduce your monthly wage to one-third for six months, put you on hard labor under restriction, and finally hand you a bad conduct discharge.

>> A *general court-martial* doesn't have a maximum sentence; it depends on the offense. However, the military has the ability to sentence you to life in prison with hard labor, and it does reserve the right to use the death penalty.

Picking up civilian criminal charges

Civilian criminal charges can throw a wrench in your ETS plans. After the civilians are through with you, the military may have a chance to prosecute you, too. In a case like that, the military can extend your contract without your input in order to investigate you and use non-judicial punishment (such as an Article 15) or try you through a court-martial.

If you're suspected of or accused of a crime, your best bet is to seek qualified legal advice (barracks lawyers don't count) before anyone — civilian or military — has a chance to question you.

REMEMBER

A civilian conviction, even without a subsequent military conviction, can change the type of discharge you receive, taking you from honorable to other than honorable with a few taps of a keyboard. With a subsequent military conviction through a court-martial, you may even be looking at a dishonorable discharge.

Chapter 2

Diving into Transition Programs

G etting out of the military is a huge deal, and it's something that the Department of Defense has only recently seemed to care much about. Just a generation ago, the military would release veterans into the wild and hope for the best. Although the DOD is a big bus to turn around, it's made some incredible progress in helping servicemembers during and after transition, including the creation of the Transition Assistance Program.

The *Transition Assistance Program* (TAP) is a combined effort by the Department of Defense, Veterans Employment and Training Service, Department of Homeland Security, and the Department of Veterans Affairs. DOD Instruction 1332.35 requires each of these agencies to pitch in to help prepare you for life outside the main gate. Within a five-day window, you get briefings on the types of 9-to-5 jobs (and others) available, guidance on creating a resume and finding gainful employment, info on veterans benefits you may be eligible to receive, and money management tips you can use for the rest of your life.

The DOD TAP is designed to provide you with a basic level of understanding. If you want — or need — more help, it may be available to you through your branch, but each branch is only *required* to administer TAP. The Department of Defense says that retirees must start transition assistance as soon as possible during the 24-month period prior to retirement; all other servicemembers must start as soon as possible during the 12-month period before the anticipated discharge date.

TIP

DoDI 1332.35, Section 5.3(a)(j) says that the military's responsibility is to "Release eligible servicemembers during duty hours to complete the TAP and exempt from normal duty for the full 24-hour period of each workshop or briefing day and the 12 hours immediately preceding and following each workshop or briefing." Do what you will with that information.

Getting in the Trenches with Your Branch's Transition Program

The following list explains what each transition program is called and where you can go to start meeting your requirements:

>> **The Army Transition Program, SFL-TAP:** The Army's Soldier For Life Transition Assistance Program, or SFL-TAP, provides transition assistance to eligible soldiers who have at least 180 days of continuous Title 10 active-duty service (except those in training status). Nearly every active-duty military installation, CONUS, and OCONUS has SFL-TAP Centers.

>> **Air Force Transition Program:** The Air Force Personnel Center runs the Transition Assistance Program for its servicemembers. In the Air Force, TAP is administered locally at your Airman and Family Readiness Center.

>> **Navy Transition Program:** The Navy used to call its program Transition GPS, but these days, it's plain old TAP. Sailors use the Fleet and Family Support Center to access transition assistance programs.

>> **Marine Corps Transition Program, TRP:** The Marine Corps' TAP is called the Transition Readiness Program. It's divided into three pillars: Transition Readiness Seminar, Marine for Life Cycle services, and Career Services and Advising. You can attend the courses at Marine Corps Community Services.

>> **Coast Guard Transition Program:** The USCG's Office of Work-Life runs TAP for Coast Guard personnel. To participate in the program, you must contact your Transition/Relocation Manager, or TRM, to schedule your seminars.

You can also access the TAP core curriculum online with CAC access through your branch's website or without CAC access through the U.S. Department of Labor's website. Get connected to your branch's TAP and stay up-to-date on the most current transition assistance program information at www.dodtap.mil.

TECHNICAL STUFF

Each branch puts its own spin on the program to help servicemembers bridge the gap between military and civilian life. Under DOD instruction, each is permitted to tailor the program to meet its members' needs and reflect the branch's culture. That's why the Army, for example, calls its program Soldier For Life, and why the Marine Corps refers to your entire career as the "Marine For Life Cycle."

Checking in with the Curriculum of Transition Programs

The Department of Defense-wide Transition Assistance Program requires you to kick off your military transition with a mandatory pre-separation assessment and individual counseling and then attend a one-day pre-separation seminar and a three-day TAP core curriculum program. You don't have to attend all the sessions back-to-back. You can spread them out over the course of your remaining time in the military, and you're allowed to attend each program more than once.

The first part of your TAP process includes a pre-separation or transition counseling. This individualized counseling, conducted by a TAP official, covers all the requirements outlined on DD Form 2648. Your counselor asks you several questions, and you complete a self-assessment exercise to identify areas where you need a little extra help.

The three-day core curriculum, which gives you a springboard for your transition, includes the following:

>> **A pre-separation brief:** Gives you an overview of your transition and veteran benefits, such as education assistance, the GI Bill, employment help, and medical benefits.

>> **Resiliency training:** Covers stress management, considerations for families, support systems, the value of working with a mentor, and special issues you may overlook during the transition process. Essentially, the resiliency training is designed to connect you with agencies and organizations that can provide you with support and guidance.

>> **Individual transition plan preparation:** Requires you to complete a personal assessment like the one pictured in Figure 2-1 so you know exactly what special considerations you need to address before you leave military service.

>> **Employment Fundamentals of Career Transition:** Involves a five-and-a-half-hour course that explains how you can weigh your career options, learn about civilian employment, and discover the fundamentals of the employment process. (Check out Part 2 of this book to find out more about getting a job in the civilian sector.)

>> **Military-to-Civilian Job Skills Crosswalk:** Involves a 45-minute course that helps you identify your skills and explains how to translate them into civilian credentialing you can use to get a civilian job. (The Army calls it the MOS Crosswalk; the Air Force, Navy, Marines, and Coast Guard call it the MOC Crosswalk.)

>> **Financial Planning Support:** Involves a three-hour course that gives you a look at how transition will impact your finances. This block of instruction also gives you budgeting tips and financial advice that, if you use it (and if everything goes to plan), prevents you from going flat-broke after you get out.

>> **A VA benefits briefing:** Lasts about four hours. This brief describes various benefits you may be entitled to from the Department of Veterans Affairs, explains services available at the VA, and covers things like finding a place to live, staying healthy, and connecting with your community when you become a veteran.

Your spouse or caregiver can attend classes with you as well. Additionally, most of these modules are available online, and spouses and caregivers are welcome to take them at any time.

Section I. Identify Post-transition Personal/Family Requirements

A. Taking Care of Individual/Family Member Needs

❖ Identify individual/family needs such as medical care, expenses, and location of potential providers.

Notes:

❖ Identify extenuating individual/family circumstances (e.g., need to provide care for elderly parents, family business, exceptional family member needs, etc.).

Notes:

❖ Assess impact of individual/family requirements on relocation options (e.g., quality of local schools, availability of medical care, spouse employment opportunities, etc.).

Notes:

❖ Evaluate your immediate post-transition housing requirements. Determine how much living space you will require to safely house yourself, dependents, and personal items. Consider whether you may need to make more than one move or need to utilize temporary storage. Contact the housing referral office to identify local and remote housing options. The installation transportation office can provide detailed information about planning the movement and storage of your household goods. Visit the VA website: http://www.benefits.va.gov/homeloans/ to get information on the VA home loan program.

Notes:

❖ Consider your post-transition transportation requirements. Determine if you have adequate reliable personal transportation to take you to and from your place of employment of school. Evaluate your commuting options and whether you need to purchase another vehicle(s) for your spouse and/or dependents. Identify your post-transition transportation expenses to include: purchase costs, vehicle registration, insurance, maintenance, fuel, etc. If you are disabled, determine if you are eligible for assistance in purchasing a vehicle and/or automotive adaptive equipment by visiting http://www.warms.vba.va.gov/regs/38CFR/BOOKB/PART3/S3_808.DOC.

Notes:

• What person or persons do you go to for advice, personal counsel and/or mentoring when facing a difficult challenge or decision? Will you still have access to those persons after you separate from active duty? Consider what steps you need to take now to maintain contact.

Notes:

• With whom do you spend your leisure time now? Who is a part of your social network? How did you meet them? Determine the steps you need to take to continue these relationships or establish this type of support in the community where you will live post-separation.

Notes:

B. Assessing Benefits and Entitlements

❖ *** Evaluate the benefits (e.g., additional income, promotions, leadership and professional development opportunities, travel) associated with continuing your military service in either the Reserves or National Guard (if applicable). Consider the financial impact of continued entitlements such as medical and dental coverage, life insurance, military exchange, commissary, club privileges, recreational and athletic facilities. Contact the installation/local recruiter to schedule an informational counseling session and identify potential units/positions.

Notes:

Recruiter counseling date: _____   Financial impact: _____

© *John Wiley & Sons, Inc.*

FIGURE 2-1:
Sample personal assessment for the military's Transition Assistance Program.

After completing the three-day core curriculum, you must choose one of four two-day transition tracks: Employment, Education, Vocational, or Entrepreneurship. You can participate in more than one track, and you can go to courses for the same track multiple times.

TIP

Want my advice? Go early and go often. It's paid time off work, you'll certainly learn a few things, and you'll have plenty of opportunities to ask questions.

You aren't authorized to attend TAP in person if you're discharged or released before you complete 180 days of active duty, although you can avail yourself of the virtual curriculum at any time.

WARNING

DoDI 1332.35 says that if you receive a punitive or under other than honorable conditions discharge, commanders can prevent you from attending the two-day tracks (but not the first three days of briefings).

Putting your nose to the grindstone on the Employment Track

The Department of Labor's Employment Track is for people pursuing civilian employment immediately after leaving military service. This track builds on the one-day DOL overview course that's part of the standard TAP curriculum. The program helps you do the following:

>> Identify and develop effective career goals

>> Discover how to market yourself effectively to employers

>> Learn about how employers choose to hire candidates

>> Figure out how to manage your online presence

>> Understand how to evaluate future job offers

>> Develop a private or federal resume

The primary goal on the Employment Track is to walk away with a shiny new resume that you create on your own. I cover effective resume-writing and provide a variety of examples of civilian and federal resumes you can use in Chapter 7.

Testing the Education Track

The Departments of Defense and Labor joined forces to create the Education Track, which is for people who aspire to higher education. This two-day course includes a MY Education workshop from the DOL and takes aim at helping you figure out what type of education you need for your desired career. It also teaches you to

>> Understand the vocabulary of higher education

>> Compare and contrast military and civilian education (and how you can use your military education to your advantage)

>> Choose a potential career and its corresponding degree program

>> Find the right school for your needs

>> Research admission requirements for colleges and universities

>> Find funding to cover your school expenses

After you complete the Education Track, you'll be able to create a customized action plan that helps you get into the school of your choice. Check out Chapters 15 and 16 for more information on finding, getting into, and paying for your educational career.

Getting technical with the Vocational Track

The Department of Labor's Vocational Track lets you zero in on the benefits of vocational training and how you can use that training to find a rewarding career in the field of your choice. You discover how to identify your career options based on what you're already good at (and what you have an aptitude for), and by the end of the course, you'll be able to

>> Define the concept of vocational training

>> Complete your own self-assessments on skill, knowledge, and values so you can make the right decisions for your career

>> Identify and explore career opportunities in each of the nationally recognized career clusters:

Agriculture, food, and natural resources	Architecture and construction	Arts, audio/video technology, and communications	Business, management, and administration
Education and training	Finance	Government and public administration	Health science
Hospitality and tourism	Human services	Information technology	Law, public safety, corrections, and security
Manufacturing	Marketing, sales, and service	Science, technology, engineering, and mathematics	Transportation, distribution, and logistics

>> Determine the training requirements and the types of credentials and qualifications you need to break into a new occupation

>> Identify the costs and benefits associated with apprenticeships, credentialing, or licensing

>> Develop a plan of action you'll use to accomplish your career goal

This track goes hand-in-hand with the Department of Defense SkillBridge program, which connects servicemembers to career job training opportunities. You may be able to use the SkillBridge program within the last 180 days of your service to get real-world experience through training, apprenticeships, or internships. (You can find out more about SkillBridge and how to use it in Chapter 6.)

Striking gold on the SBA Entrepreneurship Track

The Introduction to Entrepreneurship by the U.S. Small Business Association helps prepare you to own your own business upon leaving the military. It's designed to provide you with an introductory understanding of business ownership, and you may find it helpful if you're ready to hang up your shingle. When you complete the program, you can choose to further your study through online courses such as the following (B2B stands for Boots to Business, in case you're wondering):

- >> B2B: Market Research
- >> B2B: Business Fundamentals, Special Topic Tracks
- >> B2B: Revenue Readiness

The SBA also encourages participants to take advantage of resources and services the administration provides, including Veterans Business Outreach Centers, Small Business Development Centers, and Women's Business Centers.

After you complete the three-day curriculum and two-day track, you "graduate" the program — provided that you

- >> Create and turn in a criterion-based post-transition financial plan that includes information on your total household income, expenses, insurance information, household debt and assets, a financial action plan, and short- and long-term goals

- >> Register on eBenefits, the VA's online portal to apply for and manage the benefits you're entitled to as a veteran

- >> Complete the continuum of military service opportunity counseling (active component only)

- >> Complete a gap analysis or provide verification of employment

- >> Have created a completed private or federal resume if you don't have verification of employment

Head over to Chapter 14 for more information on opening a veteran-owned business and explore resources designed to help you (including funding options).

INVOLUNTARY SEPARATION AND TAP

If you're being involuntarily separated from the military, regardless of the reason, your pre-separation counseling will inform you that you're entitled to transitional medical and dental healthcare for 180 days after your discharge. It'll also include information on extended use of military family housing (subject to overseas status of forces agreements) for up to 180 days on a space-available basis and potential rental charges, your overseas relocation assistance, and excess leave for a period of no more than 30 days or permissive temporary duty for up to 10 days to carry out necessary relocation duties. Your counseling will also cover the use of commissaries; military exchanges; and Morale, Welfare and Recreation facilities.

Exploring Pre-Separation Resources

In addition to your branch's mandatory TAP (see the earlier section "Getting in the Trenches with Your Branch's Transition Program"), several resources are available to transitioning servicemembers. Various organizations have offerings to help you through the transition process, including the VA, Military OneSource, the Department of Defense, civilian veteran service organizations, and a number of private, for-profit companies. You can use these resources throughout your entire transition process, and in some cases, you can even use them after you leave military service. You can find comprehensive information on a wide range of programs at your branch's community service organization as well.

Many military-affiliated organizations provide in-person and online transition help before you leave the military. These organizations offer services such as guidance and mentorship, emergency financial support, mental health help, and a variety of other resources before, during, and after your separation:

>> **Disabled American Veterans (DAV.org):** Transition Service Program

>> **American Legion (Legion.org):** Local help, mentorship, and job search assistance

>> **American Red Cross (RedCross.org):** Emergency financial support and referrals

>> **AMVETS (AMVETS.org):** Warrior Transition Workshops

>> **Hire Heroes USA (www.hireheroesusa.org):** Online seminars for job-searchers

>> **Jewish War Veterans (JWV.org):** Mentorship, job placement, networking, and transition help

>> **Military Officers Association of America (MOAA.org):** Career consulting

>> **United Service Organizations (USO.org):** Transition programs, mentorship, and access to veterans benefits for up to 6 months after separation

>> **Veterans of Foreign Wars (VFW.org):** Separation benefits help, financial grants, and student support

>> **Wounded Warrior Project (WoundedWarriorProject.org):** Family support, peer support, connection to legal services, and career counseling

TIP

Register with the Department of Veterans Affairs before you leave military service or shortly after you have your DD-214 in-hand. The agency's Solid Start Program will keep in touch with you after you transition. It'll attempt to call you 90, 180, and 365 days after separation to check in and see whether you need help with any of the resources it provides.

Using mental health resources for transitioning servicemembers

Your mental health is extremely important — not just during the transition process but also before and after you leave the service. While you're still in the military, you can take advantage of your branch's behavioral health services. You also have access to the VA's mental health service (now and for at least a year after you leave military service). You may receive emergent or routine mental healthcare from the VA or through a VA partner.

REMEMBER

If you're a veteran in crisis, or if you're concerned about one, you can get free, confidential, and *immediate* support through the Veterans Crisis Line at 800-273-8255 (press 1). You can also send a text message to 838255 or chat online through www.VeteransCrisisLine.net/get-help/chat.

Military and Family Life Counseling

Military and Family Life Counseling provides free, confidential, non-medical counseling on most military installations. Counselors help servicemembers and their families develop coping skills; work on behavioral techniques to address challenges; assist with stress management and anger management issues; and help with crisis intervention for individuals, couples, and families. Your base or post directory should have a phone number or email address for your local MFLC team.

inTransition

inTransition (www.PDHealth.mil) is a free and confidential program available to active duty, reservists and Guardsmen, veterans, and retirees that provides mental health support and transition assistance through coaching. Its services are available to all military members, regardless of length of service or discharge status. It has no expiration date for enrollment; you can sign up years after leaving military service.

VA PTSD Treatment Programs

The Department of Veterans Affairs (www.PTSD.VA.gov) provides help to some active duty and all veteran servicemembers with post-traumatic stress disorder. Anyone who completed active military service and was discharged under anything other than dishonorable conditions (see Chapter 5 for more on types of military discharges) or is a National Guardsman or reservist who completed a federal deployment to a combat zone may use the VA's PTSD treatment service. Its programs offer education, evaluation, and treatment, including medications and one-on-one, family, and group therapy.

Military OneSource

Military OneSource (www.MilitaryOneSource.mil) provides nonmedical counseling to servicemembers, veterans, and their families. You can take advantage of confidential online or phone counseling, or you can find out whether face-to-face counseling is available to you.

Vet Centers' Readjustment Counseling

The VA's Vet Centers (www.VetCenter.VA.gov) are community-based counseling centers that provide a number of social and psychological services, including professional readjustment counseling that can help you transition from military to civilian life. Counselors on-staff are trained to deal with PTSD, alcohol and drug assessment, individual counseling, group therapy, and a number of other issues, and all the services they provide are free and confidential.

Moving Forward

Moving Forward (www.VeteranTraining.VA.gov/movingforward) is an online, self-paced program that focuses on stress management, school and family balance, relationship problems, financial difficulties, physical injuries, and adjustment issues. This self-help program is completely free and self-paced (and it has an app you can download to your phone or tablet). It includes problem-solving worksheets, helpful videos, and even interactive games you can use to gauge your own stress levels and responses.

Military OneSource's Transitioning Veterans Consultation

Military OneSource's Transitioning Veterans Consultation is a free service designed specifically for servicemembers returning to civilian life. You can (and definitely should) take advantage of this personalized transition support within 365 days of your separation; you can schedule your first of a series of coaching and counseling appointments through Military OneSource's website. Each personalized session with a trained consultant covers things like the following:

>> Goal-setting

- » Reviewing benefits you're eligible to receive
- » Getting help from the VA
- » Exploring your educational opportunities
- » Getting ready to join the civilian workforce
- » Finding and using online resources available to you

Resources for spouses

During your transition period, your spouse faces big changes, too. The military and several civilian organizations have created a number of resources to help spouses and other dependents through the process.

MySTeP

The Military Spouse Transition Program (MySTeP) is an excellent resource for family members. Run by Military OneSource, MySTeP empowers spouses to understand and use all the resources, benefits, programs, and tools available throughout the military spouse experience. MySTeP's "Stepping Beyond" program gives spouses and dependents a number of course modules and downloadable information on the separation or retirement process, outprocessing, benefit plans, relocation help, financial guidance (including access to personal financial counseling), and even mentoring through an experienced military spouse network.

TEAMS

The U.S. Department of Labor's Transition Employment Assistance for Military Spouses program, or TEAMS, is a series of TAP workshops targeted toward helping military spouses plan and prepare for a new job search. All the classes are free and open to transitioning military spouses so they can pursue their own employment goals. They're conducted virtually, so you can access them at any time through www.Veterans.gov/milspouses.

MySECO

The Department of Defense, in conjunction with Military OneSource, offers a wide range of programs and information through the Military Spouse Education and Career Opportunities, or MySECO, program. You can create an individual career plan by exploring your passions, goals, and skills; find out about education, training, and licensing options; prepare to join or return to the workforce; connect with mentors and certified career coaches you are; and find employment opportunities as you build your network.

Chapter **3**

Organizing to Prepare for Civilian Life

When I was a young cadre for new recruits, I hammered the five Ps into junior soldiers: Proper planning prevents poor performance. It's still true; if you want to be successful, you have to map out your future. That includes taking advantage of the programs the military offers you, hammering out the details on a financial plan so you land on your feet, and preparing to get healthcare coverage for you and your family. It also means taking care of your mental health throughout the transition process (such as setting up a care plan you can use when you're a bona fide DD-214-holder) and getting ready to move into a new home (specifically, a home that you find while you're still collecting that military paycheck). Nobody said that ETSing was easy, but I guarantee you that if you don't do the right things now, life after ETS will be much tougher.

TIP

Remember that you can extend your contract or reenlist for another couple of years before your contract expires. Provided you're eligible, continuing your military service while you prepare to take on the civilian world is always okay. *Don't let anyone make that decision for you.* You're the one who gets up and puts on the uniform every day, so you should be the one to choose whether continuing military service is your best option, even if it's temporary.

REMEMBER

The military offers you a five-day introduction to the civilian world through the Transition Assistance Program (TAP). You get a rundown on looking for jobs, create a working draft of your financial plan, and even take stock of your personal strengths so you can create a strip map to follow after you put your combat boots in the closet for the last time. The service Uncle Sam provides you through TAP can be incredibly valuable (plus, who doesn't want at least five paid days off work?), so take advantage of it. I cover TAP and pre-separation resources from entities such as Military OneSource, the DoD, and the VA in Chapter 2.

Replicating Your Military Records

The military runs on paperwork. You'll need copies of *all* your military records for various purposes throughout the rest of your life, so now is the time to gather them. You should have an "I Love Me" book that contains all your awards, certificates, promotion orders, and other information. Go through it and ensure it's accurate, right down to all those one-hour certifications on harassment, cybersecurity, and driving on a military installation. Make sure this portfolio matches what your personnel office has in your file and fill in the gaps if anyone is missing information that belongs in your records.

If you're still in the military and hold a common access card, you still have access to your Official Military Personnel File, or OMPF. You can use your CAC to log in to your branch's human resources website at one of the following addresses:

>> www.hrc.army.mil

>> www.afpc.af.mil

>> www.mynavyhr.navy.mil

>> mol.tfs.usmc.mil/mol

>> www.dcms.uscg.mil

Make two (or more) hard copies of every order, award, and certificate you have. You need them during the rest of the ETS process (particularly when you pick up your DD-214, which I cover in Chapter 4). You also need digital copies, so save them to a hard drive, email them to yourself, or do whatever else you need to do to keep tabs on these files.

Another item you need: copies of all your medical and dental records, which you can get from your providers. Remember, you get additional documentation when you have your final medical screening during out-processing, and that may be the most important medical documentation to keep. (I cover that out-processing physical in the later section "Managing Your Medical Past, Present, and Future.")

While you're hunting down documents, get your Joint Services Transcript, or JST. Your JST shows all your military education, including your training history, rate or rank history, correspondence course completion, college credit exam history, and certifications you've earned. Even if you're headed straight for the workforce, keep a few copies of your JST on hand. (You can get yours at jst.doded. mil/jst.) If you're in the Air Force and have attended school through a military-funded program, grab some copies of your Community College of the Air Force record as well.

If your spouse or children are part of the Exceptional Family Member Program, or EFMP, you need records of previously managed care; if your children have individualized education plans or other, similar plans, you also need copies of those.

TIP

Go ahead and schedule kids' sports physicals for the next school year, women's wellness appointments, routine dental cleanings, vision screenings, and other run-of-the-mill appointments for yourself and your family now. That way you don't have to pay for them out of pocket soon after you leave military service.

Banking on Financial Preparation for Your First Days as a Civilian

If you have terminal leave to burn, you'll keep receiving a military paycheck until your leave runs out. However, you can't kick back and relax this time around. You need to use those days and weeks to look for a job (head to Part 2 of this book to get the scoop on that phase of transition), file for unemployment, create a budget, and ensure you're fiscally prepared for your life's next chapter while you're still on the military's payroll.

TIP

If you're enrolled in the Thrift Savings Plan with the Defense Finance and Accounting Service, or DFAS, and have more than $200 in your account, consider hanging on to it. After you leave the military, you can no longer make contributions, but you can still change your investment mix, transfer eligible money into your account, and earn interest.

Save as much money as you can before you get out of the military. That doesn't mean simply skipping a morning coffee or deciding not to make a major purchase (please don't go buy a brand-new car just before you ETS). It means actively going out of your way to save your present and future self some cash. A 2019 Pew Research Center study indicated that vets who experience post-traumatic stress during their time in the military are much more likely to face financial challenges during transition, including relying on unemployment, receiving food assistance, and having trouble paying bills. And that's not saying anything about the number of veterans who could've received unemployment or food benefits and never applied or were turned down for various reasons.

Developing some frugal habits

Living without basic allowances for housing and sustenance, free healthcare, and other financial benefits may mean you need to spend less money. Use these tips to keep more of your hard-earned money:

>> **Go big on small monthly debt payments now:** If you have credit card debt, you need to know that it comes with the nasty side effect of robbing you of your future income. Interest piles up quickly, so you can protect your future self by paying down as much debt as you can now. Some experts swear by the snowball method, which says that you should pay off your debts in order from smallest to largest, but making payments on your highest-interest debt is also a smart way to shave down your future interest costs. Besides, if you pay off a credit card now, you'll have your full credit limit available to you if you encounter an emergency down the road.

>> **Be a smart grocery shopper:** The average U.S. family of four spends about $929 on groceries every month. When you get out of the military — provided that you don't retire near a military installation — you have to kiss those commissary prices goodbye, so you can expect to spend around that, too. Know what you need *before* you go to the grocery store, stick to your list, and watch for budget-busters when you shop (and maybe even spend some of that terminal leave time on clipping coupons). Think about buying generic brands when possible.

>> **Flip the script on subscriptions:** Most people have multiple subscription services, like movie and music streaming or trendy box-of-the-month clubs. If you don't regularly use those things, consider canceling. Here's one way to look at it: Is streaming a movie every few nights worth $250 a year? If you have cable television, know that on average, it costs about $1,200 a year for a standard package. That's an entire mortgage payment.

>> **Pack your lunch:** The Bureau of Labor Statistics says that the average U.S. household spends between $3,000 and $4,000 on dining out every year. If that's not a good argument in favor of bringing lunch from home, I don't know what is.

TIP

If you know that money burns a hole in your pocket, check out *Personal Finance For Dummies* by Eric Tyson (Wiley).

Creating a budget

Before you leave military service, put together a budget that gives you a look at what type of financial future you're facing without your military paycheck, housing allowance, and subsistence allowance. Use the empty budget worksheet in Figure 3-1 or your favorite spreadsheet program to create your own, remembering to account for common expenses and those unique to your situation.

Housing

	Projected Cost	Actual Cost	Difference
Mortgage or rent			
Phone			
Electricity			
Gas			
Water and sewer			
Cable			
Waste removal			
Maintenance or repairs			
Supplies			
Subtotal			

Transportation

	Projected Cost	Actual Cost	Difference
Vehicle payment			
Bus/taxi fare			
Insurance			
Licensing			
Fuel			
Maintenance			
Subtotal			

Food

	Projected Cost	Actual Cost	Difference
Groceries			
Dining out			
Subtotal			

Personal Care

	Projected Cost	Actual Cost	Difference
Medical			
Hair/nails			
Clothing			
Dry cleaning			
Health club			
Organization dues or fees			
Subtotal			

Entertainment

	Projected Cost	Actual Cost	Difference
TV streaming			
Music streaming			
Movies			
Concerts			
Sporting events			
Live theater			
Subtotal			

Loans

	Projected Cost	Actual Cost	Difference
Personal			
Student			
Credit card			
Credit card			
Credit card			
Subtotal			

Savings or Investments

	Projected Cost	Actual Cost	Difference
Retirement account			
Investment account			
Subtotal			

Pets

	Projected Cost	Actual Cost	Difference
Food			
Medical			
Grooming			
Toys			
Subtotal			

Insurance

	Projected Cost	Actual Cost	Difference
Home			
Health			
Life			
Subtotal			

FIGURE 3-1: Sample budget worksheet.

© John Wiley & Sons, Inc.

Your budget doesn't have to be complicated, but it does need to be as accurate as possible. Start by filling in your known expenses; that way, you know exactly how much money you need to make to cover everything or which expenses you need to cut to make ends meet.

REMEMBER

The hardest part of budgeting is sitting down to put your finances on paper. Sure, it may seem like homework, but it can help you keep your spending on track and enable you to free up more money that you can use to meet other financial goals. This financial planning tool can help you plan, track your habits, and save money now and in the future, so it's an important part of your transition process.

WARNING

I'm fully aware that this sounds grim, but I can't overstate how important being financially prepared to get out of the military is. Money is one of the biggest problems vets face. Though I certainly hope that isn't the case for you, I know that losing a regular paycheck and housing, subsistence, cost-of-living, and other allowances can throw a big wrench in your plans — and that if you have a plan in place to make up for that lost income, you'll fare better than your battle buddies who don't.

A 2019 Pew Research study says that 35 percent of veterans have trouble paying their bills in the first few years after leaving the military. Check out the graphs in Figure 3-2, which show some serious statistics you need to be familiar with before you get out.

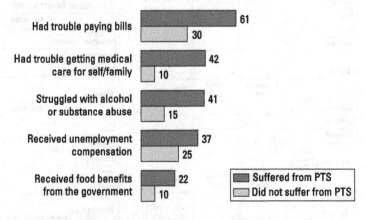

FIGURE 3-2:
Veterans in the first few years after leaving the military.

Source: Survey of U.S. veterans conducted May 14-June 3, 2019.
"The American Veteran Experience and the Post-9/11 Generation"
PEW RESEARCH CENTER

© John Wiley & Sons, Inc.

Accounting for separation/retirement pay

I had a drill sergeant who advised my whole class to "live one pay grade below your means," and that was solid advice. The same is true for your retirement pay, provided you're interested in saving extra cash for that Space-A trip to the Hale KOA or your retirement sports-car or motorcycle.

Calculating your retirement pay can be confusing. You're most likely qualified for the CSB/REDUX Retirement System or the High 36 Retirement System. Under special circumstances, you may qualify for the Blended Retirement System. You should talk to your local finance office if you're not sure what you'll receive or how much you'll get, but the following sections break down each system to give you a general overview of what to expect.

CSB/REDUX Retirement System

If you joined the military between August 1, 1986, and December 31, 2017, you qualify for the complicated CSB/REDUX Retirement System. The amount of retirement pay you receive is based on the average of your highest 36 months' base pay over the course of your career. You get a "career status bonus" after serving for 15 years, which is about $21,000 after taxes, but then you receive a reduction in your monthly payments after retirement for each year short of 30 that you fall. (If you served for 30 years, you receive 50 percent of your base pay, plus cost-of-living allowance, or COLA, for the rest of your life.) For example, if you retire at 20 years under the CSB/REDUX Retirement System, your retirement payments will equal 40 percent of your base pay from your highest-earning 36 months; if you retire at 25 years under the same program, your pension payments will equal 45 percent of your high-36.

WARNING

Your COLA amount is based on the Consumer Price Index, but minus 1 percent. A retiree under a different program may see a COLA increase of 2 percent, but under this program, you receive 1 percent. However, after you reach age 62, the 1 percent difference disappears and you receive the same COLA increase as retirees using other programs.

High 36 Retirement System

The High 36 Retirement System is available to people who joined the military between September 8, 1980, and December 31, 2017. Your retired pay depends on what you received during your three highest-paid years (that's 36 months). You receive 50 percent of your average base pay if you retire with 20 years of service or 100 percent if you retire after 40 years.

Blended Retirement System

If you joined the military after January 1, 2018, you qualify for the Blended Retirement System, or BRS. You're entitled to 40 percent of your highest 36 months' base pay after retiring with 20 years of service. The military will contribute 1 percent of your base pay to a Thrift Savings Plan, and you'll be automatically enrolled to contribute 3 percent of your base pay at the same time. (You can raise, lower, or stop your contribution at any time.) After you've spent two years in the military, the military will match up to 5 percent of your contributions. You also get a bonus at 12 years of 2.5 percent of your annual base pay at that time. If you're retiring early under the BRS, go talk to someone in your installation's finance office as soon as possible. Your payouts and program will likely differ.

Filing for unemployment

Every state in the Union (plus Puerto Rico, the U.S. Virgin Islands, and Washington, D.C.) has its own Unemployment Compensation for Ex-Servicemembers program, or UCX. This program lets you apply for benefits after you leave military service. You need your Social Security card, your DD Form 214, and probably a resume (more on those in Chapter 7) to apply for unemployment benefits. Benefits and requirements vary from state to state, with some states paying far more than others, but unemployment is a Department of Labor program that you've earned the right to use, provided that you did time on active duty, separated under honorable conditions, are actively seeking a job, and aren't on terminal leave at the time you apply. Your state's unemployment office, online or in person, can provide you with the forms you need to apply for UCX, which is a hand *up* that you're entitled to receive (even if you're using your GI Bill at the same time). Although you can't apply until your terminal leave ends, you can figure out where to go and who to talk to for this entitlement now. That way, when you leave your installation with your DD-214 in-hand, you can apply for benefits.

Exploring Employment Opportunities

The best time to start looking for a civilian job is *the day before* you decide to get out of the military. You don't have to commit just yet, especially if you're on the fence about continuing your military career, but you do need to see what's available in the civilian sector. Maybe you want to keep working for the government and build yourself a double pension, or you maybe you can't wait to see government-related work in the rearview mirror. Your best bet is to start looking at all the jobs with an open mind. It's all about keeping your options open, remaining flexible, and adapting to a new daily routine (one that doesn't involve standing in formation at 0630 and 1700 Monday through Friday). You may not find your dream job right away, and that's okay; as long as you can find a job that you can live with, you'll be in good shape to work your way toward that goal. The good news is that if you receive an honorable discharge, your military service can earn you extra points toward government employment, which I cover in Chapter 7. And even better, the Department of Defense offers a range of programs you can use to improve your employability.

Clocking into career counseling

The military has two big programs designed to help servicemembers dive head-first into civilian employment: DoD SkillBridge and VA Chapter 36. Both programs offer different benefits, so explore each and decide whether one or both are right for you.

DoD SkillBridge

You can use the DoD SkillBridge program if you're within 180 days of transition. The program matches your military training and work experience to civilian opportunities and lets you use up to the last 180 days of your service to train and learn with one of the program's partners. You continue to receive your military pay and remain covered by your military benefits while you're working in a civilian environment. SkillBridge partners offer employment in a wide range of fields, including information technology, manufacturing, transportation, civil service, retail, and energy. The catch: Release for DoD SkillBridge is mission-dependent, which means your commander must authorize your participation before you can enter into any agreement with an employment partner. However, the program is open to servicemembers of any rank, enlisted or officer, so if you can get your commander to sign off on it, this program is a great way to prepare (and maybe even land your dream job) before you get out of the military. Find out more or apply for the program at dodskillbridge.usalearning.gov.

VA Chapter 36

VA Chapter 36 (also called Personalized Career Planning and Guidance, or PCPG) provides personalized guidance and support from trained career and education counselors. Chapter 36's services include the following:

>> Career exploration

>> Resume building

>> Training support, such as locating training programs that can help you reach your career goals

>> Help finding employment

Chapter 36 is available to any service member who's six months from ETS, as well as any veteran or dependent who's eligible for an education benefit. Although you should take advantage of the program before you ETS, using it doesn't have any time constraints; whether you get out of the military today or you got your DD-214 a few decades ago, you can use the PCPG program to make a career move. And as long as you're eligible, you can use Chapter 36 as many times as you need to. You can apply for this program online at the VA's website, by mail using VA Form 28-8832, or by visiting a regional VA office or VetSuccess On-Campus Counselor.

Looking for civilian jobs that parallel your military job

Most civilian employment is a *lot* different from military service, but plenty of civilian jobs match up with military jobs. You can find some of them by using the VA Chapter 36 program (see the earlier section "VA Chapter 36") and on www.careeronestop.org, a U.S. Department of Labor website that allows you to enter your military occupational specialty, specialty code, or rating to see jobs that align with the work you did in the service. You can also get creative. Start thinking about jobs in the civilian sector that have a lot of similarities to your military role. If you were a 74D in the Army (Chemical, Biological, Radiological and Nuclear Specialist) with a couple of additional skill identifiers for biological hazards and chemical weapons, you probably earned some certifications from OSHA, such as Permit-Required Confined Space Rescue. You may be able to use those certifications to get a job in emergency management, HAZMAT removal, or a wide range of other fields.

Don't feel like you have to stick to your field, though. In some cases, finding something that's close to what you did in the military — such as combat-related positions — is tough. In that case, focus on the leadership skills and foundational knowledge you developed during your time in the military. For example, an infantry soldier can transition into corrections, civil service such as the police force or firefighting, training and development, or a number of other civilian careers that need leadership, good order and discipline, and strategic thinking. You can even find a job with the federal government working with new servicemembers, working at Range Control, or serving as a subject-matter expert for the military. (My husband swears that when he retires, he's going to get a low-stress job as a greeter in a retail store, and that's fine, too.)

Building your resume and applying for jobs

Start building your resume now; doing it correctly takes longer than you think. Gather the information you need to include; some of it will come from your "I Love Me" book (from the earlier section "Replicating Your Military Records"), your Joint Services Transcript, and your college transcripts. Write a summary about your work experience and skills and create a list of all the units you've been in. If you were only in the military for a few years, think about your prior civilian work experience; you may later want to include it on your official resume. Jot down activities you've participated in, such as clubs and societies, athletic teams and community organizations and list your education, awards, and personal interests as well. All this information goes into your first draft of your resume, which you can explore in Chapter 7.

Studying Your Educational Goals

When you're in the U.S. military, you have access to unique educational opportunities that your civilian peers don't. As long as you're in good standing, the military provides you with things like tuition assistance, the ability to take free college-level exams for free college credits, and credentialing opportunities for all the mandatory certificates you earned during your time in the service. If you plan to use your GI Bill when you get out of the military, you can get a jump on your education to save time and money later, all while you're still receiving a regular paycheck.

Using tuition assistance to get a head-start

Every branch of the military offers a form of tuition assistance to its members. Tuition assistance enables you to take college courses at the school of your choice without spending a dime (and even without touching your GI Bill benefits) while you're still on the military's payroll. Tuition Assistance, or TA, covers up to $250 per semester hour, with an annual cap. So why am I telling you this *now*? Because it's free education that'll help you in the civilian sector if you choose to remain in the military until you're really ready to get out. You also need to be enrolled in your branch's education program before you can take advantage of other benefits, like taking college-level exams for free credit, which I cover in the following section. Here are some details on each branch's offerings:

>> **Army TA:** Set up an Army IgnitEDaccount online. Then you can take advantage of the program, which allows you

- Up to $4,000 per year

- Up to 130 semester hours toward an undergraduate degree

- Up to 39 semester hours toward a graduate degree

- Up to 21 semester hours toward a certificate

- **Air Force TA:** Log into the Air Force Virtual Education Center to get access to
  - Up to $4,500 per year
  - Up to 124 semester hours toward an undergraduate degree
  - Up to 42 semester hours toward a graduate degree
- **Navy TA:** Set up a Navy College account online. With Navy TA, you get up to $4,500 per year with no semester-hour limits.
- **Marine Corps TA:** You have to complete two courses to use Marine Corps TA: Higher Education Preparation on Joint Knowledge Online and Personal Financial Management on MarineNet. Then set up an account on WebTA for up to $4,500 per year and up to two courses per semester.
- **Coast Guard TA:** The U.S. Coast Guard's TA program runs through My CG Ed, and it provides you with
  - Up to $2,250 per year
  - Up to 130 semester hours toward an undergraduate degree
  - Up to 40 semester hours toward a graduate degree

Diving into DANTES and CLEP

Head to your installation's Ed Center to take advantage of the Defense Activity for Non-Traditional Education Support (DANTES) and the completely free College Level Examination Program (CLEP). When you pass a CLEP exam, you earn college credits for it. That means if you have real-world knowledge of a subject — say, a foreign language or mathematics — you don't have to spend time or money on a college course to earn credit.

DANTES funds CLEP exams (meaning you don't pay for them) in 33 subject areas related to business, composition and literature, foreign languages, history and social sciences, and science and mathematics. These tests are available to active-duty military and reservists, as well as some eligible spouses. DANTES automatically adds your test score, pass or fail, to your Joint Services Transcript or Community College of the Air Force record. You don't have to be currently enrolled in school to CLEP a course. When you *do* enroll in college (using either Tuition Assistance or your GI Bill), turn in your JST or CCAF record to turn your CLEP scores into college credits.

TIP

Try to "CLEP out" of as many courses as you can before you leave the military.

WARNING

DANTES pays only for your first try on a CLEP exam in a particular subject. If you don't pass but want to retake a test, you have to pay for it. Additionally, some test sites that aren't on military installations charge "administrative fees," which can vary. (Taking a CLEP exam on a military installation has no administrative fee.)

Prequalifying through credentialing

You can earn certificates or credentials to use toward your civilian education or career through Credentialing Opportunities Online, or COOL, if you're still in the military. The COOL program enables you to search for credentials to earn (on the military's dime) that help you in the civilian workforce; you can get credentialed in areas similar to your current military job or in other fields — it's totally up to you. A quick search on your branch's COOL website (the Navy and Marines share one) shows you what types of credentials you can earn, how difficult they are to earn, and what agency they come from so you can make choices that will help you land the job you want after you get out of the military. You can find credentials in a huge range of areas, from becoming a certified HAZMAT practitioner or getting a commercial driver's license to becoming a certified EKG technician or certified chef de cuisine. Even if you already have a job lined up, explore your opportunities through COOL and get all the credentials you can while you're still earning a military paycheck.

Getting your feet wet with USMAP

The United Services Military Apprenticeship Program, or USMAP, helps you find apprenticeships based on your current occupation so you can get all your ducks in a row before you leave the service. USMAP has two components: formal classroom instruction and on-the-job training or mastery of competencies.

In many cases, the time you spent in Basic Training, "A" School, Advanced Individual Training, NEC, or other types of military occupational training meets the requirement for formal classroom instruction, so all that's left are work hours. These are the two types of apprenticeships you can participate in:

>> *Time-based apprenticeships* are for servicemembers who are new to an occupation and don't have much experience. Progress is measured by the number of hours spent on the job or in formal learning.

>> *Competency-based apprenticeships* are for servicemembers in the pay grade of E-5 or above who are experienced in their occupations. Progress is measured by the servicemember's ability to apply the relevant knowledge, skills, and abilities of the occupation.

After you complete all your apprenticeship hours and the U.S. Department of Labor approves and processes your report, you'll receive a Department of Labor Certificate of Completion and Journeyman card.

TIP

You can only use USMAP if you have at least 12 months remaining on active duty. Other apprenticeship opportunities may be available to you through government agencies and private employers, but unfortunately, this program is only open to people with a year left on their contracts. If you wanted to stay in the military for a couple of additional years to take advantage of USMAP and other programs, here's some unsolicited (but really solid) advice: The military takes what it wants from you. You deserve to make that a two-way street.

Certifying through civilian organizations

The military has several partnerships with civilian organizations that may enable you to get a leg up on your post-military certifications. For example, at Fort Huachuca, the Army partners with a government agency out of Fort Hood to train servicemembers in Security+. You can get information on these types of courses and certifications at your installation's Education Center — simply ask the information pro at the front desk for civilian certifications being offered on your base or post.

Lining up your GI Bill

With a discharge under honorable conditions, the GI Bill is yours for the taking — you earned it. You can apply for your GI Bill benefits online, on paper, or in person at a Department of Veterans Affairs office. Depending on the type of GI Bill you have, you may qualify to receive a basic allowance for housing, or BAH, on top of tuition; you may even qualify for grants and other forms of financial aid that help you pay for books and other school expenses. You can start the application process while you're still on active duty. Flip to Chapter 16 to read more about your GI Bill benefits and how to use them.

Managing Your Medical Past, Present, and Future

With the exception of retirement, leaving military service means giving up military healthcare. Although you may not be that impressed by a prescription for ibuprofen and the medically sound advice of "rub some dirt on it," plenty of civilians would jump at the chance to have free healthcare coverage, low- or no-cost prescriptions, the ability to visit a doctor for any old ache or pain that pops up, and high-quality preventive care. If you retire from the military, you have access to various TRICARE programs and VA medical care, but if you simply ETS, withdraw your commission, or REFRAD, those options aren't available to you unless you can show that you have conditions that developed during or were aggravated by your military service. That means you need a documented history of seeking treatment for those conditions, and you must show the DOD that as a result of those conditions, you're entitled to medical coverage through the Department of Veterans Affairs.

You may be eligible for VA healthcare if you served on active duty and

>> Were discharged under honorable conditions

>> Enlisted after September 7, 1980, or entered active duty after October 16, 1981

>> Served 24 continuous months or the full period for which you were called to active duty, unless you were discharged for a disability caused or made worse by your active-duty service; were discharged for a hardship or "early out"; or served before September 7, 1980

TIP

If you're a reservist or member of the Guard, you must have been called to active duty by a federal order, and you must have completed the full period for which you were ordered to active duty. You don't qualify for VA healthcare if your only active-duty status was related to training. However, you may qualify for six months of TRICARE under the Transitional Assistance Management Program.

The VA offers *enhanced eligibility status* to prioritize the people who qualify for VA healthcare. You're more likely to get benefits if you

>> Receive payments from the VA for a service-connected disability

>> Were discharged for a disability resulting from something that happened to you in the line of duty

>> Were discharged for a disability that became worse in the line of duty

>> Are a recently discharged combat veteran (as of this writing, that means you participated in Operation Enduring Freedom, Operation Iraqi Freedom, or Operation New Dawn)

>> Receive a VA pension

>> Are a former prisoner of war

>> Have received a Purple Heart or a Medal of Honor

>> Receive or qualify for Medicaid benefits

>> Served in Southwest Asia during the Gulf War or at least 30 days at Camp Lejeune before December 31, 1987

>> Qualify for VA care based on your income

Putting your medical issues on the map

If you have *any* medical issues, you need to put down this book and call your installation's medical appointment line. I'm talking about back pain, a scar on your neck from a hot shell at the range, tinnitus, a cough that hasn't gone away since you were exposed to a toxic burn pit in Iraq or Afghanistan, or anything else that afflicts you, especially if it occurred during or was aggravated by your military service. I'll be here when you get back. Seriously, do it now.

You should document your medical issues *before* you get out of the military. You need a paper trail to show the VA that you qualify for care. Even if you don't want to use the VA healthcare system, you may need a paper trail to share with your future doctor. Whether you broke your ankle jumping off the back of a five-ton, hurt your ACL playing flag football during unit PT, lost your ability to sleep during a deployment, still have headaches related to a TBI in Iraq or Afghanistan, or are suffering from post-traumatic stress injury doesn't matter; please do yourself a favor and get *all* your medical conditions documented by *at least* your primary care provider. If you don't document these things now, they're tougher to prove to the VA later. And right now, your medical care is completely free, so you should take advantage of it.

REMEMBER

I'm not telling you that you have to seek treatment for PTSD or moral injury right this second; I know that can be difficult and overwhelming, particularly with the military culture surrounding these serious issues. However, I am telling you that at least having these conditions documented in your military medical files is in your best interest. And when you're ready, *please do* seek treatment. Many options are available to you, and I cover some of them in Chapter 20.

Getting a VA disability rating before you get out

The VA assigns disability ratings based on the severity of service-related conditions, such as disease or injury incurred or aggravated during active military service. If the VA finds that you're partially or completely disabled, you'll receive a monthly, tax-free monetary payment. This payment is intended to compensate you for the loss of your quality of life and civilian employability.

If you think you qualify for a VA disability rating and disability pay, you can start the process of getting a rating before you leave military service. The Department of Veterans Affairs calls these types of claims *pre-discharge claims*, and you can file one within 180 to 90 days before you wrap up your military contract. Filing a pre-discharge claim can help you get your benefits sooner through the Benefits Delivery at Discharge, or BDD, program.

You can use the BDD program if you

>> Are a servicemember on full-time active duty (including full-time members of the National Guard, Reserves, and Coast Guard)

>> Know your separation date, and it's within the next 180 to 90 days

>> Are available to go to VA exams for 45 days from the date you submit your claim

>> Can provide a copy of your service treatment records for your current period of service when you file your claim

If you have fewer than 90 days left in the military, you can't file a BDD claim. However, you can still start filing a fully developed or standard claim before your discharge.

TIP

If you're wounded, injured, or sick while you're still on active duty — to the point that you can no longer perform your job duties — the Department of Defense will refer you to the Integrated Disability Evaluation System, or IDES. IDES will give you a proposed VA disability rating before you leave the service, and you'll be entitled to Veteran Readiness and Employment, or VR&E services. If you qualify for IDES but don't hear from it, reach out to the VA and explain your situation. (And flip to Chapter 20 for more information on VR&E and other wounded warrior transition programs.)

TIP

The VA sometimes pays for post-service disabilities, provided that they're related to or are secondary disabilities to an existing disability that occurred during service. Additionally, you may qualify for disability benefits for disabilities presumed to be related to circumstances of military service, even if they arise after your military service ends. For example, some veterans who were exposed to burn pits in Iraq and Afghanistan qualify for VA disability when they later develop lung problems. Troops who caught COVID-19 in a military environment, including activated reservists, National Guard members, or active-duty servicemembers who picked it up during a field exercise, may also qualify.

A lot of myths swirl around VA disability ratings. You've probably heard, "I know a guy who's getting 30 percent because he has a shaving scar on his face," or "Smith faked her back injury and now gets 70 percent from the VA." But the bottom line is that the only way to know what type of disability rating *you* qualify for — or whether you qualify at all — is to file a claim through the VA with adequate documentation that shows your treatment history.

The VA doesn't automatically award compensation, even if you're a Purple Heart or Medal of Honor recipient. You're responsible for scheduling a claims appointment, which you can do while you're still serving on active duty by using the BDD program. You can also seek help from a veterans service organization (VSO), such as the American Legion, Veterans of Foreign Wars, or Disabled American Veterans, when filing your claim — even if you're still on active duty. I cover working with VSOs in more detail in Chapter 20.

VA compensation for service-connected medical issues doesn't always go hand-in-hand with VA medical care. You may get a monthly check from the VA but remain ineligible for VA healthcare (or vice-versa), or you may be eligible for both. You need to schedule a claims appointment and apply for VA healthcare if you feel you're entitled to either.

Keeping your records on the radar

Keep copies of every medical record you ever receive during your military service. During your ETS process, you have to clear medical. That means you visit a military physician and get a complete physical exam. Request a complete copy of your medical file *before* your final physical and bring it with you to your appointment. It should contain your entire military medical history, but check it carefully to ensure that everything is properly documented. If something doesn't appear in your file, talk to your provider about it. Do the same with your family's medical records, including those from the vaccine clinic, dentist, exceptional family member program, pharmacy, specialists, and behavioral health.

If you have any medical conditions that you may later need to address with the VA, treat your military medical records like you'd treat a million dollars. Don't put them down somewhere and forget where they are. And if you don't have digital copies, make some.

Taking Control of Your Mental Health

Regardless of what anyone says, your mental health is important. (I know mental health treatment comes with a stigma in the military, but that's another topic for another book.) Even if you haven't heard about them, the military has several resources available to transitioning service members, and you're entitled to use them any time you need to. Remember, your unit's chaplain would love to hear from you during the transition process. And finally, you can rely on the Veterans Crisis Line any time you feel like you're on the edge. Call 800-273-8255 and then press 1. You can also text the Veterans Crisis Line at 838255 or chat with them online at www.VeteransCrisisLine.net, or, if you have hearing loss, call 800-799-4889.

Using the VA

Whether you're in or out of the military, you can access free VA mental health services. The VA doesn't care about your discharge status or service history; they just want to help. You can call or walk in at any VA medical center, day or night, or call or walk into a Vet Center during clinic hours. You can also call 877-222-8387. You don't need to be enrolled in VA healthcare to get mental health help from the VA.

Checking in with in-person counseling

If you're still in the military, even if you have only ten minutes left on your contract, you can get in-person counseling through your branch's behavioral health program. You don't need a referral from your doctor to get behavioral health counseling; you can simply call the behavioral health department's appointment line and schedule a time to talk.

Perusing the Veteran Training Online Portal

The VA's Moving Forward program, which you can access through the Veteran Training Online Portal (www.veterantraining.va.gov), is designed to help you manage stress, balance school or work and family, deal with relationship problems, cope with physical injuries, face financial difficulties, and handle adjustment issues. It's completely online and self-paced, so you can participate in the program from any device that has Internet access. You can also use the VA's Veteran Parenting Course, Anger and Irritability Management (AIMS) Course, or Path to Better Sleep program that involves cognitive behavioral therapy for insomnia, all available on the Veteran Training website.

Applying yourself through apps

The U.S. Department of Veterans Affairs has an entire app store dedicated to transitioning servicemembers and veterans. You find apps to address things such as PTSD, women veterans' issues, anger management, insomnia, mindfulness, couples' issues, tobacco cessation, and more, and they're all free. (A number of civilian companies have transition apps, too, but your mileage may vary with those.)

Taking advantage of TRICARE's Telemental Health Program

TRICARE covers Telemental Health, a program that enables you to get mental health help online or over the phone. If you're still in the military, you need to get a referral from your primary care provider; if you're a retiree using TRICARE, you don't need a referral or authorization to schedule an appointment with a provider.

Getting addiction help

Many people suffer from addiction, and dealing with substance abuse issues can be incredibly difficult. However, confidential help is available. If you're currently in the military, your primary care provider can help you seek treatment. But if you want to keep your situation private, which makes sense if you're on your way out the door, you can use these resources:

>> SAMHSA, the Substance Abuse and Mental Health Services Administration, which is a confidential and anonymous source of information for people who are looking for treatment facilities

>> TRICARE, provided you qualify for its coverage

>> Your branch's substance abuse program, in some cases (call a rep from ASAP if you're in the Army, ADAPT if you're in the Air Force, SARP in the Navy or SAP in the Marines, or SAPP in the Coast Guard)

>> Vet Centers through the VA

Migrating toward Your ETS Move

Whether your ETS move is your first, second, fifth, or tenth relocation through the military, it's going to be your last. Long before you schedule the movers to pick up your household goods, you need to know exactly where you're going and how much making the move is likely to cost you, among other things.

Packing up: What the military will move for you

The same rules that apply to permanent change of station moves apply to an ETS move, at least in terms of what the military will pack up and transport for you. You should address firearms, motorcycles, and other big-ticket items with your local transportation office to find out what's authorized.

If you're overseas, you're likely authorized to ship your car and the same (or greater, depending on rank and family status) overseas weight allowance you were permitted when you arrived there.

WARNING

Hand-carry everything that's important to you, including copies of all your military awards and certifications. That nice plaque your unit gave you for ETSing? Put it in your suitcase and lug it around yourself. Trust me on this one; realizing that the box containing memories of your military service is missing after a PCS or ETS move is a horrible feeling. (Can you tell I hold a grudge?)

Understanding the limits on where and how much the military will pay to ship

The military is happy to return your household goods to your home of record or the place you entered active duty, but sending them farther than that can cost you. How much the Department of Defense will pay for your ETS move depends on how much weight you're allowed (which is based on your rank) and the distance your household goods are authorized to travel. Still, if your goods are under your maximum weight allowance, thus saving Uncle Sam some money, the military may elect to send them farther at no additional charge to you.

If you're a retiree or you're separating with more than eight years of continuous active-duty service, the government covers the whole move to your home of selection, or HOS, anywhere within the United States — as long as you're being discharged under honorable conditions. If you're separating with fewer than eight years of continuous active duty under your belt, you may have to pay for some of an HOS move out of your own pocket.

You can still move out of the United States, but you're responsible for any additional costs above what it would've cost to move you within the lower 48. (Your transportation office calculates that moving distance based on the farthest possible location from your current station. If you're currently at Joint Base Lewis-McChord in Washington State, your transportation coordinator will probably be looking at the farthest-east city in Maine to figure out how much the government will pay for your move.)

Your installation's transportation office can give you exact numbers and help you calculate how much you have to pay for, which may help you make a decision about whether you want to have the military move you or you want to try a DITY move, which I cover in the following section.

REMEMBER

If you're one half of a dual-military couple and your time is up, the military immediately begins treating you as a dependent. Your stuff stays where it is, and your still-active spouse's weight allowances apply to your shared household goods.

To DITY or not to DITY: Asking the question

Do-it-yourself moves, which you probably know as DITY moves, are officially called *personally procured moves* (PPMs) by the government. Each branch has its own requirements for DITY moves, and in some cases, they're a better alternative to having the government move your stuff. In this type of move, the government reimburses you for moving your belongings yourself. In fact, you receive a payment of 95 percent of what it would've cost the government to move you, so you keep whatever you don't spend. And as a side benefit, you don't have to worry about starring in your own military moving horror story. (Everyone has them.)

Your branch may give you an advance to help defray your moving costs, although each branch's rules are subject to change at any time. Here's what you may be eligible for:

>> **Army:** Up to a 60 percent advance for retirees

>> **Air Force:** Up to a 60 percent advance for retirees or others separating from the service

>> **Navy:** No advances for anyone

>> **Marines:** Up to a 50 percent advance for retirees or others separating from the service

>> **Coast Guard:** Up to 60 percent advance for retirees and those who plan to separate; no advances for people who have already separated

DITY moves sound like real money-makers, but they aren't right for everyone. If you have a lot of goods to haul, or you don't want to deal with the hassle of renting and packing a truck before driving across the country, you may want to let the government handle it all for you. And if you're ETSing from overseas, forget it. A DITY move isn't even an option for you.

Leaving on-post or on-base housing before you have a new place

If you have to leave your on-post or on-base housing (or off-installation military-contracted housing) before you've found a new place to live, the government may elect to pay for a move that's less than 30 miles from your current installation, but you have to apply for advance approval. These short-distance local moves aren't subject to normal ETS weight limits, and they don't count against your permanent relocation. Each branch has its own rules about these types of moves, though, so contact your installation's transportation or personal property office for more info.

ETS moves and other-than-honorable discharges

In many cases, the military will still move your household goods and your dependents when you ETS with a discharge under other than honorable conditions. However, only your transportation office can address your specific case.

ETSing from an overseas duty station

Every day, people ETS from Korea, Germany, Italy, and a whole host of other nations all over the world. The ETS process you follow from an OCONUS duty station is the same as everyone else's is, but a few scenarios are game-changers, such as staying put in your host nation, taking time off at the end of your contract to find a new place to live, and making VA claims from an overseas location.

Sheltering in place

Many people choose to stick around an overseas duty station after leaving the service, and after living in some pretty sweet locations, I can see why. If that's you, you need to know that you have to take the appropriate steps to stay in your country of choice, including applying for residency, which you should start long before you leave the military. Trying to find a government job on your soon-to-be ex-installation and gaining Status of Forces Agreement status for your new job may also be worthwhile. Head to Chapter 9 for more information on continuing your employment with Uncle Sam as a civilian.

Using terminal leave or permissive TDY to find a house

You can use your terminal leave or permissive TDY to find a new place to live. In fact, you should use it before you're required to vacate your government-owned housing or civilian rental place; you stop receiving your overseas housing allowance, or OHA, when you ETS, so find a new home as soon as possible, whether you're sticking around in the same country or you're going back to the States.

TIP

Remember that some overseas property owners rent only to those who have an alien resident card or its equivalent or to people who are in the country under contract with the U.S. government. Starting to plan your move six months (or even a year) before you ETS from an overseas duty station is *imperative* if you intend to stay in your current country.

WARNING

If you plan to sell back your leave to the military, remember that you receive only your base pay for the days you sell. You don't receive OHA, subsistence allowance, special pay (which can be pretty significant if you extended to stay in a place like Korea), or other allowances.

Making VA claims from overseas

You can begin the VA claims process up to 180 days before your discharge. In fact, you *should* start it as early as possible, particularly if you're not going to live near a VA facility (which I cover in the earlier section "Getting a VA disability rating before you get out"). Your VA options are limited overseas, so begin researching where you can go for care as soon as you know it's time to get out of the military.

Chapter **4**

Eyeing Your ETS Process

Get a big, fat accordion folder at the PX, BX, NEX, or MCX and buckle up; you're about to run all over your installation picking up paperwork. Your unit gives you a clearing packet before you take terminal or separation leave, and it includes signature blocks for every organization that needs to say you're good to go. You'll swing by the library (don't steal this book, okay?), the childcare services department and schools, the veterinarian's office, all the shops and departments in your unit, and even the Department of Morale, Welfare and Recreation to get signatures from all the people you may owe something to. If you don't get all the required signatures, you're stuck in combat boots.

WARNING

I can't overstate this point: You can't officially leave the military until you clear every organization on your installation, plus every shop in your unit.

You'll also pick up a few things along the way, such as your medical and dental files, receipts for turning in your military gear, and maybe even business cards and brochures for the services that will still be available to you after you ETS. Keep all your clearing papers and the files you receive in your big, fat accordion folder and treat it like it's full of winning lottery tickets — you're going to need everything in it.

Attending Your Pre-Separation Brief and TAP Offerings

Your pre-separation brief is the "it just got real" part of the ETS process. Up to now, you've been dreaming about life on the other side of the perimeter fence. But now, it's sinking in that you're going to wake up one day in the near future and put on civilian clothes, your workdays aren't going to be measured by the amount of time left until the next formation, and you're never going to be Red in MEDPROS, MRRS, ASIMS, or SNAP again.

The *pre-separation brief* takes place in a classroom setting, and you attend it no later than 365 days before you transition out of the military. Your military spouse or caregiver can go with you on a space-available basis (if you designated a caregiver during your pre-separation counseling, that person is given priority to attend). This brief gives you the complete rundown of your transition process and veteran benefits, which I cover in Chapter 2.

The pre-separation brief is part of the Transition Assistance Program (TAP), but you don't have to attend it immediately before you tackle the rest of your TAP obligations. You have 365 days before you ETS to fit in all the classes, briefings, and other requirements you need to put your military service in the rearview. Your other TAP requirements, which I discuss in Chapter 2, include the following:

>> Participating in resiliency training

>> Creating an individual transition plan

>> Working through the Employment Fundamentals of Career Transition course

>> Completing the Military-to-Civilian Job Skills Crosswalk

>> Participating in the Financial Planning Support course

>> Getting the scoop on your VA benefits through a Veterans Affairs briefing

>> Taking one of four *tracks* — two-day courses that help you find employment, attend school, or start your own business after you separate from military service

You don't have to take these courses and participate in these briefings back-to-back. The military knows you still have a job to do, so you can spread out your attendance over the year prior to your discharge. However, you do have to participate in each block of instruction in the right order.

Clearing Your Unit: Standard Operating Procedures

After you meet all the TAP requirements, when you're just a couple of weeks out from taking terminal or separation leave, you start *clearing*. Each branch has its own clearing process, but it all starts with a clearing packet. You get a few sheets of paper with empty signature blocks that you're required to take around your installation. (Some of the blocks may be shaded or filled in — those are places you don't need to clear because they don't apply to you.) You're responsible for visiting all the places on the list and letting them know you're ETSing; then, they'll check their files and ensure you don't owe them anything before giving you a signature or stamp.

If you owe an organization something — say, a Kevlar helmet or a fine for an overdue library book — you must either settle financially or make an appointment to come back with what you owe. As you can imagine, paying a fine for a library book is a lot easier than digging up the cash for a Kevlar helmet. You can take the time before your appointment to try to find the equipment, clothing, or other items you're missing (see the later section "There's Only One Thief in the Military: Returning the Military's Stuff" for more information on that).

WARNING

The bottom line is that the military won't let you ETS if you're missing equipment you were supposed to turn in. The military will magically turn your missing equipment into a bill that you have to settle with the Defense Finance and Accounting Service. If you don't pay what you owe, DFAS reports you to the commercial credit bureaus — TransUnion, Experian, and Equifax — and may also refer your debt to a collection agency. (You may be able to make payment arrangements, though, such as forking over a monthly sum until you pay off your debt.) Head to Chapter 18 to read up on managing your money as a civilian and find out what happens when creditors are after your cash.

Raising Medical Concerns

Part of the clearing process includes a final physical. If you have other medical issues that require specialists, schedule appointments with them as well. And for the love of all that's holy, schedule a hearing appointment — especially if your ears haven't stopped ringing since your last deployment.

Getting checked out at your final physical

Your final medical appointment includes a complete physical. Your military doc goes through your past medical history with you, asks you questions about your current health, and addresses any concerns you have. If anything happened to you during your time in service that isn't documented in your medical file, talk to your physician about it. It's imperative that you and your physician document every injury and serious illness you had during your time in the service.

Leaving a paper trail

I can't stress this enough: Everything that's wrong with you — and everything that's *been* wrong with you — during your time in the military needs to be on paper.

TIP

If you still have time left on your contract, go see the doctor about that achy shoulder, tweaked back, or bad knee. Create a history of seeking treatment for any condition that occurred in or was aggravated by your time in the military.

You may not have any grounds for a VA claim when you get out of the military. Many people don't. However, you may have grounds in a year, 5 years, or even 20 years when an issue surfaces that's connected to your military service. That's why having your medical provider document everything while you're still in the military is so important; if you can show the VA that the military treated you for a particular condition, you have a better chance at a successful claim.

Keeping tabs on your medical (and dental) records

When you collect your medical and dental records during the ETS process, make multiple copies and keep them each in a safe place. If you get paper copies, you can scan them into a digital format and email them to yourself so you're sure you always have documentation. If you have a family, pick up copies of their treatment records as well.

TIP

Hand-carry your medical files — and all the documents related to your military service, including all your awards and certifications, as well as the nice plaques you've gotten each time you left a unit — when you move. Don't trust military movers with things this important. (I learned the hard way so you don't have to.)

DON'T WANT TO GO TO THE DOCTOR? GET OVER IT!

Many servicemembers put off going to the doctor for a whole host of reasons. Maybe you don't want to miss work, or perhaps you don't want your buddies to call you a *profile ranger*. That's normal, but it's not right. You currently have access to some of the best healthcare in the world, and it's completely free. Go get yourself checked out and, if possible, patched up before you leave military service. Consider it looking out for your future self. Civilian healthcare is expensive, and proving to the VA that you're entitled to care because of an injury or illness that occurred during your time in the service can be difficult if you don't have any prior treatment records.

Making Mental Health a Priority

Your mental health is one of the most important things to think about during transition. Sure, you have to keep track of your military documents and coordinate a move back to your home station, and those are big deals, but preserving your mental health is incredibly important. Military transition is one of the biggest things you'll ever go through. You've spent the last several years living a very specific lifestyle, and that's all about to change.

Sure, you faced big changes when you joined the military. You went into basic training as one person and came out as another — but then, you were surrounded by a community of people who had done the same thing. (I used to refer to my battle buddies my "Army-issued friends.") But civilians aren't going to issue you friends, and of the people you meet in the civilian world, only a few have ruck-marched a proverbial mile in combat boots. In fact, only about 1 percent of the U.S. population has been in the military, so out of every 100 people you meet out there, you'll probably find just one who has been in uniform.

If you're like the vast majority of veterans, you could use some support during the transition process, and even for some time after. Nothing is wrong with asking for help — or taking advantage of it when it's offered — so you can smooth out your switch from a military role to a civilian one.

Filling in the holes in your behavioral health file

Before you leave military service, you can visit your behavioral health clinic to talk to someone about your transition. The Health Insurance Portability and

Accountability Act, or HIPAA, protects you in most cases, so nobody is going to tell your chain of command that you're talking to behavioral health unless you display a serious risk of harm to yourself, others, or the mission.

TECHNICAL STUFF

Although you may not want to talk to someone at behavioral health about your military transition, you're entitled to do so. And if you're a leader, you can set a good example for junior servicemembers by doing so, too. In 2016, Command Sgt. Maj. Christopher Greca made a viral public social media post that said he was seeing a behavioral health professional after 30 years in the military because, as he said, "I wanted to say it was okay for servicemembers to ask for help as needed."

Even if you don't want to talk to someone about your transition, you should get your behavioral health file. You also need a list of all medications you've taken in the past, including those prescribed for sleep problems, anxiety, depression, or any other condition. If anything is missing from your file — say, treatment you received downrange, such as counseling or sleeping pills — make sure you ask your provider to help you track down the right documentation in case you need it later.

Lining up post-service treatment before you get out

The civilian world can be a huge culture shock, which may make readjustment more difficult. If you're battling your demons now, when you have access to free mental healthcare and you're surrounded by people who have known you for at least a few years, get a handle on your post-service treatment options before you leave the service.

VA-provided care

You can use the VA's mental health services free for a year after your transition — even if you wouldn't ordinarily qualify for VA healthcare. In fact, the VA's Solid Start program will contact you three times during your first year after separation (once at 90 days, again at 180 days, and finally at 365 days). It'll ask you how you're doing and see whether you need any specialized help; if you do, don't be afraid to say so. The catch: You must keep your phone number updated in eBenefits, the VA's veteran portal, so reps know how to reach you.

The VA also offers free mental health services at any VA medical center 24 hours a day, or at any Vet Center during regular clinic hours. These places can help you with problems sleeping, anger management, readjusting to civilian life, and just about anything else you need. You can visit the VA for help at any time — not just within a year of your separation. Although the VA may not be able to provide you with long-term treatment, it'll point you in the right direction.

Civilian care

As a civilian, you have two treatment options: You can pay out-of-pocket for mental healthcare or you can ask your insurance to cover it. Some mental health practitioners have set prices; one hour of therapy costs a specific amount of money. Others operate on a *sliding scale*, which means the more money you have, the more you pay for the service. (For the record, many civilian healthcare providers use sliding fee scales as well, so put that knowledge in your back pocket.) Your mileage may vary with private insurance companies; every insurer has different coverage standards and deductibles, which I cover in Chapter 18.

Heading off substance abuse issues

Substance abuse can refer to using alcohol, prescription medications, or street drugs too much or in the wrong way. A 2019 Pew Research study said that 41 percent of veterans who suffered from post-traumatic stress also struggled with alcohol or substance abuse problems during the first few years after leaving the military. An additional 15 percent who didn't suffer from post-traumatic stress have the same issues. A total of *one in five* veterans will face substance abuse issues after leaving the military.

REMEMBER

Substance abuse is different from addiction, though sometimes the two go hand-in-hand. Many people with substance abuse problems can quit or change unhealthy behaviors; addiction is a disease that requires treatment.

Here are the criteria for abuse for the most commonly abused drugs.

Alcohol	Prescription and Over-the-Counter Drugs	Illegal Drugs
Men: More than 4 drinks per day or more than 14 in one week Women: More than 3 drinks per day or more than 7 in one week	Taking medication prescribed to someone else; taking extra doses or using a drug in a way other than how you're supposed to; taking a drug for a non-medical reason	Any use not prescribed or supervised by a medical professional

WARNING

Signs that you may have a problem with substance abuse include the following:

- » Losing interest in things you used to enjoy
- » Failing to take care of yourself
- » Spending more time alone than you used to

>> Eating more or less than you used to

>> Sleeping at odd hours or experiencing sleep disturbances

>> Having problems at work or with your family

>> Changing moods quickly, from good to bad or vice-versa

>> Having cravings or strong desires to use the substance

>> Having someone you care about tell you that they believe you have a substance abuse problem

If you're currently facing substance abuse issues and you're still in the military, use your branch's substance abuse program:

>> Army Substance Abuse Program (ASAP)

>> Air Force Alcohol and Drug Abuse Prevention and Treatment (ADAPT)

>> Navy Substance Abuse Rehabilitation Program (SARP)

>> Marine Corps Substance Abuse Counseling Centers (SACC)

>> Coast Guard Substance Abuse Prevention and Treatment (SAPT)

Getting a handle on these issues now, while you still have access to free treatment options and other types of help, is absolutely essential. Each of these programs is designed to help teach you how to cope with challenges without using drugs or alcohol, too, which means that when you get out, you'll be better-equipped to handle your readjustment period.

If you don't seek help while you're in, the VA offers treatment for substance abuse that you can use regardless of whether you have VA healthcare benefits. If you've served in a combat zone, you can call or visit a Vet Center for help. If you're homeless or at risk of becoming homeless, you can call the National Call Center for Homeless Veterans at 877-424-3838 for addiction and substance abuse help.

Private treatment options can be very expensive, and depending on the type of insurance you have after you leave military service, you may have to pay out-of-pocket for treatment.

Utilizing resources that are waiting for you to use them

Several mental health resources are available to you after you leave military service. In addition to veteran service organizations, such as Veterans of Foreign

Wars (VFW), Disabled American Veterans (DAV), and the American Legion, you can reach out to these organizations for help:

>> **Veterans Crisis Line (800-273-8255, press 1):** For veterans and servicemembers in crisis, as well as their families and friends.

>> **National Call Center for Homeless Veterans (877-424-3838):** For homeless veterans and those at risk of becoming homeless.

>> **Women Veterans Call Center (855-VA-WOMEN):** Specifically for women veterans. All representatives at the WVCC are women, and many are also veterans.

>> **War Vet Call Center (877-927-8387):** A confidential call center for combat veterans and their families to talk about military experiences or issues with readjustment to civilian life.

>> **Department of Defense Safe Helpline (877-955-5247):** A crisis support service for members of the DOD community affected by sexual assault.

>> **National Domestic Violence Hotline (800-799-7233):** A service that offers help to anyone who has been affected by relationship abuse, including those who are currently in abusive relationships, friends or family of victims and survivors, and those who are out of abusive relationships.

>> **Caregiver Support (855-260-3274):** For veterans' caregivers to take training, get educational resources, and tools to help with caring for a veteran.

>> **Coaching Into Care (888-823-7458):** A VA program to guide family members and friends to help a reluctant veteran reach out for support with a mental health challenge.

There's Only One Thief in the Military: Returning the Military's Stuff

When I joined the military, my Army-veteran brother told me, "There's only one thief in the Army. Everyone else is just trying to get their stuff back." (Except he didn't say *stuff*.) He told me to keep track of all my equipment, and that was solid advice that saved me quite a bit of money.

However, I know plenty of people who were missing plenty of things while trying to clear, and they had only two options: Pay the service the monetary value of the item or find a replacement at a military surplus store outside the installation. (Obviously, they could've tried to get their stuff back in other ways, but seriously . . . *Swiper, no swiping!*) When you ETS, you bring your ID card and your installation clearing papers, plus all the equipment and clothing that the military wants back, to the necessary organizations. That means lugging three or four duffel bags to your branch's issue facility, waiting in line for your appointment, and facing down the always-cheerful worker behind the turn-in counter. (Sarcasm aside, I understand where they're coming from. Would you want to deal with raggedy military gear all day? Me neither.)

TIP

You may walk out of your installation's issue facility with a bill. If you do, remember that you may be able to find replacement gear for cheaper than what the military wants to charge you. Nearly every military installation has a few surplus stores near the main gate (even overseas), and a trip to find a used bivy cover and an entrenching tool may be worth your while.

Scheduling Your Relocation Appointments

Part of your ETS process includes scheduling relocation appointments with your branch's Relocation Assistance Office. At the relocation office, you meet with a relocation professional who asks you whether you want the military to move all your stuff for you or you want to move it yourself.

You must register with the Defense Personal Property System, or DPS, at www. move.mil if you plan to use military resources for your ETS move, including military money if you're moving yourself.

You're not eligible for dislocation allowance, or DLA, if you're ETSing from the military. However, you may be entitled to a number of other benefits, such as the following:

>> Household goods storage

>> Travel allowances, such as Monetary Allowance in Lieu of Transportation, or MALT, which the military gives you for mileage and some travel costs

>> Per diem pay, which reimburses you for meals and lodging while you're en-route to your final destination

TIP

If it's feasible, you may want to consider a do-it-yourself move (I cover those in Chapter 3). Whether the military moves your stuff or you do, you should absolutely hand-carry anything that's important to you.

When you separate with fewer than eight years of continuous active-duty service under your belt, the military will pay for your household goods to go to your home of record or the place you entered military service. If you want to go somewhere else, you have to pay the difference in transportation costs. If you served more than eight years or retire, you can go anywhere in the United States. If you move outside the U.S., you're responsible for the difference between your total cost and what it would've cost the military to move you within the contiguous 48 states.

The military will only move a certain amount of weight for you based on your rank at the time of discharge, whether you have dependents, and whether your move is completely within the continental U.S. If you go over your allowable weight, you're responsible for paying the difference. Table 4-1 shows what personal property you're allowed to bring on the government's dime and what you can bring at your own expense. Your move may have other allowances and limitations, which your relocation coordinator can explain to you.

TABLE 4-1 **What You Can Ship for Your ETS Move**

Allowed	Allowed at Your Own Expense
Firearms that comply with local and state laws	Pet travel (but in some cases, quarantine fees may be reimbursable)
Consumable items if you're going to a remote location	Privately owned vehicles, with some exceptions (such as OCONUS moves)
Appliances, including flat-panel TVs and monitors	Personal watercraft and boats
Motorcycles and dirt-bikes when shipped as household goods or when transported as privately owned vehicles	Mobile homes and tiny houses (only for CONUS and Alaska moves)
Utility trailers, sporting vehicles, and similar vehicles when shipped as household goods (with weight limits)	Residential boats (only for CONUS and Alaska moves)

TIP

Most installations have a *lending closet* — a place that allows you to borrow basic household goods while yours are in transport. You may be able to pick up a coffee-maker, some pots and pans, and a few essentials to make your last days in the military more bearable. Ask your transportation coordinator about your installation's lending closet during your appointment.

TIP

You can submit a travel voucher to the Defense Finance and Accounting Service, or DFAS, up to 180 days after you complete your travel to your home of record or the place you entered active duty if you separate from the military prior to retirement. If you retire, you can submit a travel voucher for your travel to any location within the United States for up to a year after the retirement date on your orders.

WHAT IF YOUR STUFF DOESN'T SURVIVE THE TRIP?

The military contracts out packing, loading, transportation, and unloading of your household goods. That means you're likely to get local companies on both ends with a national company in the middle — and it means three different entities will be handling your stuff. And you find no shortage of horror stories about upside-down motorcycles, moldy sofas, and damaged family heirlooms, which make a broken dish or two pale in comparison. The good news: If you follow the advice in this book and hand-carry everything that's important to you, you don't have to worry about emotional trauma after your stuff is delivered.

However, that doesn't mean you won't end up with broken or damaged goods, or that the movers won't lose some of your things. If your things are broken, you must file a Loss/Damage Report through Move.mil to get reimbursed. In some cases, the military pays you the depreciated value of your belongings; in others, you can get full replacement or repair value. You must submit a Loss/Damage Report within a specific time frame, so check with your relocation office to see how much time you have.

Working with JAG or Legal Assistance to Update Your Information

Stop by your installation's legal services office to update your information and pick up documents you may need, such as powers of attorney, before you ETS. The attorneys in your installation's office of the Judge Advocate General (JAG) can't represent you in civilian court (though some exceptions apply), but they can give you legal advice, help you prepare forms, and assist you with the following:

>> Wills and general estate planning advice

>> Powers of attorney and notary services

>> Immigration and naturalization advice

>> Divorce, legal separation, annulment, custody, and paternity advice

>> Adoptions and name changes

>> Consumer fraud and abuse advice, including identity theft

>> Leases and landlord-tenant relations

>> Basic tax advice and assistance on federal, state, and local taxes (your installation may have a separate tax office)

>> Advice on your military rights and benefits, including Servicemembers Civil Relief Act (SCRA) advice and assistance

Help from JAG or legal assistance is confidential. If these offices can't help you, they'll refer you to a specialized attorney.

You're entitled to use free military legal assistance if you're active duty, a retiree, or a dependent. Veterans can't use these services, though; if you need an attorney to look something over, create a contract, or write up a power of attorney after you're out, you have to pay for it.

Passing Your Housing Inspection with Flying Colors

If you live in military or government-leased housing, your personal space has to pass muster when you clear your installation. The military isn't going to hold you hostage if you don't pass your final housing inspection, but it will make you pay for repairs and replacements. Because military housing is largely privatized, the various companies that own the homes have different billing terms and repair requirements; at some installations, for example, you have to strip and wax the floors, while at others you simply have to sweep and mop. Before you attempt to clear housing, ask for a move-out checklist so you don't have to guess.

Some people choose to hire a professional cleaning company, which can run you a few hundred dollars (or more). Check your installation's social media pages for personal recommendations; not all military move-out cleaning companies are professional, and not all professionals are good.

REMEMBER

Whether you choose the DIY route or you hire a professional, these tips can help you pass your housing inspection with minimal (or no) charges:

>> **Schedule repairs immediately.** If you call the housing office and ask it to make routine repairs *before* you start to clear, you generally won't have to pay for the repairs. However, if you wait until you're clearing housing, you may have to pay for them. Note that housing won't repair *everything* for free; if you crash through the drywall playing beer pong, you're going to get a bill. (In a case like that, or if your dog ate your blinds, your kid soaked the bathroom ceiling with the detachable shower head, or you nuked a fork in the built-in

microwave, you'll probably save money making the repairs yourself. You'll also save money by making minor repairs on your own, such as patching nail holes or replacing lightbulbs.)

>> **Look at every item on the inspection checklist.** It includes all the items your maintenance team will check when you're ready to clear. Some installations' housing offices offer a pre-move-out inspection; if yours does, take advantage of it.

>> **Plan to get rid of items you're not taking with you *well* in advance of moving day.** Your installation's trash pickup service will most likely pick up bulk items for free if you call ahead. You can also use your installation's free and sales pages on social media to offer your items to the community. On many installations, you can also put things on the curb with a sign that says "Free" and watch them disappear. (Sometimes you can even do it without a sign — just ask any military kid who left their bike by the road overnight.)

>> **Put together a cleaning kit (unless you're hiring a cleaner) and keep it out of your household goods shipment.** Include a broom, your favorite cleaning solutions, scrubbers (including the kind that magically erase scuffs), a mop, and a bucket.

>> **Don't forget the exterior.** Some installations require you to pull weeds out of the yard, clear spiderwebs from the back porch, and clean the garage, and they *all* require you to pick up pet waste from the backyard.

TIP

Some military housing companies require you to have your carpets professionally cleaned if you have pets. If you can't afford carpet cleaning, check with your housing office; it may allow you to rent a steam-cleaner from the nearest home improvement store. Renting a steam-cleaner for 24 hours and buying special carpet-cleaning solution can cost between $20 and $50, so factor that into your moving budget. Some housing offices don't allow you to clean the carpets yourself — at least when for a move-out — so check before you rent any equipment.

Even if you live off your installation in non-government-leased housing, you still need to get the all-clear from your housing office. You won't have a housing inspection, though your landlord will most likely do an inspection and charge you for cleaning or repairs.

If you have to pay before you clear housing, the method of collection is up to the housing company that manages your installation's living quarters. You may be able to pay cash on the spot when you clear, or you may be able to request that it take the cost from your final paycheck.

WARNING

Some servicemembers do significant damage to military housing. When I cleared my last installation, the inspector told me a handful of stories about the worst houses he'd seen — much worse than a hole in the drywall from a wild game of beer pong. Animal feces, months of grime, smashed windows, and dog-eaten doors were some of the least-awful things he'd encountered. He also shared with me that one servicemember got slapped with an $8,500 bill. I can't imagine how bad the damage would've had to have been (considering a light bulb was about $2), but if your house is looking pretty rough, you need to square it away before you even attempt to clear housing. The last thing you want to do is owe more than you make — or worse, face a parade of housing inspectors, your supervisors, and maybe even the installation commander coming through your space with rubber booties and gloves on.

Reviewing Your Discharge Papers before You Walk out the Door

Your final stop in the clearing process is the office where you get your Department of Defense Form 214 (affectionately known as the DD-214 by veterans everywhere). Your DD-214 is a summary of your time in the military, and it includes information on every school you attended, every medal you earned, and every deployment you went on. Hopefully, most of that information is in the system when you show up to get your DD-214, but have your "I Love Me" book of awards, promotion orders, and such on hand to fill in the gaps just in case it's not. You should bring all your certificates, orders (including change of station, deployment, awards, and decorations), academic evaluation reports, and other documentation to back up your claims in case your branch's human resources command doesn't have all the records it should.

TIP

Visit your unit's personnel office with all your documents a few weeks before you go to pick up your DD-214. Make sure your records are up-to-date there. That way, everything should be in the system by the time you go to your final appointment to pick up your DD-214.

Before you leave the office, tuck your DD-214 into your big, fat accordion folder. You'll need copies of it later.

Reading your DD-214

The person filling out your DD-214 asks you to review it before they sign it. Ensuring that it's completely correct is your responsibility; what's on it now is what's going to stay on it forever. (You may be able to change it later through the Department of Defense, but the process is long and arduous, so why not get it right the first time?) Check out a DD-214 sample in Figure 4-1.

CERTIFICATE OF RELEASE OR DISCHARGE FROM ACTIVE DUTY
This Report Contains Information Subject to the Privacy Act of 1974, As Amended.

1. NAME (Last, First, Middle)	2. DEPARTMENT, COMPONENT AND BRANCH ARMY/RA	3. SOCIAL SECURITY NUMBER

4a. GRADE, RATE OR RANK SGT	b. PAY GRADE E05	5. DATE OF BIRTH (YYYYMMDD) 19780226	6. RESERVE OBLIGATION TERMINATION DATE (YYYYMMDD) 20140808

7a. PLACE OF ENTRY INTO ACTIVE DUTY DETROIT, MICHIGAN	b. HOME OF RECORD AT TIME OF ENTRY (City and state, or complete address if known)

8a. LAST DUTY ASSIGNMENT AND MAJOR COMMAND 0000INHHC STB P1	b. STATION WHERE SEPARATED SCHOFIELD BARRACKS, HI 96857

9. COMMAND TO WHICH TRANSFERRED USAR CON GP (REINF) 1 RESERVE WAY, ST LOUIS, MO 63132	10. SGLI COVERAGE NONE AMOUNT: $ 400,000.00

11. PRIMARY SPECIALTY (List number, title and years and months in specialty. List additional specialty numbers and titles involving periods of one or more years.) 74D2O L4 CHEMICAL OPS SP - 3 YRS 1 MOS// NOTHING FOLLOWS	12. RECORD OF SERVICE	YEAR(S)	MONTH(S)	DAY(S)
	a. DATE ENTERED AD THIS PERIOD	2006	08	24
	b. SEPARATION DATE THIS PERIOD	2010	05	14
	c. NET ACTIVE SERVICE THIS PERIOD	0003	08	21
	d. TOTAL PRIOR ACTIVE SERVICE	0000	00	00
	e. TOTAL PRIOR INACTIVE SERVICE	0000	00	00
	f. FOREIGN SERVICE	0003	00	16
	g. SEA SERVICE	0000	00	00
	h. INITIAL ENTRY TRAINING	0000	02	11
	i. EFFECTIVE DATE OF PAY GRADE	2009	03	01

13. DECORATIONS, MEDALS, BADGES, CITATIONS AND CAMPAIGN RIBBONS AWARDED OR AUTHORIZED (All periods of service) IRAQ CAMPAIGN MEDAL W/TWO CAMPAIGN STARS// ARMY COMMENDATION MEDAL (2ND AWARD)//ARMY ACHIEVEMENT MEDAL (2ND AWARD)//MERITORIOUS UNIT COMMENDATION (2ND AWARD)//ARMY GOOD CONDUCT MEDAL//NATIONAL DEFENSE SERVICE MEDAL//GLOBAL WAR ON TERRORISM SERVICE MEDAL//ARMY SERVICE RIBBON//CONT IN BLOCK 18	14. MILITARY EDUCATION (Course title, number of weeks, and month and year completed) BATTLEFIELD FORENSICS CRS, 1 WEEK, 2008//BIO INTEG DETECT SYS CRS, 4 WEEKS, 2007/ /DRIVERS TRAINING CRS, 1 WEEK, 2007//MRAP DRIVERS TNG CRS, 1 WEEK, 2009//TECH TRNS OF HAZRD MAT CRS, 1 WEEK, 2008//TECHNICAL ESCORT CRS, 4 WEEKS, 2008//TOXIC AGENT TNG CRS, 1 WEEK, 2007//NOTHING FOLLOWS

15a. COMMISSIONED THROUGH SERVICE ACADEMY	YES	X	NO
b. COMMISSIONED THROUGH ROTC SCHOLARSHIP (10 USC Sec. 2107b)	YES	X	NO
c. ENLISTED UNDER LOAN REPAYMENT PROGRAM (10 USC Chap. 109) (If Yes, years of commitment: 0)	YES	X	NO

16. DAYS ACCRUED LEAVE PAID 0.5	17. MEMBER WAS PROVIDED COMPLETE DENTAL EXAMINATION AND ALL APPROPRIATE DENTAL SERVICES AND TREATMENT WITHIN 90 DAYS PRIOR TO SEPARATION	YES	NO X

18. REMARKS
BLOCK 6, PERIOD OF DELAYED ENTRY PROGRAM: 20060809-20060823//ENLISTMENT BONUS PAID: $9000.00, 20070510//SERVED IN A DESIGNATED IMMINENT DANGER PAY AREA//SERVICE IN IRAQ 20070622-20071022//SERVICE IN IRAQ 20081013-20090922//MEMBER HAS COMPLETED FIRST FULL TERM OF SERVICE//AUTHORIZED SHOULDER SLEEVE INSIGNIA FOR FORMER WARTIME SERVICE// ADDENDUM TO BLOCK 13: OVERSEAS SERVICE BAR (2ND AWARD)// ARMY LAPEL BUTTON//CONT FROM BLOCK 13: //OVERSEAS SERVICE RIBBON (3RD AWARD)//COMBAT ACTION BADGE//EXPERT MARKSMANSHIP BADGE W/RIFLE BAR//NOTHING FOLLOWS
The information contained herein is subject to computer matching within the Department of Defense or with any other affected Federal or non-Federal agency for verification purposes and to determine eligibility for, and/or continued compliance with, the requirements of a Federal benefit program.

19a. MAILING ADDRESS AFTER SEPARATION (Include ZIP Code)	b. NEAREST RELATIVE (Name and address - Include ZIP Code)

20. MEMBER REQUESTS COPY 6 BE SENT TO (Specify state/locality) MI	OFFICE OF VETERANS AFFAIRS	X	YES	NO
a. MEMBER REQUESTS COPY 3 BE SENT TO THE CENTRAL OFFICE OF THE DEPARTMENT OF VETERANS AFFAIRS (WASHINGTON, DC)		X	YES	NO

21a. MEMBER SIGNATURE SIGNED BY:	b. DATE (YYYYMMDD) 20100415	22.a. OFFICIAL AUTHORIZED TO SIGN (Typed name, grade, title, signature) SIGNED BY: , CHIEF TRANSITION CENTER	b. DATE (YYYYMMDD) 20100415

SPECIAL ADDITIONAL INFORMATION (For use by authorized agencies only)

23. TYPE OF SEPARATION RELEASE FROM ACTIVE DUTY	24. CHARACTER OF SERVICE (Include upgrades) HONORABLE

25. SEPARATION AUTHORITY AR 635-200, CHAP 4	26. SEPARATION CODE MBK	27. REENTRY CODE 1

28. NARRATIVE REASON FOR SEPARATION COMPLETION OF REQUIRED ACTIVE SERVICE	I certify this to be a true copy of the original

29. DATES OF TIME LOST DURING THIS PERIOD (YYYYMMDD) NONE	30. MEMBER REQUESTS COPY 4 (Initials)

DD FORM 214, AUG 2009	PREVIOUS EDITION IS OBSOLETE. GENERATED BY TRANSPROC	MEMBER - 4

FIGURE 4-1:
Sample DD-214.

© John Wiley & Sons, Inc.

Most of the boxes on your DD-214 are self-explanatory, like every other military form. Blocks 1 through 3 explain who you are and where you served. Blocks 4a and 4b cover your current grade, rate, or rank (such as private, gunnery sergeant, or lieutenant colonel, plus your pay grade), and block 5 is your date of birth in standard military format. From there,

>> Block 6 shows your reserve obligation termination date. Remember, everyone who signs a contract with a military agrees to an eight-year obligation. For example, if your active-duty contract expires after three years, you still owe the Individual Ready Reserves five years. (If you've served more than eight years on active duty or in a reserve component, you don't owe the military another day.)

>> Blocks 7a and 7b show where you entered active duty and your home of record, which most likely hasn't changed since you joined the service.

>> Blocks 8a and 8b explain your last duty assignment and the station where you separated from military service. These are most likely the same place unless you have special circumstances, such as transitioning out of a Warrior Transition Unit or someplace like Fort Leavenworth.

>> Blocks 9 and 10 cover where you're transferring (if you're transferring to the Inactive Ready Reserve; if you're not, Block 9 will say "N/A") as well as whether you held Servicemembers' Group Life Insurance (SGLI) and the amount for which you were insured.

>> Block 11 shows every military occupational specialty (MOS), rating, or Air Force Specialty Code you held during your time in the service. (If you were in prior service in the reserves, those should be on there, too.) This block also includes the amount of time you served in each job.

>> Block 12 is a complete rundown of the time you spent in the military, including active duty, inactive service, and even initial entry training. It also shows how long you've been at your current pay grade.

>> Block 13 includes a lot of the records in your "I Love Me" book. All your awards, citations, and even campaign ribbons belong here; if you have too many to list, the extras go into Block 18, which is reserved for "Remarks."

REMEMBER

>> Block 14 is incredibly important, particularly if you decide to rejoin the service later (in any branch, reserve or active). All your military education belongs in this block, including NCO schools and professional development courses. If your military education doesn't fit in Block 14, it continues in Block 18.

>> Blocks 15a, b, and c cover your commission and whether you enlisted under a loan repayment program.

>> Block 16 notes how many unused leave days the military will pay you for (or has paid you for).

>> Block 17 asks whether you had a complete dental exam within 90 days of separating, and you should have. In fact, you should've had all kinds of exams and treatments by this time. After you're out, you'll be paying out of pocket for those things (if not directly, through insurance premiums).

>> Block 18 is for overflow. Everything that didn't fit in the other blocks belongs here.

>> Blocks 19a and 19b are both important; they tell the Department of Defense where you'll be and how it can reach you through your nearest relative if necessary. (Involuntary recall and the VA's Solid Start program, which I cover in the earlier section "Lining up post-service treatment before you get out," are the two main reasons the DOD wants to know where you are.)

>> Blocks 20 and 20a show whether you request that your DD-214 be sent to your home state and the VA. You should request both.

>> Blocks 21a, 21b, 22a, and 22b are for signatures and dates. You sign your DD-214 electronically by inserting your CAC into a reader and putting in your PIN. The agent at the transition center does the same.

>> Block 23 characterizes your type of separation. You may see "Release from active duty," "Retirement," "Discharge," or something else in your Block 23.

>> Block 24 tells you how the military characterized your service. Only a handful of potential categories apply to this block, and I explore them in Chapter 5.

>> Block 25 notes the regulation that authorizes your discharge from the military.

>> Block 26 gives you a separation code — a series of letters, numbers, or combinations of the two that explain the reason you're being discharged. In Figure 4-1, this block says "MBK," which is the code for "Completion of required active service." More than 800 codes exist, ranging from "MCC" for "reduction in force" to "BKK" for "misconduct (drug abuse)." *Tip:* This code can tell potential employers why you were discharged from the military if they're savvy enough to look it up.

>> Block 27 is your reentry code, which tells a recruiter whether you're allowed back in should you attempt to rejoin the military later. I cover these codes in detail in Chapter 5.

>> Block 28 contains the narrative reason for separation, which goes hand-in-hand with Block 26.

>> Blocks 29 and 30 are for any time lost (such as time spent AWOL) during your period of service and your initials saying that you request Member Copy 4, which is the long-form copy of your DD-214 (pictured in Figure 4-1). This is the copy you need to file for unemployment benefits, veteran benefits, jobs, and a variety of other things. You want Member Copy 4.

After you review every block and ensure nothing is missing, you digitally sign the document with your CAC; your signature and the date appear in Blocks 21a and 21b. Then, the government employee who compiled your form digitally signs it (in Blocks 22a and 22b) — and that means the date listed in Block 12b is officially your last day in the military.

The person completing your form stamps it as a certified true copy of the original document. *Do not lose your original copy.* If your transition center is anything like mine was, they'll shake your hand and send you to ring a big bell on your way out the door to signify the end of your service.

Reading your NGB-22

The NGB-22 is the National Guard discharge document. It's a lot like the DD-214 (see the preceding section); it shows the nature of your discharge, how much time you served, and a lot of other important information. Check out a sample NGB-22 in Figure 4-2.

Your NGB-22 starts off with personal data in Blocks 1 through 7 (including your date of enlistment, rank and pay grade, and date of rank). Then it gets into the following:

>> Blocks 8a and 8b note your current station.

>> Block 9 lists all the commands you worked under during your time in the Guard.

>> Block 10 calculates all your time in the service (including in other reserve components or active duty) as well as how much time you've served that counts toward your retirement pay.

>> Block 11 lets you know how much longer you have before you fulfill your eight-year service obligation (the time you have to spend in the Individual Ready Reserves), if any.

>> Block 12 lists all your military education, including specialty schools such as Airborne or Air Assault, additional skill identifiers you earned, and other courses you earned certifications from.

>> Block 13 describes your MOS and when you earned it. If you've had more than one MOS, each one is in this block.

>> Block 14 addresses your civilian education credentials.

>> Block 15 highlights all your military accomplishments, including decorations, awards, citations, and campaign ribbons you earned. It also includes state awards, so make sure every achievement is documented in this block.

>> Blocks 16 and 17 describe whether you have SGLI and what type of personnel security investigation was conducted for your security clearance, as well as the investigation's outcome (such as "Favorable").

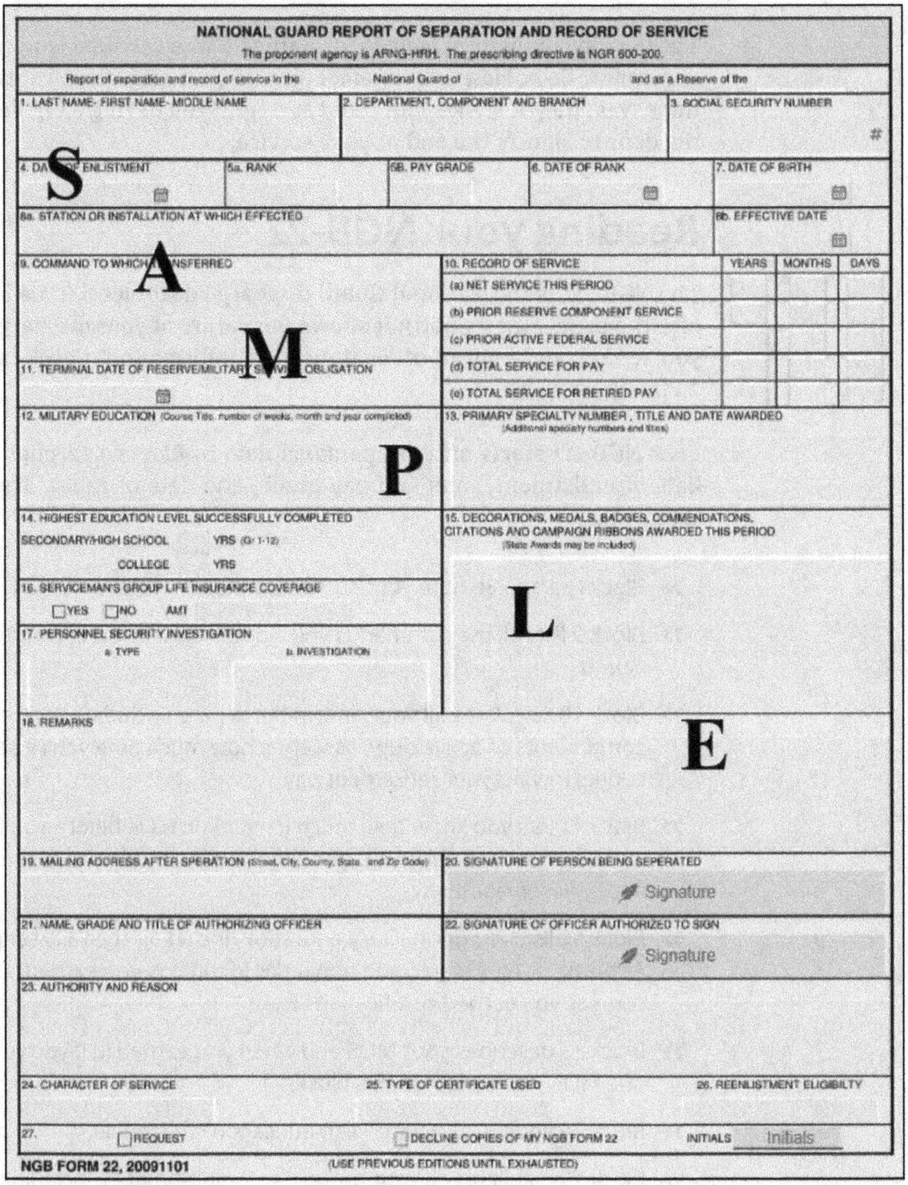

The form shown is the **NATIONAL GUARD REPORT OF SEPARATION AND RECORD OF SERVICE**. The proponent agency is ARNG-HRH. The prescribing directive is NGR 600-200.

Report of separation and record of service in the ____ National Guard of ____ and as a Reserve of the ____

1. LAST NAME- FIRST NAME- MIDDLE NAME

2. DEPARTMENT, COMPONENT AND BRANCH

3. SOCIAL SECURITY NUMBER #

4. DATE OF ENLISTMENT

5a. RANK

5B. PAY GRADE

6. DATE OF RANK

7. DATE OF BIRTH

8a. STATION OR INSTALLATION AT WHICH EFFECTED

8b. EFFECTIVE DATE

9. COMMAND TO WHICH TRANSFERRED

10. RECORD OF SERVICE | YEARS | MONTHS | DAYS
(a) NET SERVICE THIS PERIOD
(b) PRIOR RESERVE COMPONENT SERVICE
(c) PRIOR ACTIVE FEDERAL SERVICE
(d) TOTAL SERVICE FOR PAY
(e) TOTAL SERVICE FOR RETIRED PAY

11. TERMINAL DATE OF RESERVE/MILITARY SERVICE OBLIGATION

12. MILITARY EDUCATION (Course Title, number of weeks, month and year completed)

13. PRIMARY SPECIALTY NUMBER , TITLE AND DATE AWARDED (Additional specialty numbers and titles)

14. HIGHEST EDUCATION LEVEL SUCCESSFULLY COMPLETED
SECONDARY/HIGH SCHOOL   YRS (Gr 1-12)
COLLEGE   YRS

15. DECORATIONS, MEDALS, BADGES, COMMENDATIONS, CITATIONS AND CAMPAIGN RIBBONS AWARDED THIS PERIOD (State Awards may be included)

16. SERVICEMAN'S GROUP LIFE INSURANCE COVERAGE
☐YES ☐NO   AMT

17. PERSONNEL SECURITY INVESTIGATION
a. TYPE   b. INVESTIGATION

18. REMARKS

19. MAILING ADDRESS AFTER SPERATION (Street, City, County, State, and Zip Code)

20. SIGNATURE OF PERSON BEING SEPERATED
Signature

21. NAME, GRADE AND TITLE OF AUTHORIZING OFFICER

22. SIGNATURE OF OFFICER AUTHORIZED TO SIGN
Signature

23. AUTHORITY AND REASON

24. CHARACTER OF SERVICE

25. TYPE OF CERTIFICATE USED

26. REENLISTMENT ELIGIBILTY

27. ☐REQUEST   ☐DECLINE COPIES OF MY NGB FORM 22   INITIALS   Initials

NGB FORM 22, 20091101   (USE PREVIOUS EDITIONS UNTIL EXHAUSTED)

© John Wiley & Sons, Inc.

FIGURE 4-2:
Sample blank
NGB-22.

- Block 18 is the overflow block for items that don't fit in other blocks — particularly 12 and 15. If you've attended all the schools and earned all the decorations, this block will be full.

- Blocks 19 through 22 are reserved for your mailing address so the Guard knows where to find you after separation; the name, grade, and title of the authorizing officer; and both of your electronic signatures. (You and the authorizing officer will electronically sign the form by using your CACs.)

- Block 23 cites the authority for your discharge (such as a National Guard or Army regulation) and the reason you're leaving the service.

- Block 24 explains the character of your service, such as honorable, dishonorable, or something in between.

- Blocks 25 and 26 describe the type of certificate used for your discharge (such as a DD Form 256, *Honorable Discharge Certificate*) and whether you're eligible for reenlistment, and Block 27 notes whether you want or decline copies of your NGB Form 22.

REMEMBER

You do want copies of your NGB-22. You need them when you apply for veterans benefits, government assistance, and even some jobs. Keep these copies safe in a place you'd feel comfortable leaving a million dollars; getting new copies can be difficult.

Exploring the DD-215, DD-149, and DD-293

A Department of Defense Form 215 is an amendment to your DD-214. If your DD-214 has a typo, you can fill out a DD-215 to ask the government to make changes — provided you have documentation to back up your claim. Generally, you use a DD-215 to correct only spelling errors, a wrong number in your address or Social Security number, or something minor that doesn't require board review. If you want other changes to your DD-214, you must go through a board review process, which I cover in Chapter 5. You can skip the hassle of having to file a DD-215 if you review your DD-214 carefully before you sign it.

The DD-149 is the form you file if you have documentation that proves a school, an award, or other important information is missing from your service record. You can obtain a blank DD-149 if you need to apply to correct a military record, including a review of a discharge issued by court-martial. If you're asking the Department of Defense to specifically review your discharge (and possibly upgrade it), you need a DD-293. (I cover that in Chapter 5.) If you're currently in the military and concerned about the type of discharge you're receiving, you may be able to discuss your situation with your command. It can't hurt to try.

Discovering the DD-256 and DD-257

A DD-256 is a certificate of honorable discharge. You may use it to prove that you were honorably discharged from the military. A DD-257 is a certificate of general discharge. If you didn't receive either of these certificates — such as when your entire career was spent on active duty — you can ask the government to send you one through eVetRecs. Both the DD-256 and DD-257 are more for display than for applying for benefits, although some lenders will request them (along with retirement point statements) if you apply for a VA loan after service in the Guard or another reserve component.

TIP

Register your DD-214 with your local government as soon as you arrive in your new location. A copy will go to the National Archives, but getting your hands on a copy from that institution can take weeks or more. Your county clerk will allow you to register your discharge paperwork so you can access it quickly if you lose your own copies. (But after your time in the military, you know that you should have five backup copies of everything, right?) And just in case you were worried, most states have strict privacy laws on DD-214s and other military discharge documents; usually, to obtain a copy, you must prove that it's your record, or that you're an eligible next-of-kin or the servicemember's legally appointed representative.

Lining up Separation Leave

You fill out and turn in your final leave form well in advance of your first day of leave so that when the day comes, you get to sleep in and ride out the last few weeks of your military career. Your Leave and Earnings Statement contains a block that says "ETS Bal," and that tells you how many leave days you can take for terminal or separation leave; it includes the number of days you *will* earn while you're on leave. (You continue to earn 2.5 leave days every month, even when you're on terminal or separation leave.) However, the "ETS Bal" block tells you how many days you'll have when you ETS based on your current contract only. If you choose early retirement, or if you extend or renew your obligation to the military, that number will change.

If you choose to sell your leave days back to the military rather than take terminal leave, DFAS will only pay you your salary. You won't get BAH, BAS, or other entitlements. And you can only sell back 60 days of leave over your entire career. However, if you use your leave days, you'll continue receiving your base pay, BAH, BAS, and all other entitlements during the time you're still in the military.

My unsolicited advice is this: Unless you're extremely cash-strapped and need a few thousand dollars immediately, you should use all your terminal leave. You make more money doing so, and even earn some free money by accruing additional leave days while you're on leave. This is the first and last time the military's going to give you anything for free, so take advantage of it. Besides, you can use your time on terminal leave to start your job search (if you haven't already), pack up your household goods, and head home.

TIP

If you're being involuntarily separated or retiring, you may even be able to start your terminal leave a little early by requesting Permissive Temporary Duty (PTDY) leave. Transition PTDY is non-chargeable, and it may provide you with ten additional days off at the end of your contract.

Your time in the military ends on the date your contract says it ends, so plan your leave accordingly. If you have 60 days of ETS leave available and your contract says you get out of the military on June 15, your leave form should request April 15 as your first day of leave. (If you're also requesting ten days of PTDY, request that your leave begin on April 5.)

Chapter 5

Ain't No Discharge on the Ground (It's in Your Hand)

Whether you've been looking forward to framing your DD-214 or you're dreading the end of your military career, the type of discharge you get is important. Each discharge type may have a different impact on your future, from finding a new job to taking out a VA loan to buy a home when you're ready to settle in for the long haul.

The good news is that the vast majority of people in the military walk away with an honorable discharge. As long as you haven't gotten into major trouble, you leave the service with a DD-214 that can help you gain employment, use your hard-earned VA benefits, get you membership in prestigious organizations, and be authorized to wear an honorable service lapel pin on your civvies for receiving a non-adverse separation. (You didn't know about the pin? Now that you do, don't say I never told you anything useful.) If you're not happy with the type of discharge you receive from the military, you may have a way to appeal it after the fact, but you get no guarantees on how that will shake out.

Dispelling Discharge Myths: The Major Types of Military Separations

Data from the Department of Defense says that about 90 percent of servicemembers leaving active and reserve service walk away with an honorable discharge or general discharge under honorable conditions. That leaves 10 percent with what's called *bad paper* — a discharge that can negatively affect your ability to claim VA benefits, including your GI Bill and healthcare. (The VA will always provide mental healthcare for veterans in crisis, regardless of discharge status). Currently, about 125,000 veterans from the post-9/11 era have bad paper discharges, and according to the VA, only 35,000 of them have applied for the Veterans Administration to review their service characterization. Worse, only 0.07 percent of those people were deemed eligible for an upgrade.

The Department of Defense and each service branch are all working to improve their classifications to reflect changes in military culture (particularly revolving around mental health and substance abuse problems), but like most large organizations, the military is slow to change. If you're in line for bad paper (in the absence of criminal charges or non-judicial punishment), I strongly encourage you to talk to your chain of command, a behavioral health specialist, and your unit chaplain to see whether anything can be done to change your characterization of service *before* you leave the military.

The bottom line is that any discharge that isn't classified as honorable can be like a scarlet letter you have to wear for the rest of your life. The following list addresses each type of military discharge and what you can expect if you fall into that category:

>> **Honorable discharges:** Most people get out of the military with an honorable discharge. As long as you don't have any major issues while you're in, your characterization of service will be *honorable*. (Flip over to Chapter 4 to check out Block 24 of a DD-214, which is where your character of service appears.) You can use your honorable discharge to claim all your VA benefits, from a VA-backed home loan and the GI Bill to healthcare, subsidized work training, and other perks you earned.

>> **General discharge under honorable conditions:** This type is an administrative discharge (see Chapter 2). A *general discharge under honorable conditions* means that you showed up, did your job, and maybe had a few disciplinary actions. Perhaps you failed to meet some military standards, but overall, you did okay. Uncle Sam doesn't feel like you served with distinction, but he's not

going to kick you on your way out the door. If you have a general discharge under honorable conditions, you're still entitled to all your VA benefits except the GI Bill, so you're on your own paying for college or trade school.

>> **Other than honorable discharges:** *Other than honorable* — commonly called OTH — discharges are the result of misconduct during your time in the military. Security violations, big-time misconduct that endangered other servicemembers, or civilian criminal convictions can trigger this most serious type of administrative discharge. If your separation document characterizes your service as OTH, you can't join another branch (or a reserve component) except in very rare cases, and you can't access your veteran's benefits, either.

>> **Bad conduct (court-martial) discharges:** The military gives bad conduct discharges to enlisted servicemembers only, and only then when they've been court-martialed and sentenced to punishment. Often, these types of punitive discharges (see Chapter 2) are immediately preceded by a stay in a military prison. You may be required to use the leave you've accrued pending review of your conviction (it's called *appellate leave*), and if you have any leave left, you may be allowed to take a lump-sum payment based on your basic rate of pay. Additionally, you lose most of your VA benefits with a bad conduct discharge.

>> **Dishonorable discharges (enlisted only):** *Dishonorable discharges* are the worst type of discharge an enlisted servicemember can receive from the U.S. military. They're reserved for people who commit serious offenses that the military considers reprehensible — like homicide or sexual assault — and are convicted at a general court-martial that calls for a dishonorable discharge as part of the sentence. A dishonorable discharge automatically disqualifies you from receiving any VA benefits (other than healthcare for a limited number of service-connected or service-aggravated conditions), and it may even preclude you from owning a firearm if you were sentenced to spend a year or more in prison. (A dishonorable discharge with this type of conviction is a lot like a civilian felony conviction, so that's where the firearm rule comes from.)

>> **Elimination (officers only):** Officers in the military can be *eliminated* for substandard performance of duty, misconduct, moral or professional dereliction, derogatory information in their records, or in the interests of national security. Elimination won't appear on your DD-214, though. Your character of service will be honorable, general under honorable conditions, or other than honorable conditions. You may request to resign in lieu of being eliminated, but if you're discharged under general conditions, you still lose your GI Bill benefits and civil service retirement credit (although you may still be able to cash in your accrued leave).

>> **Dismissal (officers only):** Commissioned officers can't receive bad conduct or dishonorable discharges, but they can be dismissed from the service. A *dismissal* is the officer's version of a dishonorable discharge, which means you aren't entitled to VA benefits (and if you're convicted of an offense that requires you to spend more than a year in prison, your right to own a firearm is revoked, too).

>> **Entry-level separation/uncharacterized:** *Entry-level separation* can only occur during the 180 days immediately following the date you join the military. It's not characterized under any other type of discharge, so if you don't make it through basic training or job training, your discharge type is "uncharacterized." You may hear this type of discharge referred to as "failure to adapt" or something similar. You generally don't qualify for veterans' benefits with an entry-level separation (including, in most cases, medical benefits).

TIP

Although many veterans discharged under anything other than honorable conditions assume they're not eligible for any VA benefits, that's not always the case. You may be entitled to healthcare for certain service-connected conditions or conditions that were aggravated by your service. When it comes to healthcare and other benefits, the VA says, "Individuals receiving undesirable, bad conduct, and other types of dishonorable discharges may qualify for VA benefits depending on a determination made by VA." Use what you learned in the military: If a VA rep tells you that you don't qualify for any benefits, go higher up the chain until someone provides you with the right answer.

STATUTORY BARS TO VA BENEFITS

Some issues require the VA to deny you benefits after a military discharge. In fact, Chapter 38 of the United States Code (section 5303) prohibits the VA from issuing you benefits if you committed an offense that led to a discharge through a general court-martial, you were a conscientious objector, you deserted, you (as an officer) resigned for the good of the service, you were absent without official leave for a continuous period of 180 days or more, or you requested release from service as an alien during a period of hostilities. The exception is if you were declared "insane" (their language, not mine!) at the time of the offense that led to your discharge. Additionally, the VA can deny you benefits if you accepted an undesirable discharge to escape trial by court-martial or if you were convicted of mutiny, spying, or an offense involving moral *turpitude* (depravity). It can also deny you if you engaged in willful and persistent misconduct or a small number of other situations.

Recharacterizing Your Discharge

If you leave military service with an honorable discharge (which I discuss in the preceding section), you'll never need to appeal to the U.S. government to upgrade your status. But if you're among the 10 or so percent of people who exit under honorable conditions (not the same thing), other than honorable conditions, bad conduct, or another unfavorable characterization, you may later want to petition Uncle Sam. The process isn't easy, and it doesn't have a very high success rate, but it can be done.

You may be eligible for some VA benefits with a less-than-honorable discharge. In fact, you can even ask the VA for a Character of Discharge Review; when you apply for VA benefits, the agency will review your record to determine whether it was honorable for VA purposes (even if your DD-214 says something different).

You're more likely to receive an upgrade from the VA for its own purposes if your discharge had something to do with the following:

>> Mental health conditions, including post-traumatic stress disorder

>> Traumatic brain injury

>> What the VA calls *military sexual trauma* (MST), which is experiencing sexual assault or harassment during your military service

>> Sexual orientation, including things that happened while the "Don't Ask, Don't Tell" policy was in effect

If a simple VA Character of Discharge Review doesn't cut it for you because your characterization of service is impacting your ability to find a job (or affecting you in other ways), getting a bad paper discharge upgraded to general or honorable is possible, as is having your reasons for your discharge changed. Two military boards can review a military discharge: the Discharge Review Board, or DRB, and the Board of Correction for Military Records, or BCMR.

The Discharge Review Board

The Discharge Review Board can upgrade general discharges, other than honorable discharges, and special court-martial bad conduct discharges. It can also change the reason for discharge that's listed on your DD-214 (it's listed as your Separation Code in Block 26, which you can check out in Chapter 4). A DRB can only help you if you can prove that your discharge was improper or inequitable. In this case, *improper* means inconsistent with the law or factually incorrect; *inequitable* means inconsistent with the policies and traditions of the service. For example, if you served honorably but had a substance abuse issue because you were suffering from post-traumatic stress, you may be able to use the DRB to upgrade your discharge.

TIP

You have 15 years from the date of your discharge to apply for an upgrade to your status, but don't wait. Start the process now. An upgrade may make a big difference in the way prospective employers feel about hiring you, and it can make you eligible for more VA benefits.

TIP

Many people choose to work with an attorney to upgrade a military discharge. If you can afford to do so, you should find a lawyer who understands the process, has a proven track record of success, and primarily works with people in situations like yours. A general practitioner who focuses on several areas of the law may not be as well-versed in discharge upgrades as one who primarily focuses on them, so be careful whom you choose.

Applying to a Discharge Review Board

You must complete an Application for Review of Discharge From the Armed Services of the United States to petition the DRB for a discharge upgrade. You can complete the form online, get it from a regional office of the VA, or pick it up at your nearest military installation (provided you're allowed entry). The DRB can only consider what you tell it, so be as complete as possible with your application.

TIP

Provide the DRB with all the documentation that helps explain why you deserve a discharge upgrade. You may want to include things like these:

>> A personal statement, including information about your positive conduct (such as maintaining a clean criminal record, attending rehabilitation programs, or participating in mental health treatment) since you left the service

>> Your medical records relating to your upgrade request (such as documentation of post-traumatic stress disorder or military sexual trauma)

>> Statements from people you served with, ideally as high-ranking as possible

>> Educational records

>> Your employment history

The more information you can provide, the better. Again, the DRB can't consider anything you don't include with your application, so submit anything that supports your position.

Listening in on a DRB hearing

You can ask the DRB to hold a hearing or ask it to decide based on your application. Hearings often take place in Washington, D.C., and you're allowed to attend at your own expense. Most DRBs consist of five officers and senior members of the active military.

Most hearings take about an hour. You're allowed to testify or make a statement. If you testify, you do so under oath, and board members can ask you questions. Each person on the board gets one vote, and if the majority votes in your favor, you receive a discharge upgrade.

TIP

If you ask the DRB to make a decision based on your application and it denies it, you can then ask for a hearing. Strategically, that may make sense — you get two chances to make your case. But every case is different, so you should talk to an attorney to find out what's right in your situation.

Waiting for a decision

The board usually takes several weeks (or more) to rule on a case. If it rules in your favor, you receive a new DD-214 and discharge certificate as well as a copy of the board's decision. If it doesn't rule in your favor, you get a letter that explains the board's decision.

The Board of Correction of Military Records

The Board of Correction of Military Records has the power to change military discharges to or from medical retirement or medical discharge, as well as those resulting from a general court-martial. The BCMR can also review your discharge if you left the military more than 15 years ago, but you have absolutely no reason to wait that long.

Reading into Reentry Eligibility Codes

When I first left the Army, I missed it. Actually, it was more than that — I was completely freaked out and, frankly, a little surprised that people weren't lining up to hire me because I was a one-of-a-kind catch (just like every other former noncommissioned officer is). My bruised ego and I called a local recruiting station and asked what I needed to do to get back in. It turns out the first step in getting back into the military, even if you change branches, is ensuring that your *reentry eligibility code* (along with your separation code) says you can.

Your reentry eligibility code, which is located in Block 27 of your DD-214, says whether you're eligible or ineligible for reenlistment. Each branch puts its own flair on reenlistment codes by adding letters or numbers (such as RE-1A or RE-4N), so you have dozens of possibilities. Generally, though, the codes break down like this:

>> RE-1 means you may reenlist without issue.

>> RE-2 means you may reenlist, but only under certain restrictions or if the reasons that led to your receiving that code no longer apply to you.

>> RE-3 means you may reenlist, but you'll most likely need a waiver of some sort.

>> RE-4 means you're not normally eligible to reenlist or join another service, but you may be able to with an exception to policy.

Table 5-1 shows the most common RE codes for each branch and what they mean. (SM is an abbreviation for servicemember.) Because the Marine Corps is part of the Department of the Navy, they share the same codes.

TABLE 5-1   **Military RE Codes**

Code	Army	Air Force	Navy and Coast Guard
RE-1	SM is fully qualified for enlistment	SM is eligible for enlistment	SM is eligible for enlistment
RE-1A	SM has more than 6 years of service; fully qualified for enlistment but is ineligible to reenlist for 93 days after separation	SM is ineligible to enlist, but condition may be waived for enlistment	SM is eligible for enlistment
RE-1B	SM hasn't been tested to verify primary MOS during current term of service but is fully qualified for enlistment	N/A	N/A
RE-1C	SM doesn't have scores of 85 or higher in 3 or more aptitude areas of the ASVAB but is qualified for enlistment if otherwise qualified	N/A	N/A
RE-2	SM is separated for the convenience of the government under AR 635-200 but is fully qualified for enlistment	N/A	SM is ineligible for reenlistment due to status
RE-2A	SM has more than 6 years of service and was separated prior to August 15, 1977, and is fully qualified for enlistment	SM was denied reenlistment for quality reasons	N/A

Code	Army	Air Force	Navy and Coast Guard
RE-2B	SM was fully qualified when last separated but wasn't authorized to reenlist under enlisted year group management plan and is fully qualified for enlistment	SM was discharged under general or other than honorable conditions and is eligible to enlist, possibly with a waiver	N/A
RE-2C	SM was fully qualified when last separated but wasn't authorized to reenlist under reenlistment control policy but is fully qualified to enlist	SM was involuntarily separated with honorable discharge and is eligible to enlist, possibly with a waiver	N/A
RE-2E, 2F or 2G	N/A	SM is participating in a substance abuse rehabilitation program or has failed to complete the program and is generally ineligible to enlist	N/A
RE-2M	N/A	SM is separated while serving or waiting for a suspended court-martial sentence and is ineligible to enlist	N/A
RE-2N	NA	SM is a religious conscientious objector and is ineligible to enlist	N/A
RE-2Q	N/A	SM is medically discharged or medically retired and is ineligible to enlist	N/A
RE-3	SM isn't qualified for continued Army service but may reenlist with a waiver	N/A	N/A
RE-3A	SM has over 6 years of service and has declined to meet an additional service requirement but is fully qualified for enlistment with a waiver	SM is separating before 36 months or is a female learning of pregnancy prior to enlistment and may be eligible to enlist, possibly with a waiver	SM failed to meet aptitude requirements but may be eligible to enlist if mental criteria are met
RE-3B	SM has lost time during last period of service but may enlist with a waiver	SM has an ineligibility condition and isn't eligible to enlist unless the condition no longer exists	SM is restricted on assignments due to parenthood or pregnancy but may enlist with a waiver
RE-3C	SM has been denied enlistment under the qualitative screening process in AR 600-200 but may enlist with a waiver	SM wasn't yet considered to reenlist under Selective Reenlistment Program and may be able to enlist	SM is a conscientious objector but may enlist with a waiver

(continued)

TABLE 5-1 *(continued)*

Code	Army	Air Force	Navy and Coast Guard
RE-3D	N/A	N/A	SM failed to meet disciplinary standards and is ineligible to enlist without a waiver
RE-3H	N/A	N/A	SM discharged for hardship and is ineligible to enlist without a waiver
RE-4	SM separated with a non-waiverable disqualification and is ineligible for enlistment	N/A	SM wasn't recommended for reenlistment and is ineligible to enlist
RE-4A	SM didn't meet eligibility citizenship requirement of AR 601-280 at time of last separation and is ineligible for enlistment	SM is discharged for hardship or dependency reasons and is ineligible to enlist without a waiver	N/A
RE-4B	N/A	SM is discharged due to exceeding body fat standards and is ineligible to enlist without a waiver	N/A
RE-4K	N/A	SM is medically disqualified for continued service and is ineligible to enlist without a waiver	N/A
RE-4M	N/A	SM breached enlistment or reenlistment agreement and is ineligible to enlist without a waiver	N/A
RE-4R	SM retired after 20 or more years of active federal service and is ineligible for enlistment	N/A	N/A
RE-6	N/A	N/A	SM has high year tenure and was denied or ineligible for reenlistment but may enlist if all other applicable criteria are met
RE-7	N/A	N/A	SM completed the initial 2-year active duty obligation under the 2x8 Navy Reserve Program and is eligible to enlist if all applicable criteria are met
RE-8	N/A	N/A	SM has temporary medical conditions or unsatisfactory initial performance and conduct but may be able to enlist with a waiver

Registering Your Discharge Documents with the Local Government

After you receive your DD-214, you may choose to register it with your local county clerk's office. This step is a way to safeguard a certified copy of your discharge document in case you lose it. Regardless of whether you choose to file your DD-214 with your county clerk, you should keep digital copies in multiple storage locations — one in the cloud, one on your hard drive, and one in an email to yourself that you won't accidentally delete — so you have easy access if you need it. Remember, though, that your digital copies aren't certified; they're only digital copies, and you may need a certified copy in the future.

TECHNICAL STUFF

In 1973, a huge fire tore through the National Personnel Records Center in St. Louis, Missouri. The water firefighters used to tame the blaze destroyed between 16 and 18 million military records of servicemembers who were discharged from the Army between November 1, 1912, and January 1, 1960, and the Air Force between September 25, 1947, and January 1, 1964. Those records are gone forever, which is why registering yours with the local government *and* keeping several digital and print copies of your own is a good idea.

REMEMBER

Some veterans will tell you that registering your DD-214 with the county clerk opens you up to identity theft, but that's simply not the case. Military discharge information isn't a matter of public record, even if it's in your county's archives. Only you, someone with a power of attorney signed by you, or your next-of-kin (with appropriate documentation, such as a death certificate and proof of your relationship) can get a copy of your DD-214 from the county clerk.

HELP! I LOST MY DISCHARGE DOCS

The National Personnel Records Center will have your entire official military personnel file, or OMPF. You can request replacement copies of your DD-214 by mailing or faxing (yes, the government still uses fax machines) Standard Form 180 through the NPRC or by using eVetRecs, the National Archives' portal to veterans' records. However, receiving your records through the NPRC or eVetRecs can take several weeks.

2

Finding a Job

Immerse yourself in employment programs designed for veterans returning to work.

Create an attention-grabbing resume that makes employers want to hire you on the spot.

Find out about various types of civilian employment so you can start on the path that's right for you.

Consider continuing your employment with Uncle Sam by getting familiar with government work.

Make yourself more marketable by building professional and personal relationships with civilians.

Pick up the skills you need to ace any type of interview and assimilate into the civilian workforce.

Crunch the numbers so you can negotiate the salary you deserve after you receive a job offer.

Arm yourself with knowledge of employee rights, including minimum wage and overtime, and get tips to smooth your workplace transition.

Explore the ins and outs of starting and running a veteran-owned business so you can work for yourself.

Chapter **6**

Engaging Yourself in Employment Programs

I f you're like many people (me included), you bring a pretty big ego with you when you leave the military. You're a veteran, and you're (mostly) sure that employers will be thrilled to hire you. After all, you're "disciplined, physically and mentally tough, trained and proficient," or maybe you're a "guardian of freedom and justice, your nation's sword and shield." Perhaps you're "committed to excellence and the fair treatment of all." Maybe you'll "always be on time to relieve and shall endeavor to do more, rather than less, than your share," or you may "know what counts in this war is not the rounds you fire, the noise of your burst, nor the smoke you make." You know how it goes.

But no matter your past — and regardless of how many websites you scour for information, books you read, or friends you interrogate — getting a civilian job may be a lot tougher than you think it is. Veterans face some unique challenges that civilians don't (including difficulty assimilating in a completely different culture). If you're like most people, you can use a little nudge in the right direction when finding the right job, or even a job you can tolerate until you find the right career path, and fortunately, you've earned the privilege of using a number of resources that will get you there.

TIP

You most likely qualify for Personalized Career Planning and Guidance, or PCPG, from the Veterans Administration. You probably also qualify for VA Chapter 36, a program that helps you find a training program or field of study that's right for you. Provided you're eligible, you can start using these programs if you're going to be discharged in the next six months, you separated less than a year ago (but not under dishonorable conditions), or you're currently eligible for VA education benefits. These programs provide you with the following:

>> Career counseling that helps you decide which types of civilian jobs are the best fit for you

>> Educational counseling that helps you find a training program that puts you into the labor force or a field of study that will help you earn in the future

>> Academic and adjustment counseling that helps you deal with obstacles you're not used to facing

>> Resume support and goal planning

You can take advantage of these benefits by applying online, by mail, or by visiting a VA regional office or VetSuccess on-campus counselor. This chapter introduces you a number of available employment programs for veterans and walks you through how and when to best take advantage of them.

Pinpointing Helpful Programs

I'm not going to pretend that the U.S. government has a solid track record of treating veterans well. In fact, it still struggles to provide consistent resources and care for vets all over the country. But it certainly does *some* things right, like employment programs. In 2009, Executive Order 13518 created an interagency Council on Veterans Employment. As a result, a number of government agencies, including the Department of Labor and the Veterans Administration, along with several private companies, developed a well-rounded set of initiatives to put vets back into the labor force. I explain some of those initiatives in the following sections.

Apprenticeship.gov

Apprenticeship.gov has special resources set aside for active-duty servicemembers and veterans who want to develop workplace and technical skills. If you're active-duty, you can use USMAP to improve your technical skills and fulfill apprenticeship requirements, and if you're separating soon, you can use DoD

SkillBridge (more on both of those programs in the later sections with the same names). If you're already a veteran, you can use your GI Bill for up to 36 months to complete an apprenticeship, which allows you to receive a monthly housing allowance in addition to your apprenticeship wages. And if you're a vet with a service-connected disability, you may be eligible to use your VR&E benefits (see the later section "VR&E" for more on those) rather than your GI Bill, which you can then save for something else.

Compensated Work Therapy

Compensated Work Therapy, or CWT, is a clinical vocational rehabilitation program run by the Department of Veterans Affairs. All VA medical centers have an active CWT program, which provides support for vets living with mental illness or physical impairment that creates barriers to employment. Your issues do *not* have to be service-connected to use CWT services. You simply must face barriers to finding or holding a job. CWT partners with government agencies and civilian companies that want to hire veterans. The program offers the following:

» **Community Based Employment Services, or CBES:** This program leads to direct placement in competitive employment.

» **Transitional Work, or TW:** TW is a pre-employment vocational program that matches participants with actual work assignments for a limited time.

» **Supported Education, or SEd:** The SEd program provides individualized supports for vets in education and training programs, and it links veterans with educational institutions that help them achieve their goals.

» **Supported Employment, or SE:** Supported Employment is only for vets with significant barriers to employment, such as post-traumatic stress disorder, traumatic brain injury, and spinal cord injury. You may be eligible for SE if you can't work independently without intensive, ongoing support services. The program includes job placement and follow-along supports through clinical treatment.

» **Supported Self-Employment, or SSE:** The Supported Self-Employment program provides guidance on owning your own business, as well as connecting vets with networking opportunities, guidance on business practices, training and a few other services.

» **Vocational Assistance:** Vocational Assistance is an umbrella term for assessment, counseling, guidance, and other related services. They're all short-term services and designed to enable you search for and find a job, participate in interviews, and remain successfully employed.

Disability employment with a Selective Placement Program Coordinator

If you have a disability, regardless of whether the VA says your disability is service-connected, you may be eligible to use a Selective Placement Program Coordinator, or SPPC, if you're applying for federal jobs. Nearly every federal agency has an SPPC (or equivalent role) whose job is to help people with disabilities get information on current job opportunities, obtain reasonable accommodations (flip to Chapter 13 to find out more about those), and guide disabled applicants through the entire employment process with a government agency.

IVMF's Entrepreneurship Programs

The Institute for Veterans and Military Families at Syracuse University, or IVMF, offers several nationwide programs to help your business get off the ground and remain successful, including these:

>> **VetNet:** VetNet is an online resource that provides networking tools, career training, job opportunities, and even entrepreneurship classes.

>> **Entrepreneurship Bootcamp for Veterans, or EBV:** This training program teaches you the steps and stages of business creation and management, and it focuses on the challenges you'll face — as well as the opportunities you'll get — as a veteran business owner.

>> **Entrepreneurship Bootcamp for Veterans (EBV) Accelerate:** EBV Accelerate is a bootcamp-style program that teaches you about the financial, management, marketing, and strategic planning challenges that established businesses often face.

>> **Entrepreneurship Bootcamp for Veterans (EBV) Spark:** This all-virtual training program lets you test out your business ideas and develop the basic skills you need to hang up your shingle.

>> **Boots to Business, or B2B:** This program leads you through the process of evaluating business concepts and gives you the knowledge you need to develop a business plan if you're interested in becoming an entrepreneur.

>> **Veteran EDGE:** This program's acronym stands for "Engage, Develop, Grow, Evaluate." Veteran EDGE is a four-day annual conference that teaches you about the latest opportunities, best practices, and resources available to your new company.

>> **Veteran Women Igniting the Spirit of Entrepreneurship, or V-WISE:** This women-focused training program covers entrepreneurship and small business management. You get free tools, ongoing support, and business mentorship.

Onward 2 Opportunity

Onward 2 Opportunity, or O2O, is a national partnership between the Department of Defense and Syracuse University that helps transitioning servicemembers and vets get the skill sets they need to work for leading U.S. companies. The best part? It's free. You can attend classes in person if you're near one of a couple of dozen military installations or take an online-only version if you're not. It's even available to spouses of servicemembers, vets, and members of the National Guard and Reserves.

O2O used to be called the Veterans Career Transition Program, or VCTP, and today, it offers

» A direct connection to more than 400 military-friendly employers

» A comprehensive assessment tool that helps you line up your training plan with your skills, interests, and professional goals

» Career path selection, interview prep, and even employment services support

» Free industry-recognized certifications with exam fees and courses included

» More than 30 free courses in three in-demand career tracks (which are subject to change)

» In-person and virtual support along the way

Pathways Recent Graduate Program

The Pathways Recent Graduate Program offers federal internship and employment opportunities for current students, recent graduates, and people who have an advanced degree through one of three paths:

» **Internship Program:** The Internship Program is open to current students, and it offers paid opportunities to work in federal agencies while you complete your education.

» **Recent Graduates Program:** This program is for those who have graduated from a qualifying educational institution or certificate program within the past two years. It offers career development with training and mentorship.

» **Presidential Management Fellows Program:** The Presidential Management Fellows Program through Pathways is for recent graduates with an advanced degree (such as a master's, PhD, or JD) earned in the past two years, as well as current grad students who will complete their programs by August 31 of the following year.

USMAP

The United Services Military Apprenticeship Program, or USMAP, is open to active duty enlisted servicemembers (including members of the Reserve, Guard, and Air National Guard). You must have at least 12 months left on active duty, and the apprenticeship you choose must be related to your military occupational specialty and your current primary duty. The military isn't going to release you to work for another company; you're simply going to earn credit toward your apprenticeship while you're on Uncle Sam's clock. You enroll online or submit a paper application, log your supervised hours, submit a competency job function evaluation to your apprenticeship supervisor, and submit your final report to your command for approval. Dozens of apprenticeships are available through the Army, Navy, Marines, and Coast Guard (but not the Air Force), and you can find out which ones apply to your career by visiting USMAP.netc.navy.mil.

Veteran Employment Program Offices

The Department of Education runs the Veteran Employment Program Office, or VEPO, which promotes veteran recruitment, employment, training and development, and retention within several government agencies. These agencies have special programs that actively look for veterans to hire. You can find a complete list, as well as information on each agency's VEPO, at www.fedshirevets.gov.

VR&E

VR&E (officially called the Veterans Readiness and Employment Program, and sometimes called Chapter 31 or Voc-Rehab) helps veterans with service-connected disabilities and employment handicaps. You must have at least a 10 percent disability rating from the VA to use VR&E, and you must receive a discharge that's anything other than dishonorable. This program gives you guidance on employment, self-employment, and even independent living. Check out Chapter 3 for more information on getting your disability rating before you leave the military; that way, you can jump right into the VR&E program.

Support for dependents' employment

The VA offers career counseling support for dependent family members of current service members and veterans with service-connected disabilities. Your spouse, child, or other dependent must be eligible for a VA education benefit to use this program.

Tackling U.S. Government Career Transition Programs

The government has two career transition programs specifically for displaced or surplus veterans: the Career Transition Assistance Plan and the Interagency Career Transition Assistance Plan. Both plans give you selection priority over other applicants. Additionally, the Department of Defense runs SkillBridge, which is one of the most overlooked — but most valuable — programs available.

Career Transition Assistance Plan (CTAP)

The Career Transition Assistance Plan is an intra-agency program helping surplus or displaced federal employees get jobs within the same agency (so, for example, a soldier who was forced out of the military can become a DA civilian). To qualify, you must have been discharged from the military under a reduction in force, or RIF, or have retired or suffered an injury that qualifies for compensation. You must meet eligibility requirements and your agency must be accepting applications from within or outside its permanent workforce.

Interagency Career Transition Assistance Plan (ICTAP)

You may be eligible to use ICTAP to get a job with a different federal agency — not the one you just left — if you were a surplus or displaced federal employee. For example, if you're a Marine veteran, you can use ICTAP to get a job in the Department of Education, Homeland Security, the U.S. Postal Service, or any other federal agency by using the preference this program gives you. Like the CTAP program (see the preceding section), you must meet all the job's qualifications and other requirements. Additionally, with ICTAP, you must live within the job's local commuting area.

DOD SkillBridge

If you're six months out (or less) from your transition date, you can use DoD SkillBridge — a program that matches you to civilian opportunities while you're still in the service. That means you still get your military pay and benefits while you're participating in an industry training program or an apprenticeship during your transition. Hundreds of companies partner with the Department of Defense to provide these opportunities for servicemembers, including big-name online shopping retailers, aerospace and defense companies, healthcare companies, and even a famously green tractor company.

It's open to all active-duty servicemembers, National Guard members, and Reservists of any rank, but not to veterans or spouses. You can only use it while you're on Uncle Sam's payroll, and then only with approval from the first field grade commander with the authority to impose non-judicial punishment under Article 15 of the UCMJ in your chain of command. (Usually that's an O-4.)

The SkillBridge program offers you several opportunities for internships and apprenticeships, which you can find on the program's website, or you can use a program such as Hiring Our Heroes by the U.S. Chamber of Commerce.

TIP

Participation in SkillBridge is always mission-dependent. That means your commander reserves the right to tell you no. You can't enter into any agreement with a SkillBridge partner until you have your commander's authorization. Start talking to your command about taking advantage of this opportunity as early as you can — the sooner, the better — because doing so may increase your chances of being approved. Your commander may feel better about letting you go train six months from now rather than next week.

» Sizing up different resume types

» Zeroing in on your strengths by reviewing your achievements

» Making sure to include the necessary details on your resume

» Creating unique and effective cover letters

» Focusing on the special features of a federal resume

» Tracking your resume after you've submitted it

Chapter **7**

Getting Your Foot in the Door with a Strong Resume

Before you can land your dream job, you have to put together a resume that makes people want to hire you. In fact, that's the whole purpose of a resume: It's a quick snapshot of how awesome you are and why you'll be a great asset to a particular company. (Yep, I said "a particular company." You need to switch up your resume based on the job you're applying for — tailoring it to match specific job descriptions is one of the best ways to boost your chances of getting hired.)

Your resume takes a lot of work, but it's certainly worth doing right. Prospective employers may receive hundreds of applications for one position, and many of the other applicants are just as qualified as you are. That means your application packet needs to be the best one each hiring manager has ever seen.

Fortunately, as a veteran, you have some advantages right out of the gate. First, you're most likely entitled to claim veterans' preference, which I cover in the later section "Capitalizing on your military service." You also have a unique skill set, and even if you weren't in a leadership position in the military, you probably picked up some leadership abilities that civilian companies really value. (You can learn something from every leader in the military, even if it's how *not* to lead!)

Creating your resume is a process that involves taking stock of all your military achievements and maybe the things you did before you joined, too. It also requires getting familiar with common resume formats, translating your military skills into civilian terms, and putting together customized cover letters for specific employers, all of which I cover in the following sections. And if you need more resume help, I strongly recommend *Resumes For Dummies* by Laura DeCarlo (Wiley).

Identifying the Four Most Common Types of Resumes

REMEMBER

Different jobs require different resumes. Most notably, you don't use the same type of resume for a federal job that you'd use for a civilian job — but usually, with civilian jobs, you can choose which type of resume best explains your qualifications. I outline four main types of resumes here, and although yours may be a bit different, it should fall (at least loosely) into one of these categories.

Chronological resumes

Like its name implies, a *chronological resume* displays your work history and accomplishments in order. You begin with your most current position and work backward to end with your earliest. A lot of civilian employers prefer chronological resumes because your most recent experience is at the top, and that's far more relevant than what you did when you worked at the car wash before joining the military. Usually, these resumes date back 10 to 15 years.

These resumes are best if you have a solid employment background and a steady work history, especially if most of your recent experience relates to the job you're applying for.

TIP

You can still use a chronological resume if you've been in the military for a long time or if you've never had a job outside the military. Instead of listing your military branch as your employer, create separate points for every assignment you held. Check out an example of a chronological resume in Figure 7-1.

JOE SNUFFY

123 Any Street · 202-555-1212
JoeSnuffy@Email.com · LinkedIn.com/JoeSnuffy

Energetic, motivating leader with a proven ability to manage staff on short- and long-term projects. High-achieving independent worker who excels at analyzing projects to generate new ideas and improve efficiency agency-wide.

EXPERIENCE

AUGUST 10, 2021 – PRESENT
PLATOON SERGEANT, 23RD CHEMICAL BATTALION
Manage day-to-day operations, train and supervise 43 subordinates, and maintain mission readiness in a chemical company based at Camp Humphreys. Responsible for $1.3 million in equipment. Maintain secret-level security clearance. Instrumental in providing chemical, biological, radiological and nuclear support to the South Korean government, as well as ensuring the success of all subordinates in my care.

FEBRUARY 10, 2018 – AUGUST 10, 2021
OPERATIONS SPECIALIST, 3RD BRIGADE SPECIAL TROOPS BATTALION
Planned, coordinated and directed military educational opportunities for soldiers stationed at Schofield Barracks. Monitored, communicated and assisted in enforcing mission-critical plans; received and handled fragmentary orders and serious incident reports. Managed accountability, maintenance and readiness of equipment in excess of $2 million, as well as readiness of eight subordinates.

FEBRUARY 10, 2015 – FEBRUARY 10, 2018
SQUAD LEADER, 44TH CHEMICAL BATTALION
Supervised, trained, mentored and managed six subordinates; received and relayed orders; delegated responsibility as required; mentored and counseled squad members on personal and professional topics. Maintained accountability and ensured compliance with Army standards. Ensured five out of six subordinates started college-level coursework to further their personal and professional development.

EDUCATION

AUGUST 2021
BS, CRIMINAL JUSTICE, UNIVERSITY OF HARD KNOCKS
Earned GPA of 4.0; Dean's List; National Honor Society

SKILLS

- A member of a time-honored corps
- Never use grade or position to attain pleasure, profit or personal safety
- Competence is my watchword
- Officers of my unit will have maximum time to accomplish their duties

FIGURE 7-1:
Sample chronological resume.

© John Wiley & Sons, Inc.

WARNING

If you have anything other than an honorable or general discharge from the military, you may want to avoid the chronological format — especially if you weren't in the military for very long. A functional resume (see the following section) may be best for you.

Functional resumes

Functional resumes focus on your skills and experience. Your work history is still important, but these resumes let your abilities shine. If you have lapses in employment, or if you have very limited employment experience (such as a short-term stint in the military being the only job you've ever had), a functional resume may be your best choice. See a sample functional resume in Figure 7-2.

David Highspeed

123 Any Street, Your Town   202-555-1212   DavidHighspeed@Email.com

Objective
Experienced and versatile paralegal with strong experience in research and documentation seeks a challenging position with The Law Offices of Attorney, Lawyer & Barrister.

Skills & Abilities
Exceptionally skilled in fact-finding, document preparation, working directly with attorneys, developing and maintaining index systems for case files, and developing legal arguments, motions and other case filings.

Experience
Paralegal, U.S. Navy
February 26, 2018 – February 27, 2021
- Developed and maintained case file indexing system
- Monitored changes to U.S. Navy regulations
- Utilized existing files and research resources to develop information for pending cases

Education
Oakland Community College – Farmington, Michigan
4.0 GPA

Administrative
Lead coordinator for daily processing of forms, motions and client communication

Leadership
Oversaw operations of an expanding legal services office and managed four subordinates

References
Joseph Radcon
Lieutenant, U.S. Navy
202-555-1312

FIGURE 7-2: Sample functional resume.

© *John Wiley & Sons, Inc.*

Combination resumes

A *combination resume* highlights all your skills and traits, plus provides a chronological listing of your work experience. It's an overall snapshot of what kind of worker you are, so a lot of candidates feel they're more likely to be hired after submitting one. A combination resume is a great choice if your job history is limited. The tricky part of these resumes is keeping them short and sweet. If yours is too long, prospective employers and hiring managers won't even make it through the whole thing. Get a peek at a combination resume in Figure 7-3.

LS

LANCE SCHMUCKATELLI
TRANSLATOR AND MILITARY LINGUIST

OBJECTIVE

To effectively facilitate communication between Russian-speaking patients and their families at Walter Snead Medical Center

SKILLS

Reading, writing and fluently speaking Russian

Excellent interpersonal communication skills

EXPERIENCE

LINGUIST • U.S. MARINE CORPS • JUNE 6, 2011 – PRESENT
Identifying foreign communications, interpreting between English- and Russian-speakers during high-level meetings, and translating mission-essential documents between Russian and English. Monitoring, transcribing and translating intercepted target communications. Analyzing translated communications. Supervising four subordinates. Maintaining over $1.3 million in sensitive equipment.

EDUCATION

DEFENSE LANGUAGE INSTITUTE FOREIGN LANGUAGE CENTER • JULY 13, 2010
Graduated among top 10% of class.

MICHIGAN STATE UNIVERSITY • BACHELOR OF ENGLISH • MAY 5, 2010
GPA 3.7

VOLUNTEER EXPERIENCE

Earned the Military Outstanding Volunteer Service Medal by tutoring ESL students in a local high school.

GYSGT214@EMAIL.COM   @CRAYON1121   202-555-1212   /CRAYON1121

FIGURE 7-3: Sample combination resume.

Targeted resumes

Targeted resumes, such as the one in Figure 7-4, are customized to the job you want. Everything in this type of resume is a reflection of the job requirements, including your work history, education, and the abilities you highlight. These types of resumes can quickly and easily show prospective employers that you're a perfect fit. (You use a form of a targeted resume if you apply for a government job. Read more about those jobs in Chapter 9.)

Taylor Lowdrag

123 Any Street
Your Town, Any State 12345
(202)555-1212

Professional Qualifications

- Commercial Certificate: Rotorcraft-Helicopter (#1234567), issued May 27, 2020
- Instrument Rating: Rotorcraft-Helicopter, Airplane, issued July 14, 2020

Professional Experience

United States Army

- Flew 84 successful combat missions in Iraq and Afghanistan in AH-64 Apache attack helicopters
- Successful completion of Survival, Evasion, Resistance and Escape Course (SERE-C)
- Successful completion of Helicopter Overwater Survival training

Education

Bachelor of Science: Aviation
Embry-Riddle Aeronautical University
Major: Aeronautics
3.7 GPA, awarded Honor Roll and Dean's List every semester

Training

Harry's Huge Helicopter, Inc., Detroit Metropolitan Airport (DTW), Romulus, MI

- High Altitude Training
- Endorsement: SFAR 73

Zoellner Helicopters, Detroit Metropolitan Airport (DTW), Romulus, MI

- Certificate earned: Private Pilot's Certificate

FIGURE 7-4:
Sample targeted resume.

© John Wiley & Sons, Inc.

INCLUDING MILITARY SERVICE ON JOB APPLICATIONS

Not all jobs require resumes. In fact, many great jobs simply require you to fill out an application and attend an interview (find more on acing interviews in Chapter 11). When you fill out applications, you'll most likely see the question "Are you a protected veteran?" If you're reading this book, the answer to that question is probably "Yes."

The Vietnam Era Veterans' Readjustment Assistance Act of 1974, or VEVRAA, was created in response to the employment discrimination many Vietnam vets faced. Even if you're not a Vietnam vet, the law applies to Gulf War-era veterans, too (an era that started on August 2, 1990, and doesn't have an end date). However, not all employers must comply with the law; it only applies to those that work with the federal government or that have a certain dollar amount in federal contracts. Even companies that don't work with the federal government may ask whether you're a veteran, though, because they're serious about hiring vets and want to increase the number of veterans who clock in every day.

Employers are legally allowed to ask you whether you're a veteran, but they shouldn't ask to see your DD-214 or other discharge papers except when the question directly relates to the job or the employer needs to verify your veterans' preference. They also shouldn't ask you why you were discharged from the military. If they do, you're not required to answer.

Detailing Your Achievements to Find Your Strengths

Employers need to know why you're the best candidate for a job, and the best way to show them is to put your achievements on paper. Whether you earned a handful of Good Conduct Medals, led your team successfully through a deployment, or planned your battalion commander's retirement ceremony, all your achievements count in this phase of the resume development process. Open up your favorite word processing software (or a notebook) and spell out every achievement, no matter how minor, connected to your time in the military. You may want to grab your "I Love Me" book, flip through it, and reminisce a bit about the awards you earned during your time in the service to get some inspiration.

After you've listed your achievements, pick out the five biggest or most impressive — the things that make you proud. Ask yourself these three questions about each one:

>> How did I get involved in the circumstances surrounding this achievement?

>> What, exactly, did I do to earn this?

>> What did I enjoy about this achievement?

For example, if you ensured that your entire platoon passed a physical fitness test, you may write the following:

>> I was a platoon sergeant, a position that I earned through promotion. When I took over, the platoon had a 70 percent pass rate on physical fitness assessments, and I wanted them all to pass.

>> I conducted physical training with my platoon five days a week, talked about their goals with our unit's fitness trainer, implemented plans to help them reach their goals, took them on four-mile runs once a week, and did special PT once a week, like playing soccer or completing difficult hikes.

>> I enjoyed the time I spent getting to know my platoon, coming up with new ideas to keep them engaged, and becoming healthier and more fit along with them.

Because you're repeating this process for each achievement, you'll start to see patterns emerge. Maybe you really enjoy having your boots on the ground and working with others; perhaps you're driven to make sure other people meet their goals or you love coming up with creative solutions to problems. If you're having a tough time finding patterns, ask someone close to you to look at your achievement lists; sometimes patterns are easier for other people to spot.

Hang on to these lists, and if you're up for it, make more. You can likely use them to conduct a solid self-assessment, and you may find that you come up with more information to include on your resume.

Filling in All the Details on Your Resume

After all your accomplishments are dress right, dress (see the preceding section), you're ready to fill in the blanks. For most resumes, you need the following:

>> A job-focused *objective statement* to tell your prospective employer what you're looking for

>> Your most recent (and most relevant) job history

>> A list of your relevant skills and qualifications for the job

>> A list of your educational credentials

>> Your volunteer work, memberships in distinguished organizations, and, in some cases, contact information for references

Brevity is the soul of a good resume. You have only a limited amount of space, and unlike your school writing assignments, changing the font size probably isn't going to get you very far. Ideally, you'll show hiring managers that you're a perfect fit in one page (not counting the cover page, which I cover in the later section "Composing a Compelling Cover Letter").

Every part of your resume needs to show prospective employers that you're more qualified than other applicants are and that you're a better fit with the company's culture. That's why you should customize every resume you send out. Sure, editing your resume for each job you want is a pain, but it's worth it — especially because a lot of job candidates don't bother to do so. Customization can make a tired, bored, and frustrated hiring manager do a double-take on your resume and maybe even get it into the "let's-take-a-closer-look" pile.

Creating a good objective

The objective statement on a resume is important; it's your first chance to make a good impression with a prospective employer by describing your career intentions and who you are. Hiring managers often scan the objectives first, just to get a "feel" for each applicant (or to decide whether to keep reading or put the resume in the recycle bin). Remember, people are clamoring for good jobs, so you need to stand out. And if the company you're applying to work for uses software to scan resumes for keywords (most big companies do), the objective statement is a great place to add them.

TECHNICAL STUFF

Many employers use artificial intelligence to sort through resumes before a real person reads them. AI weeds out generic resumes that don't have much potential through software technology known as *applicant tracking systems*, or ATSs. Hiring managers and recruiters set up the software to look for specific keywords in resumes. If the keywords appear in a resume, it gets a second look; if not, it's never even opened.

Before you write an objective statement, study the job description so you can create one or two customized sentences that show you're worth considering for the job. For example, if the job description reads, "Private clinic hiring medical assistant in Valrico, Florida. Candidate must be experienced, reliable, and able to multitask. Phlebotomy experience desired," you can craft an objective statement that says, "Reliable phlebotomist with 7 years of experience seeking a medical assisting job in a Valrico health clinic." That objective statement wouldn't work well if you were submitting your resume to become a chef, a daycare provider, or even an administrative assistant in a doctor's office, but it's very specific to this job. That's why customizing your objective statement for each job is so important.

TIP

You can make your objective statement stand out by bolding or italicizing it, or by placing it inside a shaded box. As long as it's noticeable and right below your name and contact information, it should be fine.

If you're feeling bold, you can swap out your objective statement for a skills summary that highlights how amazing you are and what you're capable of doing. For example, you may change out your objective from "Seeking a challenging position as a paralegal" to "Accomplished and enthusiastic paralegal with extensive military experience. Versatile background includes will preparation, case research for court-martial proceedings, and transcribing witness interviews."

You can also replace your objective statement with a skills table that highlights your abilities, like the one in Figure 7-5.

FIGURE 7-5:
A skills table for an education professional's resume.

• Curriculum Design	• Special Needs Instruction	• Standardized Testing
• Classroom Management	• Technology Integration	• Imaginative Lesson Planning
• Student Assessment	• ESL and ESOL Instruction	• First Aid/CPR

© John Wiley & Sons, Inc.

You don't have to include an objective, skills summary, or skills table at all if you don't want to. Just remember that you need everything on your resume to show hiring managers why you're a great fit, and that you should avoid saying the same thing twice.

Surveying skills that follow you after military service

Regardless of your job in the military, you learned a lot about leadership, being a team player, and getting results. You probably possess several skills that'll follow you for the rest of your life, even if you draw a blank when you sit down to create your resume.

If you're having a tough time coming up with ways to describe your skills, use some of those listed here to get started.

Advising	Conceptualizing	Consulting	Creative problem-solving	Critical thinking
Decision-making	Discipline	Encouraging	Forecasting	Goal-setting
Identifying problems	Improving	Insight	Interpersonal skills	Leadership
Management	Motivating	Multicultural perspective	Negotiating	Organizing
Perseverance	Reviewing	Self-confidence	Supervising	Teaching ability
Team-building	Time management			

TIP

Consider your military achievements. (I cover brainstorming a list of these in the earlier section "Detailing Your Achievements to Find Your Strengths.") If one of your achievements was that you got your whole platoon to pass a physical fitness assessment, some of the skills you used included these:

» **Identifying problems:** You saw that the platoon was struggling to pass the test, so you knew you needed to do something about it.

» **Advising:** You gave your subordinates the guidance they needed.

» **Creative problem-solving:** You came up with creative ways to do PT so it wasn't boring.

» **Discipline:** You showed up five days a week and instilled that value in your subordinates, too.

» **Encouraging:** You motivated your subordinates and kept them going when it got tough.

» **Improving:** You improved the outcome for 100 percent of your platoon — not just those who couldn't pass, but those who could, too.

» **Leadership:** You displayed leadership by not only encouraging your platoon to pass but also getting out there and doing the work with them.

You can probably apply several other skills you learned in the military to that achievement, too. And that's not even counting the skills you gained by performing your job, whether you spent your time as a multimedia specialist, a culinary expert, or anything else.

Chalking up character traits you can include on your resume

Pinpointing your own character traits isn't always easy, but if you want your resume to be effective, you need to include them. Prospective employers are usually looking for very specific traits in employees. In fact, you can often find what characteristics employers are looking for in their job descriptions. Check out the following table to see character traits that employers look for in workers and pick out a few that apply to you.

Adaptable	Adventuresome	Assertive	Astute	Calm
Candid	Competent	Cooperative	Creative	Diligent
Diplomatic	Discrete	Easygoing	Effective	Efficient
Empathetic	Enthusiastic	Expressive	Firm	Flexible

Honest	Innovative	Loyal	Objective	Orderly
Outgoing	Patient	Perceptive	Persistent	Precise
Punctual	Receptive	Reliable	Resourceful	Sincere
Successful	Tactful	Tenacious	Tolerant	Versatile

Several of these terms probably apply to you just by virtue of your being a veteran, including *adaptable*, *loyal*, *persistent*, *punctual*, and *versatile*, among others.

Matching a prospective employer's needs with your strengths

Every job description tells you exactly what an employer is looking for in a candidate (discover more about finding the right job for you in Chapter 8), but showing an employer why you're the perfect fit is up to you. You can do that by tailoring your resume to each employer. Pick out words and phrases from each job description that interests you and see how you can integrate them with your resume.

EXAMPLE

Here's a sample job description for a dispatcher you may see on a hiring website:

Qualifications: High school or equivalent; 2 or more years dispatching experience preferred; 2 or more years customer service preferred.

Full Job Description: Looking for a dispatcher with at least 2 years of experience dispatching harbor and rail. Fast-paced environment. Must be able to multitask. Looking for swing shift, 3 p.m. to 12 a.m. M–F, weekends off.

Pay: $45,000 to $60,000 per year

Schedule: 8-hour shifts

The job description has some keywords that tell you what kinds of strengths the ideal candidate has. Specifically, it mentions "fast-paced environment" and wanting a person who can multitask. You can also infer that regardless of whether you have customer service experience, you need to have traits that make you a good customer service representative (such as being outgoing, patient, perceptive, and sincere, all of which I mention in the preceding section). Even if you don't have two years of dispatching experience (but you're a fast learner), you can still apply for this job by tailoring your resume — including your objective statement or skills table, plus your relevant job experience. Your objective statement may say something like this:

> Fast-learning, highly adaptable, outgoing, perceptive, and skilled communicator seeks a job in a challenging, fast-paced environment.

Although you'll probably be up against some serious competition (including people who have more experience than you do), that kind of objective statement can really catch a hiring manager's eye. It's your one chance to make a first impression that gets the hiring manager to keep reading.

Translating military experience into civilian terms

You're used to acronyms and industry-specific lingo that civilians aren't familiar with. If I tell you that you're a "tore-up-from-the-floor-up blue falcon," you'll know exactly what I mean (and I wouldn't blame you for being mad, but I'd never call you that). I probably won't tell you to grab a fuel nozzle using familiar terminology; if I tell you to Charlie Mike after you get a rejection after an interview, that the area around the motor pool's smoke pit needs to be police called, or that you need to show up for mandatory fun day 15 minutes prior to 15 minutes prior, you can pick up what I'm laying down. But a civilian wouldn't have a clue what I was talking about, and that's why you have to keep acronyms and military jargon off your resume.

That goes for your job title, military job description, and military experience, too. For example, my job description in the military included terms like "conduct CBRN sensitive site exploitation" and "operate and perform operator maintenance on assigned CBRN defense and individual CBRN protective equipment." Although a defense contractor would be fine with these terms, they mean nothing to civilians (especially in fields unrelated to chemical operations), which means you need to develop your translation skills to make your resume a DMZ.

I can demilitarize my resume by saying that I have experience in "collecting information and material from chemically contaminated areas," "analyzing samples using hand-held chemical identification equipment," and "maintaining and disseminating highly sensitive chemical detection equipment." Depending on the job I'm applying for, I can be even more generic and say I "prepared reports related to compliance matters," "developed emergency response plans," and "established interpersonal business relationships to facilitate work activities."

REMEMBER

Even your job title can be misleading or confusing to a civilian. Mine was Chemical, Biological, Radiological and Nuclear Specialist. That means nothing to a civilian (and it sounds a lot more impressive than it actually is), so I'd tell a prospective employer that my functional job title was "Chemical and Biological Weapon Defense" or "HAZMAT Response," depending on the job I was applying for. Other job titles, like Quartermaster (Supply Clerk), Cyberspace Defensive Operator (Cybersecurity Expert), and Yeoman (Office Manager or Administrative Assistant), also need translation so prospective employers know what you're talking about.

Also consider describing your job within your organization using civilian terms. For example, rather than "platoon sergeant," you can say "unit supervisor," "training supervisor," or "maintenance supervisor," depending on the job you're trying to land. Because the terms you used in the military don't carry the same (or any) weight with civilians, calling yourself a team leader rather than a platoon sergeant is fine; most civilians don't know where a platoon sergeant or team leader sits within the military hierarchy, but they understand that a team leader is responsible for subordinates.

Several websites can help you translate your military experience into civilian terms. One of the most popular is O*NET (www.onetonline.org), which asks you to enter your branch and military job before providing you with a comprehensive list of translations. You can also flip to the Appendix of this book, where I list a number of civilian terms for the skills you may have picked up in the military. The Department of Labor's site (www.careeronestop.org) has a similar tool.

Perusing phrases to use (and avoid) on your resume

Hiring managers scour through dozens of resumes (or more) every day to fill open positions, and as you can imagine, that gets pretty boring. With that said, you should — and shouldn't — use some words and phrases on your resume because *nobody else is* and *everybody else is*, respectively.

Think about using creative words to describe your duties and tasks. Words like those listed here may attract hiring managers' attention because they're precise (and less-common) than their synonyms are.

Achieved	Advised	Created	Developed	Empowered
Established	Ideas	Improved	Increased	Influenced
Launched	Managed	Mentored	Negotiated	Profits
Resolved	Revenue	Trained	Under budget	Volunteered

Use a thesaurus or a thesaurus website to come up with other great words. For example, synonyms for the word *responsible* include *able, capable, competent, conscientious, effective, efficient, loyal, rational, reliable,* and *sensible*. Those are all excellent alternatives that may make great additions to your resume.

Merriam-Webster says the English language has somewhere around a million words, though only several hundred thousand are used commonly enough to make it into the dictionary. That means you can likely find something to say other than the tired words and phrases in the following table.

Accomplished	Ambitious	Bottom line	Buy-in	Core competency
Detail-oriented	Duties included	Ecosystem	Go-getter	Go-to person
Hardworking	Move the needle	On time	Proactive	Responsible for
Results-driven	Rockstar	Self-motivated	Strategic thinker	Synergy
Team player	Think outside the box	Thought leadership	Value add	Wheelhouse

Composing a Compelling Cover Letter

When you submit a resume, include a cover letter with it (unless the job description specifically says not to include one). A cover letter is your first chance to make a great impression on a hiring manager, but keep a few caveats in mind. First, you can't make a good impression with a generic cover letter that you use among multiple employers. Second, you need to personalize the letter to the person who will eventually read it, and third, you must use the cover letter to provide information that *isn't* in your resume — don't just rehash your work history and experience.

TIP

Some employers require you to submit a cover letter with your resume, and others don't. You're better off having one and not needing it than needing one and not having it. If you're in doubt, add a cover letter.

Think of your cover letter like a quick introduction that makes a person want to find out more about you. It should do the following:

>> Be addressed to the right person

>> Include an attention-grabbing hook that makes the reader stick around for a few more sentences

>> Be tailored to the job you're applying for

>> Address why you're the right person for the company (not why the company has the right job for you)

>> Have a clear end that shows the reader that you're a serious candidate they should consider interviewing

Using a new, personalized cover letter with every resume

A generic cover letter that says, "Dear hiring manager, I would like to apply for the open position at your company" is pretty boring; it doesn't stand out. In fact, it shows that you're using the same cover letter for every employer, which means you're likely sending your resume to everyone without carefully reading job ads. (Applying to *all* the jobs is fine, but you need to show prospective employers that you're actually interested in the job they have open instead of doing the job-seeker's equivalent of spray-and-pray.)

A good cover letter shows a prospective employer that you read the job description. A *great* cover letter shows that you read it and that you're confident that you're the best possible person they can hire.

Address your cover letter to the hiring manager listed in the job description. If the description doesn't list a name, do a little digging. Look on LinkedIn, the company's website, or even search by the email address listed. Still can't find the right person? Try addressing your cover letter to the head of the department you're applying to using only the person's first and last name (such as *Dakota Warner*), which should be on the company's website. Even if that's not the right person, this approach shows you did some research — and it's infinitely better than "Dear hiring manager," or worse, the old-fashioned and stuffy "Dear Sir or Madam." As a last resort, you can use a specific department with "hiring manager," such as "Dear paralegal hiring manager."

Don't stop personalizing after the salutation. Personalize your *entire* cover letter by tailoring it to the job. If you're applying for an event coordinator job, for example, you want your cover letter to include specific information on why you'd make a great event coordinator. Maybe you're known as a creative party planner, or you're energetic and enjoy entertaining. That's information that may not show up in your resume, but it should definitely be in your cover letter.

TIP

Often, the most important requirements for a job are listed first in the job description. For example, a job description that says, "We're looking for an event coordinator to facilitate our paint-and-sip events and private parties. Ideal candidate should be positive, patient, energetic and enjoy being around people" tells you exactly what the employer wants from the ideal candidate.

Dropping in a winning one-liner

Grab the hiring manager's attention with a great opening line. Now's your time to shine, so ditch the cookie-cutter "I am writing to apply for the position of event coordinator with your company" in favor of something far more enticing. You can start by doing the following:

- >> **Explaining why you love the company or the brand:** "Your delivery service saved my mom's birthday, so when I saw your job opening, I couldn't help but get excited about the prospect of helping other forgetful hostesses (like me)."

- >> **Noting a personal attribute that will help the company:** "After spending three years providing individualized fitness advice to soldiers in the U.S. Army — I'm a Master Fitness Trainer — I'm excited to bring my motivational skills and in-depth knowledge to your gym so I can help your members reach their goals."

- >> **Being funny, but only if it's appropriate for the job *and* you're truly funny:** "All your servers know me by my order — angel hair pasta with marinara sauce — so I'm looking forward to supporting them as a general manager at your Sierra Vista location and helping them build an even larger base of loyal guests." (But again, only if it's appropriate for the job. If you're applying for a job as a funeral director, an attempt at humor may be the final nail in your coffin.)

WARNING

Don't make your cover letter all about you and why the position is a good fit for you. Every hiring manager knows that people are glad to have a job and earn money, and usually a dozen (or more) other applicants are trying to get their feet in the door. Instead, make your cover letter about why the employer will be glad to have *you* and how you'll help further the company's goals.

Balancing all the right details to make a great pitch

Your cover letter should include some personal information, but don't give away the farm — you want the employer to want to meet you, so be brief and interesting. Besides, all your relevant employment information is in your resume, and your cover letter gets the hiring manager to scroll through it. A quick explanation of how your skills will be an asset to the company is generally enough. Ask yourself what details you'd include if you had ten seconds to explain how you crushed a military responsibility related to this job. Maybe you were innovative enough to develop a PT plan for your entire company, or perhaps you took initiative and brought in a subject-matter expert to teach your squad how to do something that furthered your unit's mission.

The key here is relating your experience or skills to this particular job. You wouldn't write about developing a PT plan if you were applying for a job as a chef because it's completely unrelated, but you can use the fact that you identified a problem, found a creative solution, and implemented it so that your whole team's performance improved.

Use these tips to get hiring managers even more interested:

» **Use numbers:** If you brought in 50 percent more recruits than any other recruiter in the office, or if you were responsible for 140 Marines, say so! Numbers show how you made a measurable impact on the military, and hiring managers can see that you may be able to bring measurable results to their company as well.

» **Don't apologize for your lack of experience:** Everyone has to start somewhere, so don't say "Despite my limited experience . . ." Instead, say, "I'm excited to translate my experience as a mid-level manager in the military to this position."

» **Avoid excessive formality:** Being too formal makes you seem stiff and, frankly, unapproachable. Your personality can't shine through. Be genuine and friendly in your cover letter, and avoid saying "ma'am" or "sir," despite what you're used to.

» **Keep it quick:** Don't go over one page. In fact, try not to go over 250 words. Hiring managers sometimes read dozens of cover letters in one day, so the shorter, the better.

WARNING

Avoid gushing about the job or the opportunity. It seems fake and insincere, and even if you really do mean it with all your heart, take it easy on the compliments. And whatever else you do, don't use exclamation points. That's as bad as liking your own social media status.

Signing off

After personalizing your entire cover letter, you can't just say, "I look forward to hearing from you." Remember, this letter is your pitch to get a prospective employer to actually look at your resume. Use your closing sentence to re-emphasize how enthusiastic you are and how you're a great fit for the job. You may say, "I really believe in what your company is doing, and I look forward to bringing my managerial skills to the position."

Surveying sample cover letters

The kind of cover letter you need varies depending on the situation. The following sections break down the three main types: traditional, impact, and career-change.

Traditional cover letters

A *traditional* cover letter is generally best if you're applying for a job in a traditional company (such as a major retailer, law firm, or big healthcare company) or for a very traditional role (such as an accountant), or when you want to play it safe.

Figure 7-6 shows this type of cover letter for an entry-level paralegal job with the following job description:

Dear Abby Nash,

During my six-year contract as a paralegal in the U.S. Army, I honed my legal research and writing skills, learned the value of efficiency, and assisted with a number of high-profile cases, including a few that made national news. I even worked on a case similar to *Zoellner v. Babcock*, one of your firm's most notable cases. As a stickler for proper legal terminology and grammar, I earned an Army Commendation Medal for my contributions to the Judge Advocate General Corps.

I genuinely look forward to bringing my excellent organizational skills, efficient research capabilities, and strong interpretation experience, which I developed in pursuit of my bachelor's degree from Loyola University, to your firm. As I prepare to leave the military next month, I hope to contribute to your firm's success in a meaningful way.

Sincerely,

Sarah Haab
S.Haab@Haab.com
202-555-1212

FIGURE 7-6:
Sample
traditional
cover letter.

© *John Wiley & Sons, Inc.*

Responsibilities:

>> Drafting, reviewing, proofreading, and editing routine legal documents for attorneys

>> Researching references such as appellate records, commercial legal publications, and court reports that bear on particular legal issues

>> Maintaining evidence such as PDF files, image files, audio files, bank records, and other file types

Requirements:

>> Background investigation, credit check, and drug test required

>> One full year of specialized experience performing paralegal or legal work that demonstrates a basic knowledge of legal research and the ability to interpret legal decisions

>> A bachelor's or equivalent degree or two full years of progressively higher level graduate education leading to such a degree

In the example, note the phrases that correlate with the job description:

» "Proper legal terminology and grammar" in the cover letter ties in with "drafting, reviewing, proofreading, and editing routine legal documents for attorneys."

» "Honed my legal research" in the letter matches up with "researching references" in the job description.

» "Strong interpretation experience" in the cover letter goes hand-in-hand with "the ability to interpret legal decisions" in the job description.

» "My bachelor's degree from Loyola University" in the letter addresses the job description's requirement for a degree.

Additionally, the second sentence — the one that says, "I even worked on a case similar to *Zoellner v. Babcock*" — shows that the writer has done their research on the firm. (Out of all the elements of the cover letter, that one may stand out the most!) Finally, it's short and to-the-point, which hiring managers definitely appreciate.

Impact cover letters

Impact cover letters work best for jobs that demand specific results, such as sales or successful marketing campaigns. This type of letter requires you to put a lot of focus on your past ability to deliver results. Figure 7-7 shows a sample impact cover letter that you can add to your resume for the following job description for a social media manager:

Responsibilities:

» Create and implement programming and channel strategy for Social Media Fire's owned social handles (IG, FB, and TW)

» Monitor chatter, trends, events relevant to our audience, and campaign launches to act on moments that engage audiences

» Test and innovate content formats that we can turn into repeatable formats or series

» Produce weekly reports on social analytics that enable data-led programming and content decisions

» Respond to comments from fans, talent and notable influencers and quality-check all social media posts

Requirements:

» Familiarity with major social media sites

» Experience with photo editing software

» Excellent oral and written communication skills

» Team player with strong interpersonal skills

» Excellent problem solving, time management, and project management skills with the ability to multitask efficiently and effectively

---

Dear Mike Stenman,

My social media feeds are filled with unengaging, uninspiring and, frankly, boring content – when I scroll through, very few of the updates (other than those from friends or family) have what it takes to get me to interact. I know that the last thing you want is to churn out meaningless content that doesn't inspire people... and I also know that I'm the right person to create the posts you're looking for.

During my time in the Marine Corps as a public affairs representative, I was responsible for generating engaging social media posts for our battalion's Facebook, Twitter and Instagram pages. I created hundreds of social media posts across dozens of campaigns, many of which brought in record-breaking "Likes," sparked interesting discussions, and generated thousands of shares. Some of my most-shared, most-engaged posts were based on timely events, including regulation changes, vaccine availability and special news stories relating to the Marine Corps. I also monitored comments and engaged with our audience when it was appropriate, as well as responded to questions and directed people to the resources they needed.

Using Canva Pro, Photoshop and a variety of other tools, I worked with my entire public affairs team to develop exceptional content while managing six subordinates with various duties. I prepared and provided weekly briefings to my commander to ensure that we were all on the same page and achieving the goals our team set.

I've followed your Social Media Fire accounts on each platform, and I'm confident that I can produce attention-grabbing content that makes people stop scrolling and start engaging. I take content production seriously – and ensure that it gets serious results.

Sincerely,

Dave O'Neil
Dave.Oneil@Email.com
202-555-1212

FIGURE 7-7: Sample impact cover letter.

The letter is tailored to the job and shows the reader that the candidate read the job description and did some research of their own. Some of the tie-ins that will grab the hiring manager's attention include these:

» "I was responsible for . . . Facebook, Twitter and Instagram pages" goes with "Familiarity with major social media sites."

>> "Using Canva Pro, Photoshop and a variety of other tools" shows that this person has "Experience with photo editing software."

>> "I prepared and provided weekly briefings" translates to "Excellent oral and written communication skills" (and so does "monitored comments and engaged with our audience").

>> "Worked with my entire public affairs team" and "achieving the goals our team set" both mean that this person is a "team player with strong interpersonal skills."

The opening paragraph touches on how boring, uninspiring content so commonly appears on social media. It also shows that the writer knows how important social media engagement is, which is a key part of the advertised job.

Career-change cover letters

There's a 100 percent chance that you're making a career change right now, so this type of cover letter may be your best shot at getting your foot in the door to the job you want. These kinds of cover letters are a little trickier than others are because you have to focus on transferable skills that show a hiring manager that you're an excellent candidate for the job. You also have to connect your military experience and the responsibilities your new career requires, as well as explain why you're getting into this new field rather than another field. Figure 7-8 shows a sample career-change cover letter for the following job description for a car salesperson:

Responsibilities:

>> Present vehicle attributes, options, features, purchase, and finance options to customers

>> Maintain strong relationships with previous and prospective customers

>> Stay on top of new products, features, and accessories by attending product and training courses

Requirements:

>> Excellent interpersonal communication skills

>> Working knowledge of computers

>> Self-motivated with the ability to set and achieve specific goals

Dear Mary Ray,

My battalion commander was in a tight spot — he needed a subject-matter expert to teach soldiers about a new vehicle system the Army had just rolled out, and we couldn't find anyone. I volunteered to learn everything I could about the system and created a half-day familiarization course that soldiers could use to gain user-level proficiency on the vehicle. I covered the vehicle's capabilities and features during the course, and I connected students with the appropriate licensing authority so that each of the 250 soldiers who participated could become licensed to drive these new vehicles.

For eight years, I worked in a busy, constantly changing environment. I was responsible for teaching and mentoring new soldiers, helping them set and achieve goals (as well as setting and achieving my own), and consistently keeping up with new Army standards so that I could uphold the standard.

Like many others, my career path hasn't always been straightforward. Now that I'm leaving the military, I'm looking forward to applying the same drive I had during my time in the service to a civilian company. I'm an aspiring sales representative who understands that there's no limit to what I can do for Abe's Auto Sales Dealership. My experience supporting, teaching and mentoring others will be an excellent addition to your team. Thanks for considering me for a sales position in your organization.

John Snuffy
JohnSnuffy1991@Email.com
202-665-1212

FIGURE 7-8:
Sample career-change cover letter.

This cover letter mentions — but doesn't dwell on — the fact that this person has no automotive sales experience. It draws parallels between the job's requirements and military service in these ways:

>> "I volunteered to learn everything I could about the system and created a half-day familiarization course," which covers the two requirements to "Present vehicle attributes, options, features, purchase, and finance options to customers" and "Stay on top of new products, features, and accessories."

>> "I volunteered" shows that the writer is "Self-motivated," and "helping them set and achieve goals (as well as setting and achieving my own)" directly says so.

ANALYZING SPELLING AND GRAMMAR

Before you click Send on your cover letter or resume, use your computer's spelling and grammar checker. Having a real person read over your documents to look for typos, misspellings, or grammatical errors is also a good idea.

Warning: Don't use military tricks to format your documents (such as typing a lowercase o to make a bullet point) because they don't come out right when you save in other formats. Just use your word processor's built-in tools.

Drafting a Federal Resume

Federal resumes, which you use to apply for jobs in the federal government, are a lot different from civilian resumes. In some organizations, they're first scanned by artificial intelligence software (though most agencies use real people), and they're usually a lot longer than civilian resumes are because they're overflowing with details on your knowledge, skills, and abilities (sometimes referred to as KSAs), as well as your accomplishments, previous job positions, and even duty locations. You also include your Social Security number on a federal resume so that the agency you're applying with can check your service status.

When you put together a federal resume, you need your complete military history, including your evaluation reports, training transcripts, awards, and everything else that you keep in your big book of accomplishments.

REMEMBER

Federal hiring managers look most closely at your prior work experience on your resume. They don't want to see that you generally get results; they want to see actual numbers. Additionally, hiring managers want to see that you've engaged in professional growth (that's where your education and certifications come in), and they look at the quality of your application — no typos or misspellings allowed.

Capitalizing on your military service

As a veteran, you may receive preference over non-veteran applicants during the hiring process. You can use your veterans' preference when you apply to permanent and temporary jobs in competitive service or excepted service of the executive branch. *Competitive service* jobs are subject to civil service laws passed by Congress to ensure that everyone gets fair and equal treatment in the hiring process, and *excepted service* jobs require someone to appoint you, such as attorney positions, Presidential Management Fellows, and some foreign service positions. You don't compete with the public by applying for excepted service positions.

Here are the three types of veterans' preferences:

>> **Disabled:** If you have a service-connected disability or received a Purple Heart, you get a 10-point preference for jobs.

>> **Non-disabled:** You're eligible for a 5-point preference if you joined the military for more than 180 consecutive days (other than for training) between September 11, 2001, and August 31, 2010; served between August 2, 1990, and January 2, 1992; or served in another time frame that involved the Vietnam and Korean Wars.

>> **Sole survivorship:** If you were released from active duty after August 29, 2008, because you're your family's only surviving child (and you have or had another military family member who was killed, missing, or permanently 100 percent disabled), which is a very rare circumstance, you're entitled to zero preference points, but the agency you're applying to work for will recognize you as a veteran. If it comes down to you and one other equally qualified candidate with no veterans' preference, you get the job.

The points are used in competitive service positions when agencies use a numerical rating and ranking system to determine who's best-qualified for a position. Under these circumstances, your veterans' preference points are added to your numerical score on an employment assessment questionnaire. Then, the agency sorts applicants by score and sends those with the best scores to the next step of the hiring process.

Digging up the documents you need

Before you begin composing a federal resume for each job you want, gather these documents:

>> Evaluation reports

>> Certificates you earned in the military

>> List of medals, awards, and citations you earned

>> Your VMET document

>> Joint Services Transcript

>> Your DD-214 or similar discharge document

>> A copy of your military job description

>> Professional organization memberships

>> College transcripts

These documents help you fill in the blanks as you put together your federal resume. If you're missing anything, you may be able to get a copy of your Official Military Personnel File, or OMPF, from the National Personnel Records Center or, if you're currently in the military, from your personnel office.

GETTING YOUR HANDS ON YOUR VMET DOCUMENT

Your Verification of Military Experience and Training, or VMET (Department of Defense Form 2586), can be a helpful tool to use when you put together a federal resume. The VMET consolidates all your reported demographic, training, and experience records and describes your military service in civilian terms. You can get a copy of your VMET document through milConnect (milconnect.dmdc.osd.mil/milconnect/). However, if you joined the military before October 1, 1990, your file may not be complete. You also need to know that VMET uses information from your service to update your file just four times a year, so if you only recently left military service, your record may not be complete (though you probably remember what happened in the past three months, so you can fill in the gaps yourself). Finally, the U.S. Coast Guard doesn't participate in the VMET program, so if you served in that branch, you need to use your Joint Services Transcript and other documentation to get a complete picture of your service.

Using keywords from job announcements

Every federal job announcement contains keywords that are important to the hiring manager, but federal agencies don't make these keywords obvious. They're usually in the job title, required and desired qualifications, job duties, and specialized experience sections. When you see words appear more than once in a job announcement, they're likely very important to the position.

Figure 7-9 is a sample "Responsibilities" section of a job announcement for a cook position at the U.S. Air Force Academy, and possible keywords are underlined.

Responsibilities

- Prepares and cooks a variety of menu items including regular and special diet entrees and dessert items using standard recipes and cooking techniques.
- Adjusts standardized recipes for large quantity cooking.
- Provides assistance in kitchen management.
- Uses, maintains, and cleans tools and specialized equipment such as cook tank, agitating kettle, pump fill station, tipper tie, blast chiller, vacuum packer, slicer, chopper, and convection oven.
- Utilizes health, safety, and sanitation practices, procedures, rules, and regulations to maintain a safe and clean work environment.

Figure 7-10 shows a "Job Elements" section from the same announcement with more keywords underlined. Some of the language is the same or very similar to what's in the "Responsibilities" section, such as *standardized recipes, sanitation,* and *adjust standardized recipes.*

JOB ELEMENTS: Your qualifications will be evaluated on the basis of your level of knowledge, skills, abilities and/or competencies in the following areas:

1. Knowledge of food preparation principles; the physical changes that occur during the processing and cooking of food; food handling and storage practices; regular and special diet menus; and standard formulas used in yield testing.

2. Knowledge of cold food presentation; how to prepare specialty sauces; and carve and use fruits and vegetables as garnishes.

3. Knowledge of health, safety, and sanitation standards and procedures in order to maintain a safe and clean work environment.

4. Skill in arithmetic computations to determine quantities needed to prepare required amounts by multiplying ingredients and calculating servings per container; and operating, breaking down, and cleaning kitchen tools and specialized equipment.

5. Ability to adjust standardized recipes for the number of servings required in large quantity cooking.

6. Ability to communicate effectively, both orally and in writing; and to read and understand menus, recipes, worksheets, food labels, computerized food production sheets, and metric conversion tables.

FIGURE 7-10:
Job elements for a cook position at the U.S. Air Force Academy.

When you suspect that you see a keyword, see whether you can fit it naturally into your resume. For example, if you were an Army cook and wanted this job, you may say that your experience includes adjusting standardized recipes, working with convection ovens and agitating kettles, and maintaining a safe and clean work environment.

Read more about federal job announcements in Chapter 9, where I cover how to interpret the whole announcement (and meet all its requirements) before you decide that it's the right job for you.

Choosing the outline format with headlines

An outline format for federal resumes is easy for hiring managers to read, and it works with all the major resume builders (including the one used by USAJobs, the federal government's job posting site). This format gives you room to write a short, targeted paragraph where you can list information on every duty position you've held as well as your key accomplishments (which are required on federal resumes).

Use USAJobs's (or any other platform's) resume builder instead of uploading your own resume. Reviewers usually want to see all requested information in a specific order, and they may jump to specific sections while ignoring others. You don't want to make those people's jobs any harder. Additionally, the USAJobs resume builder requires you to include all the information the hiring manager is looking for; if you leave anything out, the software won't accept your resume. The best way to approach resume builders is to create your own resume in a word processor document and then copy and paste the appropriate sections into the resume builder. That way, you can tailor each section as necessary without messing up the "bones" of your resume.

Your federal resume should include the following:

>> Your citizenship status (whether you have U.S. citizenship or a work visa)

>> Special hiring authority, such as through veterans' preference or on the basis of a disability

>> Federal experience, where you indicate that you were in the military and whether you worked for the government in any other capacity

>> Your objective

>> A skills summary

>> Your employment history

>> Accomplishments

>> Computer software you're experienced with (if applicable)

>> Additional training

>> Education

>> Honors and awards

>> Volunteer work and community involvement

>> Professional associations

>> Personal references

Writing your objective and compiled skills summary

Your *objective* on a federal resume is simple: *to obtain a* (full-time or part-time) *position in public service with* (the federal agency and sub-agency offering the job) *as a* (job title, including the announcement number if it has one).

Every federal resume also needs a *skills summary* that includes an introductory paragraph, a list of skills you have that directly relate to the position, and skills you've acquired throughout your career that you think the hiring manager should know about.

Your introductory paragraph must be specific and highly detailed to match the job you're applying for. This paragraph is the first place to use the keywords you identified in the job announcement. If you were applying for the cook position at the U.S. Air Force Academy described in the earlier section "Using keywords from job announcements" yours may look like this, with the keywords underlined:

> Focused and highly motivated cook with 10 years of extensive experience in <u>safe food handling</u>, <u>large quantity cooking</u>, <u>kitchen management</u>, and <u>specialized equipment</u>. Strong background in working in kitchen environments, extensive <u>knowledge of</u> <u>food preparation principles</u>, <u>regular and special diet menus</u>, and <u>ability to adjust standardized recipes</u> to cook for a significant number of people based on the employment needs and mission of the U.S. Air Force Academy. I'm an innovative, energetic team player and a highly <u>effective communicator</u>.

The list of skills you have that directly relate to the position should also include keywords. For the same job, you may choose to write a paragraph like this, which also includes quantifiable results that you achieved:

> As a culinary specialist in the U.S. Army, I trained a staff of 25 soldiers on safe food handling, large quantity cooking, and specialized equipment such as cook tanks, agitating kettles, pump fill stations, blast chillers, and convection ovens. My food handling training led to a 100% score for 36 months running on my dining facility's food sanitation inspection.

REMEMBER

You must quantify and qualify every statement you make; you can't just use abstract ideas to impress a federal hiring manager.

Finally, you need acquired skills. These are skills that may not directly relate to the position you want but that your future employer should know about so they understand that you're a model employee, like this:

> Analyzed, developed, tested, and incorporated new recipes using locally sourced ingredients to enhance dining options on a small contingency operating base in Afghanistan and developed and implemented a new supply inventory program that resulted in a 20 percent decline in expired ingredients.

Showcasing your employment history

Your employment history can't simply say "U.S. Marine Corps, 2020–Present." You need to include every job title and description you worked in over the past decade. (You can include things from more than ten years ago, but generally, federal employers don't care too much about them. The things you learned back then may be obsolete now, or your experience may be too far in the past to make you qualified for a modern job.)

Every employment history section should be similar to this:

U.S. Army
Platoon Sergeant
2 Years

As a platoon sergeant, I manage our unit's dining facility, which serves roughly 1,500 soldiers and civilians daily. My primary focus is on <u>food safety</u> and <u>sanitation</u>, <u>kitchen management</u> functions (including scheduling), and <u>preparing and cooking a variety of menu items</u>, including <u>regular and special diet entrees</u>, appetizers, and <u>dessert items</u>. I also monitor and maintain the welfare of 23 soldiers, ensure personnel accountability, and serve as the platoon's senior trainer. I maintain the soldiers' physical fitness program, mentor and teach my soldiers, and enforce Army regulations.

Sharing your accomplishments

Your accomplishments for each job, which can give a prospective employer a better understanding of what you may be able to accomplish in a new organization, should cover all your accolades. Yours may look like this:

2020: Saved the Army $22,000 by creating a food storage system that minimized food waste

2016: Taught 1,756 new soldiers proper food handling techniques as an instructor at Fort Lee, Virginia

2011: Restructured vendor contracts with local nationals to purchase locally sourced food for a dining facility in Afghanistan, resulting in savings of over $1,200 per month

Adding other federal resume requirements

A successful federal resume contains a number of sections that don't belong on civilian resumes (other than education and professional associations), including these:

>> **Computer software:** List all the software and applications you're experienced in, as well as at what level. If you're an expert in Microsoft Excel because you used it for ten years, say so. (And I *know* that if you spent more than ten minutes in the military, you're an expert in PowerPoint, so that definitely belongs on your resume.)

>> **Additional training:** List any formal or informal training, including accreditations, that you've earned. If you have additional skill identifiers or something similar, or if you earned certifications for skills outside your job description, they belong here. That includes all the cybersecurity certificates, driving certificates, and other mandatory training you did in the military.

>> **Education:** List the type of degree, what it's in, where you earned it, the year you earned it, and your grade point average. It should look like this: *BA – Business Management, Thomas Edison State University, Trenton, New Jersey: 2011 (GPA 3.93)*

>> **Honors and awards:** List your formal awards (even if they don't relate to the position) following the year you earned them, like this: ***2021:*** *Earned a Meritorious Service Medal for outstanding and exceptional leadership in support of dining facility operations at Schofield Barracks, Hawaii*

>> **Volunteer work and community involvement:** Describe your volunteer work, if you have any, in this section. Include the dates you performed this work, like this: ***(2010–present)*** *Assistant Den Leader for Boy Scouts of America. I plan and implement training programs, facilitate transitions between Boy Scouts' ranks, and host classes that help young Scouts learn new skills.*

>> **Professional associations:** If you belong to any professional associations, list them here. Maybe you belong to the Air Force Sergeants Association, Marine Corps Association, or Association of the United States Army, or perhaps you belong to another association related to your field of work.

>> **References:** List at least three references (and their contact information). You may not need to include them when you use USAJobs' resume builder (it depends on what the hiring authority wants to see), but it'll save you time in the event that an employer does want them. Try to choose people who know you well (and who are familiar with your work ethic), such as former commanders or other superiors.

EYEING CONTRACTOR RESUMES

If you're aiming for a job as a contractor — which is often a smart choice — your resume looks just like a federal resume (minus your Social Security number and veterans' preference status). Contractors usually want the same information that government agencies need to make a hiring decision. The same rule applies about using resume builders, too: If the site where you found the job offers a resume builder, use it. The hiring manager for that job will want information presented in a certain order, and you can pull information from the resume you wrote yourself to fill in the blanks.

TIP

Save a copy of every job announcement you apply for so you have a record of its details (including the hiring manager's contact information).

Keeping Tabs on Your Federal Resume After You Submit It

Your federal resume usually follows the same path as everyone else's does. First, it lands in an agency's database. Human resources professionals assess it, review the automated score of the Assessment Questionnaire you must fill out on USA-Jobs, and compare the questionnaire to your resume. Someone determines whether you're eligible for the job (and rejects your resume if you're not) and starts distinguishing all the other resumes in the database. People who are the most qualified make it to the selecting official's desk. The selecting official makes the final decision on whether to reject your resume or further assess you through an interview. Sometimes candidates are selected without interviews, too, but that doesn't happen very often.

TIP

You should absolutely follow up on your federal resume. If you haven't heard anything within 30 days, find the hiring manager's contact information and call. Sometimes a technical error prevents a resume from getting to the right person, sometimes the job opening is cancelled, and sometimes a job just has too many applicants for one person to slog through. You can usually figure out what's going on with a simple phone call. (Just have the job title and vacancy number handy so the person on the other end of the line knows what you're talking about.)

IN THIS CHAPTER

» Narrowing down what you want in a job (and the realities of the job market)

» Understanding how civilian workplaces differ from the military

» Discovering types and levels of civilian employment

» Cashing in on pay concepts, including overtime and tax brackets

» Digging into trade unions and civilian job listings

Chapter **8**

Familiarizing Yourself with Civilian Employment (and Pay)

n the military, you know what to expect on the 1st and 15th of every month. Your pay changes only if you're promoted, your January 1 raise comes through, or you hit the next two-year mark in your current pay grade. In the civilian sector, things work a little differently. Other than pay, the biggest (and maybe the most uncomfortable) difference is that in most cases, a civilian employer can fire you without reason. On the flipside, if you don't like your job, the company you work for, or even the people you work with, you can quit and find another job.

It's not just about pay and hanging onto a job, though. The civilian workforce isn't under constant threat of punishment, so people act differently in some ways. In the civilian world, you may notice a lack of structure. Interpersonal skills are more important, because people don't have to obey you or even listen to you simply because of the rank on your chest, and people walk really, *really* slowly. You have a lot of personal autonomy in the civilian workforce, whereas in the military, someone tells you where you're supposed to be, when you're supposed to be there, and what uniform you're supposed to wear. All commands come from the tower, and if you follow those commands, you're on your way to the next phase your career (or at least, you aren't in danger of being yelled at).

REMEMBER

Although you may experience some culture shock, everyone has to get out of the military sometime. The best thing you can do is arm yourself with a stockpile of information on what it's like out there.

Getting the Job You Want versus Getting the Job You Need

Unless you're independently wealthy, you're going to need a job when you leave the military. Maybe you aspire to become the next Bill Gates, Oprah Winfrey, Steve Jobs, or Elon Musk, or perhaps you just want to get a job that pays the bills, finish earning your college degree, and stay out of debt. Although I'll never discourage you from following your dreams, I do encourage you to carefully weigh holding out for your dream job against taking a job that pays the bills — especially if your dream job is unrealistic right now. You may find that taking a job you like (or that you don't hate) and working your way up, or taking a job knowing that you only have to keep it until you're better-equipped to get your dream job, is a better approach.

TIP

Many veterans face issues that make finding — and keeping — a job tough. If you're dealing with personal issues that affect your ability to work, you need to know that a lot of people are on your side. I cover some of the resources available to you in Chapter 21.

Being realistic about your job prospects

Some areas have better job markets than others do, so hopefully you asked the military to ship your household goods to a city where you can relatively easily find employment with your skill set. If you're an investment professional, you may not have much luck in Stanley, Idaho, with its population of 63. You need to be in a big city — maybe even New York — to have a shot at the job and the pay you really want. (Don't forget about the cost of living, though. That's a whole different ball-game, which I cover in Chapter 18.)

Aside from the job market, your skill set is the strongest factor at play when you're looking for a job. It's not that you *can't* do some things; it's that you can't do some things *right now.* If you don't have the street cred (or educational credentials, as some employers prefer) to get your dream job, you may have to "settle" for a job that's just okay. And nothing's wrong with that. In fact, civilians face the same issue.

Are you going to hate your civilian job at first, even if it's a good job? Maybe, but give yourself some grace; it's going to be a lot different from what you're used to. Are you going to regret your choice to leave the military and become a little discouraged? You may; career changes on top of culture changes can be uncomfortable. (Are you going to gain weight? Probably, but that's another topic for another book.)

The bottom line is that taking a job you don't love is okay if it means putting food on the table. Remember, leaving the military almost always means your living expenses increase. Finding a job is priority number one, and you should start the process long before you get your last paycheck from the government. You have a better shot at finding a good job — one you actually like — if you take time to examine your work values, the things that make you dislike a job, and your vocational interests, which I outline in the following sections.

Figuring out what makes you happy

The first thing you do in land nav is orient the map. The same is true with your job search: You orient your map so you're looking for jobs in the right places (in this case, career fields). Point yourself in the right direction by figuring out your what makes you the happiest when you're working (other than making money). Check off all the work values that are important to you in Table 8-1 and, if you want, add your own. After you've checked all the boxes that apply to you, rank them in order of importance.

This exercise shows you what makes you happiest in a job. When you find any of these phrases in a job description (or synonyms of these phrases, like "management" for "leadership"), you know that the job may be a good fit for you.

TABLE 8-1   **Work Values to Look for in Your Next Job**

✓	Ranking	Work Value	✓	Ranking	Work Value
		Adventure			Authority
		Being a recognized expert			Competing with others
		Contributing to society			Creativity
		Flexible work schedule			Gaining recognition for your work
		Having frequent contact with others			Helping others
		Independence			Influencing others
		Leadership			Learning new things
		Making decisions			Paying attention to detail
		Persuading others			Self-expression
		Solving problems			Supervising others
		Taking risks			Working alone
		Working at your own pace			Working outdoors
		Working under pressure			Working as a team

Pinpointing work-related dissatisfaction

Every job has its ups and downs, including the military. But as a civilian, you're free to pick any job that'll have you. When you choose a job with minimal work frustrations — the things that really get under your skin in the military — you have a better chance of enjoying it. And who doesn't want to enjoy going to work every day?

Check off all the things that frustrate you most (or that you simply dislike) about your military job in Table 8-2. Feel free to add your own, too. Then, rank them in order of importance. If working under direct supervision without being able to exercise independent judgment really bothers you, you may want to steer clear of jobs that require you to answer to someone for every step you take. After completing this checklist, you have a good idea about which types of jobs to scroll right past in your search.

TABLE 8-2   ## Work-Related Dissatisfactions

✓	Ranking	Dissatisfaction	✓	Ranking	Dissatisfaction
		Additional duties and responsibilities			Attention to detail
		Bureaucracy			Competing with others
		Deployment			Early work hours
		Giving up time with family and friends for work			Holding subordinates' hands
		Inability to make independent judgment calls			Late work hours
		Making decisions			Paperwork
		Physical fitness training			Routine
		Solving problems			Time spent away from home for training or work
		Tradition over innovation			Working alone
		Working independently			Working indoors
		Working on weekends or holidays			Working outdoors
		Working through lunch and breaks			Working under pressure
		Working under supervision			Working with a team

Identifying your vocational interests

Everyone has things they like to do, and finding an employer that gives you money for doing something you enjoy is a big win. Identifying your vocational interests can help you find a job you'll like more than dislike. The job you choose doesn't have to meet *all* your vocational interests; even matching a few will make going to work easier. Use the list in Table 8-3 to identify and rank the things you're interested in. Then, pick your top five before you start looking for a job.

You have no guarantee that you'll find a job you like, and sometimes you take a job only to later discover it's not the right choice for you; in the words of Forrest Gump, "It happens." But as a civilian, you're free to leave one job for another any time you want. (And you didn't hear this from me, but if you only work at a job for a short time and discover that you hate it, no law says you must include it in the employment history section of your resume.)

TABLE 8-3   **Vocational Interests**

✓	Ranking	Vocational Interest	✓	Ranking	Vocational Interest
		Acting			Advising others
		Applying First Aid			Artistic pursuits
		Building models			Building or fixing computers
		Campaigning for causes			Coaching kids in sports
		Crafting			Helping animals
		Helping people with their needs			Influencing others
		Manual labor			Mentoring people
		Mentoring people			Mechanical work
		Organized, clearly defined activities			Performing experiments
		Playing music			Protecting people and things
		Repairing broken items			Science
		Selling products or services			Working with animals
		Working with plants			Writing

Contrasting the Military Ladder and the Corporate Matrix

Civilian employment is structured differently than military employment is. If you're like many veterans, you never held a civilian job because you enlisted in the military right after high school. Even if you had civilian jobs in the past, you may not be familiar with the way civilian companies are typically structured, which I outline in Table 8-4.

Despite the culture shock you may experience, civilian jobs can be extremely rewarding (financially and emotionally). In many cases, civilians pay better than the military does while making fewer demands. Of course, in order to find and keep one of these jobs, you have to be able to translate your military skills into marketable skills that employers want (I cover that in Chapter 7 and the Appendix), ace an interview (that's in Chapter 11), and assimilate into the civilian workforce (Chapter 13).

TABLE 8-4   **Major Differences between Military and Civilian Jobs**

Military	Civilian
Hierarchical structure for management: In the military, you know your complete chain of command (and subordinates) and report to your first-line leader. Although there is oversight, there's very little overlap in direct leadership. If your subordinate messes up, the military holds you responsible.	**Matrix structure for management:** Your workplace may have more than one line of supervision, and you may have more than one boss. You may also share responsibility for subordinates with others in leadership positions. If your subordinate messes up, the responsibility lies with your subordinate.
Explicit rules of conduct: Military regulations dictate what you can and can't do. Consequences are severe under the Uniform Code of Military Justice, including forfeiture of pay and detention, for violating the rules of conduct in a military workplace.	**Implied rules of conduct:** The civilian workforce has unwritten rules of professionalism, and those rules sometimes run counter to your military training. Generally, the worst consequence you ever face is losing your job.
Defined roles with precise job descriptions: You have an assigned career field in the military, and with each rank you earn, you take on a very specific set of additional responsibilities.	**Flexible roles with tasks that may overlap with other jobs:** Many civilian jobs blur the lines of who's in charge of which tasks and have various levels of management.
Obvious rank and status distinctions: You always know who you're dealing with in the military because of the rank on their chest, and you know how you're expected to behave in every situation. Military customs and courtesies dictate your behavior.	**Sometimes unclear status distinctions:** Civilians don't stand at attention or parade rest and have no clear-cut rules for what to call a superior or subordinate or even how to react to requests from superiors.
Consistency from one unit to the next: The military runs like a machine, and you always know what structure to expect when you change units. You have a chain of command that goes all the way to the president, and when you change units, it's as simple as swapping out a few names and photos on the wall. Squads, squadrons, platoons, battalions, wings, and divisions all run the same way.	**Variation from one team or division to the next:** Transferring to another location of the same company may be a complete culture shock; consistency isn't as rigid in the civilian sector as it is in the military. Additionally, you have the freedom to change jobs whenever you want, which can bring about even bigger changes.
Clearly defined career progression: You go from the lowest pay grade to the highest, and it's all linear; E-1 to E9, O-1 to O-10, or WO-1 to WO-5, your career path is defined for you. There's no deviation from the norm. Your pay goes up with every promotion.	**More opportunity for lateral assignments and less-defined career progression:** In the corporate world, you may have to take baby steps toward your next big pay raise, or you may take a giant leap.
Shared bond in traditions, values, and the importance of structure: The military is steeped in history and tradition, and the military impresses its values on you from day one of basic training. Everyone in your organization has been through the same training and, for the most part, shares the same values.	**Corporate culture dictates corporate values:** People from all walks of life join the civilian workforce, and they carry their own previous training and values with them along the way. The company you work for dictates the organization's values while the people you work with have their own.

Civilian workplaces don't enforce "hard times" the way the military does (you're not going to be cutting the grass with nail clippers or moving oddly shaped rocks from one side of the parking lot to the other if you show up late to a morning meeting). If you needed the military's rigid disciplinary structure to succeed, you have to become more of a self-starter to thrive in the civilian workforce.

Veterans often have special opportunities, including using veterans' preference to get a government job (more on that in Chapter 9). Although the civilian workforce is structured differently from the way the military runs things, you can thrive in the civilian sector. In fact, you'll probably thrive if you're resilient and ready to adapt.

Comparing Types of Employment

In the military, everybody puts on a uniform and gets paid on the 1st and 15th of every month (except the small handful of people who opt for once-a-month paychecks). It doesn't matter whether you work three days a week or seven, or if you work from 5 a.m. to 10 p.m. every day without a single break. You're paid the same as every other servicemember who has the same time-in-grade as you do, and you're all full-time employees on salary. But in the civilian sector, several different types of employees all have different rights and payment terms, and a single company may employ people who fall into all the employment categories.

An *employee* is an individual who's hired by a person or business (the employer) to perform work under certain conditions. A person is an employee if

>> The employer can control the work performed

>> The worker is on the company's payroll and receives a specific wage or salary

>> The worker is eligible for benefits the employer offers

>> A written or implied contract of employment exists

>> The worker has the right to legal protections on wages and employment rights

The United States has five major employee classifications: part-time, full-time, seasonal, temporary, and leased. Your employment status makes a big difference in the way your employer pays you, how you pay taxes, whether you're entitled to benefits, and how much liability you carry. Independent contractors, gig workers, and interns aren't employees; they fall into categories all their own.

Part-time employees

Part-time employees are people who work less than full-time, which most employers recognize as 40 hours per week. Because no federal law regulates the minimum or maximum number of hours a person can work while still being considered a part-time employee, employers can make up their own rules to distinguish part-time from full-time.

Usually, part-timers are paid hourly (instead of receiving a salary). Although part-time workers are officially employees, they may not be eligible for employer-offered benefits. For example, some employers have a rule that you must work for them full-time to use the company's health insurance benefit or earn vacation time.

Full-time employees

Full-time employees are employees who work an average of 40 hours each week and are eligible for benefits. Employers that have 50 or more full-time employees are legally required to offer healthcare coverage to all their full-time employees (and their employees' dependents).

Seasonal employees

Seasonal employees are workers a company employs based on its seasonal needs. For example, a store at the mall may hire a dozen seasonal employees leading up to the holidays; a large farm corporation may hire a hundred seasonal workers to plant or pick crops.

Temporary employees

Temporary employees are those hired for only a specific period of time. For example, if a company's receptionist will be out of the company for three months and is expected to return, the company may choose to hire a temporary employee to fill the position temporarily. Sometimes employers work through staffing agencies to find temporary help, and sometimes they hire temporary employees directly.

Leased employees

Leased employees are hired (and paid) by staffing companies and then leased to a company or organization to complete a specific job. Leased employees' benefits come from the staffing company, not the company they're performing work for.

Independent contractors

Independent contractors aren't employees. Instead, they're self-employed people a company pays to perform specific work or services. Independent contractors are responsible for paying their own taxes, and they're not entitled to benefits the company offers. Freelance writers, actors, and ride-sharing drivers are typically independent contractors. Table 8-5 shows some of the most important differences between independent contractors and employees.

TABLE 8-5   ## Differences between Contractors and Employees

Contractor	Employee
May work for more than one company at a time performing the same, similar, or different services	Usually only works for one (or maybe two) employers, and usually performing different jobs
Sets their own hours	Works according to the employer's schedule
Works from any location	Typically works in a place assigned by the employer
Works independently often, or at least most of the time	Works under the employer's control
Can perform tasks in any manner, without input or direction from the employer, as long as the job gets done	Is subject to the employer's guidelines and rules on performing tasks
Bears the costs associated with performing the job (such as purchasing supplies)	Doesn't incur personal costs while performing a job or make personal investments
Pays their own taxes	Employer withholds taxes and gives employee net pay
Isn't eligible to claim unemployment compensation benefits	Is usually eligible for unemployment benefits if fired or laid off
Is ineligible for workers' compensation benefits	Is eligible for workers' compensation benefits
Receives pay according to a contract's or agreement's terms and conditions	Receives at least federal or state minimum wage
Doesn't receive overtime pay	Receives overtime pay after working overtime

WARNING Some employers intentionally misclassify workers as independent contractors when they should be employees. If your future employer tells you that you're an independent contractor but you're performing like an employee would, you may have legal recourse (including an entitlement to health insurance, additional pay, and benefits).

Gig workers

Gig workers — also sometimes called *contract workers* — are hired for a specific task or duty. They're paid for completing (or partially completing) a job. Like independent contractors (see the preceding section), gig workers are responsible for paying their own taxes and don't get benefits from the company they contract with. Some examples of gig workers are people you hire on a social media site to help you complete tasks, like cut your grass or help you fix a hole in the wall. You can read more about gig work in the later section "Searching for Gig Work to Tide You Over."

Interns

Interns perform work for a company to gain work experience. Some companies pay interns, while others simply consider work experience to be sufficient payment. Most internships last for a few months, and after the internship is over, the employer may ask an intern to become a permanent employee. If you're looking for a professional learning experience, an unpaid internship may be right for you. But if you need money to pay the bills, you're better off looking for a conventional job.

CONTRASTING BLUE-COLLAR AND WHITE-COLLAR

You've heard of blue-collar and white-collar workers, but these terms are largely based on stereotypes. Generally, *blue-collar* refers to people who get their hands dirty at work; *white-collar* refers to those who don't. Really, what the two terms do is imply that people belong to different social classes, and though some people still use them, they're old and outdated. The terms originated in the 1920s, when manual laborers wore darker-colored clothes to hide dirt and office workers wore suits with white-collared shirts. However, the differences that once existed between blue-collar and white-collar workers, such as education levels, pay scales, and mentally engaging work, have faded. These terms just don't have as much meaning as they used to, and if you can find a job you like, who cares whether you get dirty, wear a suit, or wear a dirty suit (or what others think)?

Starting on the Bottom Rung of the Ladder

You can't stroll into a business and say, "I'm ready to be your CEO." Well, you can, but it's probably not going to work. (If it does, you're probably about to be framed for insider trading or something similar.) Realistically, you have to start your new civilian career at the bottom and work your way up — and that can be a bitter pill to swallow for someone who's earned some rank in the military and is used to being higher up on the food chain. Civilian workplaces don't function on rank, but they do have seniority levels that include entry-level, mid-level, and senior-level.

REMEMBER

Seniority — how long you've been with a particular company — matters in the civilian world in terms of compensation, benefits, job duties, and things like lay-offs. People in more senior positions certainly make more money, and they're often entitled to increased benefits (that's how companies build long-term loyalty). New employees may only get access to benefits after a probationary period, for example, and they may not be entitled to paid time off until they've worked for the company for a certain number of years. Additionally, higher seniority at a company may get you special benefits like being asked which projects you want to work on (rather than being assigned the next project in the pipeline). Finally, if the company you work for restructures and has to lay off employees because it can't afford to keep paying them, it may have a "last-in, first-out" policy that requires managers to let go of the most recently hired workers first.

Entry-level jobs

When you do a complete 180 in the career department, you can expect to start with an *entry-level job*. Think of it this way: Your military career may have very little (or nothing) to do with your new career field, so you're essentially starting from scratch. You have a lot to learn, just like everyone else who's never worked in that field before. Entry-level jobs are a way to get your foot in the door and work your way up, and they generally pay the least out of all the jobs on the market.

Civilian entry-level workers are comparable to junior enlisted servicemembers and junior officers in the military (with a lot less yelling and a lot fewer push-ups). In an entry-level position, you work under an experienced supervisor who directly oversees your work. And if you're lucky, your supervisor will mentor you, too. Some examples of entry-level jobs include

>> Interns

>> Apprentices

>> Administrative assistants

>> Customer service

>> Research assistants

>> Underwriters

>> Analysts

>> Dental assistants

>> Sales representatives

>> Home health aides

If you don't have experience in a field (or related qualifications, such as management), you'll likely start at entry-level. And taking an entry-level position is nothing to scoff at, especially if it offers room for advancement or you're taking a job that pays the bills while you work your way toward something bigger and better.

TIP

Although these aren't considered entry-level jobs, you need to know that even a brand-new brain surgeon, lawyer, helicopter pilot, or plumber has to start at the bottom in a new place of employment. Entrepreneurs and independent contractors start small, too. Regardless of your qualifications, you'll be on the bottom of the pile until you work your way up. Nobody gets to fast-forward, so in that way, the civilian workforce is a lot like the military: You can only work your way up as you gain experience.

Mid-level jobs

If you take a civilian job that's very similar to your military job, or if your new job relates to management and leadership skills you learned in the military, you may be able to start somewhere in the middle. *Mid-level jobs* generally pay better than entry-level jobs, regardless of your field.

Civilian mid-level jobs are equivalent to the jobs of junior noncommissioned officers and field grade officers. These jobs are typically reserved for people who have prior experience in the field. Sometimes these jobs involve managerial tasks and/ or supervising entry-level workers, but they all involve answering to a higher authority. Mid-level workers may be assigned larger projects because they've proven their worth in their field. A subset of mid-level workers are sometimes called *mid-senior*, and these are people who have been mid-level workers for a while, may have more seniority than others in the same department or field, and haven't yet been promoted to senior-level jobs.

Some common mid-level jobs include the following:

>> Account managers

>> Team leaders

>> Project superintendents

>> Regional managers

>> Supervisors

>> Underwriters

>> Outside sales reps

>> Marketing managers

>> Product development engineers

>> Associate brand managers

Getting a mid-level job based on your military experience is completely possible, so if you find something you're qualified for, I highly encourage you to apply. The worst that can happen is that they don't hire you (and you already *don't* have that job, so you're no worse off than you were before applying).

Senior-level jobs

Senior-level jobs, also known as *executive-level jobs*, require a high level of knowledge, experience, and responsibility. People filling these positions have generally worked a long and illustrious career in the same field, and their responsibilities include providing leadership within the organization. These are usually the highest-paying jobs in a field. With that said, some fields pay much more than others do (and that's true at all levels). A senior-level job in retail has a different pay scale than a senior-level job in investment and finance.

The military equivalent of a senior-level job is that of a senior noncommissioned officer or a general officer. Some common senior-level jobs include

>> President or vice president of a company

>> Chief executive officer or chief financial officer

>> Executive director

You can start your own company and be its CEO, but most people don't start at the top. Unless you're an entrepreneur or a prodigy, you have to work your way up to these senior-level jobs, just like you did in the military.

AT-WILL EMPLOYMENT AND TERMINATION

Most U.S. states are *at-will* employment states, which means that workers are free to quit with no reason — and employers are entitled to fire workers for any reason (unless the reason has to do with discrimination or retaliation, which I cover in Chapter 13). Generally, unless you have a written employment contract that says your employer will only fire you for certain reasons (or you have proof of oral statements your employer has made), the law presumes that you're employed at will. As of this writing, Montana is the only state that protects employees who have completed an initial "probationary period" from being fired without cause. Still, although the other states allow employers to fire people for any reason, some cases do exist in which an employee *is* wrongfully terminated from a job. If an employer fires you for a discriminatory reason, or because you were a whistleblower, you refused to commit an illegal act, or it's retaliating against you for filing a complaint (including about sexual harassment), that may be wrongful termination, and you may be entitled to compensation from your former employer.

Making Sense of Money Matters

In the military, you receive your pay the same days everyone else does (have you been in line at the commissary on payday weekend?). Your Leave and Earnings Statement (LES) shows your deductions, taxes, and special pay, your housing and sustenance allowances, accrued leave, and everything else associated with your assignment, pay grade, and duty station, such as your cost-of-living allowance. An LES is the military version of a *pay stub* — the document that shows civilian workers how much money they earn in one pay period, how much they contribute in taxes, and how much they've put into a retirement plan.

Civilian pay can be quite a bit different from military pay. For one thing, civilian jobs often pay better, at least when you're calculating an hourly rate — maybe not so much when you count insurance, housing allowance, and other perks of being in the military. You may be paid hourly (imagine how much you'd have in savings if the military paid that way!) or you may be paid a salary, and you may be entitled to overtime pay and double-time pay.

Salary and hourly pay

Some jobs pay a salary, and others pay an hourly rate. The main difference between the two is how much money you take home after selling a company your time and skills.

Workers who earn a salary aren't paid according to the number of hours they work. They're paid the same amount every pay period, based on their total salary. That's what you received in the military — a salary. Even if you worked 60 hours a week, you received the same base pay.

Most companies figure out salaries based on a presumed 40-hour (full-time) workweek. For that reason, salaried employees aren't entitled to overtime pay when they work more than 40 hours in a week. On the flipside, if you're a salaried employee who works 30 hours in a week, you get 40 hours' worth of pay.

Hourly workers are paid by the number of hours they work. If your hourly pay rate is $15 and you work 30 hours in a week, you earn $450 that week (before Uncle Sam takes his cut, of course). If you work 40 hours next week at the same rate of pay, you earn $600.

Companies that pay workers hourly can set the number of hours you work each week. They can regularly schedule you for 34-hour weeks to limit their costs, which may also prevent you from qualifying as a full-time worker who is entitled to benefits like health insurance, or they can ask you to work 50 hours a week and pay you overtime.

Civilian overtime rules

Federal law calls some employees *exempt* and some employees *nonexempt*. These two terms refer to whether a worker is exempt from the worker protections outlined in the Fair Labor Standards Act, or FLSA. Exempt employees aren't entitled to overtime, but nonexempt workers are.

Exempt workers

Often, if you receive a salary, you're exempt from FLSA's protections. However, it's not always that simple. Your salary must meet a minimum threshold (which is subject to change, so check the U.S. Department of Labor's website for the most current dollar amount) for you to be exempt from overtime protections. You must also meet the criteria outlined in DOL employment tests. The criteria refer to the actual work you perform, not just what your job description says. Generally, the following apply:

>> **Executives:** Executives must have a primary duty of managing an enterprise or a department or subdivision of the enterprise. They must also usually and regularly direct the work of at least two employees, and they must have the authority to hire or fire (or make heavily relied-upon suggestions and recommendations when it comes to hiring, firing, or changing the status of other

employees). If an executive position fails any part of this test, the employee filling the position is most likely nonexempt (and eligible for overtime pay).

» **Administrative professionals:** Administrative professionals must have a primary duty of performing office or non-manual work that's directly related to the company's management or general business operations. An administrative professional's primary duty must also include the ability to use discretion and independent judgment on important matters. If the actual work performed (not just the job description) doesn't meet the criteria for this test, the worker is most likely nonexempt.

» **Professionals:** Professionals must primarily perform work that requires advanced knowledge in a field of science or learning that you can usually only get through "prolonged, specialized, intellectual instruction and study," or must specialize in a highly specialized field, like computer analytics, engineering, or teaching. Otherwise, this worker is probably nonexempt.

» **Highly compensated employees:** Highly compensated employees who earn an annual salary over a certain amount (current information is available on the DOL's website) and perform office or nonmanual work, plus at least one of the duties of an exempt executive, administrative, or professional employee *may* be exempt (but not always).

» **Computer professionals:** Computer professionals who are employed as computer systems analysts, computer programmers, software engineers, or other similarly skilled workers in the computer field and who regularly apply systems analysis techniques and procedures, or who design, development, create, or test programs, as well as meet some other criteria, may be exempt. If they don't meet all the criteria, the U.S. government considers them nonexempt, and they're entitled to overtime protections.

» **Outside sales professionals:** Outside sales professionals must have a primary duty of making sales or obtaining orders or contracts, and the work must be conducted away from the employer's place of business. If you're on the phone in your employer's workplace selling products or services, or if selling or obtaining contracts isn't your primary responsibility, you're most likely nonexempt and entitled to receive overtime pay.

There are some very specific exceptions to exemptions, aside from these main categories. Those are listed here, but remember that these people *are not always* considered exempt from overtime protections:

» Some commissioned employees or retail or service establishments

» Auto, truck, trailer, farm implement, boat, or aircraft sales workers

- >> Parts clerks and mechanics who service automobiles, trucks, or farm implements who are employed by nonmanufacturing establishments that primarily sell these items

- >> Railroad and air carrier employees

- >> Taxi drivers and certain employees of motor carriers

- >> Seamen on American vessels

- >> Local delivery employees who are paid on approved trip rate plans

- >> Announcers, news editors, and chief engineers of some nonmetropolitan broadcasting stations

- >> Domestic service workers who live in their employer's residence (such as nannies and housekeepers)

- >> Employees of movie theaters

- >> Farm workers

Receiving overtime pay as a nonexempt worker

Unless you're exempt from the protections provided by FLSA (see the preceding section), you're entitled to overtime pay for hours worked over 40 in a single workweek. *Overtime pay* is 1.5 times your regular pay rate. For example, if your hourly rate is $15 and you work 45 hours, you're entitled to your regular pay ($600) plus an additional $22.50 per hour for the five extra hours you worked ($112.50). Your paycheck should be $712.50 before taxes and other deductions.

Some states have even stronger overtime protections for workers. For example, California says that if you work more than 8 hours in a day, you're entitled to overtime for those hours on that day. California law also requires your employer to pay you overtime for the first 8 hours you work on the seventh consecutive day in one workweek *and* double your regular rate if you work more than 12 hours in one day (or for every hour over 8 hours on your seventh consecutive day of work). Many states don't have these protections, though. If you're curious about yours, you can search the internet for your state's overtime laws. (Or skip all that and start searching for hourly jobs in California.)

REMEMBER

When a state's labor laws differ from federal laws, the law that provides more protection for employees wins out. For example, the federal minimum wage is ridiculously low, and some states are fine with that. However, many worker-friendly states have implemented laws that set their own minimum wages higher than federal law requires. If your state has its own minimum wage, your employer has to pay you *at least* the state minimum wage for every hour you work. This principle is a lot like the military, where a commander can add to, but never take away from, military regulations.

WARNING

The Fair Labor Standards Act forbids employers from asking you to waive your right to overtime if you're a nonexempt worker. *You're entitled to that pay.* Your employer can't announce that no overtime work is allowed, or that it won't pay for overtime if you work it, either. If you work more than 40 hours in a week, you earned overtime pay and your employer must give it to you. If you ever find yourself in a situation like that, contact your state's labor commissioner.

Commission pay

In some jobs, your pay primarily comes through commissions your employer pays you. Commissions are usually a percentage of your sales total or a fixed amount for each product you sell. Many commission-based jobs have a low base salary (enough that your employer won't get into trouble for paying you too little, but typically not enough to reasonably live on).

Some workers who regularly rely on commissions include the following:

>> Salespeople who work at car dealerships

>> Alcohol distributors

>> Insurance agents

>> Real estate agents

>> Stockbrokers

>> Entertainment agents

>> Loan officers

>> Investment bankers

Generally, the more sales you make, the more you earn in commissions. Sales jobs often require you to seek out new clients and reach specific sales goals after becoming intimately familiar with the product or service you're supposed to sell. A word of advice: If you find a job description for a sales position that seems too good to be true, it probably is, even if it's for a brake part manufacturer in Sandusky and David Spade is going to help you.

WATCHING OUT FOR MLM AND PYRAMID SCHEMES

Multilevel marketing (commonly called *MLM*) isn't illegal, but it doesn't always work out well for people who get involved in it. Some direct sales companies use MLM to encourage existing *distributors* (people who sell products for them) to recruit new distributors. Then, the existing distributor earns a percentage of their *downline* distributors' sales. Theoretically, if you recruited a lot of really good distributors, you'd make a fortune — but statistically, very few people actually earn a meaningful income through MLM.

Usually, you can determine whether an MLM company is legitimate by seeing whether it sells its products mostly to consumers or to its distributors, who are then responsible for recruiting new distributors to buy the products. If a company primarily sells its products to its distributors, it may actually be an illegal *pyramid scheme,* where only the people at the top rake in the cash (which the people at the bottom provide). The bottom line is that if a program costs you money for an opportunity to "be part of something big" or promises that you'll get rich quickly, you should research it extensively before making any kind of investment.

Tipped employees

Some employees receive a small hourly pay rate and have the potential to earn tips. The Department of Labor considers a person who regularly receives more than $30 per month in tips to be a tipped employee.

When a business employs a tipped employee, federal law requires the employer to pay that person $2.13 per hour (though that amount is subject to change, and many states have stronger minimum wage protections for workers). However, if the employer pays an hourly rate less than the federal minimum wage and the tipped employee fails to make enough in tips to bring their pay up to that level, the employer is responsible for making up the difference.

Here's an example: A restaurant server works a four-hour shift and makes $10 in tips. The server works in a state with a $2.13-per-hour minimum wage for tipped employees but a $10-per-hour minimum wage for all other workers. The server earned $8.52 in regular pay plus $10 in tips for a total of $18.52. However, according to federal law, the server must be paid at least $40 for working four hours at minimum wage. That means the employer must pay the server $21.48.

Wondering how the Defense Commissary Agency gets away with hiring baggers who work for tips only, with no base salary? Baggers are considered self-employed, and they work in the commissary by getting permission (license) from the installation's commander. That's legal due to a footnote in the Fair Labor Standards Act, which says, "Notwithstanding any other provision of law, an individual who performs bagger or carryout service for patrons of a commissary of a military department may not be considered to be an employee by virtue of such service if the sole compensation of such individual for such service is derived from tips." Essentially, baggers at the commissary are gig workers with permission to show up at the commissary to bag and carry out groceries for anyone who wants to hire them for that job. What you give them isn't technically a tip; it's payment for a service.

Fitting into tax brackets

Parts of military income are taxed, so you're sitting somewhere in one of the United States' handful of tax brackets — and you probably haven't paid much attention to the rate you pay. However, in the civilian world, where pay varies widely between different jobs and different employers (and you don't get tax-free money for housing), tax may matter to you a little bit more.

The United States operates on a progressive tax system, which means people who earn higher taxable incomes pay higher federal income tax rates. The government decides how much you owe by dividing your income into pieces, and those pieces are called *tax brackets*.

Tax brackets are adjusted for inflation each year, so the numbers change (and you can find the current numbers on the Internal Revenue Service's website, if you're interested). The higher your income is, the more you pay in taxes, but you don't pay the highest rate on all your income. You pay the highest rate on only the portion of your income that falls into that bracket.

Figure 8-1 shows three tax brackets on a taxable income of $60,000 to illustrate how tax brackets work.

The reason tax brackets may become more important to you when you leave the military is that generally, all your civilian pay is taxable. In the military, the income you bring in through your basic allowance for housing, overseas housing allowance, family separation allowance, and basic allowance for subsistence are nontaxable. That money goes directly into your pocket without the government taking its share.

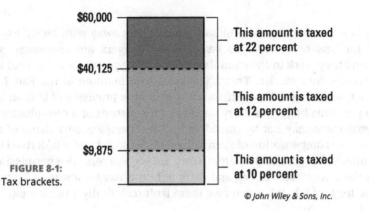

$60,000 — This amount is taxed at 22 percent

$40,125 — This amount is taxed at 12 percent

$9,875 — This amount is taxed at 10 percent

FIGURE 8-1:
Tax brackets.

© John Wiley & Sons, Inc.

If your military base pay is $3,500 per month, your BAH is $1,000, and your BAS is $500, you bring in $5,000 per month. That's a total of $60,000 in income in one year. However, you only pay taxes on your base pay, which totals $42,000 per year. The remaining $18,000 is yours, free and clear.

In the civilian world, you pay more in taxes if you bring in $60,000 per year, which you can see in Figure 8-1.

Delving into Job Market Statistics

The Bureau of Labor Statistics (BLS) maintains an Occupational Outlook Handbook, or OOH, that compiles employment data from all over the United States. The OOH contains information on most of the occupations that exist and divides them into categories, such as "Highest Paying," "Fastest Growing (Projected)," and "Most New Jobs." The BLS does this, in part, to give job-seekers a heads-up on the job market. You can check out the OOH at www.bls.gov/ooh.

The numbers can (and do) change frequently, but it's worth checking out the current highest-paying and fastest-growing jobs if you're mapping out your future. Jobs in the medical and behavioral health fields typically take the top spots for pay, and over the past several years, the fastest-growing jobs have to do with wind and solar power, medicine, and information security.

Some fields do, and probably always will, employ more people than others. The following table shows jobs that have statistically been the most common over the past several years, along with their national average salaries. Remember, national averages include those who are just starting out *and* those who have been in the field for decades, but this table can give you some guidance if you're thinking about going into a particular field.

Cashier ($10–$12 per hour)	Food preparation worker ($11–$12 per hour)	Janitor ($11–$12 per hour)	Bartender ($11–12 per hour)
Restaurant server ($11–$12 per hour)	Retail sales associate ($12–$13 per hour)	Stocking associate ($12–$13 per hour)	Laborer ($13–$14 per hour)
Customer service representative ($13–$14 per hour)	Office clerk ($13–$14 per hour)	Administrative assistant ($14–$15 per hour)	Line supervisor ($15–$16 per hour)
Medical assistant ($15–$16 per hour)	Construction worker ($15–$16 per hour)	Bookkeeper ($18–$19 per hour)	Mechanic ($20–$21 per hour)
Carpenter ($21–$22 per hour)	Electrician ($26–$27 per hour)	Registered nurse ($33–$34 per hour)	Marketing specialist ($51,000–$52,000 per year)
Police officer ($53,000–$54,000 per year)	Truck driver ($59,000–$60,000 per year)	Operations manager ($70,000–$71,000 per year)	Lawyer ($74,000–$75,000 per year)

Data from https://www.indeed.com/career-advice/finding-a-job/most-common-jobs-in-america

Joining Forces with a Labor Union

A *labor union* or *trade union* is an organized group of workers who come together to make decisions about conditions that affect their work. Generally, union workers make higher wages, enjoy better benefits, and work in safer places than their peers do; that's because unions have what's called collective bargaining power. *Collective bargaining* is the process by which workers (through their unions) negotiate favorable contracts with employers. The union acts as an intermediary between its members and the business that employs them.

Unions can fight for things like healthcare coverage, paid sick leave, parental leave, and other benefits. In fact, unions are the reason that you're entitled to overtime pay if you work more than 40 hours, you don't work on Saturdays and Sundays, and the United States implemented child labor laws that prevent kids from being exploited by businesses. Unions are also partly responsible for employer-sponsored health insurance, workers' compensation, and the Family and Medical Leave Act.

If a company with union employees does something that negatively affects its workers, the union can take action, like organizing a strike that continues until the situation is remedied. In exchange for union protections, workers pay monthly dues that vary between unions.

In some industries, unions are common; in others, they're nonexistent. The most unionized industries are education, steelwork, public service, auto work, and electrical work.

TECHNICAL STUFF

The freedom to form or join a union is part of the United Nations' Universal Declaration on Human Rights. In fact, the UN considers it a fundamental right that ensures the ability to protect other rights.

Even if you're not part of a union, you still have rights. I cover employee rights in extensive detail in Chapter 13.

Finding Civilian Jobs

The U.S. government has a handful of job search websites (some just for veterans) that can help you find employment. Several civilian companies operate massive online job boards as well. Sometimes websites overlap; one company may advertise an open job on more than one site. However, some companies have contracts with specific websites and only advertise their jobs there. I cover some of the major job search engines in the following sections, but dozens more are out there, and I encourage you to search for them if you're having a hard time finding employment by using those outlined here.

USAJOBS, apprenticeship.gov, and other job boards

At some point during your Transition Assistance Program coursework, someone will probably tell you to create a profile on USAJOBS, the federal government's official job search website. After you complete your profile, you can search for jobs, review job announcements, and prepare entire job application packages through the website. If you're interested in getting another government job as a veteran (which is a great idea, because government jobs come with pension plans), head to www.usajobs.gov to start scoping out the territory.

If you're interested in an apprenticeship to pick up a trade, you can use www.apprenticeship.gov, the federal government's tool for connecting searchers with opportunities. You may be able to use your GI Bill to pay for your training in a wide range of fields, including IT, engineering, healthcare, plumbing, electrical, carpentry, and others.

Other useful online job boards include these:

>> **Military.com:** This job board (www.military.com/veteran–jobs) is full of job listings created expressly for veterans. You can search by job title or keyword, or you can search by location to see what's available near you.

>> **Indeed.com:** The massive job website at www.indeed.com posts thousands of job descriptions each month. You can run a search for "military veteran" or "veteran" to turn up jobs that may be a good fit for you based on the time you spent in the service, as well as searches for specific job fields or locations.

>> **CareerBuilder.com:** The job board at www.careerbuilder.com enables you to search by job title, skills, or military occupational code, as well as city, state, or ZIP Code.

>> **Monster.com:** You can search www.monster.com by keyword, job title, or location (including work-from-home), as well as get access to free career self-assessments, sample resumes, top interview questions, and other valuable information.

LinkedIn

LinkedIn is a popular social networking and job search site, and it's unique because it enables you to directly connect with other professionals. By the same token, it enables other professionals to find *you*. You can get the most out of LinkedIn by using the following tips:

>> **Keep your profile updated.** Stay on top of your profile information. Include a professional photo of yourself, update your skills and objectives, and use your headline to let prospective employers know you're looking for work. Highlight all your recent experience in the military as well. Use your LinkedIn page like a resume.

>> **Build your network.** LinkedIn shows you how you're connected to others by way of degrees (like the Kevin Bacon game). If you and I both know Joe Snuffy but not each other, we're second-degree connections. Joe Snuffy is a link between us. People who are connected to your second-degree connections are considered 3rd degree connections. Because you and I know Joe, you see people who are connected to me as third-degree connections, and I see people who are connected to you as third-degree connections. (It's basically "My friend's friend knows this person.") You want as many first-degree connections as you can get because every first-degree connection has the

ability to introduce you to someone who may be helpful in your job search. With that in mind, search for people you personally know from the military, family friends, and people your spouse knows.

>> **Follow companies you're interested in.** Start searching the site for companies you want to work for, no matter how big or small. When you follow a company, you'll get a notification when it posts an open position, and you'll be able to keep tabs on company updates.

>> **Use a search to find people in your network who are connected to companies you're interested in working for.** You may find that people you actually know are connected to one or more of the companies you're interested in working for, which can give you an in later. You can ask your connections questions about the company culture, what it's like to do business with the organization, or whether they know of upcoming job openings. You can even ask for introductions to the right people if you're ready to reach out to the company.

>> **Be active on the site.** Don't lurk in the shadows — feel free to comment on posts, put up articles you've written or videos you've done, and share other information as updates on the site. Join professional groups related to your job interests and add your voice to lively discussions. But be careful: Prospective employers will be able to see your profile (and many of them will go out of their way to look at it when you apply for a job) as well as the groups you're in, so don't add anything personal. And above all else, *keep your political and social opinions to yourself*.

TIP

Research shows that most people don't use LinkedIn during business hours — they use it after work (only about 8 percent of people are on it during the day). When you're updating your page, connecting with people, and commenting in groups, try doing so after-hours to get more exposure.

LinkedIn has been known to offer special deals to veterans, such as a free year of premium membership. You can get more information at https://socialimpact. linkedin.com/programs/veterans/premiumform.

Cruising into Career Fairs

Career fairs — commonly called *job fairs* and *career expos* — are recruitment gold mines for employers. Companies pay to set up booths or tables inside large halls and expo centers, and HR professionals answer questions about current job openings and how to apply, as well as provide other important information job-seekers need.

Career fairs give you the chance to get your foot in the door and find out about opportunities you may have with participating companies. Although you're unlikely to walk away with a job, you can get in-depth information on what a company has to offer and gather contact information from hiring managers.

Many cities hold career fairs throughout the year. So do colleges and universities, some large companies, and organizations such as the Disabled American Veterans, the American Legion, and the Veterans of Foreign Wars. Many organizations even hold virtual job fairs. You can search the internet for "career fairs near me" to get a rundown of what's in the works right now.

Planning your participation

If you want your first foray into the world of career fairs to be successful, you have to prepare. Before you go,

>> **Find out which companies will be there:** That way, you can create strong, customized resumes (see Chapter 7 for more information on those) for each field. Bring at least 20 copies of your resume to the career fair.

>> **Develop and practice your elevator pitch:** Your *elevator pitch* is a quick, 30-second description of your skills and abilities that you use to introduce yourself to hiring managers and other people you meet at a career fair. I cover elevator pitches in more detail in Chapter 10.

>> **Get professional clothing:** If you don't have business attire, get some. More than half of any face-to-face interaction is visual, so you have to dress the part when you meet hiring managers who are evaluating whether you're a good fit for a company.

>> **Pick up a professional-looking planner with pockets inside:** Keep your resume, a pen, some note paper, and business cards (if you have them) inside.

>> **Clean up your social media profiles and make sure everything is locked down tighter than Fort Knox:** Hiring managers can, and do, look at people's social media profiles, so those embarrassing things you posted while you were in high school, during the last presidential election, and all the memes you've shared need to be deleted or made completely private. That goes for Facebook, Twitter, and every other social media site you've ever used.

Fitting in while standing out

You don't want to stick out like a sore thumb, but you do need to distinguish yourself from everyone else at a career fair. These tips can help you while you're visiting with prospective employers.

>> **Leave your phone in the car.** If you must have it with you, put it in "Silent" mode and tuck it into your pocket, purse, or planner.

>> **Get there early so you spend less time waiting in line to talk to prospective employers.**

>> **Remember to shake hands firmly, make eye contact, and smile.** I know — you typically had to turn off your smile while communicating in the military, but civilians expect and appreciate it.

>> **Ask thoughtful questions, provide candid answers, and leave your resume (and business card, if you have one) with every representative you meet.** Ask each rep for their business card, too, or at least get a contact name. If a prospective employer doesn't take your resume but tells you to apply online, don't take it personally; many companies only accept electronic resumes.

Concocting thoughtful questions on the fly

As you meet with prospective employers' representatives, you have to think on your feet, and that means coming up with thoughtful questions that show you're an interested (and already-informed) candidate. Never ask, "What does your organization do?" That shows that you didn't bother to do any research on the company. Instead, think about asking questions like these:

>> What qualities and characteristics do successful candidates possess?

>> What are common career paths in your organization?

>> I see that you have an open position for a [name a job the company has available]. What does a typical day look like in that position?

>> I don't have a traditional background in [name a specific open position], but I do have experience with [something relevant from your military career]. Would that make me a good fit for the position?

>> What does your hiring process for [specific job] look like?

>> What kind of person is most successful at your company?

>> What does communication look like at your company?

- How does the company commit to employees' professional development?
- How long have you been with the company?
- What do you like best about working for this company?
- What have been your biggest challenges working with this company?
- What's the best way to stay in touch with you?

Creating a list of questions and carrying it through the event is perfectly fine. You can refer to it and take notes when appropriate.

TIP

Asking the company's representative questions about their experiences with the company makes you more authentic and personable. It also shows that you're "interviewing" the company before you dive in with both feet, and that makes you more memorable.

Following up when you're interested

Follow-up is critical when you find a company you're interested in working with. If an employer asks you to submit your resume online, do it within two days of the career fair — when you still have a chance that the recruiter will remember you.

Send a thank-you note as soon as possible (preferably the same day). You don't have to get in-depth with it, but you do want to carry over the great first impression you made. Here's an example.

APPLYING FOR JOBS THROUGH COMPANY WEBSITES

Many companies list open job positions right on their own websites. Often, open positions are listed under menu items like "Work for Us" or "Careers." Applying for jobs through companies' websites rather than through job search websites (even if the positions are also listed there) has a few benefits. For example, companies often provide more detail about open positions on their own websites. Even better, you can find out more about the company with a few clicks, and that's helpful when you're customizing your resume and cover letter. You can also submit your application in the company's preferred format rather than the standard templates that many job search websites use, and your resume will most likely go directly to the hiring manager (rather than to a catchall email account that may not be checked very often).

Hello, Ms. Smith,

Thank you for the opportunity to discuss ABC Company's entry-level communications position at the VFW job fair this morning. It was nice getting to know another veteran.

I appreciate your insight on the future of media broadcasting, and I believe my experience as a public affairs liaison in the U.S. Army makes me a good candidate for ABC Company. I look forward to submitting my resume this week.

Thanks again for your time.

Queiana Jones

Using an Agency to Find Work

Some people use employment agencies to find work. Agencies are firms that companies hire to bring in new talent, and they come in three main varieties: personnel placement services, staffing services, and executive search firms. Agencies are responsible for helping millions of people find work every year.

One of the largest but least-known agencies is the U.S. Department of Labor's Employment and Training Administration, or ETA. The ETA operates almost 2,400 American Job Centers all over the country, and you can find one near you by visiting www.careeronestop.org, an official DOL website. American Job Centers have experienced career counselors on staff who can help match you with jobs and training opportunities that may be right for you (and many offer recruiting events, job search help, and resource rooms that have phones, free internet, and resume writing tools). They also provide you with access to your state's job bank (where employers in your state can post job openings for free) and the CareerOneStop Job Finder tool.

SHOULD YOU PAY TO FIND A JOB?

You can hire people, like a resume writer, to help you find employment, but generally, you shouldn't pay to find a job. Employers pay recruiters and staffing agencies big bucks to look for candidates like you, so unless you're a high-level executive (you will be in a few years, but patience, young grasshopper), you don't need to spend your hard-earned savings on hiring someone to find you work.

To work with an agency, you have to fill out an application, provide your resume, take qualifying tests, and interview with the agency so it can complete your file. The reps from the agency then attempt to match you with jobs.

TIP

If you're thinking about using an agency to find work, you may as well go big by working with more than one. Different agencies have access to different employers, which means you'll broaden your opportunity by working with multiple companies.

Personnel placement services

Personnel placement services specialize in certain industries, like healthcare or law. You don't pay for these services; employers do. (Usually, a placement service gets a commission or percentage of an employee's annual salary in exchange for providing a new hire.)

Businesses use personnel placement services to test, interview, and recommend candidates, so you may still have to go through an employer's hiring process to get a job. That may mean submitting your resume and attending one or more interviews before you receive an offer of employment.

Staffing services

Staffing services provide temporary employees, not permanent hires. They're often called *temp agencies*, and companies use them when they know a permanent employee will be gone for a specific amount of time, which can range from a few days to several months. Some companies also use staffing services to hire extra help around the holidays or during their busy seasons.

When you work for a staffing service, you work for the company that runs the service — not the company where you show up and perform work every day. The staffing service pays you out of the money it receives from the employer (the rest is the staffing service's fee).

Some people enjoy working for staffing services because they get a lot of variety. You may be a receptionist at a law firm one week and a customer service rep at a plumbing company the next, depending on your skill set. However, the kind of work that staffing services provide is temporary and intermittent — you may not have work every week (or even every month). If you turn down too many available jobs, the staffing agency you work for may stop asking.

WALKING AWAY FROM A POTENTIAL JOB

It's okay to say no to a job or an employer if you just aren't feeling right about it. Maybe the compensation isn't high enough, you're worried about the long drive to and from work, or you just didn't like your experience during the application or interview process. But turning down a job can be scary; what if you don't get another offer, or what if your other offers are *worse*? Unless you're desperate for a job (which you probably won't be if you start your search before you get out of the military), you don't need to be afraid to turn down employment offers that give you a bad feeling. Whether an interviewer shows up late or bad-mouths the former employee you'll be replacing, you find out about a company's bad reputation after applying, or you just get a gut feeling that taking the job is a bad idea, feel free to graciously thank the employer for the opportunity and let them know you aren't the best fit for the job.

Working for a temp agency can lead to a permanent job, particularly if an employer likes you and is happy with the work you perform. The experience you gain can be good for your career, too. The downside is that the employment and the pay are typically unstable.

Executive search firms

Executive search firms are specialized recruiting services that companies hire to find good candidates for senior, executive, and highly specialized positions. Businesses often use these firms to minimize their risks in hiring; hiring an employee (especially a highly compensated one) who doesn't work out is expensive and wastes valuable time. As with other agencies, you need to submit your resume and qualifications, as well as go through an interview process, before an executive search firm begins matching you with job prospects. Additionally, you still have to go through the company's hiring process before you actually land a job.

Searching for Gig Work to Tide You Over

Holding out for the perfect job — or waiting to find any type of permanent job at all — is a great way to end up in your old room at your parents' house. And although your parents may be awesome, living with them isn't a permanent solution. To avoid that, you may choose to look for gig work to tide you over until you find a full-time job.

You can apply for gigs you find online, or you can market your skills yourself, pick up work through apps, or list your skills on a website dedicated to keeping the gig economy moving. You may consider the following options:

>> Becoming a ride-share driver

>> Doing freelance work, such as photography

>> Tutoring

>> Helping with household projects through a gig app

>> Delivering food, groceries, or retail products

>> Virtual assisting

>> Pet-sitting or babysitting through apps

>> Using sites like Fiverr.com to offer your services in things like graphic design, marketing, or writing

TIP

If all else fails, even if it's not your cup of tea or wasn't part of your original plan, go to school full-time while you look for work. You have a GI Bill that pays a housing allowance at the E-5 with dependents rate for your location, whether you attend a community college or a nationally renowned university. (But take my advice: If you do this, you may want to relocate to Hawaii; Washington, D.C.; or another place that pays tremendous BAH.)

Getting Two (or More) Jobs

Leaving the military often means taking a pay cut or losing benefits, and that may mean you have to work harder to earn the same. Some people do this by taking on two jobs. Statistically, nearly a third of veteran job-seekers are *underemployed*, meaning they don't have enough paid work or aren't doing work that makes full use of their skills or abilities.

It's no secret that the federal minimum wage is abysmally low. It's also no secret that although everyone is supposed to have three months' worth of pay set aside in an "emergency fund," more than half of all Americans don't have the resources to deal with an emergency that costs $1,000 or more, and fewer than 40 percent have enough money in savings to cover a $500 emergency.

But this section isn't a lecture on building up your savings, because that isn't easy (or even realistic) in every situation. Instead, it's a gentle nudge telling you that if you have to take a job that doesn't pay well enough for you to pay the bills, you may need to get an additional job. You may have to work more than 40 hours per week across separate jobs. Nobody wants to work their life away, but having a second job may be necessary to keep food on your table and your lights on. Think of it as an opportunity to use another one of your military skills: your ability to embrace the suck.

I'm not going to pretend that being in the military is easy, because it's not. But I am going to tell you that until you get established, working in the civilian sector can be a rough ride for a while. It may require you to tighten your belt, work harder, and compromise when you don't really feel like it. If you're adaptable and prepared, you can — and will — be successful. However, you do need to know that you may not find fair winds and following seas right away.

REMEMBER

You can avoid a lot of headaches by looking for and finding a job *before* you get out of the military. And if you're not well-equipped for civilian employment just yet, use the military to get yourself there. You can use tuition assistance to go to college for free while you're in, gain more work experience, or get your foot in the door with the civilian agencies that work with your branch.

IN THIS CHAPTER

» Considering the appeal of government employment for veterans, including veterans' preference

» Looking for government jobs in all the right places

» Understanding federal job vacancy announcements and the selection process

» Classifying government job categories and pay structures

» Jumping through pre-employment hoops like background checks

Chapter **9**

Getting the Skinny on Government Jobs

Getting a government job after you leave the military may be a smart choice. The U.S. government is one of the few entities that offer a great retirement plan, free health insurance, and a wide range of other benefits that most employers don't. Government jobs offer plenty of job security (people working civilian jobs are three times more likely to be terminated by an employer than government employees are), and they run the whole spectrum of fields. Federal or state jobs as a cook, a data scientist, a computer programmer, a maintenance professional, a doctor, or nearly anything else are all possibilities. Hundreds of government agencies exist, so whether you want to work for a common veteran-employing agency like Border Patrol or a more obscure agency like the Weights and Measures Division, you're likely to be able to find something you enjoy.

The catch: You need to be able to decipher government job vacancy announcements, understand the differences between general schedule (GS) and other types of government positions, and become familiar with the assessment and selection process. But don't worry; I explain each of these things in the following sections so you can apply for the government job of your dreams.

Investigating Why Some Troops Choose Federal or State Government Jobs

If you retire from the military, you probably have plenty of time to get another job and continue working while you draw your retirement pay. Retiring from the military somewhere around the age of 40 means you still have 27 years before you can even start collecting Social Security, so although playing golf, video games, or scratch-offs for 27 years may sound good right now, getting another government job may be the wisest choice. That's because you can work for the federal government for another 20 years, retire, and get another pension.

That's not all, though. Government agencies, both state and federal, offer some of the best compensation packages around. In addition to healthcare benefits, paid vacation, stable employment, and a pretty decent pay schedule, working for the government almost always means your job is clearly defined, you usually have room for advancement, and you typically clock out at (or before) 1700. (Have you ever visited an office manned by Department of Defense civilians at 16:57? Neither have I, because the door has always been locked.) Also: No PT.

You may choose to work for the federal government, which includes hundreds of departments and agencies ranging from the AbilityOne Commission to the Woodrow Wilson International Center for Scholars. Federal jobs in Customs and Border Patrol, the FBI, Citizenship and Immigration Services, and a huge array of other agencies are always hiring — and many agencies actively recruit veterans. You can find a complete list of federal agencies at www.usa.gov/federal-agencies. And at www.usa.gov/states-and-territories, you can get information on all the government agencies in your state, which is helpful if you want to work for the Department of Motor Vehicles, an emergency management agency, the state Attorney General's office, or another state-run office.

Using Veterans' Preference to Get a Government Job

As an honorably discharged veteran, you're entitled to use veterans' preference to help you get a job with the federal government. All 50 states give veterans preferential treatment in hiring, too.

When agencies use a numerical rating and ranking system to figure out who's best qualified for a position, federal employment has three types of veterans' preference (and only two that are likely to apply to you): 0-point preference, 5-point preference, and 10-point preference. You have no limit on the number of times you can use veterans' preference to get a government job; you can use it as many times as you want. (And if you're applying for jobs *before* you get out of the military, first, good for you; second, you can prove that you're eligible for veterans' preference with a Statement of Service from your personnel office. Everyone else has to supply a DD-214 to prove eligibility.)

When an agency uses a category rating system, you fall into a *preference category* of CPS, CP, XP, TP, or SSP, all of which I cover in the following sections. The points or preference categories are calculated based on pre-employment assessments that distinguish the most-qualified candidates, and the more points you have, the more likely your application packet is to make it to the hiring authority's desk.

TIP

Retirees at the rank of O-5 or higher aren't eligible for preference unless they're disabled, and no matter what type of preference you use, you must have been honorably or generally discharged from the military to qualify.

0-point preference

You're 0-point preference eligible if you were released or discharged from active duty after August 29, 2008, because you're the only surviving child in a family in which the father, mother, or one or more siblings served in the Armed forces and were killed; died as a result of wounds, accident, or disease; are in a captured or missing-in-action status; or are permanently 100 percent disabled or hospitalized on a continuing basis *and* aren't employed gainfully because of the disability or hospitalization. The death, status, or disability can't have resulted from intentional misconduct or willful neglect of the parent or sibling or have been incurred while the person was AWOL from the military.

So why bother with claiming 0-point preference? Though you don't get any points, claiming this preference entitles you to be listed ahead of people with the same score on an examination or in the same quality category who aren't preference eligible.

5-point preference

You're 5-point preference eligible if your active-duty service meets at least one of the following conditions:

>> You served for more than 180 consecutive days (other than for training), and any part of that term occurred between September 11, 2001, and August 31, 2010.

>> You served during the Gulf War (between August 2, 1990, and January 2, 1992).

Other veterans of earlier wars are also entitled to claim this preference, but the next-earliest date of service must have occurred before October 15, 1976; if that was you and you're still in, both of the other conditions apply to you as well.

10-point preference

You're 10-point preference eligible if you served at any time and have a service-connected disability *or* a Purple Heart.

You must submit Form SF-15 if you're claiming 10-point veterans' preference. You can get a fillable SF-15 from the Office of Personnel Management's website at www.opm.gov.

Preference categories

Agencies that use a category rating system for applicants typically divide candidates into preference groups. The candidates are called *preference eligible* and put into five basic groups:

>> CPS, which is for those with a disability rating of 30 percent or more (10 points)

>> CP for those with a disability rating of at least 10 percent but less than 30 percent (10 points)

>> XP, which is for applicants who have a disability rating less than 10 percent

>> TP for people with no disability rating (5 points)

>> SSP, which is for those with sole survivorship preference

Under this category rating system, CPS and CP are highest on the *referral list* (the list of which applications will be forwarded to the hiring authority) except for scientific and professional positions at the GS-9 level or higher. XP and TP preference eligible are given precedence over non-preference eligible in the same category. SSP preference eligible can also be given precedence.

States and preference points

Most states use a preference point system like the federal government uses, but some states use "absolute preference," which gives vets an advantage over other, more-qualified non-veteran candidates. In those states, simply identifying yourself as an honorably discharged veteran (with proof, of course) pushes your application to the top of the second-look pile. Sure, that doesn't guarantee you'll land the job, but having that benefit on your side doesn't hurt.

Your state's labor office can give you the most up-to-date information on whether your area uses preference points or absolute preference.

Applying for jobs only open to federal employees through VEOA

The Veterans Employment Opportunity Act of 1998, or VEOA, is a special hiring authority that gives eligible vets access to positions that are generally only available to current competitive service employees (meaning you must already be a federal employee to qualify for the job). To be eligible for these jobs, you must fall into a preference eligible category (see the earlier section "Using Veterans' Preference to Get a Government Job" to see how to fit into those categories) or you must have separated from the military after three or more years of continuous active service performed under honorable conditions.

You can't use veterans' preference to get these jobs, but you can join the pool of other applicants while other non-competitive service employees are locked out. The government considers that your veterans' benefit in this case.

Applying for government jobs under VRA

Veterans' Recruitment Appointment, or VRA, is an excepted authority that allows agencies to appoint eligible veterans without competition. You're eligible for VRA if you meet any of the following conditions:

>> You served during a war or have earned a campaign badge for service in a campaign or expedition.

>> You're a disabled veteran.

>> You have an Armed Forces Service Medal (including the Global War on Terrorism Service Medal) for participation in a military operation.

>> You're within three years of your military discharge and separated under honorable conditions.

These types of jobs are excepted service appointments, which means that the government doesn't require agencies to list them on USAJobs. You may only find them on individual agencies' websites or through word-of-mouth.

Applying for a government job under a disabled veteran program

If you're 30 percent or more disabled with a service-connected disability, you're eligible to be non-competitively appointed. That's true whether you were retired from active service or you have a disability rating by the Department of Veterans Affairs showing a service-connected disability of 30 percent or more that qualifies for compensation. Disabled vets who are eligible for training under the VA's vocational rehabilitation program (VR&E, which I cover in detail in Chapter 20) may enroll for training or work experience at a government agency that offers either, as well. And Schedule A authority for people with disabilities — a program designed to help federal agencies hire differently abled people quickly without going through the traditional competitive hiring process — is available to vets who have a severe physical, psychological, or intellectual disability.

Skipping the Confusion with O*NET

When you want a government job that's similar to your military job but minus the PT and uniforms, use O*NET's Military Crosswalk tool (www.onetonline.org/crosswalk). O*NET is the Department of Labor's Employment and Training Administration's website, and it lists all kinds of occupations that relate to your former line of work. All you have to do is choose your branch of service and enter your job code to find out which civilian jobs may be a good fit for you. It also provides job descriptions for each.

For example, choosing "Army" and "11B," the military occupational specialty code for an infantryman, the Department of Labor tells me that related jobs include the following:

>> Emergency management directors

>> Probation officers and corrections officers

>> Communications equipment operators

>> Police and other law enforcement officers

>> Firefighters, fire inspectors, and fire investigators

After you've read the job descriptions and found a few that seem interesting, you can search for jobs in those fields on USAJobs or your state's government hiring website.

Ferreting Out Government Jobs

Most federal positions are listed on USAJobs or on specific agencies' websites. If you have something specific in mind — say, Customs and Border Patrol — you can (and should) look on both sites to see what's available.

To find your state's government hiring website, type your state's name and "government jobs" in your search bar. Look for sites that end in *.gov*. You may have to do a little digging, but generally, the sites you want are called "Office of Career Services," "State Personnel Board," or something similar.

The following sections explain the most popular places (aside from state government websites) to find civil service jobs.

USAJobs

USAJobs (www.usajobs.gov) contains, by far, the most comprehensive listing of federal government jobs available. You can browse USAJobs, an official government website, without creating an account. However, if you want to apply to any jobs, you must create a profile with the service. Basic profile information includes your U.S. citizenship information, which hiring paths you can follow (such as those for U.S. citizens, veterans, military spouses, and others), what type of federal or military service you've completed in the past, and whether you qualify for veterans' benefits or VEOA or completed a VA training program. All that information is mandatory. After you complete your profile, you can begin applying for jobs.

DONHR

The Secretary of the Navy's Department of the Navy Human Resources (DONHR) site contains listings of civilian job openings within the Navy and Marine Corps. You can also find most of these listings on USAJobs, but you may find some that the Department of the Navy doesn't advertise there (such as excepted appointment positions).

Agency websites

Whether you want to apply for a federal, state, or local government job, you can go directly to a specific agency's website to look for open positions. Some jobs are *only* listed on agency websites, so if you have a particular field in mind, looking can't hurt. You may consider working for your former military branch; the FBI, CIA, or NSA; the Defense Finance and Accounting Service; or a whole host of other government agencies, such as the U.S. Postal Service, the Government Accountability office, the judicial branch, the legislative branch, or the executive branch.

If you're going hyper-local, look at agencies such as the following:

>> State college and university health systems

>> Police agencies, fire departments, and other public safety organizations

>> Department of motor vehicles

>> Town, city, and county boards

>> Emergency management

>> Health departments

>> Early childhood education, including licensed or regulated healthcare, Head Start, and state-funded pre-kindergarten

>> Public library services or school library services

FINDING A CONTRACTOR POSITION

If you don't want a civilian job and you're not too keen on working for the government, consider a happy medium: You can be a civilian contractor. As a contractor, you perform work that helps the government, but you work for a civilian company. Many contractor positions pay exceptionally well, let you transfer within the company if you want to move, and offer benefits that are very similar to what the government offers (and sometimes pay more). You can use a site like ClearanceJobs (www.clearancejobs.com) to connect with companies like Lockheed Martin, KBR, General Dynamics, Boeing, and hundreds of others if you have an active government security clearance. Job listings for clearance-required contractor positions (as well as those that don't require security clearances) may also appear on other websites, such as Indeed.com, CareerBuilder.com, and Monster.com.

Interpreting Federal Government Job Vacancy Announcements

Vacancy announcements for government jobs are often more complicated than civilian job ads are, but if you know how to read them, you can get important clues on what needs to be in your resume. (See Chapter 7 to get the scoop on creating job-winning federal resumes.) Even better, you learn enough about the job to find out whether it's likely a good fit for you. The following bullets explain each part of a federal job vacancy announcement so you know what you're looking at before you apply. Most federal vacancy announcements contain all of these sections thanks to government regulations.

>> **Overview:** The overview of a federal job announcement, which you can see in Figure 9-1, covers a lot of information you need before you can apply. An "Accepting applications" status means it's time for you to apply for the job, and open and closing dates let you know the first day you can apply and exactly how much time you have left to send in your application, respectively. (The site operates on Eastern Time, so you have until 23:59 ET on the closing date to submit your packet.) The pay scale and grade information, which I cover in a later section, explains what type of pay schedule you'll be on if the agency hires you, as well as what "rank" you'll be in the government's grand scheme of things. The appointment type lets you know how long the job will last, and the service portion shows whether the job is competitive, excepted, or senior executive. Your future salary and work schedule are also included.

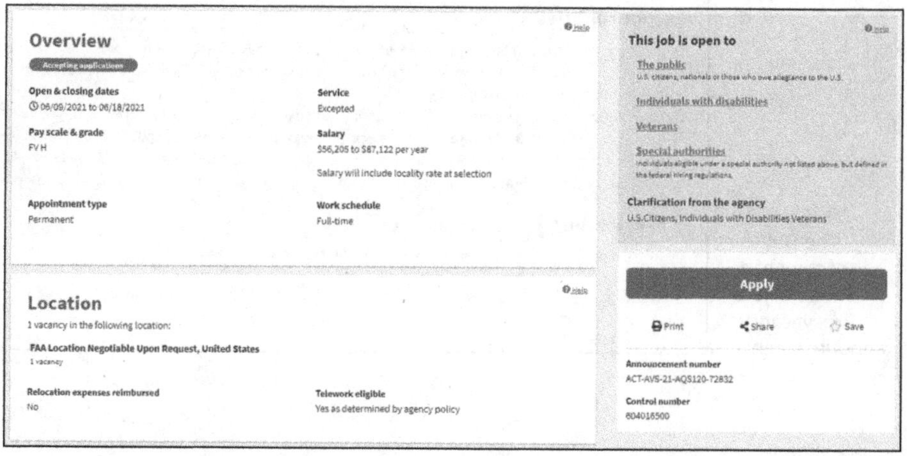

FIGURE 9-1:
The first four sections of a federal job announcement.

© John Wiley & Sons, Inc.

>> **"This job is open to:"** The "This job is open to" section tells you who can apply. Some agencies accept only applications from people who already work for them (unless the job is accepting VEOA applicants), or from any U.S. citizen, veteran, military spouse, current federal employee, surplus or displaced employee, or others. You can see this section in Figure 9-1.

>> **Locations:** The Locations section of a vacancy announcement, like the one in Figure 9-1, tells you exactly where open positions for this specific job are. It also explains whether the agency will pay for you to relocate and whether you can telework or you must go to work in person (like an essential worker).

>> **Announcement numbers and control numbers:** Figure 9-1 includes the announcement number and control number, which you need to track your application.

>> **Duties:** The Duties section of a federal job announcement, which you can see an example of in Figure 9-2, offers a quick summary and tells you exactly what your job will entail. It also lets you know whether travel is required (and if so, how much), whether you'll supervise others, and whether the position has any promotion potential.

@ Help

Duties

Summary

This position is located in the Department of Commerce, Bureau of Industry and Security, Office of Strategic Industries and Economic Security (SIES), Defense Programs Division (DPD), Washington, District of Columbia.

| Learn more about this agency |

Responsibilities

The Incumbent will support the office's Defense Priorities and Allocations System regulation, Offsets in Defense Trade, Department of Defense international agreements review, excess defense article review, NATO, defense trade advocacy, and National Defense Stockpile Market Impact Committee responsibilities.
Conducts research using available industry and government data to support office programs.
Assists senior staff members on more complex issues; conducts research; develops options; assists in document review; and recommends further action. Prepares written products to inform leadership of findings and/or recommendations for actions.
Expresses ideas both orally and in writing to leadership and representatives within the interagency and industry.

Travel Required

Occasional travel - You may be expected to travel for this position.

Supervisory status	**Promotion Potential**
No	12

© *John Wiley & Sons, Inc.*

FIGURE 9-2:
The Duties section of a federal job vacancy announcement.

>> **Requirements:** The Requirements section describes what experience you must have to be hired, conditions you must agree to, and how the agency will evaluate your application. You can check out a sample Requirements section in Figure 9-3.

One of the most important parts of this section is "Preview Job Questionnaire." You must read and answer the questions on the employment assessment questionnaire before you can apply for the job; if your resume doesn't support your answers to the questionnaire, you won't be considered for the position.

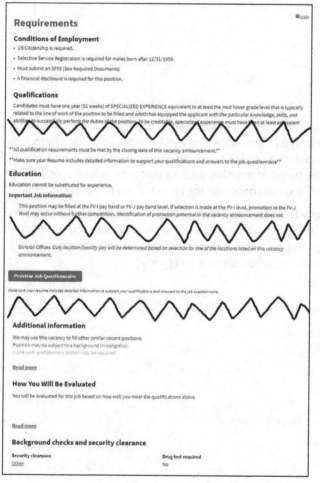

FIGURE 9-3: An abbreviated Requirements section of a federal job vacancy announcement.

>> **Required Documents:** The Required Documents section lists all the documents you need to send in with your application. These documents may be used to prove your eligibility and qualifications for the job. If you're missing any information, your application packet probably won't make it to the hiring authority. Every job requires different documents, but you can see an example of this section in Figure 9-4.

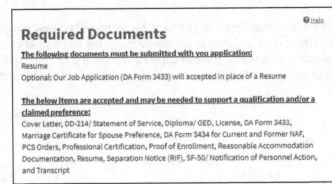

FIGURE 9-4:
A sample
Required
Documents
section of a
federal job
vacancy
announcement.

>> **Benefits:** The Benefits section of a federal vacancy announcement typically offers you a link to the agency's benefits, which usually include health and life insurance, vacation time, and a retirement plan. Your benefits will probably vary based on whether you're a part-time, full-time, or intermittent worker, and you can check with the agency if you need more specific information.

>> **How to Apply:** The How to Apply section is one of the most important parts of the announcement. It outlines exactly what you need to do to submit your application. It also includes the agency's contact information and your next steps, which you can see in Figure 9-5.

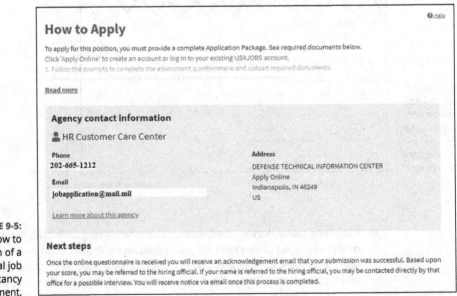

FIGURE 9-5:
A sample How to
Apply section of a
federal job
vacancy
announcement.

Eyeing the Differences between Competitive and Excepted Service

Competitive service positions are jobs subject to civil service laws passed by Congress to ensure that everyone receives fair, equal treatment in the hiring process. These positions are open to all applicants, and candidates have to go through a competitive hiring process. The process may include a written test, evaluations of your education and experience, and an evaluation of other attributes that would make you successful in the job.

Excepted service positions are federal or civil service jobs that aren't competitive. Agencies can set their own qualification requirements and aren't subject to appointment, pay, and classification rules outlined in U.S. Code. (They're subject to veterans' preference, though.) These appointment-only jobs are often only open to people who already work for a specific agency.

Another type of service, called *Senior Executive Service* (SES), comprises executives who have been selected for positions because of their leadership qualifications.

Acquainting Yourself with OPM Assessment and Selection

The Office of Personnel Management, or OPM, is in charge of how government agencies size up job candidates and choose the most qualified (or, in some cases, the most eligible) for the job. Government agencies can use assessment tools, such as qualification tests, assessment questionnaires, and other tools to zero in on the right candidates before investing more time in any one candidate. That's part of the reason that your resume and cover letter need to be on point before you send them. You need to make it past the initial gatekeeper, and possibly one or more additional gatekeepers, before you can fight — I mean, *work for* — the final boss.

One of the most common tools that government agencies use to assess your fitness as a job candidate is the *occupational assessment questionnaire.* The first few questions revolve around your special circumstances; they ask whether you claim veterans' preference and whether you've worked in federal service before. The next several questions confirm whether you're willing and able to submit to drug testing, maintain a security clearance (if applicable), and meet other criteria.

After those are out of the way, the questionnaire lets you coordinate your answers with your resume. You may see questions that look like this:

1. Please select one response that best describes how you meet the minimum qualifications for a GG-1083-07, Technical Writer-Editor.

○ A. I have one year of specialized experience equivalent to the next lower grade level (GS-05) or pay band in the federal service or equivalent experience in the private or public sector.

○ B. I have successfully completed a four year course of study leading to a bachelor's degree. Education must have included a total of 15 semester hours in an appropriate scientific, technical, or social science field(s), and at least one course above the introductory level in the field(s) covered by the position.

○ C. I have successfully completed one full year of graduate level education. Education must have included a total of 15 semester hours in an appropriate scientific, technical, or social science field(s), and at least one course above the introductory level in the field(s) covered by the position.

○ D. I have a combination of experience and education as described above that equates to one year of experience. My percentage of the required education plus my percentage of the required experience equal one hundred percent.

○ E. I do not have the experience and/or education described above.

Following questions may ask about your training and experience, and finally, you see a question that asks you to certify that all your responses are true and accurate and states that you must accept that if your supporting documentation doesn't match your answers, your application may be rated lower (or that you may be removed from further consideration). All the answers you provide on the questionnaire need to match what's on your resume or in your military records; a minor mistake can cause you to miss out on your chance at a great job.

During this part of the hiring process, a person compares your resume against your assessment questionnaire to ensure they match; if they don't, your resume is discarded. In agencies that use a point-scoring system (covered in the earlier section "Using Veterans' Preference to Get a Government Job"), your veterans' preference points are added to the score you receive on the assessment questionnaire.

Distinguishing Government Pay Scales and Grades

In the military, you received pay based on your rank, which corresponded with a pay grade, such as E-4 or O-5. You used the Defense Finance and Accounting Service's military pay tables to figure out how much money you'd earn with your next promotion or when you hit your next two-year mark in your current grade. Similarly, government agencies have their own pay grades. The following sections address the most common of them.

Getting familiar with GS grades and pay

Most government agencies use the *general schedule* (GS) pay schedule. However, about 40 agencies and agency subcomponents use special pay schedules within the GS system. That's often because they have to establish higher base pay rates for some jobs — especially in the medical, scientific, and technical fields — so they can compete with the civilian sector. Some agencies that use different pay schedules include the Environmental Protection Agency, the National Aeronautics and Space Administration, and the Internal Revenue Service.

The GS system works on a system of grades. The grade level assigned to a position determines its pay level. In a way, grades are like military ranks; people working in higher grades receive higher pay, but they have more responsibility than those below them do:

>> GS-3 and GS-4 are generally internships and student jobs.

>> GS-5 to GS-7 are mostly entry-level positions.

>> GS-8 to GS-12 are mid-level positions.

>> GS-13 to GS-15 are top-level supervisory positions.

Salaries under the GS system typically have two separate parts: base pay and locality pay adjustment. *Locality pay adjustment* is like the cost-of-living allowance you may have received for living in an expensive area in the military, or in your retirement pay for the same reason (you know it as COLA). For example, a GS-9 employee in Tacoma, Washington, makes more money than a GS-9 employee working at Fort Rucker, Alabama, and that's because of the locality pay adjustment. Pay rates outside the continental United States can be as much as 25 percent higher than standard GS pay rates, too, because the government offers some people COLA on top of their locality pay. (Am I telling you to look for a GS job in Hawaii? No, of course I'm not. I'm telling you to let *me* know if you find one.)

Many agencies that hire employees on a *temporary* or *term* basis (which means for a limited amount of time), and sometimes those that offer excepted service jobs, may use a *general government*, or GG, pay schedule. It's very similar to the GS pay schedule and includes the same benefits (including locality pay and COLA, when applicable).

Navigating FWS grades and pay

The *Federal Wage System*, or FWS, is also sometimes called *wage grade*. This hourly pay system generally aligns with the private sector as far as wages and benefits. This schedule has three classes: WG for workers, WL for leaders, and WS for supervisors. WG and WL have 15 grades and, WS has 19. All three classes have five steps in each grade.

The pay system in the FWS is locality based, so jobs that use this schedule are competitive with those in the civilian sector regarding how much cash you bring home each week. Each higher step within your class earns you more hourly pay. You can advance to higher steps within your grade with time in service and time in grade, kind of like you did in the military. For example, being hired as a WG-08 Step 1 making $25.50 per hour and then, five years later, being paid as a WG-08 Step 5 making $35.75 per hour is possible. (The pay rates vary by locality, though, so you can expect to make the same amount that civilians in your area with similar experience are making for the same work.)

Getting a big 10-4 on GL grades and pay

Law enforcement officers are paid according to the *General Law*, or GL, pay schedule, which is a derivative of the GS program. The GL pay schedule has eight grades, and each grade has ten steps of its own. On the GL schedule, your pay is determined based on your grade level and step and then adjusted with locality pay (if it's authorized). These are salaried positions, like the military.

Doing recon on FS grades and pay

The State Department, the Department of Commerce, and the Department of Agriculture use the *Foreign Service*, or FS pay schedule. The FS pay schedule consists of 9 pay grades with 14 steps in each grade.

Scrutinizing SES grades and pay

The SES doesn't have grades. Instead, it has five levels. They're in fancy Roman numerals, too, with Level V being the lowest and Level I being the highest. Employees in these positions are typically paid based on their performance, education, and experience, just like they are in the private sector. Usually, these positions work under (or are) presidential appointees. Most of the heads of federal agencies are on the SES pay schedule.

Bringing in Background Checks, Drug Tests, and Security Clearances

Some jobs in the government require background checks, which means someone will be looking very closely into your past to determine whether you have any issues that may make you a less desirable (or completely undesirable) candidate.

For example, if you've ever been convicted of robbing a bank, you're probably not going to land a job guarding the door to the gold bars at Fort Knox. Drug tests and security clearance are factors, too. If you can't get a Top Secret security clearance, the Department of Energy isn't going to hire you to maintain nuclear weapons hidden in secret locations.

Bombing (or not) your background check

Government background checks can range from simple to complex, and they're often based on information you provide (such as your Social Security number). Some agencies take things farther by using fingerprint-based background checks to delve into a person's criminal history, which enable a search through the Federal Bureau of Investigation's national database as well as other federal and state databases.

Many agencies use both types of background checks. They use your name and Social Security number to look for publicly available criminal records and to verify your professional certifications, educational credentials, past employment history, and even your driving record. They use your fingerprints to look for matches in criminal record databases.

Running a name-based background check can take a few hours to a few days, and getting the results of a fingerprint-based background check may take several weeks (or even months).

REMEMBER

If you got a waiver for a criminal record to join the military, that record will still be there waiting for you when you get out. You may want to consider having your record expunged or sealed in the state where it exists before you apply for federal employment. You can petition the courts to clear your criminal record on your own, and most state and local governments provide the forms you need on their government websites. You generally don't need to hire an attorney to clear your criminal record, but you do need to be aware that it'll take some work.

Getting all As on your drug test

Executive Order 12564, signed in 1986 by President Ronald Reagan, says, "Persons who use illegal drugs are not suitable for federal employment." As a result, many government agencies — especially those in the national security, law enforcement, protecting life and property, and public health arenas — require pre-employment drug testing. The most common type of drug test is a urinalysis, but generally, you don't have to perform in front of an observer like you did in the military. Additionally, some people in specific jobs are subject to mandatory random drug testing, just like you were in the military, and all federal employees can be drug tested if they have an accident at work or if they're suspected of using drugs.

CAN THE GOVERNMENT RUN A CREDIT CHECK ON YOU?

The U.S. government may assess your credit profile to determine whether you'll be a security risk in a job it may offer you. If you remember any of your threat awareness training from the military, you know that someone with a poor credit history can be a target for espionage, terrorist actions, and potential insider acts of violence. Many agencies have a credit check requirement in place because they want to hire employees who are less susceptible to financial pressure that may make them vulnerable to bribes. People known for "poor financial conduct" as evidenced by their credit reports may have a tough time getting a job involving defense, money-handling, or security. That means when you apply for a federal job, Uncle Sam may want to have a peek at how much you owe and how often you pay your credit card bills. If the job you want requires a credit check, you can expect to sign a form authorizing it; if you don't sign, you may not be eligible for the job.

Which drug test you get depends on the agency's policies. Some government agencies use a standard, five-panel drug urine test. Five-panel drug tests check for commonly abused substances, including marijuana, opiates (including heroin, codeine, and morphine), phencyclidine, cocaine, and amphetamines (including meth and Ecstasy). Others use a ten-panel drug urine test, which also tests for benzodiazepines, barbiturates, methadone, propoxyphene, and quaaludes. Still others use a different number of panels. No way is an agency going to tell you what it tests for before you're hired (unless you're applying for a job as the person who runs the drug tests), so play it safe and don't do anything your last commander wouldn't do. If you refuse or fail a pre-employment drug test, you have a 100 percent chance of not getting the job.

Scouting out a security clearance

Having an active security clearance can be a tremendous benefit to you when you're looking for a federal or state job or when you want certain contractor positions. In fact, a person with a current security clearance may make between 5 and 20 percent more than a person whose clearance has expired (or who never had one at all). Check out the three basic levels of security classification:

>> **Confidential:** If you have a Confidential security clearance, you're allowed to see materials that, if improperly disclosed, can be reasonably expected to cause measurable damage to national security. Most military personnel have at least a Confidential security clearance. You must be reinvestigated for a Confidential clearance every 15 years.

>> **Secret:** If you have a Secret security clearance, you can view materials and information that, if disclosed without authorization, can cause grave damage to national security. You must be reinvestigated for this type of clearance every ten years.

>> **Top Secret:** If you have a Top Secret security clearance, you have access to information and material that can be expected to cause exceptionally grave damage to national security. You must be reinvestigated for a Top Secret security clearance every five years.

If you enter federal service without a break, your military security clearance can carry over. However, if you have a significant break in service, which means you get out of the military, hang out for a while, and reenter federal service more than two years after you separate, you have to go through the tedious and time-consuming security clearance process again. You may not have a full two years, though. For example, a Secret-level security clearance lasts only ten years. If it's been longer than that since the government investigated you, you have to be reinvestigated immediately.

If you don't have a U.S. security clearance, your prospective employer has to set up the process for you. Unfortunately, most organizations don't want to do it unless it's essential (meaning you're the best candidate they've seen in a long time). It's a lengthy process that requires you to fill out Form SF-86. You may remember it from the last time you were investigated: It's dozens of pages long and you have to list every place you lived over the past decade, provide contact information for people who know you well, and fill in information for your spouse and every close relative you have (including places of birth, residence addresses, citizenship, employer information, and whether they have contact with foreign governments or foreign military personnel). Just about the only thing this form *doesn't* ask is what type of frosting your third cousin's cake had on their eighth birthday.

After you complete and turn in your SF-86, the Defense Security Service (DSS) conducts very thorough background checks — not just on you but also on people who know you and who are related to you. When the DSS is finished with its investigations, the findings are evaluated based on 13 factors determined by the Department of Defense, including your personal conduct, any criminal conduct you may have been involved in, whether you've had any substance abuse issues, and whether you have any mental health issues. Based on the results of the evaluation, your security clearance will be approved or denied.

REMEMBER

The entire investigation can take months to complete, so if you have a current security clearance, making sure it doesn't lapse before you try to get a government job that requires it is in your best interest.

TIP

Getting a job that requires a security clearance later is possible even if you don't have a clearance right now. You may want to consider applying for jobs with your desired agency that don't require security clearances at first; then, after you've established yourself, let your supervisor know that you're interested in pursuing a clearance job.

IN THIS CHAPTER

» Getting into the right mindset for networking effectively

» Writing and executing the perfect elevator pitch

» Networking through events, social media, and informational interviews

» Making connections with all the right people in military associations

» Leaving a mark on the people you meet

Chapter 10

Connecting with Civilians in Your New AO

N etworking is the act of getting your name and face out there, letting people know you're looking for work or that you're available to help others, and building relationships with other people. It makes you noticeable, keeps you relevant, and provides you with pathways to new opportunities that wouldn't have existed otherwise. Networking even helps you build self-confidence and develop communication skills that you can use in the civilian workforce. And unlike the military, civilians expect you to rub elbows with those who are above your pay grade; it's part of being a professional.

Networking isn't only about attending professional events, though many organizations host big face-to-face meet-and-greets. Any time you're out in public may be an opportunity to network. Good networking happens at family events, parties, the grocery store, kids' sports events, and anywhere else you find people you don't already know. You can join veterans and military associations, professional organizations, and clubs to grow your network quickly, or you can grow it one person at a time by introducing yourself to new people.

If you're an extreme extrovert who wants nothing more than to talk to strangers, networking may come easily to you. But if you're an introvert, it's hard; the best advice I can offer you is to embrace the suck. It gets easier with time, and I explain how you can hone your networking skills in this chapter.

Making a Great First Impression

The ultimate goal of networking is to build connections, and you can't do that effectively unless you make a great impression on others. Successful first impressions hinge on how you carry yourself, how well you communicate, and whether you appear to be genuinely interested in others rather than interested only in promoting yourself.

Preparing for success

The way you present yourself sets the stage for all your future interactions with the people you meet, so remember the following:

>> **Networking is a two-way street:** The most essential thing to remember about networking is that it's not about what people can do for you; it's an exercise in relationship-building, and relationships involve give-and-take. You're not there only to make connections that can help you in your career; you're also there to help others in any way you can.

>> **Be curious:** Try to learn about each person you talk to. Generally, the more you allow a person to talk about themselves, the more favorable their impression of you is.

>> **Listen to understand, not just to respond:** Most people listen to respond, but genuine interaction shows that you actually care about what the other person is saying; you're not just politely waiting for your turn to talk.

>> **Keep things light and friendly:** Don't be overly competitive or feel like you have to show that you're the best at everything. The civilian world doesn't typically work that way (and official networking events *certainly* don't). Try to find things you have in common with the people you meet.

>> **Have a great elevator pitch ready to go:** An *elevator pitch* is a quick description of who you are and what you do as well as why you're a valuable person to know. I cover these quick introductions in the later section "Cooking up a Good Elevator Pitch."

>> **Bring your best attitude:** The military literally frowns upon smiling in professional interactions, but the civilian world thrives on it. Show that you're

friendly, optimistic, and genuine, and people gravitate to you in public and at networking events.

>> **Look for the loners:** Professional and social events are hard for a lot of people, so look for the quietest people in the room — even if you're one of them. Be the person who engages others who may be struggling.

When you network, you're not only after individual connections; even if you don't have an obvious connection with the person you're with, they may know someone who can help you. Likewise, you may not be able to help people directly, but you may know someone who can.

Minding social cues and body language

In less than one-tenth of a second after seeing someone new, your brain gets busy processing information about their face. Neurons fire to start evaluating facial features for friendliness, trustworthiness, competency, dominance, honesty, and even morality. That snap-judgment skill leaps into action in less time than you take to blink, and it comes from humans' biological roots, when it paid to know whether a stranger was an ally or enemy right off the bat. After it finishes evaluating a stranger's face, your brain absorbs information about their body language, accent, age and gender, physical appearance, posture, perceived economic status, and even the number of people around them so it can form a first impression. That impression, which is influenced by the stereotypes that live in your head, then serves as a filter for your first interactions with that person.

Although you can't change your facial features (at least not without several thousand dollars and a few weeks off work), you can improve your chances of leaving a great first impression with others by

>> **Keeping your face relaxed:** Avoid scowling, squinting, or furrowing your eyebrows, and smile when you make eye contact with others.

>> **Maintaining a relaxed and upright posture:** Don't fold your arms over your chest, stand at attention, or slouch. If you feel like your posture is poor, do a quick shoulder roll to fix it. Then raise your chin a notch.

>> **Holding eye contact when someone is speaking with you:** That means *casual* eye contact; if you stare intensely, things get weird.

>> **Wearing clean, appropriate clothing, and making sure you're at a high level of personal hygiene:** Your clothes should fit the situation (and you) properly.

>> **Speaking a clear, warm, and calm voice:** You may need to work on lengthening your sentences and trying to be less brusque than you had to be in the

military; civilians often prefer gentler, more roundabout conversation. Tell people that it's nice to meet them and use their names. "It's great to meet you, Greg. I'm Mike," is better than "Hey, I'm Mike."

» **Using a firm, professional handshake:** Find the happy medium between the "dead fish hand" and squeezing the other person so tightly that they think you're ready to throw hands.

» **Being open, confident, and positive:** Try to stay as relaxed as you can. If it helps, know that the other person may be more anxious than you are.

» **Giving your conversation partner some space:** Don't crowd in or invade anyone's personal space. Most North Americans maintain a *proxemic bubble* — that's the psychological term for comfortable personal space — of about two to three feet in every direction. If you get too far into a stranger's proxemic bubble, they see you as an intruder and become defensive. Stay an arm's length away to keep everyone comfortable.

Your body language matters a lot when you meet new people. Experts suggest trying on these moves for size:

» **Jumping into a powerful pose before (definitely not after) you step into the room:** That means puffing up your chest and standing like a superhero, putting your hands on your hips, or flexing your biceps a few times. It may feel weird, but it can give you a natural confidence boost.

» **Keeping an open posture by rolling your shoulders back and keeping your head up:** Raise your chin a bit and stand up straight so people see you as welcoming and friendly. (And as a bonus, standing with good posture helps you breathe easier.)

» **Gesturing with your hands, but only occasionally:** An upward-turned hand, for example, makes your requests more inviting to the recipient; punctuating a statement with a pointed finger or hand gesture can help emphasize your point.

» **Steering clear of fidgeting:** Don't stand so incredibly still that you become invisible to the eye, but avoid tapping your foot, pacing around, or anything else that makes you seem nervous or unconfident.

Overall, people take about seven seconds to size up another person, so that doesn't give you much time to check all the blocks. Don't be ashamed to practice if you need to; stand in front of the mirror or get face-to-face with someone you trust to work on your first impression skills. And if it still seems hard, don't worry too much; it gets easier with more practice.

Pushing through Discomfort in Social and Professional Situations

As a veteran, the way people treat you in social situations may make you feel like an oddity —some strange animal (have you ever seen a quokka?) or a roadside attraction in the middle of nowhere. That may make you feel like you have to perform or act a certain way, and it may increase the pressure you feel to fit in. When you walk into an unfamiliar situation, feeling uncomfortable is normal.

"What if they don't like me? We're so different. Nobody's going to want to talk to me; I don't have anything valuable to say. And what if I say something stupid?"

Sound familiar? You're not alone. These are things that many people think before stepping into a new situation, whether it's a new platoon in a new unit, a party with unfamiliar people, or a professional networking event. They plague different people to varying degrees; if you aren't used to making small talk or conversing with people who aren't wearing the same uniform, you may struggle a bit at first. But with enough practice, you can become more comfortable meeting new people and holding meaningful conversations.

TIP

If you're in a social situation that seems like too much to handle, if you're shy, or if you're feeling uncomfortably out of place, experts suggest that you try the following:

>> **Find something helpful to do:** Whether you volunteer to hand out name tags, offer to help people find things, or point others in the right direction, having a "job" may make you feel more comfortable in that environment.

>> **Time your entry in a conversation:** Don't burst on the scene and blurt out an opinion to join in; listen for several minutes and get the gist of what people are talking about, and then ask a question. Questions are icebreakers that can help you build credibility as a genuine person.

>> **Know when to fold 'em:** When you hit your limit, making a graceful exit is okay. Forcing yourself to stay is going to make you miserable (and stressed), so you're better off leaving the scene and giving it your best shot next time.

You can use these tips anytime you find yourself in a new situation with unfamiliar people. The key is practice; social skills can get rusty, so using them from time to time is important.

MEETING NEW PEOPLE WHEN YOU HAVE SAD

Between 14 and 46 percent of people with post-traumatic stress suffer from something called *social anxiety disorder* (SAD), a psychological diagnosis that results from a frequent and unending fear of social situations. (You can have SAD without PTSD, too.) If you have SAD, you may have a hard time talking to others, meeting new people, and hanging out in social gatherings. You may worry excessively about coming into contact with others or be afraid that people will judge or scrutinize you, and you may even fear that you'll *look* anxious or act in an embarrassing or humiliating way. Sometimes, the closer the clock ticks toward a new social interaction, the more your anxiety grows. You may even try to avoid social situations entirely (and if you can't, you may try to blend into the background and dip out early). If this sounds like what you experience, you need to know that treatment options may be able to help you. I cover some of the ways you can get help in Chapter 21.

Cooking up a Good Elevator Pitch

The term *elevator pitch*, which you hear a few times during your Transition Assistance Program, refers to a short speech that explains who you are and where you're going. The name stems from the idea that you can rattle off the whole thing in the short amount of time you spend in an elevator with someone else. A good elevator pitch lasts no more than 30 seconds, makes people want to know more about you, and provides strangers with a good basis for a lasting impression of you. You use it when someone asks, "What do you do?" or "What's your story?" You may even use it during a job interview, which I cover in Chapter 11. The best way to come up with your own elevator pitch is to identify the most important things a person should know about you and practice delivering the details quickly and efficiently.

Asking yourself the right questions

Get a pen and paper and write down the answers to these questions:

>> **What have I done in the past that makes me awesome now?** If you're not the type to look in the mirror and tell yourself that you're amazing, look at yourself from someone else's eyes (and if you have to, ask someone you trust what makes you awesome).

- >> **How did I add value to my military workplace?** Many of the ways you added value to your workplace are outlined in your resume. If you haven't written one yet, head to Chapter 7 to get inspired.

- >> **What skills did I develop during my military career?** Leadership and thinking on your feet are definitely two skills you picked up. Add those to the other soft skills you learned, plus the skills necessary to complete your military job.

- >> **What are my current goals?** Whether you're looking for part-time work so you can head back to school or you're ready to launch your new career or start a business, figure out where you're heading next so you know what to include in your elevator pitch.

- >> **How can I explain military concepts in civilian terms?** Civilians don't know the difference between a private, a gunnery sergeant, and a major, but they do understand terms like *team leader, management,* and *specialist* (not the Army kind). Find additional help translating your experience to civilian terms in the Appendix.

Perfecting your delivery

What you say in your elevator pitch is just as important as *how* you say it. You have a limited amount of time to capture your conversation partner's interest, so being engaging pays off. I explain how to make yourself more memorable in the following sections.

Delivery in 30 seconds or it's free

If your elevator pitch clocks in at under 30 seconds, you're on the right track. It's not a sales pitch; it's a means to earning a second conversation with someone. Try to include all your information in fewer than 75 words (that's about a half-minute of talking). Keep it as short as possible! Check out the later section "Listening in on exceptional pitches" for a few examples of solid elevator pitches that can spark conversation.

Finding the right pitch for your pitch

Ever heard a third-grader read a report in front of a classroom or watched an elementary-school play? Now you know what *not* to sound like when you deliver your pitch. Practice reciting your pitch with natural inflections in your voice.

Keep it upbeat and jargon-free

Use an upbeat, happy tone when you practice your pitch, and rattle it off with a normal speech rhythm. Too fast, and you sound like an auctioneer; too slow, and your listeners lose interest. Replace military terminology with more familiar terms, like *operations supervisor* (Ops NCO), *hazardous conditions* (combat), *data collection* (recon), and *objective* (mission).

Practicing your way to perfection

Get in front of the mirror and practice your elevator pitch. Watch (and modify, if necessary) your facial expressions, and time yourself to make sure you're not as long-winded as your first sergeant during a Friday afternoon safety brief. Rambling is a horrible idea when you want to develop connections with other people.

Giving recipients the opportunity to respond when you talk

Make eye contact while you rattle off your elevator speech to a real person, and if the person you're talking to looks as if they want to ask a question, pause so they can. A good elevator pitch is flexible enough to allow for on-the-spot conversation.

Listening in on exceptional pitches

Check out these examples of successful elevator pitches before you create your own:

>> **The problem-solver**

"I got so tired of seeing boring, repetitive ads on my social media feeds, so one day I decided to put my graphic design skills to use. Now I freelance and create attention-grabbing ads that actually get people to buy from my clients, and what I'd really love to do is turn my skill into full-time work."

>> **The reality check**

"A lot of companies hire office coordinators who don't have enough experience with organization, but that was my specialty in the military. I developed a system for my office to keep track of which soldiers were scheduled to go to schools, what requirements they needed to meet, and all their deadlines, and that system ensured everybody made it."

>> **The one-liner**

"I run digital X-ray machines to help detect injuries and abnormalities, and I'm interested in using my skills to help athletes train better."

>> **The connection**

"Don't you know Sienna Jackson? She's a veteran. I served with her at Quantico. We both drove fuel trucks, and now she's working for XYZ Company and loves it. Now I'm looking forward to bringing the same skill set to the civilian sector."

>> **The background check**

"I'm an attorney with the Judge Advocate General's Corps, and when I leave the military, I want to relocate closer to my roots. I'm from Michigan, so I'd like to find a firm near Detroit where I can use my estate planning skills."

Knowing when to give someone the rundown

You don't simply walk up to someone and give them an elevator pitch. You use it when someone says, "Tell me about yourself," or when it comes up in casual conversation. You can use your elevator pitch when you introduce yourself at career fairs, veterans groups, or in everyday conversation when you meet new people.

Look at your elevator pitch as a conversation-starter. Say hello and introduce yourself, and when it's appropriate, give the other person the rundown. Remember that communication is a two-way street, so listen to hear and understand (instead of waiting for your turn to talk) when the other person describes their work and interests as well.

TIP

Put your elevator pitch in your LinkedIn bio. It's a great way for prospective employers or clients to get to know a little bit about you, and it's short enough to hold people's attention on the web.

Checking out Networking Events

Networking isn't restricted to formal networking events; you can do it anywhere. But if you want to make connections with others, you need to put yourself out there. Some of the best places to meet new people and make professional connections include the following:

>> Conferences

>> Exhibitions

>> Seminars

>> Training courses

>> Volunteer events

>> Local networking events

>> Career fairs

>> Clubs and societies, particularly those related to hobbies

>> Online forums

Develop a networking strategy before you commit to anything. You need to know which types of events are relevant to you (and where you can be useful to others), whether you should attend hard or soft networking events, and which people you can form mutually beneficial relationships with.

TIP

Start every event knowing that it's about what you can do for the people you meet, not about what they can do for you. That begins with finding ways you can be supportive of the people you meet; the rest will fall into place. Networking shouldn't be purely transactional!

Exploring relevancy

Not all formal networking events are relevant to you, so deciding to forgo attending one that won't help you advance your career is fine. Many organized events are designed for people in certain fields or with certain backgrounds. If you're nervous about attending networking events in general, look for those that host only veterans. Decide which types of groups and contacts will be most helpful — and which groups and contacts you can help the most — before you fill up your schedule with networking events.

And remember, networking isn't only about attending formal events; you can make relevant connections at kids' sports events, when you meet new acquaintances through your friends, at career fairs, and even while you're working at your current job.

Giving people the business (card)

Before you start attending networking events, order yourself a small stack of business cards. Some companies offer free design tools you can use to create your own style, and if you're just starting out, a small package may be sufficient. Don't overload your cards with information; include your name, job title (you can use your military job title if you're still looking for work), email address, phone number, and social media handles. And if you're starting your own business, include its name and your website URL.

TIP

Here's a pointer that may save you some cash: Head to a locally owned print shop and ask if it offers any discounts for soon-to-be vets. Even if it doesn't, you get a chance to practice your networking skills on the shop's owner (so you still kind of win).

Coming in hot (or not)

Hard and soft networking are different. A *hard networking event* is one that's designed for people to produce business referrals for each other. A *soft networking event* is one where you don't have to make any connections and there's no expectation of referring business.

When you see something billed as a networking event, you should likely go expecting hard networking (so take your business cards). Other events, like club get-togethers and association meetings, are soft networking events. Be careful not to pitch yourself too hard at a soft networking event; you may come off as pushy, which can drive away your potential connections.

Finding the best people to network with

A successful networking strategy helps you make connections more efficiently, and it helps you build relationships rather than a collection of business cards. When you start with a "how can I help you" attitude, the people you meet are more inclined to reciprocate.

And while you're out meeting new people, don't forget to introduce others. For example, if you meet a professional chef who's interested in starting a local restaurant and you already know someone who owns a great little café, introduce them to each other.

Following up with connections

You don't have to (and shouldn't) wait for others to reach out to you. Make an active effort to reach out to the people you meet while you're networking, whether you send a quick email with a link to a relevant news article or a text to ask whether they'll be attending the next big networking event. If you find out that a person you met has a specific need, see whether you can fill it with a follow-up, from introductions or referrals to information on a specific topic. You can even send a handwritten note to express your thanks for a person's time after a formal networking event if you feel it's appropriate.

Using Social Media to Your Advantage

It turns out that social media sites are good for more than determining what type of garlic bread you are and whether a dress is blue and black or white and gold. You can use your social media accounts to make valuable connections that help you in the real world. For most professionals, that means setting up and maintaining an active profile on LinkedIn. *Note:* It can also include Facebook, Twitter, and whatever other network you're most active on, but the information in this section mainly refers to LinkedIn because that site is specifically designed for people to make business-related connections.

The first step to successful social media networking is having a complete (and squeaky-clean) profile of your own. Your profile should be completely free from *anything* controversial, including your personal opinions, language that's unwelcome in civilian workplaces, and photos or comments that may be considered risqué. And please, if you only take one piece of advice from this chapter, make it this: Keep your political opinions off social media. If that means you have to lock down the accounts you currently use and start new ones, do it.

TIP

Fix your personal (non-work-related) social media privacy settings now. Don't allow others to post on your timeline or feed without your reviewing posts first, and ensure that you take down anything that may come back to haunt you later. Remember, the Internet is forever — so be extremely careful about keeping your accounts free from things that can hurt your future prospects.

After you establish a complete and professional profile, start looking for connections among the people you know in real life. You may be surprised to discover that the people you know likely have large networks of their own. When you're as connected as you're going to get, branch out by joining trade-specific groups and looking for high-level networkers.

Knocking on the doors of trade-specific groups

Join one (or several) of the many veterans groups on LinkedIn to get your feet wet. Then join groups in the industry you're interested in working in. These groups can give you valuable insight on industry trends, best practices, and job openings as well as provide you with opportunities to share your knowledge. These groups have two types of online networkers: those who want to share knowledge and those who are looking for knowledge. You can, and should, be both.

If you're interested in becoming a freelance copywriter, for example, you can join groups related specifically to search engine optimization (SEO) that allow you to ask and answer questions. Use the search function on LinkedIn or your favorite networking site to find these communities. Simply typing in "SEO" in LinkedIn's search box yields lists of professionals in that field, open courses you can take, job openings, and groups you can join.

Rubbing elbows with high-level networkers

Start looking for high-level networkers in your target field right away. They're easy to spot; they usually have hundreds of connections, they're very active in groups and post frequently, and they have complete and current profiles. High-level networkers are often executives and decision-makers within companies, and if you personally know someone who knows them, you have a good chance at connecting.

TIP

Go out of your way to find people you served with in the military, including your former leaders and subordinates. When you connect, stay in touch. People take all kinds of different paths through the military and when they leave the service, and reinforcing your connections with them now can be mutually beneficial in the future.

Introducing yourself to strangers

You can introduce yourself to people you don't personally know on social media in a few ways, but one of them is far and away the worst: sending someone a connection request with no explanation. You absolutely *must* have common ground with a person you're requesting to connect to (even if you only have similar interests or served in the same branch of the military). Always send a note explaining why you think that you should connect.

You can say things like "Hi, Kitrell. I wanted to reach out to you as a fellow veteran of the 25th Infantry Division who's interested in networking with other online security professionals. Let's connect so we can stay in touch about future opportunities to work together" or "Hello, Dana. I saw you speak at the XYZ networking event last month and was really inspired. I hope to connect with you here as well."

Nurturing your connections

Making one-time connections isn't good enough. You need to build relationships; that's what successful networking is. That means reaching out to the people you've already met; you can do so online, over the phone, or in person. Any relationship, from the most casual to the most serious, disintegrates if you ignore it for long enough. You don't want people to forget you (or the amazing skills you bring to the scene), so go out of your way to maintain your network. That's easy to do when you're connected online; you just have to find a reason to reach out to someone — such as an interesting article or piece of data that the other person may find useful — and write a one-line note to remind them that you're a valuable connection to keep, too.

Posting regular updates

Keep your page fresh by posting regular updates related to your field. If you find a new study or a relevant article on something that other professionals would find useful or you've developed a well-reasoned opinion about something that's happening in your field, go ahead and post it. Remember not to get too personal, though. When you're networking to find a job and enhance your career, your social media profiles should remain professional. And if you're using LinkedIn, you should *always* keep it professional (even after you find a job and are happily working in your new field).

Joining Military Associations

If you're not already part of a military association, now's a great time to sign up with one. These associations are designed for active-duty military personnel and veterans of the armed forces, and many offer a number of benefits to their members. The following sections break down a couple of different types of these organizations and introduce you to several specific groups that may work for you.

Understanding service organizations

You can choose to join a general military organization or one specific to your former branch (or several organizations in several categories). Many offer military transition help, such as resume writing and job search assistance, mental health support, and the sense of belonging that you most likely start to miss as soon as you get your DD-214.

Some — but not all — military associations are *veterans service organizations*, or VSOs, that advocate on behalf of and provide resources to veterans. Some are federally chartered, which means they're officially recognized by Congress, and most are private, nonprofit organizations staffed by volunteers. You can work with a VSO for help with filing a VA claim. But be aware that not all VSOs are federally chartered, and an organization can lose its charter at any time. You can get the most current list of federally chartered VSOs directly from the Veterans Administration.

TIP

An association doesn't have to be federally chartered to be a good organization, but you should only file a VA claim with help from one that is.

Among the many great reasons to join a VSO or military association is the ability to network with people who have backgrounds similar to yours. Even better, though, is that you get an opportunity to make a positive impact on other veterans' lives.

These types of associations are ideal for people in your shoes, no matter your background. That's because the people in them have been where you are right now, and they're willing to reach back and lend you a hand as you navigate the big shift from military to civilian life. They also often offer benefits to your dependents, which means your spouse and kids can benefit from them too. Many veterans service organizations and military associations offer things like scholarships and fellowships, employment and education help, assistance with discharge upgrades, caregiver support, and even legal and financial assistance in some cases. Some are even accredited by the VA to help you out with disability claims (even if you're still in transition).

If you're not sure whether a veterans service organization is right for you, either because you don't know whether you'll fit in or because you have the impression that everyone is older than you, let me put your mind to rest: You will fit in, and yes, a lot of the members are probably older than you are. (In my mind, that's even more reason to join. I know an active-duty soldier who's in the VFW and DAV, and the older members rely on him for heavy lifting and a fresh perspective.)

And to put your mind even more at ease: Women are also welcome in these organizations — even if it doesn't feel like it at first. Simply ask about the sign-up process, prove your eligibility, and join.

General military organizations

These organizations are open to servicemembers and veterans regardless of branch, though you may have to meet other qualifications to join (such as being a reserve officer or a Purple Heart recipient). Most require you to pay annual membership dues, though some offer fee waivers.

>> **American Legion (www.legion.org):** The American Legion is the largest wartime veterans service organization, and it's open to anyone who has served on active duty in any branch since December 7, 1941.

>> **AMVETS (amvets.org):** AMVETS is open to anyone currently in the military (including the Reserves and National Guard) or who has honorably served.

» **Armed Forces Communications and Electronics Association** (`www.afcea.org`): Anyone engaged in or a veteran of national defense, security, or related technology disciplines can join AFCEA.

» **Disabled American Veterans** (`www.dav.org`): Disabled American Veterans is open to anyone who sustained an injury or illness during their time in the military, or who aggravated a previous injury during their time in service (even if it's not service-connected by the VA) *and* who wasn't dishonorably discharged.

» **Fleet Reserve Association** (`www.fra.org`): The FRA is open to current and former enlisted members of the Navy, Marine Corps, and Coast Guard.

» **Jewish War Veterans of the United States** (`www.jwv.org`): You must be an honorably discharged American Jewish veteran who served in the Armed Forces during a U.S. war or conflict to join JWV.

» **Military Officers Association of America** (`www.moaa.org`): The Military Officers Association of America is open to active duty, former, retired, and National Guard and Reserve commissioned and warrant officers as well as their surviving spouses.

» **Military Order of the Purple Heart** (`purpleheart.org`): You can join the Military Order of the Purple Heart if you were awarded the Purple Heart medal, are a person of good moral character, and are active duty or have an honorable or general discharge from the military.

» **National Association of Black Veterans** (`www.nabvets.org`): You must be active duty or honorably or generally discharged from the U.S. Armed Forces to be eligible for membership in the National Association of Black Veterans, which has state and local chapters all over the country.

» **Noncommissioned Officers Association** (`www.ncoausa.org`): Don't let the name fool you; anyone who held the grade of E-1 through E-9 and was separated from any branch of the military under honorable conditions is eligible to join the NCOA. It's also open to any individual who actively supports the organization, and an international auxiliary is open to spouses and former spouses, widows and widowers, and family members 18 years of age or older.

» **Paralyzed Veterans of America** (`pva.org`): Membership in the Paralyzed Veterans of America is open to anyone who's a veteran with a discharge other than dishonorable and has a spinal cord injury or disease (even if not service-connected).

» **The Retired Enlisted Association** (`trea.org`): Any enlisted person who has retired from an active or reserve component of the U.S. Armed Forces, whether retirement stems from length of service or permanent medical disability, is eligible to join The Retired Enlisted Association.

- » **Reserve Organization of America (www.roa.org):** You can join the ROA if you served in the Army, Air Force, Coast Guard, Navy, Marine Corps, U.S. Public Health Service, or the National Oceanic and Atmospheric Administration.

- » **Veterans of Foreign Wars (vfw.org):** You must be a United States citizen or U.S. national who served in the armed forces and received an honorable or general discharge or who is currently serving. You must have served during a war, campaign, or expedition on foreign soil or in hostile waters, which you must prove with an authorized campaign medal, a pay statement showing your receipt of Hostile Fire Pay or Imminent Danger Pay, or service in Korea for 30 consecutive or 60 nonconsecutive days.

Army, Reserves, and National Guard

If you served in the United States Army, these organizations may interest you:

- » **Association of the United States Army (www.ausa.org):** Anyone can join the Association of the United States Army (even civilians who support the Army).

- » **Enlisted Association of the National Guard of the United States (eangus. org):** You're eligible to join EANGUS in your state if you were an enlisted member of the National Guard.

- » **U.S. Army Warrant Officers Association (usawoa.org):** Only currently serving and retired U.S. Army warrant officers and their family members are eligible to join this organization.

- » **Women's Army Corps Veterans' Association (www.armywomen.org):** Women of any era who can provide evidence of honorable service in the Army, Army National Guard, or U.S. Army Reserve are eligible to join the WACVA, regardless of rank.

Air Force, Navy, and Marine Corps

If you were in the Air Force, Navy, or Marine Corps, these organizations may be a good fit for you:

- » **Air Force Association (www.afa.org):** The Air Force Association is open to current and former Air Force members of all ranks.

- » **Navy League of the United States (www.navyleague.org):** The Navy League is open to veterans and civilians.

» **Naval Enlisted Reserve Association (`nera.org`):** You can join NERA as an enlisted or former enlisted member of the Navy, Marine Corps, or Coast Guard.

» **Marine Executive Association (`marineea.org`):** You can join the Marine Executive Association as a Marine, former Marine, or Navy Corpsman regardless of rank.

» **Marine Corps Reserve Association (`usmcra.org`):** Any member of the Marine Corps Reserve or any USMC veteran who received an honorable discharge, or any regular officer or enlisted member of the Marines in retired status is eligible for membership in the Marine Corps Reserve Association.

» **Marine Corps League (`www.mclnational.org`):** To be eligible to join the MCL, you must be currently serving or have served at least 90 days in the USMC or Reserves and have earned no less than 90 reserve retirement credit points, or you must be a Navy Corpsman who has trained and served with the United States Marine Fleet Marine Forces for at least 90 days and have earned the Marine Corps device, have earned the Warfare Device authorized for FMF Corpsmen, or be a U.S. Navy chaplain who has earned the FMF Badge while serving with the Marines.

Coast Guard

You may be eligible to join the Coast Guard Combat Veteran Association (`www.coastguardcombatvets.org`) if you're active-duty, retired, a reservist, or an honorably discharged former member of the United States Coast Guard who served in or provided direct support to a combat situation recognized by a military award during your time in the service.

Doing Your Own Informational Interviews

Networking takes place at several levels of human interaction, from casual and informal gatherings to formal career fairs and hiring events. It even includes conducting your own *informational interviews*, which are talks with people who currently work in the industry you're aiming for.

If you want to become a successful networker, you have to approach the right people, ask the right questions, and review your own performance, which I cover in the following sections.

TIP

It may help you to realize that when you're networking, you're an interviewer *and* an interviewee. Essentially, you conduct your own informational interviews with each person you meet. The questions you ask give you insight into how to further develop your new relationships, what a particular job role entails, or what a company's driving philosophy is; those things can all help you further your civilian career. Besides, asking questions shows that you're adaptable and ready to learn, which are both characteristics employers love to see. Being inquisitive also helps people like you more, and being likable is an essential part of successful networking.

Approaching the right people

Bouncing your questions off the right people is the only way to get the right answers. The questions you need answered can help you figure out who to ask. If you're interested in finding out more about a particular job, you ask someone who's done it; if you want to discover new job opportunities, you talk to hiring managers.

Start by asking people you already know. If you don't know anyone who can answer your questions, ask your friends and family to point you in the right direction; they may know someone who can help you. When you get a name, contact the person by email or phone, mention how you're connected, and ask whether they have a few minutes to talk to you. If you're at a networking event, zero in on other participants you can talk to, such as specific company reps or people who identify as employees of the companies you're interested in working for. If it's appropriate (and true), you can emphasize that you're simply looking for information rather than a job offer.

Getting off on the right foot

When you meet with someone (or talk over the phone) for an informational interview, first thank them for their time. Assure them that you understand how busy they are, too. Try something like "Thanks again for scheduling this meeting with me; I know you're very busy, so I appreciate that you're taking the time to help me."

Restate your purpose right off the bat and let your interviewee know that you value their opinion. You may say, "As you know, I'm leaving the military and need to explore my career options. I know what I do well, and I hope that you can provide me with some insights so I can make the right decisions."

Asking the right questions

Your goal in an informational interview is to learn as much as you can. Ideally, you ask open-ended questions that spark conversation. Consider asking things like

» How did you get into this type of work?

» What do you enjoy most about your job?

» What do you *not* enjoy about your job?

» What kinds of people do best in this industry?

» What do you wish someone had told you before you got into this industry?

» How can someone position themselves for success in this industry?

REMEMBER

As you continue your conversation, ask thoughtful questions (not questions you can easily find answers to by whipping out your phone and searching the Internet). The real purpose of having these conversations is to build a long-lasting, mutually beneficial relationship with another person. Don't look at it as a one-off meeting where someone gave you a few minutes of their time; you're in the long game to develop a future ally.

Conducting an after-action review

After you conduct your own informational interview with someone (or several people), review your performance. Did you ask the right questions? What did you leave out? Did you say something that you shouldn't have? Did you sound like you'd already done your research, or were you a little amateurish? Identify three things you did right and three things you did wrong, just like you would in a military after-action review, and let your assessment guide you the next time you're on a mission to find information.

Following up after an informational interview

Send a handwritten thank-you note if you spoke with someone outside a professional networking event. It's good manners, and it makes you more memorable. Simply thank the person for their time, write a line about something you discussed, and let them know you're interested in staying in contact.

If you haven't already, connect with the person online. And remember to maintain your relationship with them (see the earlier section "Nurturing your connections" for more information on how to keep in touch); networking is a process of developing relationships over time.

Standing Out from the Crowd

In the civilian world, you don't want to fly under the radar. You want to be noticed, especially if you're out there looking for a job. In that way, it's extremely different from military culture (especially among junior ranks, where you *never* wanted the higher-ups to know your name).

Because drawing attention to yourself may be unfamiliar territory, set a goal of becoming a valuable resource to at least two people at every networking event you attend. Think of it this way: Are you more likely to remember someone who has nothing to do with your job search or your career advancement or someone who has your dream job, works for the employer you want to work for, or has some other type of connection with you? You're more likely to remember someone that may be a valuable resource, and the people you meet are the same way.

When you introduce yourself to someone new, no matter how informal your meeting is, ask yourself these questions:

>> **What can I do to provide something of value to this person?** Try to determine what you can do to help the person you're talking to, even if it's something that seems small.

>> **Do I know anyone who can benefit this person?** If you know someone in a similar job or the same industry, you can all benefit from an introduction. When you introduce someone to your network, you're opening up a whole new arena for them, and they may also return the favor.

>> **Can I offer any good advice that matches this person's needs?** Based on your past experience, you may be able to provide a fresh perspective or give them advice that can help them reach their goals.

>> **Does this person's company have a job opening that I can help them fill?** People always remember those who have given them a hand, so if you know someone who'd be qualified for a job, don't hesitate to refer them.

>> **What do I know about this person's industry?** Do you have any insight to share on current trends, data, or information? If you have any questions that the other person can answer, ask; if you have information to share, do it. That way, you can engage in a more meaningful conversation.

>> **Am I speaking to this person with a genuine desire to help them or to gain something from them?** Genuine people are more memorable than others are.

When you're networking, the last thing you want is for your business card to end up in the middle of a dusty pile. (At the very least, you want your card to be at the top of a dusty pile.) You can ensure that people remember you by being genuinely interested in them, shaking hands firmly, making eye contact, and following up with those you may be able to work with in the future.

IN THIS CHAPTER

» Diving headfirst into different types of interviews

» Making a lasting impression on your interviewer

» Getting the low-down on interview do's and don'ts

» Recognizing warning signs that a company may not be for you

» Staying in touch with your interviewer

Chapter **11**

Working Your Way through Interviews

A fter your resume helps you land a job interview, you come face-to-face with the person who has the power to hire you or recommend that the company hires you. (You can read more about resumes in Chapter 7.) You have only one shot at your first interview, so you need to perform well. If you don't, the company calls in the next candidate and tosses your file into the recycle bin; that means you have to start from scratch elsewhere.

You rarely know ahead of time what an interviewer is going to ask you. In fact, you may not even know which of the many types of interview you're facing, and you may have to think on your feet. The best thing you can do during any interview is to be genuine and honest; the person interviewing you will appreciate both.

Getting Familiar with Common Types of Job Interviews

The goal of any interview is to give a company an opportunity to find out more about you and your skills. A good interviewer pays attention to more than your answers to questions; they evaluate your mannerisms, body language, communication style, and personal attributes to determine whether you'll be an effective employee and a good member of their team. An interviewer may ask you questions that don't have any "right" answer or that require you to explain points on your resume or solve problems on the spot or to determine whether you have a shot at being a productive employee.

Some interviews are very structured, while others are informal. Still others require you to solve problems so the interviewer can assess your thought processes, solutions, and behaviors. No matter what type of interview you walk into, the interviewer is there to determine whether you're more or less likely to succeed in the company when compared to other candidates — so right now, your job is to show them that you're worth a shot.

TIP

Before you walk into any interview, reread the original job description and review your resume. Try to remember as much of the job description as you can so you can use the important parts to help you answer questions during the interview.

REMEMBER

Most interviewers ask *open-ended questions* (those that require more than a yes or no answer) to get a sense of your personality and determine whether you're a good fit for their company. These questions put you on the spot; you have to come up with a complete, non-rambling answer that doesn't make you look confused or incompetent. The best way to approach this type of question is to first make sure you understand what the interviewer is asking and then weave a story about something that's already in your resume. Try the STAR technique, which I cover in the later section "Using the STAR method to answer questions."

Taking a turn with traditional interviews

Traditional interviews are the old standby for many employers. The interviewer wants you to give answers that tie into the job description, so they may ask you broad questions like "Tell me about your background" and "What are your strengths and weaknesses?" Most of the answers should be in your resume, which is what landed you the interview in the first place. (Read up on drafting a winning resume in Chapter 7.)

Traditional interviews can be structured, unstructured, or somewhere in between, which I explain in the following sections.

Structured interviews

Structured interviews are the same across the board: Every candidate gets the same questions in the same order. Each person's answers are scored against the job's requirements. You can tell you're in a structured interview if the interviewer reads your questions from a tablet or a piece of paper and doesn't ask follow-up questions.

These types of interviews can be really tough on interviewees because they feel like one-sided conversations. However, they do give you a great chance to stand out by giving you an opportunity to explain how well you match the job description. If you can remember the must-have attributes from the job description, use them to describe yourself as you answer questions.

TIP

Try your hardest to tell a memorable story during your interview so the interviewer doesn't view you as just another application in the pile.

Unstructured interviews

Unstructured interviews are those in which the interviewer lets the questioning lead wherever it will. Instead of sticking to standardized questions for every candidate, interviewers allow the conversation flow based on your answers to previous questions. But be warned: Although these types of interviews may feel like casual conversations, you're still being evaluated. The way to succeed in an unstructured interview is to structure it yourself; try to remain focused on what the interviewer needs to know about you, and ensure that all your answers to questions lead to the obvious conclusion that you're the best possible candidate for the job.

You can, and sometimes should, ask your own questions during an unstructured interview — especially if the conversation starts getting off-track. These interviews are more conversational than structured interviews are, which means you have the chance to show that you're a detail-oriented, thoughtful, and methodical candidate.

Semi-structured interviews

Semi-structured interviews are hybrids. They use some preplanned questions, but the interviewer can ask follow-up questions as appropriate. In this type of interview, your safest bet is to ensure you know what the interviewer is asking, provide anecdotes that match the job description and requirements, and ask questions that ensure you're engaging in a two-way conversation when appropriate.

Running through serial interviews

Serial interviews involve more than one interviewer, but you don't sit with them all at once. Instead, you have one interview with an initial screener, one or more interviews with other people, and your final interview with the person who has the authority to hire you (or to recommend that the company hires you). Often, the initial interview is generic; it's a back-and-forth to find out whether you may be a good fit for the company. Subsequent interviews may be more technical or even more intense, with each interview delving into a different area of your expertise.

These types of interviews are most commonly used for senior-level positions, or when a candidate comes in from out of town. You may face multiple interviews back-to-back over the course of a day, or you may have a few days (or longer) between interviews.

TIP

If you know you have another interview coming up, see if you can find out a little bit about the next person you'll talk to. You may ask things like, "Does the next person interviewing me feel the same way about teamwork and collaboration as you do?" This can give you a head-start on finding common ground with each of the people you'll sit down with during upcoming interviews.

Working under a microscope with assessment interviews

Assessment interviews are designed to show an employer your personality, motivation, interests, and practical skills. Like the name implies, these interviews are like tests that you must complete so a prospective employer can decide whether you're a good fit for the company.

Behavioral interviews

Behavioral interviews give you an opportunity to share how you react in specific situations. Employers often use these types of interviews because they believe that past behavior predicts future performance, so finding out how you behaved in the past can show them whether you're likely to do the right thing for their company in the future.

Behavioral interview questions often look like these:

>> Give an example of a time you used logic to solve a problem.

>> Describe a time when you had to convince team members to work on a project they didn't want to work on.

>> How do you handle things when your schedule is interrupted?

>> Tell me how you work effectively under pressure.

>> Provide an example of a goal you reached and how you achieved it.

>> How have you handled difficult situations with coworkers in the past?

The best way to answer these types of questions is through the STAR method I outline in the later section "Using the STAR method to answer questions." Remember that these types of questions have no right or wrong answers; your interviewer is trying to understand your behavior to find out whether you're the right person for the job.

Competency-based interviews

Competency-based interviews are designed to show an employer whether you have the necessary soft skills to perform a job. These types of interviews are typically very structured and can show employers whether you're adaptable, able to resolve conflict, flexible, and resilient, as well as whether you have leadership qualities the company needs.

Questions in these types of interviews may include the following:

>> Can you describe a situation where you successfully used your leadership skills?

>> Tell me about a major decision you recently made and how you went about it.

>> What has been your biggest professional achievement?

>> Tell me about a time when you showed integrity.

>> Explain a time you made a decision and changed your mind.

>> Describe a time when you succeeded despite adversity.

Taking a moment (but not much longer) to think about your answer before you blurt something out is okay. When you're ready, rely on the STAR method; you can read about it in "Using the STAR method to answer questions" later in the chapter.

Puzzle interviews

Puzzle interviews are increasingly popular among employers that want to evaluate prospective employees' cognitive abilities — that is, they want to make sure that employees can figure things out when faced with challenges. Originally popularized by Microsoft in the 1990s, these types of interviews ask an applicant to solve puzzles or unusual problems; they're often used in the information technology field.

REMEMBER

Your answers to puzzle interview questions often aren't as important as how you arrive at those answers because prospective employers are simply trying to watch your brain work.

When someone hits you with a puzzle interview question, follow these steps to answer:

1. Think about the problem.

Is it a riddle, or does it deal with a real-world scenario? Is it realistic, or do you have some creative license to come up with an answer?

2. Ask for clarification if you're not exactly sure what the interviewer is asking you.

Some of these questions can be complex, and in some cases, interviewers *expect* you to ask for clarification. Asking questions shows that you're the type of person who wants all the data before working on a problem.

3. Use what you already know.

Many puzzle interview questions require a mathematical approach or prior knowledge of a subject.

4. Explain your reasoning.

When you work through one of these questions, show the interviewer your process; that lets them see, in real-time, how you plan solutions and solve problems under pressure. And again, the way you solve a problem is often more important to the interviewer than getting the "right" answer is.

5. Provide a solution.

When you reach the answer to the question, even if it's wrong, share it with your interviewer.

Check out these examples of common puzzle interview questions and try to come up with your own answers, just for practice:

>> You have 12 identical-looking coins. One is counterfeit and is lighter than the genuine coins. What is the minimum number of times you need to weigh the coins to identify the fake one with a two-pan balance scale without weights?

>> A building has 100 floors. If you drop an egg from the Nth floor or above, it will break. If you drop it from any floor below the Nth floor, it will not break. You have two eggs. Find N while minimizing the number of drops for the worst case.

>> A hallway has 100 closed doors in a row. A hundred monkeys are nearby, and the first monkey runs and opens every closed door. A second monkey closes all the even-numbered doors. A third monkey either closes or opens every third door, depending on whether it's currently open or closed. When all 100 monkeys have done their work in this way, how many doors will be open?

During a puzzle interview, your interviewer may ask you to solve a logic puzzle, such as this one:

Six people (Michaela, Nancy, Oscar, Perry, Quincy, and Rob) have the following attributes:

- >> Michaela is richer than Nancy but shorter than Rob.
- >> Nancy is richer than Quincy but taller than Rob.
- >> Oscar is poorer than Perry and taller than Michaela.
- >> Perry is poorer and shorter than Quincy.
- >> Quincy is poorer and shorter than Michaela.
- >> Rob is richer than Michaela and taller than Oscar.

Who is the richest person of them all?

(And for the record, if you can't figure out a mathematical answer, try a *The Hitchhiker's Guide to the Galaxy* approach and tell your interviewer that the answer to everything is 42. If nothing else, the fact that you're well-read may help you land the job.)

Case interviews

Case interviews rely on questions that revolve around specific job scenarios. Your interviewer gives you a hypothetical business situation and asks you how you'd handle it. Like many other interview questions, these don't typically have a right or wrong answer. Your interviewer wants to see you process the information you're given and figure out how to solve a problem. And in many cases, the interviewer doesn't give you complete information right off the bat; they expect you to ask follow-up questions so you can come up with a well-informed, reasonable response. Your entire response doesn't have to be verbal, either. You can sketch a chart, graph, or illustration to explain your solution.

REMEMBER

Always ask questions to clarify the problem (in fact, that's probably what your interviewer expects you to do). Take your time answering each question and explain how you arrived at your solution.

A case interview may present you with a problem like this:

> DRJ3, a game-designing company, has been in the industry for several years. However, sales have been declining each year for the past five years. The company wants to understand what's causing the decline and what it can do to generate more sales. DRJ3's CEO wants our recommendation on how to proceed, so what should we do?

Group and panel interviews

Group and panel interviews are two different things, but both involve multiple people interacting at the same time.

Group interviews involve two or more candidates and one interviewer. The candidates are interviewed at the same time. Sometimes companies use these types of interviews to figure out which prospective employees will fit in best with company culture by evaluating how each person interacts with the others in the room and who performs well under stress.

Panel interviews involve one candidate and two or more interviewers. Each member of the panel is free to ask the candidate questions, just like a military promotion board, Soldier-of-the-Month board, or any other competitive board. These types of interviews allow multiple professionals from various departments to evaluate whether a person is a good fit for the company by asking their own questions.

Taking it easy with informal interviews

Informal interviews are those that take place outside the workplace in a casual setting. You may attend an informal interview at a coffee shop or over lunch. But informal interviews are still interviews, so don't let down your guard; be professional the whole time. Some employers (particularly those that pride themselves on a laid-back company culture) prefer informal interviews because they're a great opportunity to observe candidates' personality types and communication styles without the rigid structure of an office environment.

You can still expect to hear standard interview questions during an informal interview, such as "What kinds of issues did you deal with in your last job?" and "What did you like most about your work while you were in the military?" Answer those questions with the job description in mind, just like you would any other interview question. You should show up with some questions of your own as well; you may consider asking your interviewer what they like about working for the company and what challenges the company is facing right now.

You can also use these tips to increase your likelihood of getting the job (or a second, more formal interview):

>> Bring a pen and paper so you can take notes.

>> Use active listening techniques, such as nodding your head, leaning slightly forward, and making eye contact.

>> Show that you're engaged by providing thoughtful responses, including rephrasing important points the interviewer has made in your own words.

>> Dress in business casual clothing.

>> Avoid speaking too freely; no matter how much it feels like a social outing, it's still a job interview.

TIP

If you don't have business cards yet (see Chapter 10), now's the time to invest in some. Several online companies allow you to design your own, and they'll print and ship them to you. Leave a business card with each interviewer you talk to, even if you've given them one in the past.

Getting your comms online with remote interviews

Distance, global pandemics, and a whole host of other issues can force you into a *remote interview* — one that takes place while you and your interviewer are in different locations. Sometimes remote interviews are used as initial screening tools, too; you talk to an interviewer who decides whether the company should spend time interviewing you in person. You may have to participate in a phone interview or a video interview, and each has its own pros and cons.

Phone interviews can be tough because you can't see how your interviewer reacts to the things you're saying. That works both ways, so this interview type isn't always ideal. Video interviews give you a little more to work with, but they're still not the same as in-person interviews.

If you know you have a remote interview coming up, prepare just as you would for an in-person interview. For these interviews especially, reread the job description, review your resume, and prepare a list of questions you want to ask your interviewer. You can do your best on these interviews if you

>> **Answer the phone or online call yourself:** Don't let someone else pick up! Kick everyone else out of the room and close the door so there are fewer distractions. When you answer the phone, say, "This is [your name]," so the interviewer knows they reached the right person.

>> **Follow your interviewer's lead:** That may mean having a few minutes of small talk or it may mean diving right into interview questions. Prepare yourself for both.

>> **Listen carefully, and don't cut off your interviewer while they're speaking:** Thinking for a moment before you respond to questions is okay as well.

>> **Don't smoke, chew gum, eat, or drink during your remote interview:** But do keep your water bottle handy in case you need it.

>> **Smile, even if you're on the phone:** Smiling changes the tone of your voice and indicates to your interviewer that you're happy and energetic.

>> **Give short, appropriate answers:** Don't get chatty; stay focused, just like you would if you were participating in an in-person interview.

>> **Dress to impress, particularly if you're doing a video interview:** Putting on business clothes can jazz you up for a phone interview, too.

>> **Test your technology before the interview:** Make sure that your Internet connection is good and that the clothing you plan to wear looks appropriate on camera. Ensure that you won't be looking down at the camera — you want to look at it head-on — and check for glare, too.

>> **Make sure the area around you is clean and appropriate for a video conference:** You don't want anything unprofessional in your camera's field of view (like an open bathroom door, a cat's litterbox, or a box fort that your child has spent a week building). Try not to use built-in digital backgrounds or a blurring feature during a video interview; your interviewer will know you're not on the beach or in front of the Eiffel Tower and may wonder why you're covering up the real world behind you.

>> **Show up early:** Don't even cut it close. Have the phone in your hand or the online meeting program open ten minutes before your interview is scheduled. Take that time to relax by doing some deep-breathing exercises so you're ready to go when your interviewer arrives.

Breezing through career fair interviews

Attending a career fair may get you an on-the-spot interview. Most commonly, these interviews are simply quick screening tools that employers use to find out whether a candidate is even remotely suitable for a position. However, sometimes employers conduct mini-interviews; more rarely, they conduct full interviews that result in job offers.

Screening interviews

Screening interviews only last a couple of minutes, and employers usually conduct them to find out which candidates are worth interviewing further. A prospective employer may ask you questions about your past work experience, what type of job you're looking for, and what level of education you have. A screening interview is the perfect place to use your elevator pitch, which I cover in Chapter 10.

Mini-interviews

When a career fair employer asks you to sit down and chat, you're probably about to participate in a mini-interview. These talks usually last five to ten minutes, and during that time, your interviewer may ask you to expand on the information you included in your resume. You may also be asked a few behavioral, case, or puzzle interview questions. If you perform well during a mini-interview, the employer may well invite you to participate in a full interview.

Full interviews

If an employer is particularly excited about you, you may be asked to sit down for a full interview. These interviews are usually held behind a curtain or screen near an employer's booth at a career fair, or they may be held in another location in the same venue. Sometimes these interviews last 20 minutes (or more). Your full interview may be structured, unstructured, or semi-structured, and it may fall into any of the categories I outline in the preceding sections.

Creating a Favorable First Impression in Your Interview

Unless you already met a prospective employer at a networking event or career fair, your interview is your first chance to make a great impression. Research suggests that an interviewer's first impression of you shapes that person's perception of how competent you are, and that can directly affect whether you walk away with a job offer. . .or just walk away. That includes the way you dress, the expression on your face, and your body language and posture. Although you can improve on a first impression, making a positive splash when you show up is really important. (And for the record, you can in fact destroy a good first impression.)

Doing recon on your interview location so you're on time (that is, early)

Even if you're pretty familiar with the area where your job interview will be held, drive by and scout out the area a few days ahead of time. Scope out potential parking areas, figure out how long you need to get from the parking lot to the office, and gauge the traffic at various times of day.

TIP

You heard some variation of this in the military: If you're five minutes early, you're already ten minutes late. Part of the reason you should do recon is so you don't chance being late, which will definitely tank your chance of being hired. Try to arrive 15 minutes before your interview begins so you have time to check in, get the lay of the land, and relax before you get face-to-face with a hiring manager.

Outfitting yourself for employment

Employers expect job candidates to dress appropriately during job interviews and after they're hired, but doing that can be complicated. What if you're interviewing at a company where people wear board shorts and ride skateboards with their dogs around the office? What if you're being interviewed by a law firm, a restaurant, or a Fortune 500 company?

It's simple: Dress for an interview, regardless of what everyone wears to work. Candidates wearing professional attire make a better impression than those in relaxed attire do. Corporate interviews require formal clothing, such as a suit or pantsuit, and interviews in less-formal workplaces often prefer business-casual dress. However, you won't go wrong if you opt for conservative clothing, such as the following:

» A suit or pantsuit in a solid color, with a tie if appropriate

» A long-sleeved, button-down shirt or conservative blouse

» Slacks, or a skirt that's no shorter than just above the knee

» Closed-toe shoes

» Limited (or no) jewelry

» A professional, neatly done hairstyle

» Light makeup and limited (or no) aftershave, cologne, or perfume

» Clean, neatly manicured nails

» A professional-looking bag or briefcase, but only if it's necessary

Your interviewer begins forming an impression of your physical appearance within just a fraction of a second. It's not even a conscious process; the human brain forms an impression of a stranger's face in less time than it takes to blink, and within the next seven seconds, it sizes up everything else that's visually apparent.

Modeling professional behavior from the get-go

The things you do and say even before your interview starts can determine whether you get the job, so use these tips to ensure you kick things off with the right foot:

» **Wear appropriate clothing.** Different industries have different expectations; corporate interviews require you to wear a suit or pantsuit, while less-formal workplaces often favor business-casual interview attire. When in doubt, err on the conservative side by wearing a suit or pantsuit.

>> **Walk confidently when you enter the room.** Keep your head up, smile, and say hello to your interviewer as you shake hands. (Firm, but not dominatingly tight, is the way to go when you meet someone who can offer you a job.)

>> **Be interested in the opportunity, even if you aren't sure it's the right job for you before, during, or after your interview.**

>> **Carry a portfolio with hard copies of your resume, business cards, and blank paper and a pen for taking notes.**

>> **Leave your phone in the car to prevent distractions and empty the change from your pockets so you don't jingle when you walk.**

Navigating through Interviews

Interviewing with prospective employers is vastly different from joining the military; you have to impress a hiring manager rather than earn a passing score on the ASVAB, get a physical, and sign the dotted line. But the good news is that job interviews give you an opportunity to shine; they're the perfect place to show a prospective employer that you have the talent, skills, and knowledge to help their company outperform its competitors. The good news is that your interview doesn't have to go perfectly for an employer to offer you a job. The bad news is that if it doesn't go reasonably well, you're back to square one.

Acting like a civilian in public

You may be pleased to know that civilians tend to view veterans as more disciplined, loyal, and hard-working than other civilians are. That can certainly work in your favor when you're applying for jobs, but you still need to make an effort to blend into the civilian world, and that means leaving some of your military mannerisms, terms, and actions at the door.

Dropping military vernacular

Military terms like *counseling*, *SHARP training*, *ROE*, and *blue falcon* can be confusing to civilians. Some of the words you use every day may mean something different to civilian ears, or they may not mean anything at all. Drop military vernacular from your vocabulary and replace it with terms that translate well. For example, when you refer to a counseling, simply say *evaluation report*; when you refer to SHARP or your branch's equivalent, say *anti-harassment training*.

While you're at it, get comfortable with the fact that civilians don't have rank. They're *Mr.*, *Mrs.*, or *Ms.*, and if you're not sure whether a woman is married, default to *Ms.* Although saying *ma'am* or *sir* is usually okay, it can be viewed as a little old-fashioned (particularly in fast-growing sectors like tech), so use your best judgment.

WARNING

Be realistic; don't expect civilians to completely understand military culture and military-related issues. You only understand these things because you've spent time in the military, and even *you* may make mistakes from time to time. When you demean, belittle, become frustrated, or "vetsplain" things to civilians (who shouldn't be expected to know everything about the military), you look like a simple-minded jerk who's never developed social skills. And if you act like this during an interview, you're definitely not getting the job.

Cleaning up your language

Civilians' vocabularies are colorful, but they're not usually as four-letter-word colorful as some servicemembers' are. Because you're coming from a culture where few people even flinch at profanity, you may not even be aware of how often you swear. You may need to make a concerted effort to clean up your language so it's appropriate for job interviews and civilian workplaces. Ask your spouse or someone else you trust to redirect you when you slip up if you're concerned about it.

Saying goodbye to standing at attention, parade rest, and ease

As a vet, you're used to standing at attention or parade rest when you're talking to someone who outranks you, and during a job interview, you may consciously or subconsciously feel as if the person interviewing you is one of your superiors. Though you should be respectful at all times (in and out of job interviews), the way to show your respect to civilians isn't through drill and ceremony; it's through politeness, proper greetings, and appropriate language. If you knock three times, stride to the interview chair while swinging your arms, do facing movements, and render a salute before you sit down, you're doing it wrong.

Getting your postural feedback effect on

Power posing, also called *postural feedback*, is a hotly debated topic. Essentially, a *power pose* is a movement that raises your self-confidence and positively enhances your mental state, and it may be enough to help you succeed during an interview.

Some people swear it works, but your mileage may vary. An early study suggested that the postural feedback effect increased testosterone levels and reduced cortisol (the stress hormone), but the jury's still out on those points. However, some scientific evidence suggests that postural feedback can make you feel and look more confident for a short period of time.

If you want to give it a shot, try rolling your shoulders back and down and putting your hands on your hips, or raising your arms high while swinging them around (kind of like a silverback gorilla chasing off a predator). Moves like these are called *expansive postures,* and when contrasted against *contractive postures* (like hugging yourself and slouching), they certainly can make you feel more powerful. But if you're going to try the gorilla move, I advise you to do so in the parking garage rather than in front of the receptionist.

Speaking the right body language

Body language is the way you communicate your feelings with your posture, facial expressions, gestures, and movements. When you're face-to-face with your interviewer, your body language probably says a lot more about you than you think it does. In fact, a seasoned interviewer will probably be able to tell if you're nervous, whether you're not sure you want the job, and even whether you think you're not qualified for the position.

When you use confident, self-assured body language, you make a better impression on your interviewer (and everyone else you meet). You appear more confident, competent, and secure if you

>> **Maintain good posture:** Keep your chin up and shoulders down. Don't stick out your butt; try to keep your spine neutral and your feet slightly apart. Remember that gem of wisdom you learned in the military about not locking your knees, too; falling out is *not* good body language.

>> **Keep your palms open:** Use your hands to make small gestures as you talk, but don't use closed fists or keep your fingers and thumb extended and joined. Your knife hand is a little too stern for gesturing in a job interview.

>> **Use effective, but not weird or aggressive, eye contact:** Act like you're sitting across from an old friend, not your base or post commander. Make regular eye contact and look away when it feels natural to do so; don't stare or glare.

>> **Show that you're actively listening:** Nod, smile, and shake your head as appropriate. Lean forward slightly to express interest. Take cues from what your interviewer says, as well as their facial expressions and body language.

>> **Don't cross your legs when you're sitting down:** If you must, cross your ankles only. Crossing your legs creates a closed-off body position and shows that you're guarded; worse, it can get uncomfortable quickly, causing you to need to shift or stretch, which the interviewer can misinterpret as disinterest in the interview.

>> **Avoid bouncing your foot up and down or fidgeting, even if your brain is working a mile a minute:** Restless habits can make you look nervous or disinterested.

>> **Put your personal items, such as your purse, briefcase, or portfolio, on the floor beside your chair so you can reach them easily after the interview:** Don't plop your stuff on the interviewer's desk or put it somewhere it can spill over and make a mess.

Dissecting common interview questions (and how to answer them)

You probably haven't had a job interview in a while (or, if you're like many veterans, ever). Regardless of what type of interview you're in, some questions and requests are pretty standard, such as the following:

>> Tell me about yourself.

>> Why should we hire you?

>> What are your greatest strengths and biggest weaknesses?

>> What do you do when you don't get along with a coworker?

>> Where do you see yourself in five years?

>> Give me an example of a time you solved a tough problem at work.

>> Why did you leave the military?

>> When were you most satisfied in your job?

>> What can you do for our company that others can't?

>> What are three positive things your previous boss would say about you?

>> What salary are you looking for?

>> Do you have any questions for me?

Interviewers ask you these questions to evaluate not just your answers but also your communication skills and your ability to think on your feet. They also want to see that you've done your research on the company.

Using the STAR method to answer questions

In most cases (other than for requests to talk about yourself, which you can answer with the elevator pitch I explain in Chapter 10), the best way to answer interview questions is to use the STAR method. Each letter in the acronym stands for an important part of the answer your interviewer expects:

>> **Situation:** Set the scene by explaining a situation you've been in. That means you have to think quickly and find a relevant story from your past, so reviewing some of your accomplishments in the military before you show up for an interview is in your best interest.

>> **Task:** Describe the task you were responsible for executing. Use civilian terms that convey the same meaning. For example, you can explain sitting on an IED crater by saying something like, "I was responsible for maintaining the physical security of the area until the authorities arrived."

>> **Action:** Explain the steps you took to address the problem. If you were responsible for ensuring your platoon passed the Army Combat Fitness Test, explain what you did, such as helping your soldiers schedule appointments with nutritionists or working with Master Fitness Trainers to create customized exercise programs for soldiers who were struggling.

>> **Result:** Describe the outcome you achieved through your own actions. The results should be quantifiable; that is, you should be able to express a measurement of your success. For example, you may say that you recruited 68 troops for the Air Force, that you saved the Marine Corps $125,000, or that you were responsible for the health and well-being of 200 active-duty soldiers.

TIP

Questions that begin with "Tell me about a time when," "Have you ever," "What would you do," and "Describe an instance when" are typically good candidates for the STAR method. Confine each step to one or two sentences so your answers are simple and clear. You can plan out answers to these questions to get a feel for how you'll answer variations on them as well.

Turning negative questions into positive answers

Your interviewer will almost inevitably ask you a question that requires you to give what seems like a negative response. Sometimes interviewers use questions like these to see how well you respond under stress, find out what type of attitude you have, and decide whether you're a strong or weak candidate for the job.

One example of a negative question is "What's your biggest weakness?" On its face, that seems like an unwinnable question. It feels like the interviewer is asking you why you're not good enough for the job and expecting you to lay it all on the table. But the interviewer isn't looking at the substance of your answer; they're looking at whether you panic, fib and say you don't have any weaknesses, or show a lack of self-awareness and personal insight.

The best way to answer a question like this one is to choose a former weakness that doesn't apply to the job. For example, if you're interviewing for a role in management, you wouldn't say you're not assertive enough or that you're too aggressive when it comes to accomplishing the mission. Instead, say something like, "In the past, I was a bit of a procrastinator. That forced me to scramble to complete projects by performing all the work myself, at the last minute. I consulted with my mentors and learned how to properly delegate tasks so my team could meet its deadlines together."

WARNING

Don't say that you're a perfectionist or that you spend too much time paying attention to little details. Everyone says those things, so they won't make you stand out. Just be honest about a former flaw that you've taken time to correct, and you'll be on the right track.

Other negative questions you may encounter include these:

>> **"How do you handle criticism?"** Nobody likes to be criticized, but your job is to show your interviewer that you welcome it when it's constructive, that you can decide whether it's valid, and that it depends on who's dishing it out.

>> **"What makes you angry?"** You don't want to come across as someone who's easily angered or as someone who doesn't have so much as a spark. Give an answer that shows you understand there may be valid reasons to become angry but that managing difficult events appropriately is very important to you.

>> **"What's the worst mistake you've made at work?"** Nobody's perfect, and everyone has made a mistake that keeps them up at night from time to time. Explain a mistake you made that wouldn't be relevant to the job you're interviewing for and that gave you an opportunity to learn, and then follow up with the lesson you took away from the situation.

Flipping the script by asking your own questions

Your interviewer may ask you if you have any questions at the end of your interview, but in most cases, asking questions as they arise during your conversation is appropriate. You may want to find out more about the company's values or culture, what success looks like in the company, or what the interviewer believes is the most challenging aspect of the job you're interested in. Interviews don't have to be a one-way street; in fact, many interviewers expect you to use your interview as an opportunity to figure out whether the job is a good fit for *you*. You can also ask whether anything on your resume or in your background makes the interviewer question whether you're a good fit for the job, which gives you a chance to explain away their concerns.

TIP

You may also express genuine curiosity about the interviewer or the company, which can help you make a positive impression and show that you're very invested in the prospect of getting this job. You can do that by asking things like

>> "How long have you been with the company?"

>> "What made you want to work for this company?"

>> "How has your role changed since you've been here?"

>> "What's your favorite part about working here?"

>> "Where do you see this company in the next few years?"

>> "Can you tell me about the last team event the company held?"

Avoid asking questions you could easily find the answers to on the Internet. Doing so shows your interviewer that you didn't bother doing basic research.

Dodging unlawful interview questions

REMEMBER

Interviewers aren't allowed to ask you any question that can enable the employer to discriminate against you. In fact, asking questions that relate to your age, race, religion, gender, or a few other subjects can open a company up to a complaint with the Equal Employment Opportunity Commission (EEOC) or even a discrimination lawsuit. Table 11-1 outlines what's legal and illegal in certain lines of questioning.

TABLE 11-1   **Lawful and Unlawful Interview Questions**

Subject	Lawful	Unlawful
Address	What's your address? How long have you lived there? What was your previous address?	Do you own or rent your home? Who lives with you, and how are you related?
Age	Are you old enough to work in this job with state and federal age restrictions? (An employer can directly ask a person's age if the job has age restrictions, such as working in a bar.)	What year were you born, and when did you graduate high school?*
Availability	What days and times are you available to work? Is it difficult for you to travel for work, and do you have reliable transportation?	Can you work on weekends, or do you attend church? Do you have childcare arrangements? Do you own a car?**
Citizenship or national origin	Are you legally eligible to work in the United States? Can you provide proof after you're hired? Do you have any aliases?	Are you a U.S. citizen with a birth certificate? What country are your parents from? Where were you born? How did you learn English?

(continued)

TABLE 11-1 (continued)

Subject	Lawful	Unlawful
Criminal history	Have you ever been arrested for or convicted of a specific crime that relates to this job? (Employers may only ask if the job is security-sensitive, and even then only about crimes related to the job.)	Have you ever been convicted of a crime?
Disabilities	Can you perform all the functions of this job?	Do you have a disability? Have you ever filed a workers' compensation claim? Have you ever been injured on the job?
Family status	Do you have commitments that may prevent you from working your assigned shifts?	Are you married or single? Do you have children?
Financial status	Do you own a car?**	Do you own your home? Do you have good credit?
Genetic information	No questions about genetic information are lawful.	Any questions.
Marital status	No questions about marital status are lawful.	Any questions.
Military service	What experience or training did you receive that may benefit you in this job?	What was your discharge status?*** Which country's military did you serve in?
Organizations	Are you a member of a professional organization?	What sorority or fraternity did you belong to? Are you a member of any nonprofessional clubs or organizations?
Pregnancy	How long do you plan on working at this job?	Are you pregnant or trying to start a family?
Race or color	No questions about a person's race or color are lawful unless either is a requirement of the job.	Any questions.
Religion or creed	No questions about a person's religion or creed are lawful.	Any questions.
Sex, sexual orientation, or gender identity.	No questions about a person's sex, sexual orientation, or gender identity are lawful.	Any questions.

*Under federal law, age discrimination pertains to adults over the age of 40 only.

**Employers may ask whether a person owns a car if having a car is a requirement of the job.

***Interviewers may ask you about your discharge status if it's relevant to the job.

You have a few options if an interviewer asks you an unlawful question. First, you may choose to calmly and professionally point out that you're aware the question is illegal. You have the right not to answer any question, as well as the right to end your interview on the spot. Before you decide what to do, take some time to figure out whether your interviewer had bad intentions when asking. You can even ask for clarification on an iffy question.

Also be aware that interviewers can get creative. For example, if an interviewer says, "I noticed you were limping a little on your left foot — everything good?" that may be a genuine concern . . . or it may be a roundabout way of asking you if you're disabled and whether your injury is permanent. In a situation like that, you may choose to say, "Oh, I'm good. It's nothing that would impact my ability to perform this job!"

Ending things on a confident note

When your interview is over, your interviewer will likely stand up, shake your hand, and thank you for your time. This moment is your last chance to solidify the favorable impression you've made, so don't simply say goodbye and thanks. Instead, ask, "When do you anticipate making your final decision? When should I follow up with you?" Check out "Following Up after the Interview" later in the chapter for details on touching base.

TIP

Operate on the assumption that you're getting the job and it's just a matter of time before the interviewer calls you to make an offer.

Knowing When to Walk Away

Sometimes, an interview makes you realize you no longer want the job. You may end up surrounded by red flags that warn you not to take the job during the interview, such as when your interviewer

>> Asks you unlawful questions with bad intentions (the earlier section "Dodging unlawful interview questions" has more on this kind of situation)

>> Hits on you or sexually harasses you

>> Tries to be intimidating

- » Displays racist tendencies or discriminatory practices
- » Engages in inappropriate, rude, or offensive behavior
- » Speaks poorly of current employees
- » Isn't clear about the job or the company's expectations of you
- » Talks about high turnover rates
- » Seems incompetent

You should also check out the employees you encounter; if morale seems low, people look unhappy, or you witness unpleasant confrontations between current workers, you may want to keep on keepin' on in your job search. Each of these things is a big, red flag that warns you about what working for the company is like. You should probably run and never look back.

Following Up after the Interview

Follow up with your interviewer as soon as possible; don't let 24 hours slip by without sending an email. In fact, there are three times you should follow up:

1. Send a prompt thank-you to the interviewer.

When you get home after an interviewer, compose a quick, professional email to thank the person you spoke with. Your subject line can be as simple as "Thanks for your time today!"

Open your note with a formal greeting using the interviewer's name, such as Ms. Jackson or Mr. Stenman. Write something like "I appreciate your spending time with me this afternoon. I'm certainly very interested in working as a paralegal for your firm." Then, mention something you discussed during your interview that'll help you stand out and suggest that your experience and skills can help the company move past its challenges. Let your recipient know that you're available to provide additional information if necessary and that you're eager to hear from them by the date they told you they'd be in touch.

TIP

Send a thank-you email even if you don't want the job after your interview. You may come into contact with that person later.

2. Email if you don't hear back.

When you don't hear back from your interviewer by the established deadline but you still want the job, send a follow-up email. The same principles on a formal greeting apply (see the preceding section), but this time, write something like "I wanted to check in because you mentioned you'd make a final decision for the paralegal position by this Monday. Please let me know if I can provide you with additional details to help facilitate the hiring process." Thank the person again and sign off.

TIP

If you received another offer but really want to work with a particular company, mentioning that in your second follow-up is a good idea. Note that you'd be happy to turn down the second company's offer if this company wants to hire you before you commit to anything else.

3. **Send a note if you don't get the job.**

If you feel that your interview went well but you weren't chosen for the position, you may want to send an email to ask for feedback. Be brief, thank the interviewer for their time, and ask for constructive criticism that can help you do better in the future. Some interviewers won't respond, but your name is likely to stand out. That can work in your favor in the future, such as when the company is hiring for a different position or the hiring manager moves to another firm that can use your help.

Chapter **12**

Negotiating Your Salary When You Get a Job Offer

Would you be surprised to find out that you're doing an employer a favor by choosing to bring your knowledge, skills, and experience to its organization? You shouldn't be — the organization needs your help. Of course, you need its money, too, but a successful employment relationship is one in which *both* parties recognize that they have a pretty sweet deal.

Naturally, employers want to get the best possible bargain on a great worker. Many employers don't offer job candidates the highest possible salary and benefits package right off the bat. They often leave some room for negotiation.

Not all employers have room for negotiation, and large-scale negotiations are typically reserved for people with a lot of experience and special skills, but that doesn't mean you can't attempt to negotiate your salary and terms of employment after you receive a job offer. After all, the employer has already tipped its hand: It wants to hire *you*, not the other people who went through the hiring process for the same job.

REMEMBER

Before you get too excited about the prospect of negotiating, you need to know that negotiation isn't about you winning. It's about you and the employer both walking away satisfied with the outcome. The best way to negotiate is to listen to what the other party wants and come up with a solution that makes everyone happy, and I outline how you can pull that off in the following sections.

Getting Over Negotiation Fears

Negotiating a salary can be scary; nobody wants to be told that they're worth less than they think they are. You may even worry that the employer will withdraw its job offer if you're not prepared to accept an as-is offer.

Negotiating also feels like you're questioning your soon-to-be employer before you're even hired, and that can be exceptionally difficult for someone who's used to a mentality of "adapt and overcome." In the military, you take what you're given and make the best of it. But as a civilian, you're free to ask for what you're worth.

Asking for higher pay puts you in the minority. According to a 2018 survey, only 39 percent of people tried to negotiate their pay with their last job offer, and according to a 2012 study, 18 percent report *never even trying*. Those who do negotiate can increase their salaries by over 7 percent. Although that may not seem like much, the math says differently. If you take a $100,000-per-year salary and another person raises theirs to $107,000 (7 percent more), and you both receive the same raises and promotions from then on, you'd have to work an additional eight years to be as wealthy as the other person.

TIP

Still worried about it? Remember that out of all the other applicants, the employer decided it wants to hire you.

Fearlessly Asking for What You're Worth (without Demanding)

Negotiations don't begin until someone says "no." If you agree that your future employer is offering you a fair salary and benefits package to compensate you for the work you'll be doing, you're good to go. If you don't, then being the person who says "no" and kicks off negotiations is okay.

So how do you know whether you should negotiate? By knowing your worth and arming yourself with an exact number.

You can find out what others with similar qualifications and experience are making by searching sites like www.payscale.com or www.glassdoor.com, or by asking people who are already working in the field. As you search for a hard number, look at benefit packages, too. You have to look at the whole deal, including your job duties and responsibilities, flexibility in work hours, location, travel, opportunities for growth and promotion, and other factors.

That doesn't mean you gather data and then stroll into the hiring manager's office and say, "I won't do this job for less than $150,000 per year, 30 days of paid vacation that never turns into use-or-lose, and a company car." It means you use negotiating tactics to get as close as possible to what you want.

Kicking off negotiations

First things first: Try not to negotiate over email. Schedule a time to talk in person or on the phone. That enables you to have a back-and-forth conversation, which allows you to clearly communicate your requirements and make adjustments as necessary.

Lead with gratitude and courtesy. By the time you reach salary discussions, you know that the employer likes you and wants to hire you, and it has invested time and resources into bringing you to this point. Recognizing this investment is essential, so thank the other party for bringing you to the table and mention specific reasons you're excited about the job.

Listening while you negotiate

Listen carefully to what the other party is saying. In fact, you should listen more than you talk. Remember that companies don't negotiate; people do. The person you're negotiating with wants to fill an open job position (preferably with you), and if you're tuned into that person's discussion, you can understand their motivations. Then, you can incorporate those points into your side of the argument.

For example, if the hiring manager says, "We're trying to stick to our budget," you may want to come back with, "I completely understand that operating costs are concerning. However, hiring a less-qualified candidate may end up costing the company more in the long run."

Realize that the person on the other side of the table has some hard-and-fast rules they can't break (like salary caps). Your job is to figure out where the other party is flexible — and where they're not. Don't push it if the person says, "I'm really sorry, but the company doesn't pay new hires more than this amount." You can, however, negotiate other items, like vacation time, a signing bonus, or an earlier performance review than the company usually offers in an effort to get your first raise sooner.

Being likable

People aren't going to want to negotiate with you if you're not a pleasant person. Anything you do during negotiations that makes you less likable — like being demanding, arrogant, or rude — is only going to hurt your chances of getting what you want.

Make it clear that the employer has a shot at hiring you. Nobody wants to spend time and resources negotiating with a person who probably isn't going to take their offer. If you have other options through other employers, it's okay to say so, but say something like, "Your company is my first choice, so if you can meet these conditions, I'll be happy to work with you."

Choosing (and fighting) your battles wisely

The person on the other side of the table also has to believe you're worth what you're asking for, so you have to explain why your requests are justified. Don't just say that you deserve more money than other workers in the same position do; explain which of your qualifications make meeting your requirements a good investment for the company.

REMEMBER

Pick your negotiation points strategically. Although everything in a job offer may be up for negotiation, don't bother trying to haggle over things that aren't important to you just because you can. Negotiate only for things that are genuinely important to you; if you end up accepting the job, you can negotiate for other, smaller things later in your career. When a person says no, what they really mean is "Given the circumstances right now, I'm not going to accommodate that request." That doesn't mean that asking to work from home on Mondays is always going to be off the table; it means that right now, the employer isn't going to allow it. In six months, after you've proven your worth and the employer has a certain amount of trust in you, things may change.

Fielding tough questions

You don't want to face difficult questions during salary or benefit negotiations, but your prospective employer may throw some at you anyway. The other party may ask you whether you have any other offers or whether their company is your first choice. The most important thing you can do with these questions is to tell the truth.

Remember that the person asking you these questions isn't trying to back you into a corner or expose your weaknesses. That person's job is to present a happy new hire to the employer, not to tear you down or give you a bad first impression of the company. This idea can be difficult for veterans to understand, particularly after dealing with unquestionable superiors who care only about the mission. Remember, in the military, you're locked in; you couldn't quit if you wanted to. In the civilian world, hiring managers want to hire people who are willing to stick around, because the managers don't have any recourse when an employee goes AWOL.

If a question rubs you the wrong way, answer it in a way that addresses the person's intent. Usually, the person's intent is simply to determine how excited you are to work for the company or to find out how they can take you off the job market.

Negotiating multiple issues at the same time

Avoid frustration (on your part and the other party's part) by negotiating all your changes at once. Put everything on the table; don't wait until the salary issue is resolved and say, "Now let's talk about vacation time."

When you present multiple negotiation points, start with the most important first. Also, explain which are most important. If you don't, the other party may choose to negotiate things that you don't care that much about (at least in relation to your other points), and you'll walk away with an offer that's not much of an improvement over the original.

Avoid mentioning your personal needs. Don't tell the other party, "My rent is expensive, and I have three kids." Instead, focus on your performance and achievements that justify your receiving a higher salary or additional benefits.

Controlling the anchor

The first number put on the table during negotiations is called the *anchor*. It's the most important number in the negotiation because the rest of the conversation is centered on it. If the anchor is too low, you'll most likely end up with a lower final offer; that's why you should be the first one to throw out a number.

Avoid using a range, though. If you tell a prospective employer, "I can work for a salary of $70,000 to $75,000 per year," the employer will automatically gravitate toward the lower end of the spectrum. Instead, ask for the high number in your range and keep the low number to yourself. Bargaining partners feel like they're getting a better deal when they negotiate down, and besides, the worst thing that can happen is that the employer counteroffers your counteroffer.

According to a study published in the *Journal of Experimental Social Psychology*, you should use an incredibly precise number when you set the anchor. Part of the reason is that everyone uses round numbers, and using a super-specific number shows that you've done your research and you're very sure of what you want. In the study, recipients of very precise opening offers made more conciliatory counteroffers, and that effect carried through to final settlements.

Try this: "I'm really excited for this opportunity, and I'm certain that I'll bring a lot of value to the company. I do appreciate the offer of $65,000, but I was expecting to be in the $69,850 range based on my experience and past performance. Can we explore that?"

Employing the Thursday-Friday strategy

Some science suggests people are more agreeable toward the end of the workweek. Though it may not be a green light for everything you hope to achieve in negotiations, experts say that most people start the week with dominant behaviors revolving around organizing work, assigning responsibilities, and otherwise getting things done. By Thursday, people are looking forward to the end of the workweek and are generally more agreeable. If you can, schedule your negotiation conversation on a Thursday or Friday, when people are amping up for leisure time with family and friends.

Taking your time before making a commitment

You don't have to accept an offer immediately. In fact, pouncing on an offer can be a huge mistake, such as when you're waiting for another, potentially better offer to come through. You may be able to slow down the process with one company while you wait for another; that way, you can look at all your offers side by side and make the right decision. You can take this approach by letting the other party know you're entertaining other offers (but only if it's true), or by simply asking for a few extra days to consider.

Negotiating through Email

Negotiating a job offer through email isn't ideal, but it is possible. If you can't schedule a face-to-face or phone meeting, digital communication is the next best thing. The upside to email negotiations is that most people find asking for a higher salary or better benefits package easier when they aren't looking another person in the eye. Be careful, though; tone is hard to pick up through email, and the last thing you want is to come off as demanding, arrogant, or rude.

All the same principles that apply to face-to-face or phone negotiations apply to email as well. Kick things off courteously and with gratitude, know your worth (and back it up with facts), and request more than you require for the job. You can read more about in-person negotiations in "Fearlessly Asking for What You're Worth (without Demanding)" earlier in this chapter.

EXAMPLE

Here's an example of a salary negotiation email. You can use it as a springboard to create your own after you receive a job offer.

Subject: Salary question

Dear Mr. Zoellner,

Thank you for offering me the position as a lead copywriter at XYZ Digital Assets. I'm sure I'll be a strong asset to your team, and my 20 years of public affairs work in the U.S. Army has prepared me with the skills and knowledge necessary to help take your company to the next level.

Before I can accept your offer, I want to discuss the proposed salary you sent me this afternoon. As I mentioned during my interview, I spent more than 15 years in leadership roles overseeing writers, photographers, and digital media professionals in the military. In my previous role, I was responsible for getting U.S. Army Europe's message across to the global community, through both articles and press releases I personally composed and those my subordinates composed. With this expertise and proven skill set, I feel that a salary of $75,125 is appropriate, which is slightly more than the $68,500 you offered.

I'm confident that my expertise and work ethic will contribute to your organization's growing success, and I'm excited about the possibility of working with XYZ Digital Assets. Please let me know when we can further discuss the salary for this position.

Thank you for your time, and I look forward to hearing from you soon.

Sincerely,

Jesse Davids

Avoiding Negotiation Pitfalls (or, How to Lose Negotiations Every Time)

Wayne Gretzky once said, "You miss 100 percent of the shots you don't take." He was right, and that applies to negotiations, too; if you don't negotiate for what you want, you lose out. But you can also lose negotiations in other ways. Check out the five things you should never say during salary or benefit negotiations:

» **"I'm currently making. . .":** If you tell a prospective employer what you currently earn, the offer you receive probably will be somewhat close to the salary you're already making. (Sure, military pay tables are public and anyone can search for them on the Internet, but that doesn't mean you need to bring it up.)

>> **"Sorry:"** Don't apologize for asking for what you're worth. Most employers expect you to negotiate your salary (and they may be surprised if you don't). Although most people want to smooth out uncomfortable situations, like discussing money, saying that you're sorry is a signal that you're seconds away from backing down because you're not confident that you're worth the company's investment.

>> **"No" or other negative words:** Although negotiations start when someone says "no," don't come right out and say, "No, I can't accept that," after things are moving. Instead, try to find middle ground by coming up with a counteroffer. If you really want the job, get creative; if you're $2,000 away from the salary you want, ask for additional vacation time or another benefit.

>> **"Yes:"** When you receive an offer that seems too good to be true, you may have underestimated your worth to the company. For example, if you expected to be paid $55,000 a year for the job and the company offers you $65,000 and a 401k, trying a counteroffer for more is worthwhile.

>> **"Can we try. . .?":** Don't ask your negotiating partner to try to do something. Simply say, "I'd be more comfortable with X," and let them come back with a different offer. Remember, the person you're negotiating with wants you to work for their company, and by the time you've reached this stage of the hiring process, they're on your side. Your negotiating partner wants you to be comfortable with your salary and benefits, so making an "I'd be more comfortable" statement is the best way to get closer to what you want.

Closing the Door on an Un-closeable Deal

Negotiations don't always result in a favorable outcome. Sometimes you simply can't find common ground, and sometimes you get a better offer from another company after you start negotiating with someone else. The bottom line is that you're the one whose sweat and tears (but hopefully no blood) will go into your work, so it's okay to gracefully exit negotiations with a company that's just not meeting your requirements.

If you know you're waiting on an offer from another company, tell your negotiation partner so immediately. And if you realize that you're at an impasse, tell your negotiation partner that although you appreciate the time they've invested in you, you don't believe you'll be a good fit for the position at this time.

Above all else, *don't burn any bridges*. You never know when a future opportunity may arise.

Chapter **13**

Assimilating into the Civilian Workforce

Veterans often face unique challenges when they join the civilian workforce. Some of the most common obstacles that you — along with millions of other vets — may face involve relating to people who aren't used to the way you talk, getting accustomed to employee rights (particularly after not having many in the military), and not being told when and where to show up every moment of every day. You can't just switch off your military training and ditch the customs you're used to when you take off the uniform; fitting into your new role as a civilian takes time, resiliency, and adaptability, so the following sections address some of the challenges you may have to deal with on the other side of the perimeter fence.

Opening Your Eyes to the Big (Civilian) Picture

For most people, leaving the military is such a big life event that it eclipses every-thing. Maybe you have short-timer syndrome and you're counting down (30 days and a wake-up!), or maybe your separation date is farther in the future so you're getting a jump on things by preparing early. Or maybe the ink isn't even dry on your DD-214 yet and you're sitting there thinking, "Now what?" Either way, no amount of reading can prepare you for how slowly civilians walk from Point A to Point B. Of course, I'm (mostly) kidding, but walking, talking, and even joking are different in the civilian world than they are in the world you're used to.

Adjusting to the less-urgent pace of civilian work

Civilian workplaces don't typically run at the same OPTEMPO that military work-places do. Sure, some jobs are very demanding and fast-paced, but for the most part, nobody's going to die if you don't drop everything and finish one last-minute task *right now*. (Outside of jobs in national security, law enforcement and other public service occupations, and national defense, of course.) People show up to work late, don't park vehicles with their bumpers along a perfectly straight line, and can even shout back if their boss yells at them (ridiculous, right?).

The best advice I can offer you here is to draw from the deep wells of patience you developed while standing in formation for hours on end. Be patient with yourself as you get used to the slower pace, and be patient with the civilians who don't understand that you're used to working under much harsher conditions, both psychologically and physically.

Improving your interpersonal skills

Communicating effectively with civilians — or getting effective communication out of them — can be a tremendous challenge for vets fresh out of the service. In the military, the mission always comes first, and communication is supposed to cut through chaos to accomplish the mission. Military communication is fast, impersonal, and straightforward.

However, in the civilian workforce, what you say and how you say it are some-times more important than reaching goals. It's not that civilians are "soft" or that they don't like your brusque nature. It's that they simply aren't used to the mili-tary's style of communication, and they're often caught off-guard because it's uncommon in civilian workforces. Civilians may express themselves more indirectly than a military member would, and they're often focused more on creating relationships with coworkers to accomplish a mission than on accomplishing the mission and worrying about the fallout later.

TIP

Remember how stunned you were by your first shark attack in basic training or the first time a senior leader really let you have it? Keep that in mind when you think about improving your interpersonal communication skills for civilians. (I accidentally called a drill sergeant "Sir" on Day 2 of basic training, and he made sure that I — and everyone around us — knew I'd made a tremendous mistake.)

The bottom line is that if you're going to be successful in the civilian workforce, people have to like you. At the very least, they have to be able to tolerate you. You can't be as brief and impersonal as you were in the military and expect people to listen to anything you have to say; if you aren't signing their paychecks, civilians can (and will) walk away from you when they feel you're being rude or disrespectful. They're not afraid of non-judicial punishment, a negative counseling statement, or a dressing-down by the battalion commander. They don't even know what those things are.

REMEMBER

It's up to you to be adaptable, and I know that as a veteran, you possess that skill. You're in the civilian world, and it's not going to become more like the military. The best thing you can do is shift the way you communicate (including your tone, volume, and language, which I cover in the next section) to make your interactions more successful. Be patient with yourself and your coworkers, even if it's frustrating and feels like communication is an unnecessarily long, drawn-out process.

Curbing your enthusiasm for curse words

I'm willing to bet you have an amazing vocabulary of four-letter words, even if you don't use them as frequently as some of your fellow servicemembers do. You may appreciate how these colorful words can be used as nouns, verbs, adjectives, and expletives, or you may not like them so much. Either way, you'll probably go a year (or more) before you hear civilians drop as many F-bombs as you heard before lunch in a typical military workday.

In fact, a lot of words are off-limits in civilian workplaces (and for reasons that should be obvious, I don't list them here). A good rule to follow is this: If you wouldn't want someone to say a word to your toddler (or any toddler), who will most likely repeat it at the worst possible moment, don't use it in a civilian workplace.

Differentiating between military discipline and civilian workplace behavior

Watching civilians act in ways that most military members don't — like rolling into work late, dipping out to go home before the job is complete, or not having each other's back when it comes to sharing a workload — can be frustrating. Nobody's going to knock on your office door and stand at parade rest waiting for you to acknowledge them, some people are going to do what you see as fraternization, and sometimes the mission just isn't going to be completed on time. These things can be especially frustrating if you never had a civilian job before you joined the military or haven't worked in the private sector in a long time.

You may feel uncomfortable. You may feel out of place. You may even feel like you want to quit and call a military recruiter to see if you can get back in. (I know I did!) But in the military, you learned how to adapt to new situations quickly; you also learned to change your operational tempo as necessary, and you figured out that sometimes the best idea is to drive on, even when things get hard. Unless you're independently wealthy, you probably need a job, and if you stick it out past the initial culture shock, you'll probably be glad you did. (And if not, you can quit when you find something better.)

Knowing that you can quit (or be fired) at any time

Your contract with the military locked you in. Quitting wasn't an option unless you wanted to trade your camouflage service uniform for black-and-white stripes. On the flipside, you couldn't be "fired" unless you really, really screwed up. In the civilian world, it's more of a balancing act — and that can make you pretty uncomfortable. You don't have the same job security you did in the military (or the same benefits, like housing allowance and free healthcare), but you can choose to leave one job for another if you want. Just wait until you have another job lined up before you quit, please.

Taking a few tips for your first weeks on the job

In the civilian world, "something to write on and something to write with" aren't inspectable items, and that's just one of the differences between civilian and military workplaces. Check out these things tips to ensure you get off on the right foot when you start a new job:

>> **Don't overshare.** The people in your civilian workspace aren't like your military-issued friends, so take your time in getting to know them. And don't run around your workplace telling everyone you're a veteran. Remember, most of your colleagues won't understand (or be impressed by) a story that starts with, "So, no $#!@, there I was . . ."

>> **Steer clear of the water cooler.** Don't get mired in office gossip about people you don't even know yet.

>> **Participate in meetings and conversations.** Sharing your insights, ideas, and perspectives is always okay, and don't be afraid to ask questions.

>> **Be confident and approachable.** That may be easier said than done, but civilians do things like shake hands or fist-bump, and they certainly make eye contact and don't stand at parade rest. Let your body language show that you're happy to be there, you know you're going to be a great asset to the team, and you're an approachable, friendly person.

>> **Don't stereotype your coworkers.** I know what many people in the military think of civilians, and although you're very likely to meet some people who definitely live up to those stereotypes, you have to remember that you've had very different experiences than they have. You can't hold those different experiences against them if you want to be successful in the civilian workforce.

>> **Keep your political views to yourself.** Avoid all conversations that involve politics. Although you may have had many of those discussions in the military, participating in them in the civilian workforce is unlikely to work out in your favor — no matter which side you take.

>> **Don't be too hard on anyone, including yourself.** You can't yell or swear at civilians; if you do, you're probably going to lose your job faster than you got it. Be easy on yourself, too. You're adapting to a whole new environment, and that's a hard adjustment to make.

>> **Be mindful of military humor.** After spending more than ten minutes in the military, you may have developed a dark, irreverent, and risqué sense of humor. A lot of the jokes, teasing, and kidding around that are common in the military are very inappropriate in the civilian workplace.

Applying Your Military Skills in the Civilian World

You'd need a long time to list all the skills you picked up in the military, but some of the most important are those related to leadership, teamwork, resilience, and problem-solving. When you enter the civilian workforce, nearly all the expertise you built is going to help you get ahead. No, you're not going to put your least-favorite coworker in the rear naked choke. But you can use many of your so-called soft skills to become more successful.

Soft skills are things that you may classify as personality traits or good habits. They include things like dependability, flexibility, and a strong work ethic, as well as leadership ability and innovative problem-solving skills (like using gutted 550 cord to tie down everything from your weapon's sights to the hatch of a rickety old HMMWV).

Table 13-1 lists some of the best soft skills you likely picked up in the military and how you can apply them to your civilian workplace.

TABLE 13-1   ## Military Soft Skills in Civilian Applications

Soft Skill	Use in the Civilian Workforce
Flexibility and resilience	Working with people who have very different perspectives from yours; compromising so that work still gets done and your team still meets its goals; being ready to change plans at a moment's notice
Teamwork	Recognizing that every member of the team can make a valuable contribution; covering down for less-capable coworkers so the job still gets done
Planning	Understanding that changing plans is acceptable and often necessary; knowing how to manage your expectations and help your coworkers manage theirs; anticipating objections to plans; paying close attention to detail to make sure all your bases are covered
Determination	Improvising, adapting, and overcoming; finding creative ways to solve problems
Leadership	Looking out for those who work with (and for) you; fostering trusting relationships between members of your team; taking charge in difficult situations to ensure the job gets done
Effective communication	Cutting to the chase and using precise language; effectively conveying ideas and requirements

Discovering Right-to-Work Laws

More than half of U.S. states and the federal government have right-to-work laws, which are important if you plan to enter a profession that has union workers. First things first: The term *right-to-work* is a little misleading. Of course you have the right to work. But the term as it's currently used is related to membership in a labor union.

Right-to-work laws are simply laws that say you can't to be forced to join a labor union or pay union dues as a condition of employment. These laws can prohibit contracts that require businesses to hire union workers. At the federal level, the Taft–Hartley Act of 1947 prohibits *closed* shops — businesses that hire only union members. It does allow *union* shops (businesses that require nonunion members to join a union) if requiring nonmembers to join is approved by the majority of a company's employees. State laws vary, but under the Taft–Hartley Act, they're allowed to outlaw union shops.

Regardless of your personal or political view of unions, you absolutely have the right to join one (or not). I cover some of the benefits unions offer in the later section "Perusing Union Protections."

Knowing Your Rights as an Employee

In the military, you didn't have a lot of employee rights — at least not in the way they apply to civilians. Civilian employers are subject to a number of laws that protect workers, both at the federal and state levels, including requirements to prevent harassment and discrimination, provide equal pay for equal work, and make reasonable accommodations for workers.

Federal and state laws to protect workers

The federal Equal Employment Opportunity Commission, or EEOC, is responsible for enforcing federal laws that make discriminating against a job applicant or employee based on certain characteristics illegal. It investigates complaints and takes action against employers who are violating federal laws such as these:

>> **Fair Labor Standards Act, or FLSA:** The Fair Labor Standards Act standardized the eight-hour day that civilians typically work and instituted a federal minimum wage.

>> **Title VII of the Civil Rights Act of 1964:** Title VII prohibits employers from refusing to hire someone, firing someone, or otherwise discriminating against someone with respect to compensation, terms and conditions of employment, or privileges of employment due to that person's race, skin color, religion, sex, or national origin.

>> **Age Discrimination in Employment Act, or ADEA:** The Age Discrimination in Employment Act prohibits employment discrimination against people who are age 40 or older.

>> **Occupational Safety and Health, or OSH, Act:** The OSH Act requires employers to keep workplaces free from hazardous conditions (other than those inherent in the job) and gives employees the right to know about the dangers involved in their jobs, a right to file complaints with the Occupational Safety and Health Administration (OSHA) to control workplace hazards, and the right to not be punished for exercising other rights protected by OSHA.

>> **Family and Medical Leave Act, or FMLA:** The Family and Medical Leave Act lets some employees take unpaid leave for family or medical reasons without risking their jobs or health insurance. Under this law, employees are allowed up to 12 weeks off after the birth or adoption of a child, to care for a child or spouse with a serious health condition, or in the event that a serious health condition prevents the employee from performing their job. It also allows up to 26 workweeks of leave during a 12-month period to care for a servicemember with a serious injury or illness if the servicemember is the worker's spouse, child, parent, or next-of-kin.

>> **The Equal Pay Act of 1963:** This law requires employers to give people equal pay for equal work, regardless of gender, and prevents them from using job titles to determine whether work is equal (instead, it requires that job content determine equality of work).

REMEMBER

Each state has the right to enact its own worker protection laws, and some have many more laws than others do. States can add on to federal laws by increasing protections for workers, but they generally can't take away from them by decreasing protections. In the event that a state removed worker protections that were covered by federal law, federal law still takes precedence.

Together, these laws protect workers in a variety of situations as well as workers who have certain protected characteristics. *Protected characteristics* are generally things outside a person's control, including the following:

>> Age (40 or older)

>> Skin color

>> Disability

>> Genetic information (including family medical history)

>> National origin

>> Race

>> Religion

>> Sex or gender (including pregnancy, sexual orientation, and gender identity or expression)

Discrimination at work

Federal law ensures that all workers have the right not to be discriminated against based on protected characteristics (see the preceding section). *Employment discrimination* means treating someone differently or less favorably than others are treated. Employers can't discriminate during the hiring process, employment, or the termination process — it's *always* against the law.

Discriminatory practices can occur in any aspect of employment, but employers (with very few exceptions) can't do the following:

>> Exclude potential employees during recruitment

>> Choose not to hire a candidate for a discriminatory reason

>> Deny some employees compensation or benefits

>> Pay equally qualified employees in the same position different salaries

>> Discriminate when assigning retirement options, disability leave, or maternity leave

>> Deny or disrupt the use of company facilities

>> Discriminate when issuing promotions or layoffs

>> Fire someone for a discriminatory reason

WHEN PERCEIVED DISCRIMINATION ISN'T UNLAWFUL

In some cases, an employer's actions may look like discrimination, but they're not. Employers don't have to hire someone who isn't capable of performing a job, even if the person has protected characteristics. For example, if a person is blind, a trucking company doesn't have to hire that person as a driver. The company isn't discriminating; it's just not going to pay someone who can't safely perform the job. Along the same lines, sometimes it's okay for a company to hire only women, such as when it's staffing a domestic violence shelter for only women and children. As long as a business can prove that it has a bona fide need to include or exclude some people from the job, its actions aren't discriminatory. However, employers are required to provide reasonable accommodations for people who have protected characteristics, which I cover in the cleverly titled "Reasonable accommodations for people in protected classes" section in this chapter.

Harassment in the workplace

The law considers harassment to be a form of discrimination, and all workers have the right to work in a place free from harassment. *Harassment* is offensive, belittling, threatening, and otherwise unwelcome behavior directed at someone that is based on protected characteristics, and it can take the form of things like these:

>> Offensive jokes

>> Demeaning remarks

>> Name-calling or offensive nicknames

>> Slurs

>> Offensive pictures or objects

>> Bullying

>> Physical assault

>> Threats

>> Intimidation

>> Interfering with someone's ability to do their work

>> Retaliating against a person for filing a discrimination charge or participating in an investigation

A harasser can be a supervisor, coworker, client, customer, or vendor. *Note:* I'm distinguishing harassment from sexual harassment; you can read about the latter in the following section.

Harassment becomes illegal when putting up with offensive and unwanted behavior, actions, or communication becomes a condition of employment, or when the behavior is severe and pervasive enough to create a *hostile work environment*.

REMEMBER

A single incident, if it's severe enough, can create a hostile work environment; a series of less-severe incidents over time can also constitute harassment if they're so pervasive that they affect a person's ability to do their job. And you don't have to be on the receiving end of the harassment to be a victim of it; everyone who observes it happening to someone else and is uncomfortable with the situation is a victim of the harassment.

Employers are automatically responsible for harassment if a supervisor's harassment of an employee results in a negative employment decision, such as failure to promote, loss of wages, or termination. An employer is also liable if the harassment creates a hostile work environment. The only way an employer may be able to dodge responsibility is if it can prove that it took immediate and reasonable corrective action upon learning of the harassment, and at the same time, the harassed employee unreasonably neglected to take advantage of the opportunity to correct the behavior. For example, if a supervisor learns of one worker using racial slurs against another and immediately terminates the nasty-mouthed employee, the employer may not be held liable.

Sexual harassment in the workplace

There are two main types of sexual harassment: hostile work environment and quid pro quo. Both are unlawful, and like other types of harassment (see the preceding section), only one incident may be necessary to create a hostile work environment.

Like the military, employers are required to have a zero-tolerance policy on sexual harassment. In order for something to qualify as sexual harassment,

>> **The conduct must be unwelcome:** However, remember that the person a comment or a behavior is directed at may not be the only victim. Others who observe the comments or behaviors can also be victims if they're offended by the conduct or don't welcome it.

>> **The conduct must be offensive to a reasonable person:** Conduct that a reasonable person would find creepy, weird, uncomfortable, or gross may constitute sexual harassment.

>> **The conduct needs to be pervasive or severe:** Pervasive conduct seeps into the workplace and affects the way a person works, and a single incident or a series of incidents can be severe enough to do the same.

REMEMBER

You don't have to tolerate sexual harassment in the workplace, no matter what anyone tells you. If you see or experience sexual harassment in your workplace, you can and should report it to a supervisor. If your supervisor ignores your concerns, go higher. Employers can't fire you for making a complaint about sexual harassment or participating in a sexual harassment investigation. If they do, you can file a formal complaint with the EEOC or speak to an attorney about your options. You may be entitled to get your job back, plus receive pay and benefits from the time you missed at work.

Hostile work environment sexual harassment

Anyone can be a perpetrator — and anyone can be a victim — of hostile work environment sexual harassment. Neither party's sex or gender identity matters; it can occur between opposite biological sexes or the same biological sexes. It can happen between coworkers, supervisors and their subordinates, supervisors and workers in other areas, and even customers or clients and workers.

Not all instances of sexual harassment constitute hostile work environment harassment. For example, say one coworker approaches another coworker and says, "Hey, Sam, I like your outfit," and then combines the comment with lewd sexual gestures, leering or leaning in, or a follow-up comment that is unwelcome and offensive. In that situation, Sam can shut the person down on the spot by telling them that the conduct is inappropriate. If it works, that single incident isn't likely to have transformed the workplace into a hostile work environment. However, if the conduct persists, it may lead to a hostile work environment in which Sam is uncomfortable or unable to perform their job.

Sexist comments and actions may also count as harassment. Offensive conduct based on an employee's gender can create a hostile work environment, such as when a person is encouraged to live up to gender stereotypes, or when employees of one gender are routinely left out of meetings or have their work sabotaged by coworkers of another gender. Employers are also required to protect employees from sexual harassment by customers, clients, vendors, business partners, and others, as well.

Quid pro quo sexual harassment

Quid pro quo sexual harassment occurs when the harassing party is in a position of power or is able to trade employment-related benefits for sexual favors. It can also occur when a person in a position of power threatens negative consequences if the victim fails to comply. In Latin, the term *quid pro quo* means "this for that," and that's exactly what this type of harassment requires.

Employment-related benefits may include things such as hiring, promotion, a raise, desirable work shifts or assignments, favorable performance reviews, recommendations, and even continuing employment. Negative consequences can include refusing to hire or promote someone or provide a fair performance review, demoting someone, or creating an unmanageable or undesirable work schedule for that person.

A supervisor telling you that you'll get a better performance review if you take them to dinner, that you'll be transferred to an undesirable department if you don't submit to their advances, or that you'll lose your job unless you sleep with them is committing quid pro quo sexual harassment.

Equal pay for equal work

The Equal Pay Act requires employers to pay people in the same workplace the same wages for the same work, regardless of gender. The content of a job (not the job title) determines whether jobs are substantially equal. For example, an employer can't give a man a job title of "Senior Production Specialist" and pay him $50,000 per year while paying a woman, who does the exact same job under the title "Production Specialist," less than it pays the man.

All forms of pay are covered, including base pay, overtime, bonuses, holiday pay, and benefits, such as life insurance, gasoline allowances and hotel accommodations, and vacation time. The Equal Pay Act works hand-in-hand with Title VII of the Civil Rights Act, which prohibits employers from discriminating based on sex.

Minimum wage and overtime

A *nonexempt worker* is a person who is eligible to receive employee protections under the Fair Labor Standards Act, or FLSA. (On the other side of the coin, an *exempt* worker isn't entitled to such protections.) For a closer look at who's exempt and nonexempt, flip to Chapter 8.

As a civilian, nonexempt worker, you're entitled to make at least the federal minimum wage for every hour you work. If your state's minimum wage is higher than the federal minimum wage, you're entitled to make the higher amount. Your employer can't pay you less than minimum wage, even if you agree to it; that's against the law. That's a lot different from the military, where you may work a 60-hour workweek and still make the same amount of pay — and earning $400 for 40 hours is a lot different from earning $400 for 60 hours when you calculate it hourly.

TECHNICAL STUFF

The federal minimum wage is abysmally low — it's not enough to live on. The hourly rate hasn't kept pace with cost-of-living increases since the late 1960s. Today, a minimum-wage, full-time worker with a family of four falls well below the national poverty line. But the national minimum wage was originally intended (with the Fair Labor Standards Act in 1938) to keep people *out* of poverty; it was designed to create a minimum standard of living to protect the health and well-being of employees.

The Fair Labor Standards Act also requires employers to pay nonexempt workers overtime. FLSA says that you're entitled to 1.5 times your regular rate of pay for each hour beyond 40 that you work in a week. That means if you make $10 per hour and work 40 hours, you're entitled to $400. If you work an additional hour, your employer must pay you $15 for that hour (that's 1.5 times your regular rate of pay). Your paycheck for a 41-hour workweek would be $415, because you picked up an extra five bucks by working an hour of overtime. Imagine if the military paid that way when you were in the field, at Fort Irwin's National Training Center, or deployed!

Some states have additional laws that require employers to pay you overtime if you work more than eight hours in a day or seven days in a workweek, or to pay you double time (you read that right) if you work a certain number of hours in one day or one week. And some employers agree to pay people extra for working weekends or holidays — but they're not required to by federal law.

Reasonable accommodations for people in protected classes

Civilian employers with 15 or more employees and federal agencies are usually required by federal law — including the Americans With Disabilities Act, Title VII of the Civil Rights Act of 1964, and a handful of other acts — to provide reasonable accommodations for people with protected characteristics, such as disabilities and religion. (Head to the earlier section "Federal and state laws to protect workers" for details on protected characteristics.) In this context, *reasonable* means that doing something to help the employee won't cause an undue hardship on the employer. State laws on reasonable accommodations may apply to smaller companies as well.

For example, an employer that hires a person with a disability may modify their job duties, allow them to have a desk that's not hidden in a hard-to-navigate maze of cubicles, or install ramps or otherwise restructure a work site. Along the same lines, an employer has to make reasonable accommodations for people who can't work from sundown on Friday to sundown on Saturday or who are required by their religion or closely held beliefs to grow a beard or wear special clothing.

REMEMBER

Employers are only required to provide reasonable accommodations if they don't create undue hardship, though. *Undue hardship* can mean financial difficulty, or it can mean that the person's demands are unduly extensive, substantial, or disruptive or would fundamentally change the nature or operation of the business. For example, an employer doesn't have to build an elevator in a two-story, leased building or turn off all the lights and tell everyone to be silent for 20 minutes twice a day so a person can pray.

And just in case you weren't sure, an employer isn't allowed to choose not to hire you because it may have to make reasonable accommodations for you. However, an employer may decline to hire you because you're not qualified or because you can't perform the job. If a prospective employee attends an interview and says, "My religion says I can only work from 9 a.m. to 9:30 a.m. each day," and the position requires a person who can work from 9 a.m. to 5 p.m., the employer can legally decline to hire them — in this case, the work schedule did them in. However, refusing to hire that person because of their religion is illegal.

Whistleblower protections

If you're a federal employee, your employer can't retaliate against you for filing a complaint, whether it's about corruption in the workplace, sexual harassment, or something else. Retaliation can be any type of negative action, such as firing or laying off, demoting, denying overtime or promotion, or making threats, intimidating, or harassing you. Your employer also can't engage in less-obvious acts of retaliation, such as isolating you, ostracizing you, making fun of you, or falsely accusing you of poor performance. Your state may have whistleblower protection laws for government and nongovernment workers as well.

Meal and rest breaks

Federal law doesn't require employers to give people breaks during the workday, but many states do (you should check your state's rules on meal and rest breaks before you start job-hunting, just so you're familiar). However, the Fair Labor Standards Act, which does *not* force employers to allow breaks, does say that employers must pay workers for all hours worked — even if the employer calls some of the workday "break time." In order for your employer to legally avoid paying you for your breaks, you must be completely relieved of your duties.

State safeguards

When a state's legislature feels that federal protections aren't strong enough for workers, it can pass bills, laws, and acts that do better. You see this variation in minimum wages across state lines (including some states whose legislators believe the federal minimum wage is good enough), meal and rest breaks, family and medical leave, and even overtime pay protections.

THE SEARCH FOR CHEM LIGHT BATTERIES

If you've ever been sent on a hunt for chem light batteries or blinker fluid, or if someone sent you to bring them six feet of flight line, tap on a truck's armor to listen for weak spots, take an exhaust sample from a vehicle by using a trash bag, or calibrate a turret by counting the number of times it spins around before stopping, congratulations. You've been hazed. Workplace hazing isn't normally illegal in the civilian world, but it can be a violation of anti-harassment laws if the person being hazed has been singled out due to their protected characteristics, such as race or color, religion, national origin, sex, age, or disability.

If a discrepancy exists over which laws apply to a worker (federal or state), courts defer to the more protective law. For example, if you live in a state that requires your employer to pay you overtime for every hour you work over eight in a day, federal law doesn't have any bearing on your case; only state law, which requires the employer to pay you, does.

Perusing Union Protections

Labor unions are collections of people who demand adequate treatment from the employers that are profiting from their labor. The National Labor Relations Act gives you the absolute right to join a union if you want to. You also have the right to decide *not* to join a union, as I discuss in the earlier section "Discovering Right-to-Work Laws." Some industries are mainly staffed by union members, including auto work, education, steelwork, public service, and electrical work.

Unions charge their members dues — typically monthly, quarterly, or annual fees — in exchange for certain protections and benefits. The average union dues across the United States are around $400 per year, or about two hours' worth of pay per month, though every union is different. Unions have *collective bargaining power*, which is the process by which workers (through the union's democratically elected representatives) negotiate favorable contracts with employers.

For example, an auto workers' union may tell an automaker that it will keep workers on the job as long as the automaker promises to pay double-time wages for hours worked on weekends or to offer an affordable healthcare plan to its workers. If the automaker feels that agreeing is in its best interests, the two parties reach an agreement and the auto workers show up at work. If the automaker breaks its end of the deal, the auto workers may go on a *labor strike* — which means they refuse to work until the automaker does what it says it would. Many unions have strike funds that help ensure employees get at least some money while they're on strike.

The whole point behind a labor union is to ensure better working conditions for members. That may include pay, healthcare benefits, and even workplace safety. Statistically, union workers make more money than nonunion workers do (to the tune of 11.2 percent), are generally entitled to more benefits, and enjoy stronger worker protections (including more job stability) in exchange for paying dues.

IN THIS CHAPTER

» **Discovering the popularity of self-employment for veterans**

» **Exploring entrepreneurship programs designed for veterans**

» **Getting your hands on critical startup funding**

» **Looking into franchising**

» **Pursuing contracts with the federal government**

Chapter **14**

Starting Your Own Business

When you have the next big idea, the first logical step is to start your own business. Although everyone wants to work for themselves, few people realize that entrepreneurship is a full-time job (as in *full* full-time, 24 hours a day and 7 days a week). But if you're ready to put in the late nights, caffeine-fueled weekend mornings, and other investments (including financial investments) necessary to make it work, veteran business owners have several free resources at their disposal that you can use to get your business off the ground.

Running a Veteran-Owned Business

Research has shown that vets are 45 percent more likely to be self-employed than non-veterans are, but they have significantly fewer mentorship options and networking opportunities. The U.S. government attempts to fill those gaps with education and training programs run by the Department of Veterans Affairs and the Small Business Administration. Even the military's Transition Assistance Program offers a special education track on entrepreneurship, which I cover in Chapter 2.

About 9 percent of all businesses in the United States are veteran-owned, and some of them are pretty big. FedEx, GoDaddy, and RE/MAX were all founded by veterans, and so were millions of others.

TIP

Veteran-owned business enjoy some advantages that other businesses don't, including preference when competing for government contracts. You may also be eligible for special loans and other perks simply by virtue of your veteran status.

Considering Programs Designed to Help Vets Open Up Shop

In addition to private resources designed expressly for veterans, the U.S. government has a few tricks up its sleeve for helping vets hang up a shingle. Both the U.S. Small Business Administration and the Department of Veterans Affairs have programs you can use to launch a business.

Veteran entrepreneurship training programs from the OVBD

The Small Business Administration offers a lot of help to vets who want to start businesses of their own. Its Office of Veterans Business Development, or OVBD, is devoted exclusively to promoting veteran entrepreneurship. The OVBD also runs the Veterans Business Outreach Center (VBOC) Program, which has centers all over the country. And even if you don't live near a VBOC, you can use its online resources to establish your business.

Each center provides services such as the following:

>> **Pre-business plan workshops:** These development workshops help you face down some of the major issues involved in self-employment. They also teach you to work directly with a business counselor as well as to use the Internet to develop and expand your business.

>> **Business plan preparation:** A VBOC counselor can help you develop and maintain a five-year business plan, including how to legally form your business, determine your equipment requirements (and how much they'll cost), set up your organizational structure, and create a financial plan.

>> **Concept assessments and feasibility analysis:** You can work with an expert to figure out what you and your business need to be successful as well as

identify strengths and weaknesses in your business plan to increase your likelihood of success.

>> **Entrepreneurial training and counseling for service-disabled veteran entrepreneurs:** VBOCs and other SBA partners target training projects and counseling sessions to disabled vets to address special needs and concerns you may face if you're disabled.

>> **Mentorship:** If necessary, VBOCs can conduct visits to your business to check how well you're sticking to your business plan and review your monthly financial statements to determine whether you need to adjust fire.

>> **Special training:** You can access special assistance and training in areas like international trade, Internet marketing, franchising, accounting, and more through VBOCs.

VA Office of Small & Disadvantaged Business Utilization

The Department of Veterans Affairs runs the Office of Small & Disadvantaged Business Utilization, or OSDBU, which focuses entirely on helping veterans. Its Veteran Entrepreneur Portal connects you with federal services that can help you develop your ideas, find funding, access government programs, and build partnerships with others through VA Direct Access Events. It also gives you access to online training programs, career resources through national companies, and non-profit organizations that provide benefits to veteran business owners.

Vets First Verification Program

The Vets First Verification Program gives verified veteran-owned businesses the opportunity to compete for VA contracts. To qualify, your small business must be at least 51 percent owned by a veteran (service-disabled or not) and primarily controlled by that same veteran.

Boots to Business

The SBA's free business course, Boots to Business, guides you through your transition out of the military and into becoming a business owner. Classes include topics such as creating business plans, managing product launches, marketing, and developing new business concepts.

TIP

Some states offer grants to veterans who complete the Boots to Business program.

Finding Funding to Start a Veteran-Owned Business

Most businesses have *overhead* — the cost of doing daily business. You may need to rent office space, create prototypes, or buy supplies that enable you to offer your product or service to the public. Unless you have enough money in savings (and you won't miss that money if something goes wrong), you probably need to secure funding. You can get the money you need to start your business in several ways, including through grants, loans, and venture capital.

Determining how much funding you need

Every business has different financial needs, particularly for startup costs. If you're opening a *brick-and-mortar* shop (one with a physical location that customers or clients can visit), you have different financial needs than an online business or service-centered business does. However, most startups need to spend money on the following:

>> Office space and utilities, unless you plan to work from a home office

>> Equipment and supplies, such as a computer, desk, and office goods (like paper, pens, and a trash can)

>> Communications, such as a dedicated phone line and Internet connection for your business

>> Licenses and permits, which are required for some businesses

>> Insurance, which some states require for certain businesses

>> Inventory (if you plan to sell products rather than digital assets or some services)

>> Employee salaries for yourself and those who work for you

>> Advertising and marketing, including your company's website

>> Attorney and accounting services

You may not need a lot of capital to start your business. For example, if you're a freelance graphic designer or writer running an online-only business, you probably don't have a lot of overhead. However, if you're creating a product to sell, you need the materials for that product, a place to store those materials (and your finished products), and a way to give customers access to your products.

Figuring out exactly how much you need for each expense takes some research, but when you're finished, categorize them according to whether they're a one-time expense or they're recurring costs. Multiply your monthly expenses by 12 to determine how much they'll cost you over a year, and then multiply that total by 5 to determine how much you'll need to spend in five years. Then, you can determine how much funding you need to get your business off the ground.

Self-funding versus finding an investor or crowdfunding

Bootstrapping is the term for self-funding. That means you use your own financial resources to support your business. If you fund your own company, you retain complete control over everything, but all the risk is yours alone, too. You have to be extremely cautious not to overspend.

If you can't bootstrap your business, you may need to find an investor. If an investor believes in your product or service, they may be interested in partnering with you. In a case like this, your investor gives you the cash and may maintain an active role in your company while you handle the legwork of implementing your ideas. Venture capitalists — people who invest in business ideas — typically want to have some control and ownership of the company in return for funding.

If bootstrapping or finding an investor aren't good options for you, you may also turn to crowdfunding. Crowdfunding relies on several individual donors who believe in your product or service, and none of them expect a financial return; instead, they look for a "gift" from your company, such as early access to a product or other special benefits, like meeting you or getting an autographed copy of what you're selling.

Taking out a small business loan

When you take out a small business loan through a conventional lender, such as a credit union or the bank you normally use, you retain complete control over your business. However, to get funding through a conventional lender, you need a business plan, expense sheet, and financial projections for the next five years. You may need to find professional help to develop documentation that scores a lender's approval.

Using the SBA's Lender Match

The Small Business Administration offers SBA-guaranteed loans to people who have trouble getting a conventional loan or other types of funding. These loans don't come directly from the SBA; instead, the SBA guarantees all or part of them so lenders can be more comfortable letting you borrow the amount you need. The three main types of SBA loans are these:

>> **7(a) loans:** *7(a) loans* are the most common. You can use these loans for short- and long-term working capital, as well as to buy furniture, supplies, and fixtures for your business. Applicants must meet specific criteria and use the funds for a sound business purpose. You can borrow up to $5 million with an SBA 7(a) loan.

>> **504 loans:** *504 loans* offer long-term, fixed-rate financing. (*Fixed-rate* means your interest rate doesn't change over the life of the loan.) These loans can be used to buy or build facilities or to purchase long-term machinery and equipment. You can't use them for working capital or inventory. You must have a tangible net worth of less than $15 million and a net income of less than $5 million after federal income taxes for the two years before you apply (not a problem for a recently separated veteran, right?), and you must operate a for-profit company in the U.S. to borrow up to $5 million with this program.

>> **Microloans:** *Microloans* provide up to $50,000 to help your business start up or expand. The SBA says that the average microloan is about $13,000, but you can borrow more or less, depending on your business's needs. You may use money from this type of loan for working capital, inventory, supplies, furniture, fixtures, machinery, and equipment, but you can't use it to pay existing debts or to buy real estate.

Scoping out the SBA's investment programs

The Small Business Administration runs a handful of investment programs that help investors connect with people who have great ideas. These investment programs rely on investors who actively look for people to share their money with; investors register as Small Business Investment Companies (SBICs), Small Business Innovation Research (SBIRs), or Small Business Technology Transfer (SBTTs).

>> **SBIC:** *Small Business Investment Companies* invest in small businesses through debt, equity, or a combination of the two. An SBIC lends cash to a small business (with interest), and the SBIC gets a share of the business's ownership.

>> **SBIR:** *Small Business Innovation Research* partners focus on research and development of new, high-tech innovations. Through this program, you can propose innovative ideas to the U.S. government with a partner that isn't part of a nonprofit research institution.

>> **STTR:** *Small Business Technology Transfer* partners, like SBIRs, focus on research and development of new innovations. This program also lets you propose new ideas to the federal government, but to receive funding from it, you must partner with someone from a nonprofit research institution.

Getting grants designed for veteran startups

Several private organizations offer grants to new veteran-owned businesses across the country. You can use a site like www.grantwatch.com, which keeps tabs on nationally available grants for vets (and others), or you can search through your favorite veteran service organizations' websites for opportunities. Some may even be located in your state, which you can find by searching the Internet for "[state] veteran business grants."

Surveying Special Franchising Opportunities for Veterans

If you want to join a party hosted by an already-established business, franchising may be the right choice for you. *Franchising* is a form of business that enables one person to own and operate one or more locations of a big-name business, whether it's a fast-food restaurant, gym, medical facility, retail store, or something else.

In a franchise, you pay for the right to use a company's name and branding materials, as well as business-related tools, to sell its products or services. You pay a fee or royalties to do so, and the company provides you with the things you need to be successful. As an example, the next time you walk into your favorite restaurant (dine-in or fast-food), look for a sign on or near the door that says, "This location is independently owned and operated." That's a sure indication that the business is a franchise, which means someone is paying the restaurant to use its name, menu, ingredients, and processes.

You can check for franchising opportunities for veterans at www.vetfran.org or by searching for specific businesses online. Look for a menu item that says "Franchising Opportunities" or something similar to find out whether an organization offers special benefits to veterans.

Contracting with the Federal Government

If you want to do business with the U.S. government, the Small Business Administration has a path for you. Government agencies use the Dynamic Small Business Search, or DSBS, to search for small business contractors for upcoming contracts. You can get your business listed in the DSBS database by registering with the System for Award Management, or SAM. Anyone from security professionals and manufacturers of physical fitness equipment to professional writers, aircraft parts manufacturers, and information technology experts can contract with the U.S. government (sometimes to the tune of billions of dollars).

You may also sell your products to the U.S. General Services Administration, or GSA, by getting on the GSA Schedule through the SBA. The GSA also publishes a subcontracting directory called SubNet for large government contractors who need to work with small businesses.

You can get a peek at how much the federal government spends on contracts with outside companies at www.usaspending.gov. Amounts range from just a few hundred dollars to billions, and if you play your cards right, your company's name might end up on that website.

3

Gearing Up to Go Back to School

Figure out where to look for military-friendly schools and educational opportunities.

Cash in on your GI Bill, find financial aid, and discover scholarships available to veterans.

Blend in with other students and make the most out of your scholarly career by taking advantage of veterans opportunities.

Chapter **15**

Advancing on Your Scholarly Career

F ew things can make you feel as old or out-of-place as stepping into a college classroom after completing a tour or two in the military, even if you're not that much older than most of the people around you. Your fellow students may be a lot different from your military peers (have I mentioned that civilians walk very slowly around you when you're a brand-new veteran?), and your experience in civilian education will be vastly different from your experiences in military schoolhouses. But like your military education, the things you learn in civilian college courses will most likely pay off with career advancement, higher pay, and other benefits. Even better, a lot of the things you learned in the military, including the time you spent in basic training and job training, count toward college credits, which gives you a head-start on your degree.

Plus, if you use your GI Bill to attend school full-time, you're most likely entitled to receive basic allowance for housing at the E-5 with dependents rate, which is a pretty decent addition to your bank account every month.

Before you get too far ahead of yourself, you need to know that you may face challenges that your civilian peers don't (and that's okay; you can work through them). Also, not all colleges and universities are created equal; that goes for both their educational quality and their commitment to helping veterans succeed. As long as you're selective about where you go and you remain flexible throughout the process, you have a great shot at obtaining a degree that you can use to launch a long and illustrious civilian career.

Facing Down Common Challenges and Finding Military-Friendly Schools

Research shows that many veterans report difficulty making social connections with traditional students, and sometimes vets perceive traditional students as "just kids" because they haven't yet firmly established vocational, social, or family roles. It's not just about other students, though. Studies show that the differences between military and civilian education are vast. The military uses a rigid, hands-on approach to teaching a skill, and you can expect the same type of instruction regardless of which course you attend (from basic training to specialized skill courses). In a college environment, professors all have their own teaching styles, and that can make civilian education seem chaotic, confusing, and less orderly than what you're used to.

REMEMBER

If you feel that way, you're not weird; you're among thousands of other veterans who feel or felt the same way (me included). I want you to walk into your first college course with your eyes wide open, and later, I want you to walk out of your institution with a well-deserved degree in your hand.

Some schools are better-equipped than others are at helping veterans reach their higher education goals. When you're looking for a college, you may want to choose one that has veterans programs in place, including the following:

>> Strong financial support for military students, including GI Bill experts on staff who can help you when you need it

>> Military-specific career resources that can help you figure out what to do with your degree

>> An active veteran center or veteran community on campus

Some schools have dedicated military and veteran offices that can help you with every part of your educational experience, including filling out your application form and planning your academic schedule, transferring military credits, and helping you use your VA education benefits.

TIP

Some personal issues may make getting motivated to enroll in school (and, later, sticking to it) difficult for you. Resources are available to you if you're struggling, no matter the reason, and I cover many of them in Chapter 21.

Surfing for Online Educational Opportunities

Many of the most popular colleges and universities servicemembers use offer online classes, and you can use your GI Bill to pay for them. (Head to Chapter 16 to discover more about the GI Bill and how to use your benefit.) You can attend an online-only college or one that offers both brick-and-mortar and distance-learning courses — whatever works best for your lifestyle.

WARNING

The GI Bill does pay for independent and distance learning online. However, if you're taking only distance-learning courses, you're eligible for a housing allowance based on 50 percent of the national average only. You don't get your full monthly housing allowance, or MHA, entitlement unless at least half your classes are in-person.

ARE FOR-PROFIT COLLEGES SCAMS?

For-profit colleges are businesses, and many of them have well-deserved bad reputations. In 2019, the Federal Trade Commission slapped two major for-profit colleges with huge penalties for deceptive advertising. One was pretending to be affiliated with the Army, and another had to pay out $191 million in damages for misleading students about job placements. As a result, the VA banned the two schools (and two others) from enrolling GI Bill students. However, after significant lobbying by the for-profit college industry, the VA lifted the bans and allowed the offending schools back into the fold. However, the fact that the VA allows a school to take GI Bill tuition payments doesn't mean that the school is a legitimate opportunity or that it's not preying on you because you can make guaranteed payments.

If you're interested in attending a for-profit college, regardless of whether you use your GI Bill benefit, you should make sure that its credits transfer to another institution and that a degree you earn through the company is worth something to employers. Don't just take the institution's word for it, either; do a lot of research on your own to make sure a school is a good use of your limited GI Bill money. (You only get so much, and when it's gone, it's gone.) Check with the U.S. Department of Education to see whether the school has been sanctioned, read reviews from former students, and explore Harvard Law School's Project on Predatory Student Lending and Veterans Education Success's website (vetsedsuccess.org/help-for-students/find-a-school) to find out whether the school you're interested is a safe bet for your future.

If you're currently in the military and have enough time left on your contract, you may be able to use your branch's tuition assistance program to knock out a few courses online. Earning college credits now may make pursuing your degree easier after you're out.

Applying for College Admission

After you find a school that accepts the GI Bill, has a great reputation for helping veterans, and offers the degree program you want, you can apply for admission. (You apply for your GI Bill benefit after an accredited institute of higher learning accepts you, and I cover that process in Chapter 16.) Although every school has its own admissions process, you need to fill out an application, provide your standardized test scores (if applicable), share your military and previous school transcripts, and pay application fees or submit fee waivers. If you're interested in a particular school, look for admissions information on its website; every school lists its application criteria (or provides you with a way to get that information) for new students.

Filling out the Common Application or the Coalition Application

Although some colleges have their own application forms, more than 900 colleges and universities accept the Common Application. Often called the Common App, this online application requires you to create an account and fill in important details for the schools you're interested in attending. (You can create your account at www.commonapp.org.)

Some schools accept the Coalition Application (www.coalitionforcollegeaccess.org) instead, which is newer than but very similar to the Common App.

TIP

You can figure out which type of application a college or university accepts by visiting its website. Additionally, both the Common Application and the Coalition Application list their partner schools on their websites.

Lining up letters of recommendation

Some schools ask applicants to submit letters of recommendation with their applications. *Recommendation letters* are brief, formal statements that highlight your positive qualities and explain why you'll be an asset to that particular institution (and no, you can't write your own). The letter should include, at minimum, the following:

>> How the recommender knows you

>> A list of your positive qualities that relate to your success in college

>> Personal stories that illustrate your character and competence

REMEMBER

Although your friends and family members may have great things to say about you, you should choose someone who's familiar with your work ethic and how you operate when you're assigned specific tasks. Your first-line leader in the military may be a good choice, but credentials can be impressive. Go as high in your chain of command (or outside it) as you can to score a letter of recommendation that wows the admissions department at your future school.

EXAMPLE

Here's an example of a good letter of recommendation that covers all the bases.

Dear Admissions Committee,

I had the great pleasure of serving as Robert's platoon sergeant in the United States Army. From his first day in my platoon, Robert impressed me with his attention to detail and ability to provide actionable solutions to previously unidentified problems.

Throughout our deployment to Afghanistan, Robert continued to perform tasks that were above the scope of his duty position. He created a system for tracking inventory in our supply shop that our entire unit eventually adopted, earning him an Army Achievement Medal and bringing great credit upon himself and the U.S. military. Additionally, Robert earned a significant promotion through his hard work and dedication, and he rose to the challenge. He was recognized as our unit's Soldier of the Month, a designation that requires a servicemember to engage in intense study of military history and knowledge, perform flawless executions of military tasks and drills, and outperform his peers by appearing before a board to answer in-depth questions.

I am certain that Robert will continue to do great things in the future. I highly recommend him for admission to your undergraduate program. He is talented, knowledgeable, and eager to learn, and he consistently seeks out constructive feedback to improve his skill set. Please feel free to contact me if you have any questions.

Sincerely,

Kimberly Yost
SFC, USA
Platoon Sergeant

Composing college admissions essays

Many colleges and universities require you to write an admissions essay as part of your application package. Usually, they expect around 500 words; although that doesn't seem like a lot, a great essay can mean the difference between acceptance and rejection. Your admissions essay is your opportunity to tell your story, so:

>> Write about something that's meaningful to you and that has had an impact on your life. (Here's a hint: Your experience in the military both sets you apart from most applicants *and* makes for an interesting read.)

>> Mix self-reflection into your story. Instead of writing about your experience as if you were an observer, write down what you learned and how it changed you.

>> Write multiple drafts of your essay and ask friends and family to read them all. Get feedback on whether the essay is interesting, flows in a logical order, and reveals something about you; then make changes as necessary.

If you're having a tough time coming up with a topic for your essay (and your school hasn't provided one), these prompts can give you some ideas:

>> Tell your military story, including why you joined and what changed about you during your military career (for the better, of course).

>> Explain how you learned to overcome obstacles to get where you need to be and how you think ahead to avoid obstacles now.

>> Describe and reflect on something that challenged one or more beliefs you held in the past.

>> Recap and reflect on something that forced you to grow as a person.

>> Reflect on a time you bounced back from failure to become successful.

>> Describe a topic that captivates you — something you could talk about for hours — and explain why it matters so much to you.

Your best bet: Read the instructions carefully, use a great hook (such as a question) to pique the reader's interest, and be authentic as you present good examples that support your ideas. Search the Internet for great college admissions essays to get familiar with a few examples before you start. Oh, and steer clear of military acronyms and jargon, proofread and edit relentlessly, and avoid idioms like the plague.

Submitting your standardized test scores and transcripts

To get into the college of your choice, you may need to submit standardized test scores — as in the SAT and the ACT scores you got while you were in high school. Because standardized testing has been debated widely over the past several years, some schools are now switching to "test-optional" policies, which means you don't have to dig up these old test results to get in.

However, if you've completed any college coursework or have earned college credits in the past (either from another institution or by acing tests through the College-Level Examination Program, or CLEP), you definitely want to submit proof through transcripts or a certified CLEP Exam score report. That way, your credits transfer to your new school and (hopefully) contribute to your degree.

REMEMBER

Your official Joint Services Transcript or Community College of the Air Force Transcript, which contains records of all your military training and experience, is an essential part of your college application. Many of the things you learned in the military translate into civilian college credits. For example, you may get credit for learning military history and satisfy your physical education requirement for the PT you did at basic training; your job training may translate into something that relates to your degree, and so can other coursework you did. The number of credits you receive varies by institution, but every little bit helps; when your previous training turns into college credits, you spend less time in the classroom and less money on books and supplies.

Revamping your resume

Some schools ask prospective students to submit a resume. If you elect to include yours, regardless of whether your future school asks for it, head to Chapter 7 to get some killer tips on crafting a document that showcases all your skills and abilities.

TIP

If you have the opportunity to upload a resume with your application, do it.

Amassing application fees (or using fee waivers)

Even if you use your GI Bill, the VA doesn't pay for your college application fees. Most college application fees are between $50 and $60, so that's something to keep in mind if you want to apply at several schools. Some schools charge twice that, and others don't have application fees at all.

ADVANCING YOUR KNOWLEDGE WITH FREE COURSES

Though you don't receive official credit, you can take free college courses from several prestigious schools. You can apply the things you learn to CLEP out of college courses, or just for your personal edification. Several e-learning platforms can connect you with these courses, or you can sign up directly through the schools that offer them. Course topics cover the whole spectrum, ranging from medicine and business to computer programming and religion. Schools such as Princeton, Harvard, Columbia, MIT, Yale, and Stanford all participate, as do dozens of others. Some of the schools even offer certificates of completion for coursework, which you can mention on your resume.

However, some schools offer fee waivers to students who demonstrate financial need, make official on-campus visits, or apply online. Some colleges also have free application weeks. If you need a fee waiver, your best bet is to contact the admissions office and ask what you need to do to qualify. The school may ask you to submit your most recent tax return or other information.

Taking Advantage of CLEP Opportunities

If you're still in the military, you can take free College-Level Examination Program examinations that, when passed, translate into college credits. (You can still take these exams after you leave the military, but you have to pay for them out of your own pocket.)

Thanks to the Defense Activity for Non-Traditional Education Support, or DANTES, you can take these exams (commonly called CLEP exams) in your choice of 33 subject areas. Testing typically takes place in installation education centers. You can take as many CLEP exams as you want, in as many of the subject areas as you want. Successful scores can earn you college credits at around 2,900 colleges and universities, so these tests can take months off the time you need to earn your degree.

REMEMBER

If you need a second attempt to pass, you're responsible for paying the fee.

Chapter **16**

Cashing in on Your GI Bill

W hen you raised your right hand to join the military, you did so in exchange for certain benefits — and one of them may be the GI Bill. Throughout the years, the Department of Veterans Affairs has cycled through a few iterations of the GI Bill, so the type you have likely depends on when you joined and what you signed up for.

You can use your GI Bill for an undergraduate or graduate degree, to attend a foreign college or university, to train for a specific job (such as truck driving, HVAC repair, or pilot training), for entrepreneurship training or apprenticeships, and for independent and distance learning. Basically, it's there for you to get the education or training you need to start a successful career in nearly any field.

Knowing Which GI Bill Is Yours

The GI Bill has evolved quite a bit since it was introduced in 1944 by then-President Franklin D. Roosevelt. It now covers tuition and fees, money for housing in many circumstances, and money for books and supplies. You can use your GI bill only if your military discharge is honorable; if it's anything else, you need to apply for a discharge upgrade to qualify for this benefit. (Head to Chapter 12 for details on getting your discharge categorization changed.)

Forever GI Bill

The Forever GI Bill isn't an actual program; it's legislation that modified the original Post-9/11 GI Bill I discuss in the following section. This legislation modified and extended GI Bill benefits *only* for people discharged on or after January 1, 2013, by adding special protections for GI Bill users who attend schools that close before the user can finish a degree and by getting rid of the 15-year time limit to use the Post-9/11 GI Bill benefit. (People discharged before that date in 2013 have only 15 years to use their GI Bill benefit; after that time, the benefit is no longer available to them.)

Other modifications the Forever GI Bill made to the Post-9/11 GI Bill include the following:

>> Changing housing stipend payments

>> Authorizing GI Bill funds for work-study programs

>> Providing veterans with priority enrollment in educational counseling

>> Enhancing dependent and spouse access to GI Bill benefits

Post-9/11 GI Bill

Most people (you included, if you're about to leave or have recently left the military) have the Post-9/11 GI Bill modified by the Forever GI Bill legislation in the preceding section. That means you're entitled to full tuition coverage at a public university as well as tuition for private and foreign schools in most circumstances.

To qualify for 100 percent coverage through the Post-9/11 GI Bill, you must have served 36 months or more since September 11, 2001, or have served at least 30 continuous days on active duty and been discharged due to a service-connected disability, or have received a Purple Heart.

To qualify for partial coverage through the Post-9/11 GI Bill, you must have accrued 90 days of active service; that active service must have occurred since September 11, 2001. The VA covers varying percentages based on your time in service as I outline in Table 16-1.

REMEMBER

Complete, 100 percent coverage means that the VA matches 100 percent of your tuition up to the cost of the most expensive public state school's in-state undergraduate tuition. The VA pays the money directly to the school so you don't have to worry about making payments.

TABLE 16-1

Percentages the VA Covers

Length of Service	Percentage of Benefit
At least 90 days but fewer than 6 months	50 percent
At least 6 but fewer than 18 months	60 percent
At least 18 but fewer than 24 months	70 percent
At least 24 but fewer than 30 months	80 percent
At least 30 but fewer than 36 months	90 percent

The GI Bill does more than pay tuition, and schools and states can pitch in to provide even more benefits. I cover the additional perks of using your GI bill in the following sections.

The Yellow Ribbon Program

Many schools participate in the *Yellow Ribbon Program*, which provides money to help pay for higher tuition costs at private schools or for attendance as a nonresident student at a public school. (In public colleges and universities, local students are given discounted rates; students coming from outside the school's designated radius are considered nonresidents and pay more for tuition.)

If your school participates in the program and you qualify, the school contributes a certain amount of money toward your extra tuition and fees through a grant, scholarship, or similar program, and the Department of Veterans Affairs matches the school's contribution. The VA maintains a list of Yellow Ribbon Program schools on its website.

REMEMBER

You only qualify for the Yellow Ribbon Program if you served at least 36 months on active duty (you can have breaks in service and still qualify) or if any of the following applies to you:

>> You received a Purple Heart on or after September 11, 2001, and were honorably discharged after any period of service.

>> You served for at least 30 continuous days on or after September 11, 2001, and were discharged after 60 days with a service-connected disability.

>> You're a dependent child using benefits transferred by a veteran or service-member who qualifies at the 100 percent level.

>> You are a Fry Scholar (the child or dependent of a veteran whose parent or spouse died in the line of duty or was a member of the Selected Reserve who died from a service-connected disability on or after September 11, 2001).

Your school must not have exceeded the maximum number of students in its agreement with the VA. Your school is responsible for providing Yellow Ribbon Program information to the VA and certifying your enrollment as well.

Monthly housing allowance

The Post-9/11 GI Bill pays a monthly housing allowance, or MHA, based on your school's or campus's ZIP code. (If you attend more classes in one location than another, the VA gives you money based on the campus where you spend most of your time.) You're entitled to receive monthly housing allowance at the same rate an active-duty E-5 with dependents receives in basic allowance for housing, or BAH.

Like the BAH you received in the military, this stipend is a monthly amount that goes directly to your bank account. You must attend more than half your classes in-person to receive the full amount. If you take all your courses online, you're still eligible for the stipend, but you receive only half the national average stipend (which varies each year).

Your monthly housing allowance is based on the amount of active-duty service you completed. The percentages you receive are outlined in Table 16-1. For example, if you served between 24 and 30 months in the military and received an honorable discharge, you're entitled to 80 percent of the housing stipend.

REMEMBER

You must attend school more than half-time to receive MHA. That means if your school says that 12 credit hours is full-time for undergraduate training, taking classes that total 6 credit hours won't cut it; you need to take at least 7 credit hours to qualify for MHA. The VA pays your benefits for graduate training based on what your school reports your training time to be; that means if you're taking 3 graduate hours and the school tells the VA that you're a full-time student, you receive full MHA.

But wait! There's more! You only qualify for full MHA if you're attending school full-time. The VA determines your training time and pays you at the nearest 10 percent level. If 12 hours is full-time and you're taking 7 credit hours, your training time is 58 percent (because 7 ÷ 12 = 0.58). Rounded up to the nearest 10 percent, the VA gives you 60 percent of your MHA. If you had trouble calculating this, know that if your school considers 12 credit hours to be full-time, a 3-credit-hour math class will get you 25 percent of the way to full MHA.

TIP

To maximize your MHA stipend, go to school full-time and in-person. (And if the school happens to be in Hawaii; Washington, D.C.; or another high-BAH area, well, hey.)

Books and supplies

You may receive a book and supply stipend of up to $1,000 per year, which the VA pays you at the beginning of each term. The VA pays $41.67 per semester hour, up to a total of 12; that works out to $500 per semester if you take 12 credit hours.

You can receive this nontaxable books and supplies stipend if you attend a college, another degree-granting institution, or a vocational school or if you participate in technical training. You're also eligible to receive it if you attend a non-degree-granting institution or if you participate in an apprenticeship or on-the-job training program. The cash is yours to spend how you need to; the VA doesn't require you to submit any receipts.

Tutorial assistance

Tutorial assistance doesn't take away from the money you get from your GI Bill benefit. Instead, it complements it. If you're enrolled in an educational program for at least half-time and you take a difficult course that's required for your educational program, the VA may give you up to $1,200 to pay for a tutor. It doesn't pay more than $100 per month for tutoring and caps the total at $1,200; the VA will never pay more than that throughout your scholarly career. You're eligible for this payment if your course instructor writes a letter on your behalf and files a form with the VA.

Transferring the Post-9/11 GI Bill

You may be able to transfer your unused Post-9/11 GI bill benefits to your spouse or dependent kids, but only if you're still on active duty or you're in the Selected Reserve. You must also have completed at least six years of service and agree to add four more years to your contract, and the person you want to transfer your benefits to is enrolled in the Defense Enrollment Eligibility Reporting System, or DEERS. If you successfully transfer any of your unused Post-9/11 GI Bill benefits to a qualifying dependent, they get the same benefits you would: tuition, housing, and a books and supplies stipend.

Your spouse can use your GI Bill benefit right away or for up to 15 years after you separate from the military, but they don't qualify for the monthly housing allowance while you're still on active duty. Your child can't use the benefit unless you've finished at least ten years of service and they've received a high school diploma (or equivalency certificate) unless they're 18 or older (those over 18 don't need a diploma or high school equivalency certificate to use a parent's GI Bill benefits). Kids can't get MHA until you're off active duty, and they must use it by the time they turn 26 (but they don't have to use it within 15 years of your separation, which means you can transfer it to a toddler, get out of the military, and have the benefit waiting when they turn 18).

You can revoke or change a transfer of your GI Bill benefit at any time.

Montgomery GI Bill

Back before 2009, having $100 per month deducted from your paycheck for a year to pay for your access to the Montgomery GI Bill (MGIB) was a popular option; in fact, it was the *only* option. Today's new recruits can still choose that path to educational benefits, though most choose the Post-9/11 GI Bill (which doesn't require $1,200 of their own money) instead. I cover that bill in the earlier "Post-9/11 GI Bill" section.

When the Post-9/11 GI Bill came out, most troops chose to make the switch and relinquish their $1,200 buy-in. However, if you never did so, the Montgomery GI Bill is your jam. It comes in two types: one for active-duty troops and one for members of the Selected Reserve (which includes Army and Air National Guard).

Montgomery GI Bill Active Duty

Commonly known as the MGIB-AD, the Montgomery GI Bill Active Duty requires you to fall into one of four categories, all of which require you to have paid into the program. Only Category I is likely to apply to you unless you entered active duty military service before or during the 1990s.

>> **Category I:** You have a high school diploma, GED, or 12 hours of college credit and you entered active duty for the first time after June 30, 1985. You must also have served continuously for three years, or two years if that was your original enlistment agreement, or four years if you entered the Selected Reserve within a year of leaving active duty (that was called the 2 by 4 Program).

>> **Category II:** You entered active duty or signed a delayed enlistment program contract before January 1, 1977, and served well into the 1980s.

>> **Category III:** You don't qualify under Categories I or II and you were on active duty on September 30, 1990, and involuntarily separated after February 2, 1991, or involuntarily separated on or after November 30, 1993, or chose to voluntarily separate at any time under the Voluntary Separation Incentive (VSI) program or the Special Separation Benefit (SSB) program.

>> **Category IV:** You were on active duty on October 9, 1996, and had money in a Veterans' Educational Assistance Program account on that date, and you chose the MGIB before October 9, 1997, or you entered Title 32 National Guard service between July 1, 1985, and November 28, 1989.

If you do qualify for the MGIB-AD, you may be entitled to up to 36 months of education benefits each month. The amount you receive depends on how long you were in the military, what educational or training program you choose, and whether you qualify for a college fund or Kicker (the *Kicker* is an incentive to get service members to enlist or reenlist into special positions or units, and it increases the amount of money you can receive in GI Bill benefits). Your entitlement also depends on how much you paid into the $600 Buy-Up program. The catch: You have to use your MGIB-AD within ten years of separation in most cases.

TIP

If you started your military service by paying for the Montgomery GI Bill but later made the irrevocable election to use your Post-9/11 GI Bill, used all your Post-9/11 GI Bill benefits, and had entitlement remaining as the date of relinquishment of the Montgomery GI Bill, you may be entitled to a partial or complete refund of your original $1,200 investment. You should contact the VA about getting your money back.

TIP

If you have two separate qualifying periods of service, one with the Montgomery GI Bill and one with the Post-9/11 GI Bill, you may be entitled to receive benefits from both. In September 2020, the U.S. Court of Appeals for Veterans Claims issued a decision in the case *BO v. Wilkie* that allows veterans with two separate qualifying periods of service to use both programs' benefits with a 48-month overall cap. That means if you exhausted either program's 36-month entitlement, you can use the other program for up to 12 months. This ruling applies to only a limited number of vets, but if you're one of them, the VA is required to pay for an additional year of your education.

Montgomery GI Bill Selected Reserve

As a veteran of the Army, Air Force, Navy, Marine Corps or Coast Guard Reserve, or of the Army National Guard or Air National Guard, you may be eligible for the Montgomery GI Bill Selected Reserve, or MGIB-SR. With the MGIB-SR, you may be eligible for up to $384 per month in payments for up to 36 months. You can use that benefit for a degree program, remedial courses, deficiency courses, or refresher courses.

To qualify, your service obligation must have started after June 30, 1985 (and in some cases, after September 30, 1990). You must have also incurred a six-year service obligation to the Selected Reserve, or be an officer who agreed to serve an additional six years on top of your initial service obligation. You must also meet all the following criteria:

>> Complete your initial active duty for training, or IADT

>> Get a high school diploma or equivalency certificate before you finish IADT

>> Remain in good standing while serving in an active Selected Reserve unit

You're still eligible if you're discharged from your branch of the Selected Reserve if you're discharged from service for a disability that wasn't caused by misconduct.

If you join the Selected Reserve after leaving active duty, you may still be eligible for benefits under both the MGIB-SR and -AD programs, but you're not allowed to use them both at the same time. You should talk to a VA rep to find out what's best for you right now.

Finding Places to Use Your GI Bill

Most colleges and universities accept GI Bill payments. You can use your benefits at an institute of higher learning such as a four-year university, a community college, or an institution that provides an advanced degree program. You can even attend more than one college at the same time, as long as all the classes you're taking count toward your degree and the school that's granting your degree agrees to accept the classes from the other school to meet your degree program's requirements. And as long as you have an entitlement left over, you can earn one degree and get started on another.

TIP

You don't have to limit yourself to college, though. You can use your GI Bill for several other learning and training opportunities, including the following:

>> **Vocational or technical training, including non-college degree programs:** That means you can use your GI Bill to pay for trade school, vocational school, or specialized skill training schools (or a combination of these). Want to be a truck driver, HVAC professional, or EMT? You can use your GI Bill to pay for those training courses and many more.

>> **On-the-job or apprenticeship training:** Your job must meet certain criteria (including keeping you under supervision at least 50 percent of the time and leading to an entry-level position) for you to qualify. If you're setting your sights on becoming a union apprentice, such as a carpenter, electrician, line worker, pipefitter, firefighter, corrections officer, Department of Homeland Security customs or immigration officer, or other trade worker, you may be eligible to use your GI Bill for on-the-job or apprenticeship training.

>> **Licensing and certification:** You can use your GI Bill to pay for preparation courses and license or certification tests in some fields. Whether you want to become a real estate agent, mechanic, medical tech, or other professional who needs a particular license or certification, the GI Bill may have you covered.

>> **Testing:** The GI Bill can pay for nationally approved tests such as the SAT, LSAT, GRE, GMAT, and many more. You have no limit to the number of tests you can take (even if you don't pass). You can take tests you've passed in the past if they're required for re-certification or to retain a license you've already earned, too. The catch is that it's a *reimbursed* expense; you pay the registration fees, fees for specialized tests, and administrative fees and then let the VA know you want to be repaid. In some cases, the VA requires receipts.

>> **Flight training:** Your payment for flight training depends on the type you're enrolled in, such as a degree program or vocational flight training. Payments for flight training go out after you complete your training and your schools submits information to the VA.

>> **Correspondence training:** Correspondence training is different from distance learning that occurs at a college or university. In correspondence training, you receive lessons and have a certain amount of time to complete and return them for a grade. The VA reimburses correspondence students after receiving certification from the school.

>> **Work-study programs:** Full-time and ¾-time students in college degree programs or vocational or professional programs can use the GI Bill to pay for work-study with the VA. The VA chooses students for its work-study program based on job availability, ability to complete the contract before education benefits expire, disability, and other factors. As a work-study participant, you earn minimum wage (federal or state, whichever is greater), and you may elect to be paid in advance for some of your work.

>> **Entrepreneurship training:** You don't have to aim to work for someone else. As an honorably discharged veteran who qualifies for the Montgomery GI Bill or the Post-9/11 GI Bill, you may be eligible for VA reimbursement for approved entrepreneurship courses. You can even still qualify if you already own your own business, and you can use your benefits multiple times to take approved courses.

The way the VA calculates your GI Bill benefit when you use any of these options varies, but it typically depends on how much time you spend training toward a certification or licensure. Your VA rep can tell you exactly what you qualify to receive based on your specific training program.

Applying for GI Bill Benefits with the VA

Applying for your GI Bill isn't complicated, but it does require you to apply online, by mail, or in person at a VA regional office. You need basic information about the school or training facility you want to attend (or that you currently attend), your

Social Security number, bank account direct deposit information, and education and military history.

To apply online, you need a VA.gov account, DS Logon, or ID.me account; check out Chapter 19 for more on those. The VA website walks you through a series of questions, including which GI Bill benefit you want to use (the Post-9/11, MGIB-AD, or MGIB-SR, all of which I discuss earlier in the chapter) and your dates of military service. If you need help or don't understand your choices, call the VA's specialists at 888-442-4551 (that spells GI-BILL-1) Monday through Friday from 8 a.m. to 7 p.m. EST. You can also ask a veteran service organization, or VSO, to help you apply for benefits or walk into a VA regional office for assistance.

Perusing Other Programs to Get You Back in School

You don't have to rely on your GI Bill to get back to school. You may qualify for other programs that can pay your way as you develop the skills you need to earn post-military money.

Earning technical certifications through VET TEC

Veteran Employment Through Technology Education Courses, or VET TEC for short, can help you gain computer experience toward starting or advancing your career in the technology industry. The VET TEC program matches you with leading training providers without spending a dime of your GI Bill money. VET TEC covers training in computer software and programming, data processing, information science, and media applications.

TECHNICAL STUFF

Some of the certifications you can earn through the VET TEC program include "Cybersecurity Professional Penetration Tester" (that's a hacker!), "Advanced Software Development in ASP.NET Core," and "Front-End Web Designer." Dozens of other certifications are available, too, which may all be worth checking out.

You're eligible for VET TEC if you're within 180 days of separating from active duty or have already separated, you qualify for VA education assistance under the GI Bill, and you have at least one day of unexpired GI Bill entitlement. (That means even if you've used most of your GI Bill already, you can still qualify for this program.) You must also be accepted into a program by a VA-approved training provider, but don't worry; you don't have to find a provider on your own. The VA has a list for you to choose from.

If you qualify for this program, you get tuition payments that cover the cost of your program plus money for housing during your training. (But if you're active-duty, you don't get housing allowance.) If you attend training in person, the VA pays you a housing stipend equal to monthly military BAH for an E-5 with dependents, based on the ZIP code where you attend your training. If your training is online, you get half the BAH national average for an E-5 with dependents. However, this program has limited funding; you can participate only until funding runs out or when Congress appropriates new funds.

You can only apply for the VET TEC program online through the VA's website. You must apply for VA education benefits before you can apply for VET TEC because your eligibility for the program hinges on your eligibility for other VA education benefits. If the VA determines that you're good to go for VET TEC, you apply to the training provider of your choice, complete your program after acceptance, and receive a certification for your skills.

Discovering the Accelerated Payment Program

The Accelerated Payment Program can give you a lump-sum payment of 60 percent of tuition and fees for some high-cost, high-tech programs, such as biotechnology, electronics, aerospace, nuclear technology, and a handful of others. You may want or need to use this program if you can't afford a semester of school on what your GI Bill pays.

REMEMBER

You qualify for the Accelerated Payment Program only if you're using the Montgomery GI Bill Active Duty or the Montgomery GI Bill Selected Reserve and only if your tuition and fees are more than double the MGIB benefits you'd otherwise receive for that term. (You can read about the MGIB in the earlier section "Montgomery GI Bill.") This money is paid instead of those MGIB payments. The VA makes accelerated payments for only one term, quarter, or semester at a time unless the program doesn't operate that way; in that case, the VA makes an accelerated payment for the whole program.

You must also certify that you intend to seek employment in a high-tech industry (according to the VA's definition of "high-tech"). To apply, ask your school to include a request for accelerated payment to the VA, along with your certification that you'll seek employment in a high-tech industry, when it sends your enrollment information.

Finding Financial Aid

You may be eligible to use several types of financial aid outside the GI Bill, such as federal Pell Grants, which you never have to repay, and subsidized and unsubsidized student loans. You can also apply for scholarships.

Fiddling around with the FAFSA

The Free Application for Federal Student Aid, or FAFSA, is your ticket to more financial assistance for attending school. If you want to apply for any form of federal student aid, including Pell Grants, scholarships, and student loans, you must fill out the FAFSA first. You should fill out and file this form even if you're not sure whether you qualify or you intend to apply for federal student aid.

You can fill out the FAFSA at studentaid.gov. Before you do so, you need an FSA ID, which requires you to have your Social Security number and your own mobile phone number or email address. It takes a few days before the government can verify your Social Security number and other information. After your information is verified, you need personal identifying information, your federal tax returns, bank statements, untaxed income information, and documentation on assets you own to fill out and file your FAFSA.

REMEMBER

You must file your FAFSA by a certain date to be eligible to apply for aid the following school year. In fact, you may have up to three different deadlines (one for the federal government, one for your state, and one for your school). And you have to file a new FAFSA every year for which you want to apply for federal student aid.

Your GI Bill benefits may affect the amount of federal aid you can receive, but it happens in a roundabout way. Your original GI Bill benefits, such as housing allowance, tuition payments, and your books and supplies stipend, are entitlements, which means they don't count as part of your income. However, when FAFSA calculates your expected family contribution to your educational costs, other types of VA benefits, such as the work–study allowance, do count toward your income.

Many veterans service organizations, including the American Legion and Disabled American Veterans, can help you fill out and file the FAFSA. (I cover veterans service organizations in more detail in Chapter 10.)

WARNING

Don't pay someone to help you complete your FAFSA. The application process is designed for students, and if you need help, it's available on the FAFSA website, through the VA, or through a veterans service organization (and you don't need to be a member of a VSO to get help from one). If a company offers to complete your application for a fee, steer clear; plenty of free, high-quality help is available to you.

Fishing for types of federal student aid

The federal government can help you through a number of grants and loans. Some of the most common, which all require you to fill out and file the FAFSA (see the preceding section), include the following:

>> **Federal Supplemental Educational Opportunity Grants:** These grants, commonly called FSEOGs, are need-based and can cover up to $4,000 per year.

>> **Pell Grants:** You never have to pay back a Pell Grant. However, they're available only to undergraduate students who don't have a degree, and they're generally based on financial need.

>> **Perkins Loans:** Perkins Loans are federal, low-interest student loans that are available to people with "exceptional financial need." The school acts as the lender.

>> **Subsidized Stafford Direct Loans:** These are need-based loans that charge no interest for students who attend school at least half-time.

>> **Unsubsidized Stafford Loans:** These aren't need-based loans. Your school determines how much you may borrow, and interest begins on these loans from the moment they're paid.

ARE STUDENT LOANS WORTH IT?

The average college graduate has borrowed around $30,000 to pay for school, and total student debt in the United States is in the trillions (you read that right). If you can avoid taking out a student loan, you should. First, you have to pay interest, which can be astronomical (and compounds daily). That means that if you graduate with $30,000 in student loan debt, interest accrues the day after you graduate; then, the next day, you pay interest on the original loan amount plus the interest you accrued the day before. You pay interest as your balance climbs every day. Second, falling behind on payments can lead to delinquency and default, which trashes your credit score.

Student loans can also harm your debt-to-income ratio, which is important when you want to buy a home or take out another type of loan. And on average, paying off student loans (even if you don't graduate) takes 21 years. These are just a few reasons to avoid student loans. Although college *is* an investment in your future, plenty of other routes are available to you, including your GI Bill, the Yellow Ribbon Program, and free grants from the government.

>> **TEACH Grants:** TEACH is short for the Teacher Education Assistance for College and Higher Education. It may provide up to $4,000 per year to students who are going to school to become educators. To qualify for this grant, which you don't need to repay, you must agree that you'll teach in a high-need area or in a school that serves low-income families.

Petitioning for scholarships

Scholarships are financial aid awards that can help you pay for an undergraduate degree. They can be based on need, academic achievement, membership in a group, or other factors. A scholarship can be a one-time check paid to your school, a renewable benefit you can use again, or a direct deposit to your bank account. They come from a wide range of sources, including federal and state governments, clubs, charities, businesses, colleges and universities, and even individuals. Some are designed especially for veterans, and I cover the most popular in the following list:

>> **AMVETS scholarships:** AMVETS scholarships are only available to veterans, active-duty servicemembers, and Guard and Reserve members, as well as their spouses, children, and grandchildren. You must provide evidence of service status and demonstrate financial need as well as meet other requirements you can find at amvets.org.

>> **Purple Heart Scholarship Fund:** Recipients of the Purple Heart and their spouses, children, and grandchildren are eligible to apply for the Purple Heart Scholarship Program at purpleheart.org if the recipient is a member of the Military Order of the Purple Heart.

>> **Rogers STEM Scholarship:** The Edith Nourse Rogers Science, Technology, Engineering, and Math Scholarship allows some eligible veterans in high-demand fields extend their Post-9/11 GI Bill benefits for up to nine months. You must be currently enrolled in an undergraduate STEM degree program or qualifying dual-degree program or have earned a post-secondary degree or graduate degree in an approved STEM degree field while being enrolled in a covered clinical training program for healthcare professionals. Or, you must have earned a post-secondary degree in an approved STEM degree field and be working toward earning a teaching certification to qualify. You can apply on the VA's website.

>> **Women's Overseas Service League:** The Women's Overseas Service League awards scholarships annually to women who are committed to advancement in military or other public service careers and have demonstrated that commitment through life experiences. You must have successfully completed at least 12 semester hours of study in any institution of higher learning with a minimum grade-point average of 2.5 as well as meet the other requirements listed on the organization's website at wosl.org.

Chapter **17**

Fitting into Your New Role as a Student

When I first left the Army, I continued working toward the degree I had started years before, but I went in person, as opposed to the online classes I had been taking while I was in. I couldn't believe the audacity of the students who laid their heads down on their desks and drooled their way through the professors' lectures (and more than once, I was tempted to kick someone's chair leg and tell them to stand up and do cherry-pickers until they were no longer so sleepy). I was also older than nearly everyone in my classes, including some of the instructors, and I had a hard time relating to the people around me who had spent the last few years partying when I'd done a couple of tours in a combat zone. I felt like a fish out of water, and I wanted to quit.

Although I want to tell you that it'll be easier for you, it may not be. You may face some of the same issues that I and millions of other veterans have faced, and I want you to be prepared. Fortunately, you can use plenty of resources to make fitting into your new role as a student easier, and I outline them (and give you some unsolicited-but-sage advice) in this chapter.

Tapping into Your Academic Advisor's Knowledge

When you enroll in a college, you'll most likely be assigned an academic advisor. Your *academic advisor* is a professional staff or faculty member trained to help you with your academic planning. They can help you explore your academic interests, choose the right courses, and identify resources that can help you reach your college goals. An academic advisor can also refer you to other campus offices for help in several areas, including career counseling, academic skills development, financial aid, and even personal issues.

Many schools require you to meet with an academic advisor shortly after you enroll and before you register for classes. And although it may seem like an inconvenience, your advisor can help you identify your goals and reach them, as well as avoid taking courses that don't count toward your degree, find opportunities you didn't know existed, and help you map out a course schedule that works around your family and work obligations.

Visiting On-Campus Veterans' Resources

Many colleges and universities have a veterans' services office. Yours may be called a Student Veterans Resource Center, Veteran Services, or something different, but no matter what terminology your school uses, it's a place worth visiting. Some of these centers have computers, lounge areas, snack bars, and professionals who can help you get the most from your GI Bill, which I cover in Chapter 16, as well as connections with local veterans' organizations.

A lot of veterans' organizations also operate on college campuses, and your school may even have specific veterans' groups. You can most likely find information on these groups at your college or university's veterans' office or by talking to the school's veteran liaison. Student Veterans of America has a network of more than 1,500 on-campus chapters, and many schools have their own versions of these types of groups as well. They're often called something like "Student Veterans' Association at [your school's name]." Some of the organizations you find are purely social; people get together and help each other navigate academia while hanging out. Other organizations are service-based, which means the members do things together to benefit the community, such as fundraising or volunteering at nearby VFW or American Legion halls.

In addition to regular veterans' clubs and organizations, you may be able to join a fraternity or sorority that's exclusive to vets. Omega Delta Sigma is a national, coed veterans' fraternity that operates on several campuses all over the United States, and your school may have its own version as well.

Utilizing Your School's Career Services and Job Placement Opportunities

Colleges and universities typically have career services offices that help prepare students for the job market. These offices can assist you with a wide range of things that can help you prepare for civilian employment after you have your degree, including

>> **Decision-making:** A counselor at your school's career services office can help you choose the right future career, even if you have no idea where you're headed. These counselors can use self-assessment tools that help you examine your personality type, interests, values, and abilities. Think of these types of tests as ASVABs for civilian jobs. After you settle on a career path, your career counselor even helps you figure out which major you need to pursue to reach your goals.

>> **Resume-writing:** If you don't find enough help in Chapter 7 of this book, where I cover a huge amount of information on how to write amazing resumes and cover letters, your career counselor can lend you a hand. (You can also check out *Resumes For Dummies* by Laura DeCarlo, published by Wiley, for all the ingredients you need to concoct an irresistible resume.)

>> **Job interview preparation:** When you're ready for job interviews, check to see whether your school's career services office sponsors workshops that help you learn about acing an interview, which I also cover in Chapter 11. You may even be able to run through mock interviews where you can practice your skills.

>> **Job fairs and recruiting:** Many career services offices host job fairs and recruiting events, and sometimes they even have career management systems and job portals where you can look at employment listings. You may even be able to upload your resume to a searchable database that your school maintains; sometimes recruiters and employers scour these databases looking for desirable job candidates.

>> **Networking:** Your college or university's career services section can most likely point you toward networking events where you can rub elbows with people in your chosen field. (I explain how to get the most out of networking in Chapter 10.)

Getting in Touch with the VA about Problems with Your School

The Principles of Excellence program requires schools that get federal funding (such as the money that comes from your GI Bill) to follow certain guidelines. These schools must give you a personalized, written summary of the total cost of your educational program (including the financial aid you may qualify for), assign you a point of contact for ongoing academic and financial advice, and give you a timeline that explains when and how you can fulfill your graduation requirements. They must also accredit all new programs before enrolling students, have refund policies that follow Title IV rules (the rules that govern federal student financial aid programs), and avoid fraudulent, deceitful, or aggressive methods of recruiting.

No school is perfect, but you should contact the Department of Veterans Affairs if you encounter a serious issue related to an educational institution's

>> Accreditation

>> Changes in degree plans or requirements

>> Grade policies

>> Quality of education

>> Recruiting or marketing practices

>> Refund issues

>> Transfer or credits

>> Tuition and fee charges

The VA will review and investigate your complaint as well as forward it to your school for a response. The VA will review the response and, if necessary, take action to protect other students.

Finding Civilians on the Map

Civilians who go straight to college after high school often develop their identities there. That's where they learn to be adults, become entrenched in the habits that will stick with them the rest of their lives, and map out their futures. But you've already done those things, and the things that shaped you are different from textbooks, study groups, and frat parties. You're already "adulting," and you have been since the day you stepped off the bus at basic training (or maybe even before you signed the dotted line).

Individualism rules on college campuses, but you're cut from the same camouflaged cloth as all your military peers are. You may worry that the people around you have a negative view of servicemembers and the military, so you may choose to keep to yourself and avoid making much of an effort to fit in. That, coupled with issues you may be experiencing on a personal level — such as post-traumatic stress, anxiety, culture shock, and other things that affect your day-to-day life — can make fitting in seem impossible. Although you should do what makes you most comfortable, a 2017 study draws a direct correlation between veterans developing social relationships at school and their decisions to finish the requirements to earn a degree.

Re-charting your personal course

When you're suddenly immersed in an entirely different culture, you can easily feel like the odd one out. You may not understand the people around you, and you may assume that they won't understand you, either. Remember that civilians may have a tough time relating to veterans because they don't know many, and that's understandable. (You probably don't know a million civilians, either.) The fact is that, to a degree, you've been institutionalized; it happens when you live under the rules of a specific institution for a long time. You probably became used to relying on the guidance and instruction the military provided, and now that you've thrust yourself into a totally different world, you're going to experience a little bit of a culture shock.

Going to school may cause you to struggle with your own identity, so some experts suggest creating a new definition of yourself. Until now, you've been a Soldier, Airman, Marine, Sailor, or Coast Guardsman, and that's been an inextricable part of your identity. But you're a veteran, and you're a student, and you're so many other things. Maybe you're a parent, or an expert euchre player, or a gamer. Whatever you are, your life doesn't revolve around the military anymore — and your identity doesn't have to revolve around the fact that you're a veteran.

TIP

Do yourself a favor and stop toting around a digi-cam backpack with web straps, let your hair grow out or take it out of the bun, and don't try to live up to the "dysfunctional veteran" stereotype.

Adjusting your attitude

School isn't a do-or-die environment like the military is, and that means you're now exposed to a wide range of people who think, talk, and act differently than what you're used to. Where you were once surrounded by people who shared your values, traditions, and culture, you're now in the middle of a group of people who may never have even considered the military to be a viable career choice.

And if you feel like you're too different to fit in, you're superior to civilians because you've been in the military, or that nobody will understand you, you need to change your perspective before you make things harder on yourself than they need to be.

The people around you in school — stick with me here — aren't completely different from you. They may not understand what shaped your perspectives, where you've been, or the things you've done, but that doesn't mean they can't relate to you (or that you can't relate to them). In fact, holding a "we're so different" mentality can hold you back from reaching your full potential. Making generalizations about civilians, being elitist, and automatically shutting people out causes you more trouble than it's worth.

You're going to encounter people from all different backgrounds for the rest of your life, and now's as good a time as any to start getting used to it. After you're out of the military, you're likely not going back in, and you're not going to have much luck changing the civilian world to meet your expectations. Maybe you don't need the type of advice you see plastered on photos of sunsets on social media, like "Don't look back, because you're not going that way," but I am going to tell you that now that you're out of the military, it's time to embrace the fact that you're a civilian now, too.

You won't like everyone you meet; you may even dislike many of them. But don't let your ego get in the way of connecting with others. If you're still hung up on stereotypes about civilians, take some time to figure out where you learned them. (I'll give you a hint: You didn't think this way before you signed your first contract with the military.)

Oh, and don't look back, because you're not going that way.

4

Adjusting to Civilian Life

Make sense (and cents) out of financial guidance that keeps you on track.

Get access to the benefits you earned during your time in the military.

Discover each branch's wounded warrior transition programs and what they offer.

Find out where you can go when you need some additional help.

Chapter **18**

Managing Your Money as a Civilian

Money matters are different for civilians than they are for servicemembers. First, most civilians don't get housing or subsistence allowance, nontaxable combat pay, or family separation pay, and they must find and pay for their own health insurance. They don't have a first-line leader telling them that buying a sports-car with an $800-per-month payment is a terrible idea at their pay grade, nor do they have access to a military branch's community service organization to get an emergency loan when they hit a rough patch. Civilian pay doesn't come with guarantees, either; civilians can lose their jobs in the blink of an eye. That's a big contrast from the military, where you know exactly when your contract expires and you're out of a job (and even if you're involuntarily separated, military red tape causes that process to take a long time).

Unfortunately, civilians don't have a basic training program that lays it all out for you; you hang up your uniform and start fending for yourself, which can be particularly stressful (or downright scary) if you've been in the military for a long time. Maybe you've never lived on your own in the civilian world, so you're really lost in the sauce right now. If either of those sounds like your situation, don't stress too much; in this chapter, I address most of the issues you're likely to face.

Comparing Military versus Civilian Pay

As a civilian, you have to plan for regular monthly living costs that you didn't have to pay for in the military, plus surprise expenses, retirement, and travel. You have to adjust to the loss of

>> Basic allowance for housing (BAH)

>> Basic allowance for subsistence (BAS)

>> Cost-of-living allowance, if you received it

>> Subsidized childcare, if you used a military program to help you pay

>> Free healthcare coverage for you and your family

That can all be pretty challenging, particularly when you consider that only about half of post-9/11 veterans find a new job less than six months after starting their job searches. For 21 percent, finding new employment takes between six months and a year; for about 16 percent, that timeline is more than a year. That's why it's in your best interest to start looking for a job *long* before you get out of the military.

THE STRUGGLE IS REAL

The reality is that many veterans struggle financially for at least a few years after leaving the service. A Pew Research study from 2019 says that 61 percent of veterans with post-traumatic stress have trouble paying bills, and 22 percent receive food benefits from the government in the first few years after separation. The numbers are nuanced, too; about 49 percent of nonwhite veterans say they had trouble paying bills, compared with 32 percent of white vets, and overall, female vets are more likely to rely on food benefits such as the Supplemental Nutrition Assistance Program (SNAP) than their male counterparts are. The study doesn't address how many veterans qualify for government assistance (only those who apply for and receive it), and experts believe that number is much higher. If you're one of the significant number of veterans who find themselves struggling, help is available; I cover some of the resources you may be able to use in Chapter 21.

Additionally, more of your civilian paycheck is taxable. When you were in the military, the government didn't take its cut from many of your allowances (such as BAH or BAS); that money went directly into your bank account. However, for the most part, your entire civilian paycheck *is* taxable, and that means Uncle Sam takes his cut before you see a dime of your hard-earned money. And if you didn't pay state income taxes while you were in the military because your state didn't require them for military pay, you have to adjust to paying them now. Civilians don't get those kinds of exemptions, so you may need to find a job that pays more than what you made in the military to enjoy the same standard of living.

Making Rent without BAH

Whether you received basic allowance for housing or lived in the barracks your entire military career, one thing's for sure: You're going to have to pay rent or make a mortgage payment when you get out. And although you may be able to put off that expense by living with a friend or family member for a while, that's not an effective long-term solution for most people — which means you have to earn enough money through a civilian job to pay for housing. Civilian housing costs are different from those in the military; though you may have paid application fees, background check fees, and utility bills while you were in, the military is no longer able to help you with a security deposit through an emergency relief loan or provide you with on-installation housing when you want it.

Paying application fees

Landlords — the people, companies, or entities that own property that's available to rent — aren't required to charge you an application fee for an apartment or rental house, but many won't even consider your application if you don't pay one. To play devil's advocate for a moment, landlords want you to pay an application fee so they know you're not out applying all over town and wasting their time. Some landlords also use high application fees to determine whether you have extra cash to burn (and are therefore more likely to be able to pay your rent). But of course, that doesn't make coughing up $30 (or more) just to get a landlord to consider your application any easier. Some, but not all, states have caps on the amount a landlord is allowed to ask you to pay for an application fee. If you encounter a fee that's too high, you can always ask the property owner whether they can waive it.

Landlords may also charge a fee to cover the cost of running a criminal background check on you and anyone else who's going to live with you. The fees may be included in your application fee, or they may be separate charges. Landlords aren't usually allowed to make a profit from background check fees, but in some cases they are allowed to charge you a "processing" or "administration" fee for the time they spend on obtaining and reviewing the background check.

Saving for a security deposit

A *security deposit* is a sum of money you give a landlord in addition to your advance rental payment. It's a kind of insurance for your landlord; they can keep the money if you fail to pay rent or you damage the space. However, your landlord can't keep the money free-and-clear; they must return it to you when your rental agreement expires, less any fees for damages you caused or rent you didn't pay.

Security deposits are usually equal to one month's rent, but sometimes they're equal to one and a half times your rental payment (or more). If you have pets, you may also be required to pay a *pet deposit*, which is a fixed sum of money that covers potential damage your four-, two-, or no-legged family members may cause to the place. Your landlord can deduct things like carpet cleaning fees and repairs from your pet deposit, so keep in mind that you may not get any of it back, depending on your state's renter protection laws.

Making rent payments

Civilian paychecks usually don't include a housing allowance, although some executive jobs do offer company housing benefits. The vast majority of civilians have to come up with rent payments on their own.

Most people pay rent every month, though agreements exist where the period between payments is shorter or longer. Landlords have absolutely no limit on what they can charge you for rent, but most try to stick with the going rate for the area because nobody's realistically going to pay twice what others are paying for comparable homes in the same community.

REMEMBER

Only about 30 percent of your income should go toward your rental payment. If you spend that amount, maintaining a good balance between comfort and affordability is possible. On a median income, that's enough to leave some cash in your bank account after paying average bills and handling other expenses. (But do yourself a favor and be as thrifty as you can.)

WARNING

In some areas, housing costs far surpass average wages, so keep that in mind as you decide where to settle down. For example, a city with an average rent of $2,500 may not be the best place for you if you anticipate making $3,000 per month after you leave the military unless you want to pick up some roommates or compromise on the type of home you're comfortable living in. Military BAH and cost-of-living allowance help you offset high rental costs, but when you stop working for the military, those perks evaporate. Scouring rental listings in areas you want to live *before* you actually get out of the military is a smart idea.

Understanding the impact of utility bills

On some military installations, utility usage (gas, electricity, water, trash disposal, and even cable TV and Internet service) is free or discounted; on others, such as those overseas, you receive an additional utility allowance to offset the cost of your home's power use. But in the civilian world, the companies that provide those services expect you to fork over some of your hard-earned cash to pay for them; if you don't, it's lights-out (or water-, gas-, or cable-out) until you can catch up. Therefore, you have to budget for utility bills. Some landlords pay some utility costs, such as water and trash collection. Even if those add-ins aren't offered, it doesn't hurt to ask a prospective landlord when you're contemplating signing a lease.

REMEMBER

Although some local and state governments regulate utility companies' profits by limiting how much they can charge consumers, that's not the case in every area. And if there's only one electric, Internet, gas, or other utility company in town, you can expect to pay more than you would if two or more others were competing for your business. Companies that have the monopoly on these services can often charge whatever they want.

Most of your utility bills will fluctuate from month to month depending on how much you use (though some, like your phone or Internet bill, are likely to stay the same). You can usually calculate the average utility costs in the city where you intend to live on the service providers' websites or by doing a little Internet sleuthing.

TIP

You can cut out unnecessary utility costs by turning out the lights when you're not using them, canceling things you don't really need but that seem like utilities (the average cable TV bill is now over $217 per month), and being careful about things like hot water usage. And if you grew up in a house with a parent's hawk-eye on the thermostat, you may need to develop that skill yourself.

Side-Eyeing Housing Discrimination

Housing discrimination occurs when a landlord, home-seller, real estate agent, property manager, or anyone involved in the housing process takes any of the following actions because of a person's race, color, religion, sex, disability, familial status, or national origin:

>> Refuses to rent or sell housing

>> Refuses to negotiate for housing

>> Makes housing unavailable

» Sets different terms, conditions or privileges for sale or rental of a dwelling

» Provides different housing services or facilities to different people

» Falsely denies that housing is available for inspection, rental, or sale

» Makes, prints, or publishes any notice, statement, or advertisement involving the sale or rental of a dwelling that indicates any preference, limitation, or discrimination

» Charges different sales prices or rental charges

» Evicts a tenant or a tenant's guest

» Harasses the person

» Delays or fails to perform maintenance or repairs

» Limits privileges, services, or facilities of a dwelling

» Discourages the purchase or rental of a dwelling

» Assigns someone to a particular building or neighborhood or a particular section of a building or neighborhood

Housing discrimination also occurs in mortgage lending, such as when a lender does one of the following based on a person's race, color, religion, sex, disability, familial status, or national origin:

» Refuses to make a loan or provide other financial assistance for a dwelling

» Refuses to provide information on loans

» Imposes different terms or conditions on a loan (such as interest rates and fees)

Housing discrimination is illegal under the Fair Housing Act, Title VI of the Civil Rights Act of 1964, and a number of other federal laws, as well as some state laws. You can find out more about housing discrimination, as well as what to do if it happens to you, on the U.S. Department of Housing and Urban Development at www.hud.gov.

Buying a House with (or without) a VA Loan

If you decide to buy a house and stay in one place for more than three years after you leave the military, and if your discharge is honorable, you can use your VA loan benefit to your advantage. The money for this loan doesn't come from the VA;

it comes from a private lender, and the VA guarantees a portion of it. That gives your lender the warm-and-fuzzies that it'll be able to recoup some money if you walk away from making your mortgage payments, and it enables lenders to give you more favorable terms (such as more competitive interest rates) than they ordinarily would.

VA loans are packed with other benefits that can help you on the path to home-ownership, which is sometimes cheaper (especially in the long run) than renting is:

>> **No down payment:** You can purchase a home with your VA loan without coming up with a down payment, which means your mortgage covers the entire cost of the home. That can result in higher monthly payments than you'd pay if you had a down payment, but it means that you don't have to save tens of thousands of dollars to get moved into your own place. (For more on how down payments work and why you may want to make one anyway, check out the later section "Saving for a down payment.")

>> **No private mortgage insurance requirement:** The VA prohibits lenders from making you buy private mortgage insurance (PMI) if you put down less than 20 percent of the home's sales price for a down payment. PMI is business as usual with other types of loans; it protects the lender if the borrower stops making payments. It usually costs between 0.5 percent and 5 percent of the total amount of a mortgage loan per year until the buyer builds up 20 percent equity in the home.

>> **No prepayment penalty:** The VA doesn't allow lenders to charge you a prepayment penalty when you use a VA loan, which means you can pay it off as early as you want to save yourself some money on interest. With a traditional loan, you have to keep making payments for the loan's entire lifespan; otherwise, you may face a *prepayment penalty,* which is a lump-sum payment that helps the lender recoup some of the money it would've made off your paying interest.

>> **Different qualification requirements:** Lenders can't deny you a loan based solely on your credit score; the VA requires them to look at your entire financial picture when they make a determination. You still have to have acceptable credit, but it doesn't have to be perfect (or even necessarily good).

>> **Limited closing costs:** The VA limits the *closing costs* (fees such as title insurance and property tax paid when you close on the house) lenders are allowed to charge you. For comparison, if you use a conventional loan that has nothing to do with your VA loan benefit, you can expect to spend between 2 and 5 percent of the total loan amount at closing; if you're talking about a loan that's a few hundred thousand dollars, that can really add up. And as an added bonus, sellers are allowed to pay your closing costs for you on a VA loan, as is customary in some housing markets.

The best part? The process for obtaining a VA loan isn't much more complicated than any other type of loan is; in fact, you probably won't even notice the difference after you obtain your Certificate of Eligibility (COE) from the Department of Veterans Affairs.

Using your VA loan benefit has some catches. For example, you must live in the home as your primary residence for a certain period of time, and you must pay a VA Funding Fee (however, you can roll that into your mortgage amount).

The idea that you can only use your VA loan benefit once is a common myth. As long as you satisfy your current VA loan (meaning that you pay it off completely), you can take out another one as soon as the last is paid off.

You don't have to use your VA loan benefit to buy a home, but for most people, it's the smart choice. The VA also offers other home-related programs that can help you, as well, such as these:

>> Native American Direct Loan Program, which is available to Native American veterans or veterans whose spouses are Native Americans to buy, build, or improve a home on federal trust land.

>> Adapted Housing Grants, which are funds you can use to buy or change a home to meet your needs so you can live more independently if you have a service-connected disability. You don't have to pay back grants.

You can read up on these benefits (and many others) on the VA's website at https://benefits.va.gov/homeloans.

Timing your purchase the right way

Buying a home is time-consuming. It's faster if you pay all-cash for a home, but unless you have hundreds of thousands of dollars lying around, you'll need a mortgage loan. Closing on a home can take between 30 and 90 days depending on your circumstances; that means you may wait three months from the time you make an offer to the time you get the keys to your new home. You may need to find a temporary rental home if you leave the military without enough time to find and purchase a house, so keep that in mind if you intend to buy.

If you're being involuntarily separated from the military under honorable conditions or retiring, you may be eligible for up to 30 days of leave to facilitate your relocation. Your spouse may also be entitled to take a round trip on a military aircraft without you to handle housing needs.

Knowing whether you're staring down a money pit

No matter how eager you are to buy a home, you need to make sure it's not going to do you more harm than good. There's certainly something to be said for buying a fixer-upper and living in it while you make repairs, which you can do with a VA rehab and renovation loan, but you have to be extremely careful that you don't get more than you bargained for.

When a seller accepts your offer to buy, coming up with the money to hire a qualified home inspector is in your best interest. A professional home inspection can cost between $200 and $500, but only a skilled inspector can tell you whether you're about to dive headfirst into a money pit that will fall apart as soon as you bring in your first piece of furniture.

REMEMBER

Only some states require home inspectors to be licensed, so do your homework before you make a hiring decision.

Saving for a down payment

When you use your VA loan benefit, you don't have to come up with a down payment to buy a house. However, the more money you can put down when you buy, the lower your monthly mortgage payments will be.

For example, if you take out a 30-year, fixed-rate mortgage for a home that costs $300,000 and pay 3.92 percent in interest with no down payment, your monthly mortgage payments are $1,418.

But say you put down $25,000 on the same home, which means you only have to borrow $275,000. If all the other conditions are the same, your monthly mortgage payment will be $1,300.

WARNING

Some lenders add property taxes and homeowners insurance into your monthly mortgage payment, then hold the money in *escrow* (a special account for safe-keeping). The initial math you see may not include those recurring fees. Ask your loan officer if your monthly payment amount includes these payments or if you have to pay them separately.

If you don't use your VA loan benefit, your lender will likely ask you to come up with a 20 percent down payment. If you don't, you'll be subject to paying for private mortgage insurance and may not qualify for the best interest rates. However, other loan programs are available through the government that may allow you to buy a home with 0, 3, 5, or 10 percent down, such as USDA, FHA, and some Fannie Mae and Freddie Mac home loan programs. You'll likely have to purchase PMI if you use these loan products, which have nothing to do with your military service. However, they may be viable alternatives if you aren't eligible for a VA loan.

Scoring Your Own Health Insurance

You may not be a huge fan of the military's go-to medical advice ("Drink water, rub some dirt on it, and walk it off"), but free medical care is nothing to scoff at. While you're a military member, you and your dependents get no-cost access to preventive medicine, specialized treatments for injuries and disabilities, and a wide range of other types of care, including physical therapy, dental, and optical. But as a civilian, you have to pay for medical care out of your own pocket, either at the point of service (where you receive treatment, such as an urgent care center or doctor's office) or by spending money on private health insurance.

Some employers contribute to health insurance costs, and some veterans are entitled to use the VA medical system or TRICARE, the military's insurance program, but generally speaking, you're on the hook for your own healthcare costs. And I'm not going to lie: Health insurance is expensive. I cover common types of civilian healthcare plans in the later section "Clearing up civilian healthcare options."

Using the VA medical system

The VA is the largest integrated healthcare system in the United States, and you know what that means: plenty of red tape to go around. However, it also provides top-tier care in many situations, so if you qualify for VA medical benefits, you should absolutely use them.

VA healthcare eligibility

Not everyone is eligible for VA healthcare benefits, and some people qualify for some types of healthcare but not others. You may be eligible if were released or discharged from active duty with an honorable or general (under honorable conditions) discharge. You're more likely to qualify if you

>> Were discharged or separated for medical reasons, early out, or hardship

>> Served in a combat theater within the past five years

>> Are a Purple Heart or Medal of Honor recipient

>> Were a prisoner of war

>> Receive a VA pension or disability benefits

>> Receive state Medicaid benefits

>> Served in the Persian Gulf before November 11, 1998

If you received a bad conduct, other than honorable (OTH), or dishonorable discharge, you can qualify for VA healthcare with a service-connected disability or condition that was aggravated by your service. Otherwise, you have to apply for a discharge upgrade or ask the VA to review your character of discharge. I cover getting your discharge changed in Chapter 5.

REMEMBER

In most circumstances, you must apply for VA healthcare; the VA doesn't just funnel you into the program. You must fill out an application online, by mail, or in person at any VA medical center or clinic. The exception: The VA will provide you with emergency mental health treatment at any VA medical facility — 24 hours a day, 7 days a week — or at a Vet Center during normal business hours, regardless of your discharge status, how long you've been out of the military, or anything else.

Tipping the scales with TRICARE for retirees

Many military retirees choose to continue using TRICARE, the military's health insurance program that covers dependents. Retired servicemembers and their families are eligible for TRICARE Prime, Select, For Life, or Select Overseas, or the U.S. Family Health Plan, as well as dental and optical coverage. You don't have to use TRICARE if you find a better option, but you can use it in addition to other types of private insurance to provide fuller coverage.

Perusing employer-sponsored plans

Some civilian employers pay all or part of their workers' health insurance costs. In fact, employer-sponsored coverage is the most common way people get health insurance in the United States. The Affordable Care Act, which you may know as Obamacare, requires employers with at least 50 full-time employees to provide at least some healthcare coverage to their workers. If they don't, they pay a penalty to the Internal Revenue Service.

Employer-sponsored healthcare means that your employer pays at least a small percentage of your health insurance costs; you're responsible for the remainder. Choosing an employer-sponsored plan certainly makes sense (as long as it provides adequate coverage) when you consider that in 2020, the average monthly cost for private health insurance was $456 for an individual and $1,152 for families. Insurance costs vary based on factors like your age, income, location, and how often you make doctor's visits, to name a few.

Clearing up civilian healthcare options

Civilian healthcare is confusing, and figuring out what's best for you and your family can be difficult. Although you can currently go without health insurance without a penalty (as of this writing), that means you have to pay out of pocket for all your medical costs, including sports physicals, dental cleanings, and urgent or emergency treatments. You have a lot of options for civilian health coverage, including the following:

>> **Health Maintenance Organization plans, or HMOs:** These plans have their own networks of doctors, hospitals, and other providers. If you have an HMO, you can only see providers in the network; otherwise, you pay for your care out of pocket except in emergencies.

>> **Preferred Provider Organization plans, or PPOs:** These plans, like HMOs, have their own networks of providers, and you pay less if you use them. You pay more if you use doctors, hospitals, or providers outside the network.

>> **Exclusive Provider Organization plans, or EPOs:** These plans are like HMOs because they require you to see doctors, specialists, and other providers in their networks. You may use out-of-network providers in an emergency.

>> **Point of Service plans, or POS (I know):** In these plans, you pay less if you use in-network providers. They also require you to get a referral from your primary care provider if you need to see a specialist.

>> **Catastrophic coverage:** Catastrophic health coverage covers only three primary care visits per year, has higher deductibles and copayments, and requires you to be under the age of 30 or get a hardship exemption.

- » **Medicare:** Medicare is government health coverage for people who are 65 or older, or for younger people who have disabilities, as well as those who have end-stage renal disease, or ESRD. Medicare has four parts: Part A covers hospital stays and some other types of care; Part B covers some doctors' services, outpatient care and medical supplies, and some preventive medicine; and Part D covers prescription drugs. (Part C is like an HMO or PPO and is offered through private companies.)

- » **Medicaid:** Medicaid is the United States' public health insurance program for people with low income. In fact, it covers one in five people in the United States as of 2021.

- » **The Children's Health Insurance Program, or CHIP:** This government program provides low-cost health coverage to children in families that earn too much money to qualify for Medicaid. Every state offers CHIP coverage, and each has its own rules about who qualifies.

Taking a Wise Approach to Credit

If times are tough because you lost the financial perks of being in the service, you may be tempted to accept all the credit card offers you're getting in the mail or hit up a payday loan place to tide you over. Not so fast, though; I explain why these options are bad ideas and offer a better approach in the following sections.

Handling credit

Every time you shopped at the PX, BX, MCX, NEX, or another store on a military installation, you may have been asked to save 15 percent by signing up for a credit card with the Exchange Credit Program. You know it as the Military Star card. You may already have a credit card (or several), or you may be entirely new to the revolving credit scene. Although I'm not going to give you financial advice, I am going to tell you that you need to be extremely careful when you apply for and use credit cards.

WARNING

Credit isn't a good cash substitute because it comes with interest attached, it can lead you to massive amounts of debt, and it can hamper your ability to buy a car or home. Traditional wisdom says that you should only purchase things with a credit card if you have the money to pay your balance immediately.

Managing debt through consolidation

If you've already racked up a bit of debt, either during your time in the military or shortly after getting out, don't panic. You may be able to consolidate debt you owe to different organizations and roll it all into one monthly payment at a lower interest rate. (This tactic is generally only a good idea if you can get a lower interest rate.) Be wary of debt consolidation firms that charge you a fee and claim that they'll clean up your credit, though. You can do the same thing yourself by taking out a personal loan or getting a new credit card that lets you transfer all your balances without exorbitant fees.

For example, if you have four credit cards with interest rates ranging from 17.99 percent to 24.99 percent, it makes sense to apply for a personal loan that has a 10 percent (or lower) interest rate, pay off your debt with it, and make a single monthly payment to pay off your loan. You should consult with a financial professional before you make a move like this, but know that it may be a simple way for you to save money immediately.

Avoiding potentially predatory lenders

I'm just going to be frank: Payday and title lenders are there to rip you off. Pawn shops aren't much better. *Payday loans* (also called *cash-advance* or *check-advance* loans) are short-term, unsecured loans in which a lender extends you high-interest credit based on your income. *Title loans* are the same, but you give the lender the title to your car (or something else valuable) as collateral. Read that again if you have to: If you don't pay back a title loan in full (along with its very high interest), the title lender *keeps your vehicle or other property!*

Pawn shops are places you can go to temporarily sell items of value. You bring your item into the pawn shop, it offers you a fraction of the value, and you leave the object there while walking away with some cash in your pocket. If you want your item back, you have to buy it back from the pawn shop with fees attached; the fee goes up based on how long you leave the object there. After a certain period of time, the pawn shop can sell your item to another customer and keep all the profits.

WARNING

Payday lenders, title lenders, and pawn shops are often predatory; they look for vulnerable people and exploit them for their own profit. If you're in a financial crunch, other options are available to you (though prevention is the best medicine).

Creating a Smart Budget

Even if you're pretty sure you'll have plenty of cash on hand when you leave the military, creating (and sticking to) a budget doesn't hurt. Sure, it's not the most exciting thing you could be doing on terminal leave, but it can help ensure you have enough to make ends meet in the future. Planning for how much income you'll have after you leave the military and stop receiving paychecks on the 1st and 15th of the month can be tough, but do yourself a favor and create a budget based on the worst-case scenario by following these steps:

1. **Create a list of your monthly expenses, including car payments, rent or mortgage payments, childcare, and utilities.**

    Throw in everything you regularly spend money on, even if it's dining out every Friday night or going bowling every Sunday.

2. **Figure out which expenses are fixed and which are variable.**

    Fixed expenses are those that don't change, like your rent or mortgage payment, childcare services, and your phone bill. *Variable expenses* are those that cost you a different amount every month, like groceries, dining out, and gifts you buy for your favorite people.

3. **Total your monthly income and deduct your expenses.**

    Use the worst-case scenario for your monthly income (well, almost the worst; the worst would be if you weren't able to find a job). If your expenses are greater than your income, you're in danger of overspending and need to make some adjustments.

4. **Make adjustments.**

    Look for ways you can cut expenses to get yourself back in the black. (Have I told you that the average monthly cable TV bill in 2020 was $217?)

5. **Track your actual expenses every month.**

    If you spend too much in one area, cut back in another. Try to make your income and expense columns equal so all your money is accounted for (and if you have extra, put it in savings or use it to pay down high-interest debt).

TIP

You don't have to use a pencil and paper to create a budget. You can find several great budgeting apps for your phone or tablet or use spreadsheets on your computer.

Chapter **19**

Zeroing in on the Benefits You Earned

When your door to the military closes, the Department of Veterans Affairs opens a new one for you. You're eligible for a wide range of VA benefits, even if you didn't retire from military service (and even, in some cases, if you left the military under less-than-ideal conditions). You're also eligible for benefits offered by a wide range of other organizations — some governmental and some private — and if you know where to look, you can make your transition process a lot easier. I cover many of the resources available to you (and how to get to them) in the following sections.

Navigating Access to Your VA Benefits

You can apply in several ways for the benefits you earned from Veterans Affairs, and for some people, the easiest way is through a VA representative. You can find a representative at www.ebenefits.va.gov/ebenefits/vso-search or call the VA directly.

REMEMBER

If you're in a crisis and need mental health help, you can call or walk into any VA medical center, any time. You can also call or walk into any Vet Center during clinic hours, or you can call the VA at 877-222-8387.

The VA offers benefits relating to

>> Disability compensation

>> Employment

>> Pensions

>> Education and training

>> Home loans

>> Life insurance

>> Healthcare and mental healthcare (head to the later section "Using VA healthcare" for more)

To get to many of your VA benefits, you need an AccessVA account or an eBenefits account. In order to log into either of those services to create accounts, you need a Defense Self-Service Logon (commonly called a DS Logon). Alternatively, you can use your CAC or MyPay credentials to log in and create your accounts. I cover several of these in the following sections.

WARNING

If you choose to use your CAC or MyPay credentials to create an AccessVA or eBenefits account, you still need to create a DS Logon. You return your CAC to the military and lose access to MyPay (unless you're a retiree) when your contract expires.

If you're not enrolled in the Defense Enrollment Eligibility Reporting System (DEERS), you need to call or message the VA through its website or visit a VA Regional Office in person. In most cases, DEERS enrollment is automatic when you leave military service.

DS Logon

The *Defense Self-Service Logon* lets you access your information across Department of Defense and Veterans Affairs partner websites. You can use your credentials to view your financial and benefits information, personal health information, claim statuses, and records.

In order to get a DS Logon, you must be affiliated with the DOD or VA, and you must be listed in DEERS.

AccessVA and eBenefits accounts

AccessVA (https://eauth.va.gov/accessva) is your gateway to several medical-related and other benefits, including service-disabled veterans insurance, life insurance, your My HealthEVet account (your veteran health records), and the VA's Virtual Medical Center, where you can communicate in real-time with a medical provider and handle a number of other health-related issues. It's also where you go to apply for your veteran identification card, which I cover in a later section.

Before you can apply for benefits online, check your compensation or pension claim status, check your post-9/11 GI Bill enrollment status or use the VetSuccess employment search, you need an eBenefits account. This account also gives you access to your TRICARE health insurance policy, Veterans' Group Life Insurance, and your appeal statuses and lets you

>> Order prescription medications

>> Message your physician

>> Access your medical information

>> Use the VA's military skills translator and resume builder tool

>> Order medical equipment (such as hearing aid batteries or prosthetic socks)

>> Generate a VA home loan certificate of eligibility

>> Get official personnel documents, such as your DD-214

>> Register for and update direct deposit information for some benefits

TIP

Even if you don't intend to use any of your free veterans benefits, you need to set up your eBenefits and AccessVA accounts and log into them periodically. That's where you find special programs that the government is offering to people like you. For example, the VA established a very little-known, exceptionally funded program during the COVID-19 pandemic called the Veteran Rapid Retraining Assistance Program, or VRRAP, for veterans who had lost their jobs due to the pandemic. The program was designed to provide free college tuition or money for learning a skilled trade for a year, plus basic allowance for housing at post-9/11 GI Bill levels (that's the E-5 with dependents rate, in case you were wondering). The VA pushes out information on programs like this one through eBenefits and AccessVA (which is why the VRRAP program was little-known, despite its exceptional funding). While you're in your accounts, sign up for email updates so you don't miss anything that may apply to you.

ID.me account

ID.me is like a digital identification card. The U.S. government accepts ID.me credentials to log into a number of government websites, and many other organizations — including private businesses — use it as well.

WARNING

Photographing or copying your military ID card is unlawful. Don't use your military CAC to verify your identity with ID.me. Instead, use a redacted copy of your DD-214 to prove military service.

Veteran ID card

A *Veteran ID Card*, or VIC, is a photo ID that you can use to get veterans' discounts at restaurants, hotels, stores, and other businesses. You don't need one, but having one can be useful.

You're only eligible for a VIC if you served on active duty, in the Reserves, in the National Guard, or in the Coast Guard and you received an honorable or general (under honorable conditions) discharge.

When you apply for your VIC, be prepared to provide the VA with your Social Security number, a digital copy of your DD-214 or another discharge document (to prove the character of your discharge), and a copy of a current and valid government-issued ID card (such as your driver's license, state ID, or passport). You also need a digital color photo of yourself from the shoulders up, which is then printed on your VIC. The VA is very specific about what it wants; essentially, it's a passport-style photo (although you're allowed to wear glasses and smile) that's been taken against a plain background (no scenery or other people) within the past ten years.

The VA verifies your eligibility by checking up on your discharge status, ensuring your government-issued ID is valid, and determining whether the photo you sent in meets the right requirements. You get an email notifying you of the status of your application (which you can also check through your AccessVA account), and if approved, you receive your VIC in the mail.

eVetRecs

If you need copies of your military records — nearly anything from your Official Military Personnel File, or OMPF — you can get them through eVetRecs (https://vetrecs.archives.gov). Simply identify yourself, select the reason you need your records, and complete the requester information before submitting your request. The VA determines which records to give you based on your needs.

WARNING

Requesting your military records through the federal government is normally free. If you come across an ad from a company that says it will get you copies of your DD-214 or any other military records for a fee, it's almost certainly a scam. You can always access your records through eVetRecs, and if you're having a hard time doing so, you can get help from the VA.

Determining Which Benefits Are Yours for the Taking

Not all veterans qualify for all benefits. Many entitlements depend on whether you retired from the military, the nature of your discharge, and whether you have a qualifying disability. The best way to find out exactly what you qualify for is to physically visit a VA office and ask to speak with a Veteran Service Officer, or VSO. Your assigned VSO looks at your records and helps you find the benefits you're entitled to receive. If you're not near a VA office, or if you'd rather not visit in person, you can find a VSO through your eBenefits account. (See the earlier section "AccessVA and eBenefits accounts.") I cover a range of VA benefits that you may be eligible for in the following sections, but your best bet is to work with a VSO who knows your situation.

Banking on retirement pay

I can't even sugarcoat this: The military retirement pay system can be confusing and frustrating. You're only eligible for retirement pay if you've served the required amount of time for your branch, and in some cases, you may get retainer pay.

Retirement versus retainer pay

In the Army, Air Force, and Coast Guard, you're eligible for retirement pay if you've completed 20 years of military service and received retirement orders. If you're an enlisted member of the Navy or Marine Corps, you must accrue more than 30 years of service, but if you're a warrant or commissioned officer in either of those two branches, you're eligible for retirement pay when you retire after 20 years.

Enlisted sailors and Marines who don't meet the 30-year service requirement but who have completed more than 20 years of service are transferred to the Fleet Reserve or the Fleet Marine Corps Reserve, and their pay is called *retainer pay.*

Disability retirement pay

People who are determined to be unfit for military service and who have a disability rating of at least 30 percent (from the military, not the VA) qualify for disability retirement pay. Military disability retirement is different from VA disability because it comes from the Department of Defense (rather than the Department of Veterans Affairs, which pays for standard retirement pensions).

If you didn't complete the 20 years of service normally required for retirement pay, you receive a different payment than a military retiree would if you were put on the Permanent Disability Retired List, or PDRL.

WARNING

Speaking to a VA representative about disability retirement pay is essential. Only a VA rep can give you advice based on your personal situation.

The Temporary Disability Retirement List

If the medical board evaluating your disability believes that you'll get better (or worse), its members put you on the Temporary Disability Retirement List, or TDRL. When you're on the TDRL, you receive a monthly stipend and medical coverage for you and your dependents until your condition changes.

When you're placed on the PDRL (see the preceding section) or TDRL, your monthly retirement check includes your disability pay. The government calculates this amount in two ways, and you're allowed to choose either computation method.

>> **Option 1:** (years of service) × (2.5 percent) × (retired base pay)

>> **Option 2:** (disability percentage) × (retired base pay)

In the option 2 method, your disability percentage can't exceed 75 percent.

Disability severance pay is a one-time payment. It's usually calculated by multiplying your basic pay (at the time of your severance) by two, then multiplying that number by your number of years of service.

TIP

You may not qualify for this benefit now, but when you're 65 or older or are permanently disabled, served on active duty for at least one day during a period of war, and have a countable family income below a certain threshold, you may be eligible for a Veterans Pension. You must have been discharged under other than dishonorable conditions to qualify. The amount you may receive can be pretty substantial, so put that information in your back pocket for later (or to share with someone you know who qualifies).

Sheltering in place with a VA loan

The Department of Veterans Affairs can help you buy a house through its VA Loan program. One of the biggest benefits of a VA loan is that you can finance your entire purchase, including the down payment. VA loans also limit the amount you can be charged for closing costs, and they prevent lenders from requiring you to pay for private mortgage insurance, or PMI. A VA loan has no prepayment penalties, which means you can pay it off as soon as you want, and you can reuse your benefit (as long as your last loan is satisfied) as many times as you want like. A VA loan also requires no minimum credit score; most lenders do have their own minimums, but the VA prohibits lenders from denying you a loan based solely on your credit score. Lenders have to look at your entire financial situation before making a decision on your application.

The money to buy your home doesn't come from the VA. It comes from a private lender. The VA guarantees that the lender will get at least part of its investment back if you default on payments, which is why lenders are comfortable offering veterans more competitive interest rates and better loan terms than they'd offer non-vets with similar financial profiles.

Using VA healthcare

The VA is legally obligated to provide eligible veterans with necessary hospital care and outpatient care services. (In this case, *necessary* means a care or service that will promote, preserve, and restore health.) Your eligibility depends on several factors, and you should speak with a VA representative to find out whether you qualify.

REMEMBER

Regardless of your discharge status, how long you've been out of the military, or whether you're enrolled in VA healthcare, the VA will provide emergency mental health care services if you're in a crisis. You can connect with a Veterans Crisis Line responder at any time by phone at 800-273-8255 or by texting 838255. You can also chat with someone online through the VA's website (www.va.gov) or go directly to the nearest VA medical center.

The VA also provides specialized healthcare services with varying eligibility requirements, including

>> Drug and alcohol addiction treatment

>> Mental health and wellness

>> Post-traumatic stress treatment

>> Traumatic brain injury treatment

USING VETERAN DISCOUNTS

Several companies offer special discounts to veterans and their family members. Just like military discounts, they're not often advertised, so the best way to find them is to ask while you shop or dine out. You can get discounted rates on amusement park and museum tickets, food and wine, and fitness club memberships, plus a whole host of other services. You should even ask your favorite satellite TV provider and your phone company about potential savings. (That Veteran ID Card may come in handy, after all!) Several websites list veteran discounts that may be available to you, too.

Making the Most of Military OneSource and Other Avenues of Support

Military OneSource (www.militaryonesource.mil) may be the most comprehensive resource available for recently separated veterans. You can use its services for up to a year after your contract expires, and it offers the following:

>> Free, confidential nonmedical mental health counseling (including marriage counseling)

>> Adoption help

>> Health and wellness coaching

>> Spouse education and career opportunities

>> Financial and tax consultations

>> Document translation and language interpretation

>> Peer-to-peer support

>> Specialized help for wounded warriors and their caregivers

Several other organizations offer a wide range of support services for veterans, including some to help with veteran homelessness (such as the HUD-Veterans Affairs Supportive Housing program, the Supportive Services for Veterans program, and the National Coalition for Homeless Veterans) and a wide range of other issues that you may need help with. The Wounded Warrior Project, Veterans of Foreign Wars, Disabled American Veterans, AMVETS, the Women's Army Corps Veterans Association, and the American Legion are among the biggest veteran-supporting organizations that can connect you with the supportive resources you need.

GIVING BACK THROUGH VSOs

One of the most rewarding things you can do is join a veteran service organization, or VSO. (Not to be confused with the other VSOs, Veteran Service Officers, that I discuss earlier in the chapter. Same abbreviation, different concept.) In addition to connecting yourself to a supportive community, you can serve other veterans in your city or town by providing essential services, working at charity events, doing heavy lifting (literally), and helping other vets realize that they're not alone. Many members of these organizations have plenty of wisdom to share while you work on community service projects and veteran outreach together as well. Women veterans are also eligible to join many VSOs (although some of the older members may initially try to steer you toward their ladies' auxiliaries. But if you explain that you're a veteran, they'll explain your membership options — I know from experience). I cover lots of VSOs in Chapter 10.

IN THIS CHAPTER

» **Discovering wounded warrior transition programs in each branch**

» **Receiving disability pay and benefits from the government**

» **Getting help from the DOD, VSOs, and civilian resources**

» **Uncovering resources for post-traumatic stress and military sexual trauma**

Chapter **20**

Transitioning as a Wounded Warrior

W hile you're in the military, you're considered a *wounded warrior* if you have a serious illness or injury that requires long-term care. Your case may need to be looked at by a medical evaluation board or physical evaluation board to determine your fitness for duty. When you *leave* the military as a wounded warrior, you're eligible for a specific set of benefits from the U.S. government that range from disability compensation to vocational rehabilitation and employment services from the VA. In addition to government benefits you earned, you have access to several civilian organizations that provide services to people in situations similar to yours. This chapter covers all the most important information you need to know to take advantage of these benefits and services, whether you suffer visible or invisible wounds (or both).

TIP

One of the first things you should do is find the Department of Defense's *Wounded, Ill, and/or Injured Compensation and Benefits Handbook* (commonly called the *C&B Handbook*), which contains the most current information on where to go and how to get the benefits you're entitled to. It's considered a living document, and it's often updated when changes roll out through the DOD, the Departments of Veterans Affairs, Labor, and Education, the U.S. Social Security Administration, and each branch of the armed forces.

REMEMBER

The VA provides emergency mental healthcare for all veterans, regardless of discharge status or VA eligibility. It doesn't matter what's going on, what caused your crisis, or where you're located. If you're in a crisis, you can visit any VA medical center at any time for help; you can also walk into or call a Vet Center on a VA campus during normal business hours. You can also call the Veterans Crisis Line at 800-273-8255 (press 1), text 838255, or visit VeteransCrisisLine.net to get the help you need.

Tackling Transition Programs for Wounded Warriors

Each branch of the military has its own transition program for wounded warriors, and additional programs exist within the branches for elite communities, such as U.S. Special Operations Command. The Navy shares its wounded warrior program with Coast Guardsmen and their families.

U.S. Army Recovery Care Program

The U.S. Army Recovery Care Program, or ARCP, manages wounded warrior transition for soldiers and their families. Each soldier in the ARCP works with a Recovery Care Coordinator, or RCC, whether they're remaining in the military or getting out. This program helps you establish goals in six domains: career, physical, social, family, emotional, and resolve. You work with a dedicated team of professionals to take advantage of special adaptive reconditioning programs, career and education programs, and, if you intend to get out of the military, the Veteran Track; the Veteran Track is a platoon that focuses on career and education readiness while providing resources that help you transition to veteran status.

Air Force Wounded Warrior Program

The U.S. Air Force Wounded Warrior program, or AFW2, provides personalized care, services, and advocacy for seriously wounded, ill, or injured airmen, their caregivers, and their families. Like other wounded warrior programs, this program's aim is to retain servicemembers; if that's not possible, the program ensures support through retirement or separation.

AFW2 provides a wide range of support programs, including adaptive sports, "ambassador" workshops, caregiver and family support, and community partnerships that help wounded warriors find recovery-based opportunities. It also provides the Empowerment in Transition program (or EIT, which assists recovering airmen and caregivers in developing and achieving long-term career and life goals) as well as the Recovering Airman Mentorship Program and the Wellness and Resiliency Program.

Navy Wounded Warrior Program

The Navy's Wounded Warrior program is open to sailors and Coast Guardsmen who have a serious illness or injury. Enrollment is voluntary; you can self-refer, or your command or medical provider may make a referral. The program allows servicemembers to focus on recovery with a team of experts on hand to resolve nonmedical problems and help wounded warriors transition back to active duty or civilian life. Through this program, the Navy provides the Education, Employment, and Internship program, or E2I; it connects you and your caregivers with a wide range of education resources, career counseling services, benefit applications, and employment assistance.

U.S. Marine Corps Wounded Warrior Regiment

The U.S. Marine Corps's Wounded Warrior Regiment's motto is *Etiam in Pugna,* which means "still in the fight." The program's goal is to retain Marines when possible or to assist with transition if not. It's broken into four *lines of operation,* or LOOs: Mind, Body, Spirit, and Family. The Mind LOO provides access to college courses and vocational training programs, on-the-job training and internships, and professional military education. The Body LOO works on physical fitness, including medical and physical therapy and the Warrior Athlete Reconditioning Program. The Spirit LOO provides behavioral health services, religious programs, and extension outreach programs where Marines and veterans can begin healing in the civilian sector. The Family LOO provides many of the same services to dependents.

Figuring out Your VA Disability Pay

Before you leave the military for medical reasons, your physician refers you into the Integrated Disability Evaluation System, or IDES, to determine whether you're fit for continued service. Servicemembers who are processed through the IDES have only three possible outcomes: return to duty, medically separate, or medically retire (temporarily or permanently). The possible designations of your fitness for duty are

>> **Fit; Return to Duty:** If your conditions aren't severe enough to prevent you from performing your required military duties, you return to duty without

DOD disability compensation. However, you may be eligible for VA disability benefits after you separate from the military.

>> **Unfit; Separate without Benefits:** If your illness or injury is unfitting but is determined to have been incurred or aggravated "not in the line of duty," such as one that stems from intentional misconduct or willful negligence, you can be separated without benefits.

>> **Unfit; Separate with Severance Pay:** If one or more of your conditions is unfitting, the combined disability rating of all your unfitting conditions is lower than 30 percent, and you have fewer than 20 years of service under your belt, you may be separated and awarded severance pay. I cover severance and combined disability ratings in the later section " "Compensation payments and disability ratings."

>> **Unfit; Permanent Retirement:** If your unfitting condition results in a combined disability rating of 30 percent or higher or you have 20 years or service, and your condition is stable, you're permanently retired. You receive disability retirement pay, access to TRICARE, commissary and exchange privileges for you and your eligible dependents, and all other benefits of regular military retirement.

>> **Unfit; Transfer to the Temporary Retired List (TDRL):** If your condition isn't stable but may be permanent, you're temporarily retired and placed on the TDRL for a maximum of three years. Your benefits are the same as those for servicemembers who are permanently retired for disability. The military reevaluates you at least once every 18 months to see whether your condition has stabilized. At that time, you may be found fit for duty; if you're unfit for duty, you're separated if your disability rating is lower than 30 percent and retired if it's 30 percent or higher.

If your record shows you're unfit for continued service, the IDES provides you with DOD and proposed VA disability ratings before you get out. The Department of Defense only compensates veterans for unfitting conditions, which vary case by case; the VA compensates people for service-connected conditions.

TECHNICAL STUFF

You can be separated from service for a medical condition that interferes with your performance without being referred to the IDES if your condition doesn't constitute a physical disability.

If you'll separate from military service within the next 180 to 90 days, you may apply for VA disability compensation through the Benefits Delivery at Discharge (BDD) program. Otherwise, you may apply for VA disability compensation after you separate. Applying using the BDD program is in your best interest so you don't have to wait for your benefits after you leave the military.

The VA makes periodic cost-of-living adjustments (COLAs) to VA disability compensation benefits (as well as to pension amounts, which I cover in Chapter 3). Under federal law, the COLAs are the same percentage as they are for Social Security benefits.

Compensation payments and disability ratings

The VA pays disability compensation benefits based on how disabled you are. The VA makes an initial determination about the severity of your disability based on all the evidence you submit with your claim. It rates your disability on a scale from 0 percent to 100 percent in 10 percent increments.

Each year, the compensation rates change. You can use the most current veterans disability compensation rates table on the VA's website to find out how much you're likely to receive (at least for this year). You may be paid additional amounts if you have very severe disabilities or loss of limb(s); you have a spouse, kids, or dependent parents; or you have a seriously disabled spouse.

Combined ratings are a measure of how much multiple medical conditions disable you. If you have one disability rating of 60 percent and another of 15 percent, your combined rating isn't 75 percent; instead, the VA uses a Combined Ratings Table to calculate a combined disability rating. There isn't a specific mathematical formula, so visit the VA's website and search for the Combined Ratings Table to calculate how much disability pay you're entitled to receive.

Disability severance pay

Disability severance pay is a one-time, lump-sum payment you receive if your disability rating is under 30 percent. The amount is equal to two months of basic pay for each year of service; the minimum total service in the formula is 3 years (even if you haven't served that long), and the maximum can't exceed 19 years. For example, if your current base pay is $2,371.80 and you've been in the military for three years, you receive ($2,371.80 × 2) × 3, which is $14,230.80.)

If you receive disability severance pay, the U.S. government doesn't consider you medically retired.

Special Monthly Compensation

The VA pays some wounded warriors Special Monthly Compensation, or SMC. This higher rate is payable to people with very specific conditions, such as the loss of the use of a body part or function, or who need Aid and Attendance (assistance to perform normal, everyday tasks), which I discuss later in the chapter.

Exploring Extra VA Disability Benefits

The VA provides additional benefits for wounded warriors who leave the service with specific conditions or additional needs. In some cases, you must apply for benefits; others are automatically given to you based on your medical needs or special compensation status.

Disability housing grants

Vets with certain service-connected disabilities are eligible for Specially Adapted Housing grants from the VA that allow them to buy or change a home to meet their needs and live more independently. These grants can be used for things like adding wheelchair ramps or widening doorways, installing special fire alarm systems for the hard of hearing, or adding a walk-in bathtub. To qualify for one of these grants, you must have a qualifying service-connected disability. Only a limited number of veterans qualify each fiscal year.

Automobile allowance and adaptive equipment

If you have a disability related to your military service that prevents you from driving, you may be able to get a special grant that helps you buy a specially equipped vehicle. You may also qualify for a grant to change a vehicle so it has features like specialized brakes, seats, windows, power steering, or lift equipment that helps you enter and exit.

Clothing allowance

If your clothing has been damaged by your prosthetic or orthopedic device or by medications you use to treat a skin condition, you may qualify for money to purchase new clothing each year. This annual allowance is available to people with service-connected conditions; some people qualify for a one-time benefit, while others qualify annually.

Aid and Attendance and Housebound allowance

Some veterans qualify for VA Aid and Attendance or Housebound benefits, which are monthly payments tacked on to a VA pension. You may be eligible for these benefits if you need help with daily activities, such as bathing, feeding, and dressing; because you have to spend a significant amount of time in bed; or because you can't leave your home because of a permanent disability. You can't receive Aid and Attendance and Household benefits at the same time, even if you qualify for both.

Service dogs

You may be eligible for a service dog who can help you perform specific tasks. You can apply under two categories for a service dog through the VA's Prosthetic and Sensory Aids Service:

>> **Hearing, Guide, Mobility:** Your VA clinical care provider must evaluate you to determine whether you need assistive devices (including a service dog). If your provider determines that a service dog is the best tool for your rehabilitation and treatment plan, you and your provider work through your local VA to obtain one.

>> **Mental Health Mobility:** If your mental health condition creates substantial mobility limitations, and if your clinical care provider determines a service dog is the best treatment approach or intervention for you, they request the benefit on your behalf.

Service-Disabled Veterans Insurance and Veterans' Mortgage Life Insurance

You may qualify for low-cost Service-Disabled Veterans Life Insurance (S-DVI) if you have a service-connected disability. You have a time limit on when you may apply after being classified with a new service-connected disability, but if you're approved, you may get up to $10,000 in standard coverage and up to $30,000 in supplemental coverage.

Veterans' Mortgage Life Insurance offers mortgage protections to the families of vets who have severe service-connected disabilities and have adapted a home to meet their medical needs. This benefit provides up to $200,000 in coverage.

Vocational Rehab and Employment

The Veterans Readiness and Employment Program is sometimes called *Chapter 31* or *Voc-Rehab*. If you're 10 percent or more disabled and were discharged under any classification other than dishonorable, you may qualify for help learning new skills, finding a new job, starting a business, or getting educational counseling. (If you're currently on active duty, you must have a VA memorandum or an IDES rating of 20 percent or more or be going through a Physical Evaluation Board.) Some severely injured active-duty servicemembers automatically receive VR&E benefits before the VA issues a disability rating.

The 180-Day Family Housing Extension

If you live in military family housing and separate from active duty because of your injury or illness, you may be eligible for an extension of up to six months that allows you to remain in your home. Housing extensions are made on a space-available basis, so call your installation's housing office to find out how to apply for one if you need it.

Dependents' Educational Assistance

The Survivors' and Dependents' Educational Assistance program provides financial help to wounded warriors' eligible family members to use toward college programs, career-training certificates, apprenticeships, on-the-job training, and educational and career counseling. The veteran or servicemember must meet eligibility requirements, such as being permanently and totally disabled due to a service-connected disability or currently being in the hospital or getting outpatient treatment for a service-connected, permanent, and total disability. Children must be between the ages of 18 and 26 to use these benefits; spouses' benefits begin on the date the VA determines eligibility and last for ten years.

DOD Programs to Give You a Head-Start

Some Department of Defense programs can help you find employment, get an education, or obtain assistive technology that helps you function in your everyday life. These programs come from the DOD, not the VA, and require you to apply directly with the DOD division that provides them.

>> **Operation Warfighter (OWF):** Operation Warfighter is a DOD internship program that matches qualified wounded, ill, or injured servicemembers with nonfunded federal internships. The idea behind OWF is that work experience can help servicemembers reintegrate into the military or find a job using newly acquired skills as a civilian. You can find out more and apply for OWF at warriorcare.dodlive.mil/Care-Coordination/Operation-Warfighter.

>> **Education and Employment Initiative:** The Education and Employment Initiative (E2I) is available to active-duty wounded, ill, or injured servicemembers leaving the military. (This initiative is separate from the E2I program I cover earlier in the chapter as part of the Navy's wounded warrior transition.) The program helps you identify your skills and matches you with educational and career opportunities that can help you transition to civilian life. If you're interested in more info, you can visit warriorcare.dodlive.mil/Care-Coordination/Education-Employment-Initiative.

> » **Computer/Electronic Accommodations Program:** The Computer/Electronic Accommodations Program, or CAP, provides assistive technology and accommodations that support wounded warriors. Public Law 109-364 says that servicemembers who use assistive technology from CAP while in the military may keep it upon separation. Head to cap.mil for more.

Seeing about Social Security Disability

Social Security Disability Insurance (SSDI) is funded through payroll taxes; it's something you paid into during your entire military career as well as through any civilian jobs you held in the past. Receiving the VA disability payments I discuss throughout the chapter and SSDI at the same time is possible. In fact, you should apply for SSDI benefits if your disability prevents you from working, regardless of your income status, discharge status (even if it was dishonorable), or anything else. To qualify, you must be under 65 and unable to do "substantial work" due to your medical conditions. Also, your medical conditions must have lasted, or be expected to last, at least a year or to result in death.

Your spouse and children may also be eligible to receive partial dependent benefits (called *auxiliary benefits*). The amount of your monthly benefit depends on your current earnings. Your VA benefits *do not* count toward your earned income for SSDI; those payments are entitlements, not earned income. Because you're a disabled veteran, you may qualify for expedited processing for your SSDI benefits.

TECHNICAL STUFF

If you receive SSDI for two years, you become eligible for Medicare, which I cover in Chapter 18.

You may also apply for Supplemental Security Income, or SSI, but you may not qualify for it. SSI is a need-based program, and your VA income counts toward its minimum income requirements.

Exploring PTSD Resources

The VA provides mental healthcare for veterans with post-traumatic stress. In fact, you can find nearly 200 specialized PTSD treatment programs located all over the United States — in Community-Based Outpatient Clinics and Vet Centers and through Telemental Health, the VA's program for using technology to communicate. The VA's PTSD services are open to all veterans who completed active military service in the Army, Navy, Air Force, Marine Corps, or Coast Guard and were discharged under any conditions except dishonorable, or who were National Guard members or reservists who completed a federal deployment to a combat zone. That said, the VA will provide mental health crisis help to any veteran, regardless of discharge status.

The VA's PTSD programs offer education, evaluation, and treatment, providing services that include the following:

» One-on-one mental health assessment and testing

» One-on-one psychotherapy and family therapy

» Group therapy that covers specific topics or that involves veterans of specific conflicts or specific traumas

» Medication

You may also call 877-WAR-VETS (877-927-8387) 24 hours a day, 7 days a week. The people who answer are combat veterans from several eras, as well as family members of combat veterans. You can use this confidential call center to talk about your military experiences or any other issue you're facing, whether you're having difficulty readjusting to civilian life or going through a different type of rough patch.

Several private organizations also provide PTSD help, and your local veterans service organization can help you connect with the right resources. Following are a couple of examples:

» **Give an Hour:** Give an Hour (giveanhour.org/military) provides free mental health services to military members, veterans, and their families. You can use Give an Hour to talk to a licensed medical health professional regardless of your discharge status, the length of time you served in the military, or your branch of service.

» **PatientsLikeMe:** PatientsLikeMe (www.patientslikeme.com) is a network of nearly half a million people who can track and share their own experiences while connecting with other people who have the same disease, condition, or diagnosis. *Tip:* You can use the site with an alias if you want to; divulging any personally identifiable information when you use a networking site to discuss medical or mental health conditions isn't a great idea.

Getting Military Sexual Trauma Help

Veterans are eligible for free care (including medications) for mental and physical health conditions related to sexual assault or sexual harassment experienced during military service. These experiences are collectively called *military sexual trauma*, or MST. You're eligible for mental or physical healthcare (or both) even if you don't generally qualify for VA services and you didn't report the incident(s) when they happened. You don't need to have a specific diagnosis, and you have no time limit on when you can seek help from the VA. You don't need to prove that your MST really happened, either. All you need to do is contact your local VA medical center and ask to speak to the MST coordinator, who will help you get access to the resources you need.

Working with Civilian Organizations

Several civilian organizations, including veterans service organizations (VSOs), can connect you with the resources you need. They can help you file claims with the VA, search for programs that enrich your life (or simply make it easier), and get you moving in the right direction in terms of mental health help. I note the most well-known VSOs and wounded warrior organizations here, and the VA maintains a list of congressionally chartered VSOs that you can access using its website.

>> **The VFW:** Veterans of Foreign Wars (vfw.org) is a nationally recognized veterans service organization that provides a tremendous amount of help to disabled veterans. The VFW is staffed by trained professionals who can assist you in filing a VA claim, appealing VA decisions, and getting the benefits you deserve. The organization also provides financial grants to those who need them, student veteran support (including applying for GI Bill benefits and awarding scholarships of up to $5,000), and mental wellness help for veterans.

>> **The DAV:** The Disabled American Veterans organization (www.dav.org) has helped veterans access more than $23 billion in earned benefits, has provided hundreds of thousands of rides to medical appointments, and helps more than a million veterans every year. It's a chartered VSO (see Chapter 10) and has professionals on staff who can help you file VA claims, appeal decisions, and access your benefits. It also has Transition Service Offices that can help you make the switch between the military world you're accustomed to and life outside the perimeter fence.

>> **The American Legion:** The American Legion (www.legion.org) is a chartered VSO that can help you and your family understand and apply for the veterans benefits you're entitled to receive. It can aid you in filing claims and disputing decisions that don't turn out in your favor, as well as provide you with a wide array of services for integrating back into your community as a wounded warrior. It offers scholarships, financial assistance, donated goods, and several other resources, including the Legion Riders, a motorcycle club that's raised hundreds of thousands of dollars for veterans' homes, children's hospitals, and many other good causes.

>> **The Wounded Warrior Project:** The Wounded Warrior Project, or WWP (www. woundedwarriorproject.org), is a VA-accredited organization that can help you access benefits (including those you didn't even know you were entitled to). You can sit down with a WWP team member who will walk you through every step of the VA claims process and answer your questions. The WWP also offers ways for you to connect with other wounded warriors; get peer and family support; and find out how to do things like acquire a service dog, find marriage and family counseling, or get the legal services you need. The organization also provides emergency financial assistance to those who qualify, connects you with mental health help, and offers career counseling.

Finding Family and Caregiver Resources

Wounded warriors' families and caregivers can receive support from a wide range of governmental resources, including these:

>> **The VA Caregiver Support Program** (www.caregiver.va.gov): The Caregiver Support Program can provide you with travel expenses when your veteran has to travel for medical care, mental health services and counseling, a monthly financial stipend, legal and financial planning services, and comprehensive VA caregiver training.

>> **Military OneSource** (www.militaryonesource.mil): Military OneSource provides confidential support services, including wounded warrior resources, relocation support, domestic abuse prevention, and spouse education and career opportunities for servicemembers from all branches and their families.

>> **Coast Guard Support** (www.cgsuprt.com): Open to Coast Guard members, CG civilians, members of the reserves, and their family members, Coast Guard Support provides nonmedical counseling, legal and financial assistance, and a variety of other services.

>> **TRICARE Respite Care Program** (tricare.mil/respite): This program is exclusively to help care for servicemembers who were injured in the line of duty, who have a serious injury or one that has resulted in or may result in a physical disability, or have an extraordinary physical or psychological condition. It provides a break for primary caregivers, and servicemembers do not incur any out-of-pocket expenses for the service. It has no benefit cap, either.

The Defense Health Agency's Caregiver Resource Directory, or CRD, also features dozens of state and local resources for families and caregivers of wounded warriors. You can access it through warriorcare.dodlive.mil/caregiver-resources.

» **Finding emergency help in a crisis**

» **Cashing in on financial assistance when you can't make ends meet**

» **Dealing with disabilities**

» **Refusing to give in to loneliness**

» **Checking out veterans' groups**

» **Accessing resources to help you with criminal charges, addiction, and homelessness**

» **Changing your mind about getting out**

Chapter **21**

Getting Help When You Need It

Many veterans struggle after leaving the military, so if you're having a hard time, you're not alone. Military transition isn't always easy, and the process can take a long time to get through. It begins when you decide to leave the military or find out that you're being separated, but it doesn't end the day you receive your discharge documents. It ends when you're on your feet and completely adjusted to civilian life.

Unfortunately, the military probably prepared you very well for life in the service, but it's less likely to have prepared you as well for civilian life. Some of the challenges you face are unique to your period of service; as a post-9/11 vet, you're more likely to have deployed, seen combat, and experienced emotional trauma than your predecessors were. In fact, about 47 percent of post-9/11 veterans say they had emotionally traumatic or distressing experiences related to their military service, and one in three report suffering from post-traumatic stress. As much as

I wish I could tell you otherwise, your readjustment period may be more difficult than you expect it to be.

If you're having a hard time, some government and civilian resources are available to you — regardless of your discharge status, disability status, or reason — that can help you pull through a rough patch and come out better for it. The sections in this chapter address what you can do to get help if you're having a mental health crisis, how to find financial help when money's tight, and where you can turn for help with incarceration, addiction, and homelessness.

REMEMBER

The most important thing to remember is that you're not alone. People who actively want to help you are out there, and they'll do their best if you reach out.

Battling Your Demons: Suicide Prevention and Crisis Intervention

People can experience an emotional or mental health crisis for a wide range of reasons, from a pileup of everyday stresses to a major life event (such as the end of a relationship, the loss of someone close to you, or even military transition). During stressful periods, such as military transition, issues can become magnified to the point that you just don't know what to do.

The Veterans Crisis Line has people ready to talk, text, or chat online with you 24 hours a day, 7 days a week. Call 800-273-8255 and press 1, text 838255, or visit www.veteranscrisisline.net to connect with someone online.

You can use the Veterans Crisis Line anytime you're having a mental health emergency. It's completely confidential and open to all veterans, regardless of discharge status, as well as active-duty personnel, their family members, and friends. It's staffed by professional, qualified responders who know how to help you get through big problems, even if you feel that you have no way out or that your situation is hopeless. Many of them are veterans themselves, so even if they haven't experienced your exact situation, they understand where you're coming from.

TIP

In some cases, you may be able to head off an emotional or mental health crisis by talking to someone when you notice you're starting to struggle. Take a moment to do a quick self-check by asking yourself these questions:

>> Do I feel nervous or worry a lot?

>> Am I easily annoyed or irritable?

- Is my life too stressful?
- Have I been getting into a lot of arguments or fights?
- Do I feel intensely lonely, alone, or left out?
- Do people do a poor job of listening when I ask for help, or let me down when I'm counting on them?
- Do I feel intensely angry?
- Are things hopeless for me?
- Am I desperate?
- Do I feel like I have no control?
- Have I been drinking more than usual or feeling like I've been drinking too much?
- Have I been using drugs, including prescription meds without a prescription?
- Do I feel like I can't control how much I eat, or would others say I'm overly concerned about my weight if they knew how I felt?
- Am I having flashbacks (repeated, disturbing memories, thoughts, or mental images of a stressful experience)?
- Do I have physical reactions, such as a pounding heart, trouble breathing, or sweating, when I think of a stressful experience?
- Do I tend to avoid activities or situations that remind me of a stressful experience?
- Am I having a hard time concentrating, or feeling tired and having very little energy?
- Am I having a hard time falling or staying asleep, or am I sleeping too much?
- Do I feel like a failure or like I've let myself or other people down?
- Am I moving so slowly that other people may have noticed, or am I zipping around with restless energy?
- Do I still find pleasure in doing things I've enjoyed in the past, and am I still interested in those things?
- Do I feel like I'd be better off dead, or am I thinking about harming myself?
- Do I have a plan — even a poorly put-together one — about how I'd take my own life if I wanted to?
- Have I ever been knocked out or lost consciousness due to an injury?

If you can answer *yes* to any of these questions, you may benefit from scheduling an appointment with a VA behavioral health provider, a private counselor or psychologist, or a religious or spiritual leader who can help you. You can also make a confidential call to the War Vet Call Center at 877-WAR-VETS (877-927-8387) or the Women Veterans Call Center at 855-VA-WOMEN (855-829-6636).

Accessing Resources for Financial Help

Leaving the military can cause you a financial hardship. You've had a steady paycheck, additional money for housing and groceries, and free healthcare for at least a few years, and making the adjustment to a civilian paycheck (even if it's higher than your military base pay was) can be pretty tough. Fortunately, a number of programs may be able to help you and your family make ends meet until you can bounce back.

The term *public assistance* refers to government programs that provide cash help or in-kind benefits (such as food) to individuals and families. These programs are usually based on need, age, employment status, or veteran status. And just in case you were about to give me the "handout" line, let me tell you this: A VA pension is considered social insurance, which is a form of public assistance. So unless you're prepared to tell a retiree that they're taking a handout (and face the instant karma for doing so), I need you to stop thinking that anything is wrong with getting assistance from the government to feed or house yourself and your family. It isn't. Your taxes go into the programs that provide these types of assistance, and they're there for you to use.

Though I outline federal programs (and those backed by federal funding) in the following sections, keep in mind that your state may have additional benefits you can apply for.

TIP

If you don't need information about individual types of benefits but need to apply for help quickly, visit www.benefits.gov and use its Benefit Finder tool. All you need to do is answer a few questions, and the federal government offers you a list of benefits you may qualify for, such as healthcare and medical assistance, family and child services, financial assistance, and food and nutrition. Select the programs you may want to apply for and then answer more questions to determine your eligibility and apply.

Supplemental Security Income

Supplemental Security Income, or SSI, provides cash to meet your basic needs for food, clothing, and shelter. It's funded by tax revenues (not Social Security taxes), so during your time in the military, you contributed to the fund that pays for SSI. You may not qualify for SSI if you receive disability payments from the VA (though you can as long as you're under a certain income threshold).

You're eligible for SSI if you're age 65 or older, blind (your vision is 20/200 or less in your better eye or you have a field of vision of less than 20 degrees), or disabled and have limited income, limited resources, and are a U.S. citizen or national (or in one of a select few categories of aliens). You must be a resident of a U.S. state, the District of Columbia, or the Northern Mariana Islands, can't be absent from the country for a full calendar month (or for 30 or more days), and can't be in an institution (like a prison or hospital) at the government's expense.

SSI payments aren't huge. In fact, they don't provide you with enough money to live on; you may need to apply for other types of benefits to fill in the gaps until you can get on your feet.

Supplemental Security Disability Insurance

Supplemental Security Disability Insurance, or SSDI, is a kind of insurance that kicks in to help you out when you become disabled. Like SSI (see the preceding section), it's another government program that you paid into while you were working for the military (or in any other job that took taxes out of your paycheck).

You can receive SSDI and a VA disability pension at the same time. Although SSDI requires you to show your earned income, your VA pension doesn't count toward that (it's an entitlement, not an earned income). You may qualify for this program if you're disabled and your disability is expected to last for at least a year or result in death. Because of your medical condition, you must not be able to do work you did before or to adjust to other work.

You also need to have *work credits,* which are a measure of how much you've paid into the system in the past. The number of work credits you need to qualify for disability benefits depends on your age when you become disabled. Most people need 40 credits, with 20 of them having been earned in the past 10 years, but younger people need fewer credits. You earn one credit for a certain dollar amount in earnings, but no more than four credits per year. The dollar figure is subject to change, so you can check www.ssa.gov to find out how much one work credit "costs" this year. If you're disabled, you should apply for this benefit even if you're not sure whether you qualify; the worst the government can do is tell you no.

Supplemental Nutrition Assistance Program

The Supplemental Nutrition Assistance Program, or SNAP, used to be called food stamps. This U.S. Department of Agriculture-run program has come a long way since then; today, it provides nutrition benefits to supplement the food budget for individuals and families so they can purchase healthy food.

To receive SNAP benefits, you must apply in the state where you currently live. You must also meet resource and income limits, which are subject to change. Other benefits, such as SSI (which I discuss earlier in the chapter), Temporary Assistance for Needy Families (later in the chapter), and most retirement and pension plans don't count toward your resources and income for SNAP eligibility.

SNAP benefits typically come on a debit card that you can use just like a credit card. You can use your card to buy food for your household, such as fruits and vegetables; meat, poultry, and fish; dairy products; and even seeds and plants that produce food for your household to eat. You can't use them for beer, wine, liquor, cigarettes or tobacco, vitamins, medicines, or supplements. Additionally, you can't use them for foods that are hot at the point of sale or nonfood items like cleaning supplies, pet food, or hygiene items.

Even if you think you may make too much money or have too many resources, you can apply for SNAP through your state office, which can also give you the current limits. You can find your state office at www.fns.usda.gov/snap/state-directory. The experts in that office can tell you whether you qualify, and if necessary, can point you in a different direction for help.

Special Supplemental Nutrition Program for Women, Infants, and Children

The Special Supplemental Nutrition Program for Women, Infants, and Children, which is commonly called WIC, provides money to buy supplemental foods for low-income pregnant, breastfeeding, and non-breastfeeding postpartum women. It also provides benefits to infants and children up to the age of 5 who are deemed to be at nutritional risk. (You can get WIC for your children even if you're not a woman, so don't let the name of the program stop you from applying.)

The money for WIC comes through the U.S. Department of Agriculture from federal grants that are distributed by states, so WIC is another program you paid into during your time in the military. You receive a card that's just like a credit or debit card, and you use it at the checkout to buy WIC-approved foods. You can use WIC benefits to buy vegetables and fruits, milk, eggs, beans, peanut butter, juice, cheese, yogurt, and whole-grain foods like rice, bread, cereal, and pasta. Infant cereal, baby formula, and baby food also qualify. (If you're unsure, most WIC-approved foods are shelved above a sticker that says they're okay to buy with this type of assistance.)

You can apply for WIC through a local or state agency. Your state's website should provide you with a web address or phone number, or you can use the USDA's directory at www.fns.usda.gov/contacts.

Temporary Assistance for Needy Families

Temporary Assistance for Needy Families, or TANF, is a time-limited program funded by federal taxes that are distributed to states. In order to qualify for TANF, you must be unemployed or *underemployed* (which means you don't have enough paid work or are doing work that doesn't make use of your skills and abilities), have a child who's 18 years old or younger, be pregnant, or be 18 years old or younger and be the head of your household.

TANF, like other types of help, comes on a plastic card that you use like a debit card. Your state issues you one if you're approved for the program, and you can use it to buy things like supplies for your home, medical supplies, clothing, food, transportation, furniture, and anything else you need.

Every state has its own requirements; you can find your state's information on the Department of Health and Human Services website at www.acf.hhs.gov/ofa/map/about/help-families.

General assistance

Many states have general assistance programs designed to help individuals without children pay for basic needs. The program requirements vary greatly between states, and some states limit the amount of time you're allowed to receive help. The funding for these programs comes from the state that pays them, and you can find out whether a local program to help you is available by visiting your state's website or searching your state's name and "general assistance" online.

Unemployment Compensation for Ex-Servicemembers

As a veteran, you may be eligible for Unemployment Compensation for Ex-Servicemembers, or UCX. The U.S. Department of Labor runs the UCX program; the money comes from the federal government (specifically, each military branch) and is distributed by individual states.

UCX benefits are paid based on a percentage of your earnings over a recent 52-week period, and every state sets its own maximum benefit amount. Your claim is valid for a year, and you may receive the available benefits during any period when you're unemployed. However, the total number of weeks payable depends on your state's law and is tied to your state's maximum benefit amount. You may spend your UCX money on anything you need to, from rent or your mortgage payment to diapers and infant formula.

To qualify for UCX, which is paid weekly, you must have been on active duty or in active Reserve status (including the Guard) during the base period of the claim. In most states, the *base period of the claim* is a one-year range consisting of the last four out of the most recent five calendar quarters worked before filing the claim. You must have been honorably discharged and completed at least your first full term of service; if you were a Reservist, you must have completed at least 180 days of continuous active duty. You must also meet all of your state's eligibility requirements. You can apply for UCX through your state's website.

REMEMBER

You can't collect UCX along with standard unemployment, so if you intend to apply for one or the other, look into *both* programs to see which one better meets your needs. For example, if your state pays only four weeks of UCX benefits but 36 weeks of unemployment benefits, applying for standard unemployment benefits may be in your best interest in case you can't find a new job within a month.

Unemployment insurance

The U.S. Department of Labor also runs the unemployment insurance (UI) program. You may be used to hearing it simply called "unemployment." This program is a collaboration between your state and the federal government; each state administers its own program to provide cash to eligible workers, though some programs are better than others are. Every state has the freedom to pass legislation that shapes its UI program, but they all follow the same guidelines.

You paid into the UI program through your taxes while working any job, including during the time you were in the military. You can use your unemployment insurance money to buy anything you need; it's a cash entitlement. The "insurance" part of this program is just like car insurance or homeowners insurance; you paid for coverage, and now you're making a claim.

The state pays your UI benefits every week. To qualify, you must be unemployed, meet work and wage requirements (meaning you've recently worked), and meet additional state requirements.

You can apply for UI through your state's unemployment insurance program, and you can get contact information for each state at the DOL's website at oui.doleta. gov/unemploy/agencies.asp.

Workers' compensation

If you're injured at work (outside the military), you may be entitled to workers' compensation benefits. This type of insurance provides benefits to employees who have work-related injuries or illnesses. When you receive these benefits, the money goes to help pay for your medical care, wages from lost work time, and other necessities.

Workers' compensation benefits vary by state. If you were injured or became ill at work, check your state's website to determine how you can apply for these benefits.

Receiving Help for Disabilities

As a disabled veteran, you're entitled to certain benefits that many other people don't qualify for. You may be eligible for a disability pension from the Department of Veterans Affairs or for SSDI, which I cover in more detail earlier in this chapter and in Chapter 20. In addition to those two forms of financial assistance, you may be entitled to a range of other services and benefits from the VA, including the following:

>> An automobile allowance that helps you purchase or adapt a vehicle to accommodate your disability

>> A clothing allowance that pays for new clothes if yours have been damaged by your wheelchair, a medical device, or a medication you use to treat a skin condition

>> Specially adapted housing grants to help you change your existing home or buy a new one that accommodates your disability

>> Vocational Rehabilitation and Employment, or VR&E, which provides educational and training services to veterans with service-connected illnesses and injuries

I cover each of these additional services — and a few more — in Chapter 20. You may also be eligible for Supplemental Security Income, or SSI, which I cover earlier in the chapter.

Combating Loneliness and Boredom

People join the military for a wide variety of reasons, ranging from wanting to serve their country to being eager to escape Nowhereville, USA. Regardless of why you joined, the military quickly took over your entire life. You always had somewhere to be, whether it was at work for long hours, pulling staff duty or working on duty section, or mandatory fun days with your unit. When you were off work, you likely hung out with other military people; even your off-post neighbors were most likely military.

But after you leave the military with your freshly printed DD-214, things change. You may stick around your last duty station while your friends keep the same work schedules and eventually PCS or ETS. Maybe you move to an entirely new city or even go back home (to your home of record, anyway; it may not feel like home anymore).

WARNING

If you move back home, your old friends may not be the same. But if they *are* the same, and joining the military was a good excuse to get away from them so you could make something of yourself, avoiding reconnecting with them is in your best interest.

No matter where you end up, your employer doesn't care what you do outside normal work hours; you have no recall formations, mandatory 10k "fun runs" on Saturday mornings, or groups of people living on your street who wear the same uniform you do. Your social life may suffer, at least until you actively try to make new friends, and the stress from it all can torpedo you into self-isolation.

The American Psychiatric Association, as well as a host of medical professionals, say that loneliness is detrimental to your health. It can cause your stress hormones and blood pressure to rise, disrupt your sleep (which can contribute to many illnesses), and increase your risk of having a heart attack. But the definition of *loneliness* isn't just being alone; loneliness is the distress you feel when your relationships and social involvement aren't what you want them to be.

Unfortunately, the loneliest vets are also the least likely to reach out. The VA published a study in 2018 that said as much — and in recent years, it has been struggling to try to meet vets' needs for post-transition social interaction. (That's part of the reason the VA calls you six months and a year after your separation for a check-in.)

Don't try to fill the empty space you feel with drinking, staying on the Internet until the wee hours of the morning, or anything that may be unhealthy for you. Veterans have much higher rates of alcohol abuse than the general public does, and toxic veterans' groups on social media sites can suck you into an us-versus-them mentality (with "them" being civilians, other veterans who weren't in combat arms, or anyone else) while giving you the illusion of the camaraderie you miss.

REMEMBER

If you take only one thing from this book, let it be this: Don't let yourself get into a cycle of loneliness, even if you think nobody will understand you. No matter how unique your experiences have been, there are always at least some people who will understand you. Look at it this way: You can personally understand other people's unique experiences, even if you haven't been through them yourself. In the same way, others can understand and care about yours.

If you do become lonely and isolated, take active steps to recognize it and get out. Get a gym membership, meet some of your new coworkers for drinks after work on a Friday, rescue a shelter pet, and join a real-life (rather than social media) veterans' group, which I cover in the following section. Call the Veterans Crisis Line at 800-273-8255 and press 1 or get in touch with the combat veterans at 877-WAR-VETS (877-927-8387) who will shoot the breeze with you or discuss issues you experienced during your service.

Being Part of Veterans' Groups

A number of veterans' groups are open to you, including the Veterans of Foreign Wars, the Disabled American Veterans, the American Legion, and several others that I discuss in Chapter 10. These organizations often do charitable work, perform veteran outreach to help struggling vets reconnect, and provide valuable services and information that can help you in your civilian life. For example, veterans service organizations, or VSOs, offer all kinds of services for vets and their dependents. (Who would've guessed?) Some VSOs provide networking opportunities, job fairs, housing assistance, access to legal help and counseling, and help filing VA claims and appealing unfavorable decisions. You can find literally dozens of VSOs (if you don't believe me, take a look at Chapter 10), and the Department of Defense maintains a current list of organizations that may be able to help you at www.defense.gov/Resources/Veteran-Support-Organizations.

Some organizations have motorcycle clubs, places to sit and have a beer with other veterans, and even auxiliaries for your spouse to join. When you settle in after separating from service, do a little research to see what joining one takes.

TIP

Be aware that many veterans' groups and organizations charge dues. However, a significant number of them offer fee waivers, grants, and other ways you can participate.

Reaching out When Life Is Ugly: Legal, Addiction, and Housing Concerns

Sometimes life takes an unexpected turn and all you can do is try to pick up the pieces. Even if you're going through something big and life-changing, resources are available to help you get back on track.

Dealing with legal issues and incarceration

A *justice-involved veteran* is a veteran who meets any of the following criteria:

>> Has had frequent crisis contact with local law enforcement

>> Has been locked up in a local jail for brief periods of time for offenses that don't result in prison time

>> Is being monitored by the local court system

Justice-involved and incarcerated veterans may be eligible for VA benefits, including disability compensation, pension, education and training, healthcare, and life insurance. However, incarceration may affect some of the benefits you receive.

Disability compensation

VA disability compensation payments are reduced if you're convicted of a felony and imprisoned for more than 60 days. After you're released, your payments may be reinstated based on the severity of your service-connected disability at that time. If you're released to participate in a work-release program or live in a half-way house (sometimes called *residential reentry centers*), your compensation payments aren't reduced.

Pension payments

If you receive a VA pension and are imprisoned in a federal, state, or local penal institution for conviction of a felony or misdemeanor, your pension payments are terminated effective the 61st day after imprisonment. The VA resumes your payments when you're released as long as you meet eligibility requirements.

REMEMBER

All or part of the money the VA isn't paying you may be given to your spouse or children, or your dependent parents, on the basis of individual need.

Education benefits

If you're incarcerated for a misdemeanor (but not a felony), you can receive full monthly education benefits if you're otherwise entitled. Additionally, convicted felons who live in halfway houses or who are participating in work-release programs can still receive full monthly benefits.

If you're incarcerated for a felony, you may use your education benefit to pay only the costs of tuition, fees, and necessary supplies. If another federal or state agency pays for all of your educational costs, the VA doesn't make payments; however, if another government agency pays for only part of the cost, the VA can pick up the tab on the rest.

VA medical care

You don't forfeit your eligibility for VA medical care when you're convicted of a crime. However, the VA can't provide hospital or outpatient care to incarcerated veterans; the only thing it can do is provide care after you're unconditionally released from a penal institution.

The VA's Health Care for Re-Entry (HCRV) program provides a number of services for veterans who are returning home after incarceration, such as pre-release assessments and referrals to medical, mental health, and social services (including employment services). It also offers short-term case-management assistance upon your release.

The Veterans Justice Outreach Program

The Veterans Justice Outreach Program, or VJO, is in place to help incarcerated and justice-involved veterans access VA services and benefits. Though the VA can't provide legal services apart from holding periodic free legal clinics on VA campuses, the VJO's specialists can connect you with local legal resources that may help you, as well as create a reentry plan so you can be successful when you're released. You can find the most current list of the VJO's local Veterans Justice Specialists, or VJSs, in the "Contacts" section of its website at www.va.gov/homeless/vjo.asp.

Facing down addiction

The VA provides help with addiction and substance use issues, including tobacco, alcohol, illegal drugs, and prescription medications. However, in most cases, you must apply and be approved for VA healthcare to get help. If your substance abuse is related to depression or post-traumatic stress from your time in the military, or if your military service aggravated your post-traumatic stress, be sure to include that on your application.

If you qualify for VA healthcare, the services you receive depend on your needs. You may receive medically managed detox, drug substitution therapies (such as methadone and buprenorphine), counseling and therapy, intensive outpatient treatment, and residential care.

You may still qualify for some level of addiction help from the VA if you served in a combat zone. You can get free private counseling, alcohol and drug assessment, and other forms of support at one of the VA's hundreds of Vet Centers across the country. Additionally, the VA provides several self-help resources at www.mentalhealth.va.gov/mentalhealth/get-help/index.asp.

TIP

Your help doesn't have to come from the VA, though. Military OneSource (www.militaryonesource.mil) can help you with nonmedical counseling, and you can visit the Substance Abuse and Mental Health Services Administration's website at www.samhsa.gov to find facilities near you. You can also call the National Helpline at 800-662-HELP (4357) for treatment referral and information 24 hours a day, 7 days a week. The National Helpline may be able to point you toward free and low-cost programs in your area, including those run by your state. Many states also provide specialized addiction help for veterans at little or no cost to you.

Getting a hand up from homelessness

The Department of Veterans Affairs provides some services to homeless veterans and those in danger of becoming homeless. Every VA Regional Office and VA Medical Center has a Homeless Veterans Outreach Coordinator who can help you determine what benefits you qualify for, help you apply for them, and refer you to other organizations that may be able to help.

REMEMBER

If you're homeless, unsheltered, or in danger of losing your home, call the National Call Center for Homeless Veterans at 877-4AID-VET (877-424-3838) for immediate help.

Housing assistance

The VA can connect you with federal housing programs that support you and your family through the U.S. Department of Housing and Urban Development and VA Supportive Housing Program, or HUD-VASH. This program combines HUD housing vouchers with the VA's supportive services to help you find and keep permanent housing. As part of the VA's Housing First Program, you're also eligible for access to healthcare and other supports that help you stay on your feet. You can learn how to apply by calling 877-4AID-VET; a trained responder can connect you with the homeless program's point of contact at the nearest VA facility.

Employment assistance

The VA offers employment programs such as these for homeless veterans:

>> **The Homeless Veterans Community Employment Services (HVCES):** This service, provided by formerly homeless veterans who have been trained as Vocational Rehabilitation Specialists, or VRSs, offers vocational assistance, job development and placement, and ongoing support. You can discover how to participate in this program by visiting www.va.gov/homeless/hvces.asp.

>> **Compensated Work Therapy (CWT):** This national vocational program provides three programs to help you get a job: Sheltered Workshop, Transitional Work, and Supported Employment. Veterans in CWT are paid at least federal or state minimum wage, whichever is higher. Find out how to participate in this program at www.va.gov/health/cwt or by visiting your nearest Vet Center.

>> **Vocational Rehabilitation and Employment (VR&E):** This program helps vets with service-connected disabilities prepare for, find, and keep jobs. When you participate in VR&E, you get a comprehensive rehabilitation evaluation to determine your skills, abilities and interests; employment services such as assistance finding and keeping a job; and access to on-the-job training, apprenticeship, and other work experiences.

Foreclosure assistance

If you have a VA loan and have a tough time making your mortgage payments, the VA may be able to help you by offering you a repayment plan, special forbearance, loan modification, or additional time to arrange a sale. Contact the VA and your loan servicer for more information on these programs.

Community Resource and Referral Centers

Community Resource and Referral Centers, or CRRCs, can help you locate community-based organizations for help finding a home or avoiding homelessness if you're at risk. You may be able to identify a CRRC in your area by visiting the VA's directory at www.va.gov/HOMELESS/Crrc.asp.

Supportive Services for Veteran Families

The Supportive Services for Veteran Families, or SSVF, program is designed to rapidly rehouse homeless veteran families and prevent homelessness for those at risk. You can visit a Vet Center or call 877-4AID-VET to find out whether a VA professional can refer you to this program.

Domiciliary Care for Homeless Veterans

The Domiciliary Care for Homeless Veterans (DCHV) program is residential care (meaning live-in) for sheltered and unsheltered veterans with multiple challenges, illnesses, or rehabilitative care needs. The VA maintains 2,400 beds for DCHV care across 47 locations in the United States, and you can call 877-4AID-VET to find out whether you qualify.

Health Care for Homeless Veterans

The Health Care for Homeless Veterans (HCHV) program provides case management and residential treatment services that can help you transition from living on the street or in an institutional setting (such as a prison, halfway house, or hospital) to a stable housing environment. You can ask your local VA's Homeless Coordinator for more information on this program or call 877-4AID-VET to get the help you need.

Mental health help and substance abuse interventions

The VA can provide several types of interventions that help homeless veterans deal with mental health issues, including residential and outpatient care. It provides specialized addiction treatments such as cognitive behavioral therapy and contingency management, which encourages sobriety. It also provides treatment for post-traumatic stress in medical and nonmedical settings for homeless vets.

HUD Office of Housing Counseling

If you're facing foreclosure and are in danger of homelessness, you can contact HUD's Office of Housing Counseling in your state to find out what programs you may be eligible for. Visit www.hud.gov/program_offices/housing/sfh/hcc for more info.

DOL Homeless Veteran Reintegration Program

The Department of Labor, in partnership with the VA, operates the Homeless Veteran Reintegration Program, or HVRP. This program serves veterans who can't obtain help through the VA and other organizations because of severe post-traumatic stress, long histories of substance abuse, serious psychosocial problems, and legal issues, and those who are HIV-positive. Call 877-4AID-VET and ask about the HVRP to find out more about this program.

Doing an About-Face: What If You Want to Get Back In?

A lot of veterans get out of the military, get a few doses of civilian reality, and want to get right back in. That's totally normal, and if you're eligible to do so, go for it. Rejoining the military can give you more time to prepare for life on the outside, whether that means getting a college degree, lining up a higher-paying job, or working toward a military retirement.

When you rejoin the military, you're considered *prior service*. You may be able to join in your old job, but in some cases, you may have to choose a new job. (You'll definitely have to choose a new job if you enter a different branch.) Each branch has its own requirements for prior service candidates, and you must meet them all or get a waiver if you expect them to let you in.

REMEMBER

One of the biggest challenges many veterans experience with rejoining the military is the reenlistment eligibility (RE) code on their DD-214; flip over to Chapter 4 for more information on those. If your RE Code is 1, you should be good to go; if it's a 2, you may have some challenges; if it's a 3, you probably need a waiver, and if it's a 4, you're ineligible for reenlistment in any branch.

The other big challenge you may face is your branch's *prior service quota*. Every branch has its own limit on how many prior service candidates it's allowed to take.

You may have to repeat basic training, attend a specialized course for prior-service candidates, or participate in a whole new basic training experience (such as when you join the Marine Corps after being in any other branch).

The best way to find out whether rejoining the military is right for you (or is even possible) is to talk to a recruiter at an Armed Forces Career Center. Only a recruiter can assess your specific situation and let you know whether getting back in is an option (and whether you need to jump through hoops to do it).

5

The Part of Tens

Get the inside scoop on finding a civilian job that pays the bills.

Tally up financial tips to prepare you for life after the military.

Put together a successful VA claim and figure out where to go for help with your application.

Chapter **22**

Ten Tips to Help You Find a Job

F inding a job is probably one of your main priorities when you leave the military, but it's not as easy as it seems when your "must-have" date is far out on the horizon. As you count down the days to your pending unemployment, you can use these ten tips to help you find a job.

Assess Your "Work Wants"

Before you even start looking for a job, take the time to figure out what makes you happy at work. Maybe you want to be outside, you enjoy helping people, or you want to work with children. Or perhaps you prefer to work with your hands, organize paperwork, or plan big events. Although you don't have to get your "forever" job right after you leave the military, aiming for a job doing something you enjoy (or that you at least don't hate) is a good idea — particularly during your post-military adjustment period. Narrow your job search based on how it fits around the things you like to do.

Search Early and Search Often

Start your job search as soon as you're certain you're getting out of the military. You don't have to apply for jobs a year out — many of them won't still be open by the time your contract expires — but keeping an eye on companies that you want to work for, salaries and hourly pay for jobs you may like, and job descriptions for things that interest you keeps you primed for finding the perfect opportunity. When you're getting down to the wire and have only a few months before you leave the military, expect to spend two to three hours a day on reading job listings, tailoring your resume, and writing compelling cover letters.

Create Tailored Resumes for Every Job

Tweak your resume for each job you apply to. Carefully read every job listing to find out what the employer is really looking for, and make sure the employer's *keywords* (important words that indicate particular skills) are tucked wherever they read well in your resume. I cover resumes in more detail in Chapter 7.

TIP

Save a working copy of your resume on your computer so making changes is easier. If you use job listing websites to search for employment, copy and paste your resume into each site's resume builder. That helps hiring managers focus on the parts they care about most, and it helps ensure that you don't leave out anything important.

Make Your Cover Letter Count

Personalize every cover letter you write. Use an attention-grabbing hook at the beginning that shows the hiring manager you're not just another piece of paper in the pile, and then prove that you did your research on the company by bringing up something you know. Keep it simple and brief, and sign off by letting the hiring manager know you're interested in the position and look forward to exploring your options. For more on cover letters, head to Chapter 7.

Network like Crazy

Sometimes it's all about who you know, and having been in the military, you know a lot of people. Make sure you let your friends, family, and acquaintances know you're in the market for a new job, because you may be surprised at how many people have connections to open positions. Get out there and meet new people, too, whether that means going to in-person or online networking events, connecting with professionals on LinkedIn, or joining a veterans service organization. Chapter 10 has info on networking.

Dress to Impress at Job Interviews

Don't put on your most formal outfit to attend job interviews, but do choose what your grandma would call your "Sunday best." As I explain in Chapter 11, a collared shirt (with a tie if appropriate) and jacket or a pantsuit or conservative skirt and dress shirt is generally the way to go. However, you should choose what's appropriate for the job; don't wear a three-piece suit to an interview for a job working construction.

Charlie Mike without Military Jargon

Steer clear of military acronyms and slang during job interviews (see Chapter 11). Few people outside the military and veteran communities know what an MRAP, ACOG, or OPORD is, and most interviewers won't understand (or appreciate) common slang like *pogey bait, leg,* or *snivel gear.* Focus on explaining things in civilian terms. You may want to practice your interview skills with someone you know who can stop and redirect you when you use terminology a civilian won't understand. (Even if you don't use much military jargon, practicing for interviews is *always* a good idea.)

Follow Up with Interviewers

After you land an interview — unless you accidentally light a desk on fire or something else goes horribly wrong — you should follow up with the person who spent their time with you. Send a thank-you note after you leave the interview, and send an email to confirm that you're still interested in the position after the projected decision date has passed. If you don't hear back, sending another follow up to ask for an update is okay.

Look for Work on Multiple Websites

Remember to turn every stone when you're searching for a job. Look on federal and state agency websites (check the menu for a "Careers" or "Work for Us" section), or on private companies' sites if you're not interested in continuing your partnership with Uncle Sam. Some websites allow you to set up a search and receive notifications when jobs meeting your criteria hit the market, so if you find the opportunity, use it.

Consider Different Avenues

You don't have to limit yourself to traditional jobs. You need to bring in an income, so consider applying for one-time or short-term gigs, working with a temp agency, or becoming a freelancer and advertising your services if you're having a tough time finding something you want to do. Think about becoming a ride-share or delivery driver or a handy-person. Or look at changing plans entirely and going to school full time by using your GI Bill (and getting a housing allowance to supplement your income from a part-time job).

Chapter **23**

Ten Tips to Help You Score a Job

Finding a job is (or should be) one of your top priorities after you decide to leave the military. The civilian world has near-infinite career possibilities, but you have to compete with others in order to land a great (or even good) job. You can get help with your resume in Chapter 7, figure out where to dig up highly sought-after government jobs in Chapter 9, and discover how to dazzle interviewers in Chapter 11. In the meantime, these ten tips can help you find and get a job that pays the bills and keeps you reasonably happy. May the odds be ever in your favor.

Stay Flexible

Before you start your job hunt, build a little flexibility into your search. Maybe you *only* want to be a restaurant manager, an executive assistant, or roofer, but if you stay flexible and look for related or similar jobs, you have a better chance at finding something that lines up with your goals. And many jobs have the opportunity for advancement. If you can't be a restaurant manager because you lack experience or can't find any open positions, starting as a server or bartender and working your way up may be the best path for you. If that's not your cup of tea, broaden your search to include other types of jobs that have potential.

Use Your Veterans' Preference

When you're applying for jobs that ask whether you have military service under your belt, even if you're not too thrilled about your former career, let people know. Employers tend to automatically assume that vets understand the importance of teamwork, are prepared for anything, are focused and goal-oriented, and have valuable leadership skills that many civilian employees don't. And if you're an honorably discharged vet applying for government jobs, use your point preference to get an edge; if it comes down to you and another equally qualified non-veteran candidate, you'll get the job thanks to your military history.

Stay Away from the Us-versus-Them Mentality

Civilians do things a little differently than what you're used to, but that doesn't mean you're pitted against each other. Don't get caught up in an us-versus-them mindset; it's toxic and unhealthy, and it doesn't do you any favors. In fact, it can be detrimental to your job search, your ability to be happy at work, and even your ability to keep your job. Sure, you have a military background; just don't let it go to your head and prevent you from moving forward. (That goes for your work *and* personal lives.)

Work Hard at Civilianizing Yourself

Military life is all-encompassing. You live and breathe acronyms, straight-to-the-point communication, and constant connection to people you work with. (If someone doesn't text you at 2 a.m. at least once a week, you're doing it wrong.) But when you walk out of the DD-214 office with an official military discharge, you're no longer part of that world — and that means you have to work hard to assimilate back into civilian culture. I know it sounds hard, but remember this: You were part of that culture for at least 17 years before you joined the military, and you can be a successful member of it now.

That means realizing that dark humor isn't as well-appreciated outside as it is inside the military, and neither is creative use of four-letter words. Military jargon means nothing to most civilians, and some of it may actually be offensive to them. And because the military taught you to be tough (and thick-skinned), understanding that civilians haven't developed a hard-candy shell like you have can take a little work. Do yourself — and the civilians in your life — a favor and work on reeling things in a little bit. (And please stop carrying a dip spit bottle with you everywhere.)

Write an Effective Resume

Hiring managers are busy; a lot of people are jockeying for jobs right now (especially the good jobs). That may mean that a single hiring manager scrolls through dozens of resumes in one day, and after the first few, they all start to look the same. Do your best to make yours stand out by customizing it for each job you apply for, putting your most relevant experience front-and-center, hitting all the keywords you find in the job description, and keeping it brief. And remember, your resume isn't your autobiography; it's a quick look at how awesome you are and what a great asset you'd be to the company. Your goal with your resume is to land an interview.

Figure out How to Be a "People Person"

Networking with others can help launch your new career, but in order to network successfully (and to be successful in general), you have to work on how to be a *people person*. That means ensuring that you're a good, active listener; that you approach others with a "what-can-I-do-for-you" attitude; and that you genuinely care about what happens to other people.

Pay Attention to Your Body Language

Whether you're networking or sitting in a job interview, your body language says a lot more about you than you think it does. Avoid crossing your arms, squaring your jaw, and giving people the death glare when they ask you questions. (Weird — it's almost as if you saw those body expressions often in the military.) Instead, keep your face relaxed, your palms open, and your posture straight but not rigid. If you're at attention, you've taken it a smidge too far. Lean in when someone is talking to you, and make eye contact (but not the intense, weird kind that civilians find a little scary). Give people a warm, firm handshake, but not so firm that they're pretty sure you're about to put them in the rear naked choke.

Use the Career Programs Available to You

As a veteran, you're entitled to use a wide range of programs that can help you prepare for civilian work and find a job. So use them! It all starts with your branch's Transition Assistance Program, or TAP. Go early and go often to all the classes you're allowed to take. (As I explain in Chapter 2, Department of Defense Instruction 1332.35, Section 5.3(a)(j) says that the military is responsible for releasing you during duty hours to complete TAP for the full 24-hour period of each workshop or briefing day, as well as the 12 hours immediately preceding and following each workshop or briefing.) You also have free access to world-class job training opportunities, apprenticeships, and veterans' preference for government jobs. All you have to do is show up in the right place at the right time (but not necessarily in the right uniform), and you can get a tremendous amount of help from government and civilian organizations.

Don't Be Above a Job

There's no way around it: Some jobs suck. But if the one thing standing between your eating and going hungry is a sucky job, you need to find the intestinal fortitude to say yes to the employer who's offering it to you. You don't have to stay at any job forever; civilians can quit as soon as something better comes along. Nothing is wrong with taking a job that you don't like or that doesn't pay as much as you want if it keeps your family off the streets. I'm not telling you to "settle" by any means, but I *am* telling you that I know the military taught you that doing unpleasant things is sometimes necessary (NTC, anyone?). You already know that completing the mission is more important than what you had to do to get there.

Ask for Help

Because you're a veteran, help is available to you during every step of the employment process. You have access to career prep programs, resume-writing help, job search assistance, and so much more through the VA, the Department of Labor, the Small Business Administration, Military OneSource, and a handful of other government agencies, as well as through several civilian and veterans' organizations. When you're stuck on something, whether it's how to write a cover letter or how to act or dress during an interview, someone is always waiting in the wings to help you.

Chapter **24**

Ten Tips on Filing a Successful Claim with the VA

Filing a disability claim with the VA seems like a nightmare, particularly if you listen to horror stories from people who have done it. But I'm going to let you in on a little secret: Although the VA isn't perfect (or fast), many — but certainly not all — people who have horror stories about filing a claim with the VA don't listen to advice, file the appropriate forms, or provide the right type of documentation. I'm not saying the VA will approve your claim, even if you check all the right boxes, but I am saying that you improve your chances for filing a successful claim if you get professional help and follow every instruction to the letter. These ten tips can help you file your claim properly the first time so you don't get engaged in a long, drawn-out back-and-forth with the VA trying to prove that you're entitled to disability payments.

Apply for a Rating Early

Current servicemembers can apply for a disability rating and file a pre-discharge claim while they're still being paid by the military. You may use the Benefits Delivery at Discharge (BDD) program to streamline the process and avoid interruptions in payment if you have fewer than 180 but more than 90 days before discharge, are available to go to VA exams for 45 days after filing a claim, and can provide copies of service treatment records to the VA when you file.

Use a VSO

Several veterans service organizations, or VSOs, have expertly trained reps who can help you file a claim with the VA. In order to become an accredited VA representative, these individuals must pass an exam, submit to a background check, and take continuing education courses. Some of the most popular federally chartered VSOs, including American Veterans (AMVETS), Disabled American Veterans (DAV), The American Legion, and Veterans of Foreign Wars (VFW) can help you prepare your claim, track it, and act as a liaison between you and the VA. If the VA returns an unfavorable decision, your rep can help you file an appeal and continue dealing with the agency on your behalf. And even better, using a VSO to help file your claim is free; you don't even have to be a member of an organization to use its services.

Understand What's Required for Your Claim

When you make a claim with the VA, you're responsible for showing that you're entitled to a disability payment. You must show that you have the condition you're claiming (usually through a doctor's diagnosis) and that your condition was caused or aggravated during your time in the military. For example, it's possible to get VA compensation for things like scars, but only if you can meet the right criteria. (The VA rates scars based on things like pain, stability, size, shape, limitation of motion, and deepness. They're actually the sixth-most common service-connected disabilities.)

You can usually get the specific requirements for any type of claim from your VA Regional Office (and you can find a list of VA Regional Offices in the Appendix). If you have a certainly unwinnable claim (such as a tiny scar on the side of your pinky finger that doesn't cause you any trouble), save yourself the trouble of filing it and getting a rejection. If you're not sure whether a claim is *compensable* (meaning that you can be paid for it), talk to a VSO for help as I discuss in the preceding section.

Use the Right Forms

Like the military, the VA runs on paperwork. You must use the right forms to file your claim; if you don't, the VA may deny your claim or reject the whole application, which means you either have to appeal or start from scratch. You can find out which forms you need to file by checking the VA's website.

Back up Your Application with Facts

Showing the VA that you're entitled to disability payments is up to you, and a doctor's diagnosis is a good start. You should also send in any other evidence you have to increase your chances of success. You may want to include your service record, witness statements, military medical records, and any other information that can help the VA make a favorable decision.

Write a Statement in Support of Your Claim

Pen your own letter on VA Form 21-4138, Statement in Support of a Claim. You can use this form to write any information you want the VA to know as it makes a decision on your claim, including information that fills in the gaps about medical treatments you received in the past. For example, if you were diagnosed with post-traumatic stress in the military but never sought treatment, use this form to explain why — as well as how not receiving treatment has affected you. You can write separate statements for different claims or lump them all into one; you may also want to group together similar claims and keep some separate.

Go to Your C&P Exam

The VA may choose to schedule you for a Compensation and Pension (C&P) exam. If it does, you need to show up. A C&P exam is when a VA professional meets with you and decides whether your claimed condition likely really did come from your time in the military, as well as the degree to which it's disabling you. If you don't show up for your C&P exam, the VA may deny your claim outright.

Be Prepared for All Your Exams

Every VA exam is different, so know what to expect before you show up. Call the provider's office or the VA to find out what each exam will cover so you know how to explain the condition and how it's a direct result of your service. Bring all your medical documentation with you to your VA exams, and know the technical terminology for whatever ails you.

Meet All Your Deadlines

After the VA receives your claim, it may request additional information. You usually only have a limited time to provide that information or respond with questions. If you don't provide the information the VA needs, or if you don't ask for an extension, the VA may choose to deny your claim.

Don't Give Up

Keep tabs on your application's status and don't give up. Dealing with the VA can be time-consuming and frustrating, but your disability pension is on the line, so don't let it go because you're upset about the way the VA is handling your claim. You can contact a VSO for help at any time during the process; even if you've already filed your claim and feel like you're getting the runaround, it's not too late to get professional assistance. Read more about VSO help in the earlier section "Use a VSO."

Appendix

Civilian Terms for Military Experience

This appendix is your go-to resource for getting acquainted with civilian terminology you can use in your resume or in conversation, as well as a helpful key for translating common military terms into civilian ones.

Cozying up to Civilian Terminology

Straightforward, concise communication is essential in the military. Think about the last nine-line you sent up, the last award you wrote, or the last evaluation report or counseling statement you put together. Brevity matters in the military, and that often means steering clear of flowery language. However, civilians tend to use more words to say the same things, and as a brand-new veteran, that takes some getting used to. Tables A-1 through A-5 cover terminology you can use to describe your skills on your resume or in conversation.

TABLE A-1   # Basic Skills

Term	Meaning
Active learning	Understanding the implications of new information
Critical thinking	Using logic and reasoning to identify the strengths and weaknesses of alternative solutions, conclusions, and approaches to problems
Learning strategies	Choosing and using training and procedures that are appropriate for the situation
Monitoring	Keeping tabs on and assessing performance (for yourself or others) to make improvements or take corrective action

TABLE A-2   # Social Skills

Term	Meaning
Coordination	Adjusting your actions in relation to other people's actions
Coaching and developing others	Identifying other people's developmental needs and then coaching them, mentoring them, or helping them improve their knowledge or skills
Communicating with supervisors, peers, and subordinates	Providing information to supervisors, coworkers, and subordinates in any manner
Conflict resolution	Handling complaints and settling other people's disputes
Consulting	Providing guidance and expert advice to others on technical, systems-related, or other processes
Coordinating the work and activities of others	Ensuring that members of a group work together to get things done
Developing and building teams	Building cooperation, trust, and respect among team members
Guiding and directing subordinates	Providing instructions, advice, and guidance to people who work beneath you, including personally setting performance standards and monitoring your subordinates' performance
Negotiation	Bringing multiple parties together to reconcile differences
Persuasion	Convincing others to change their behavior, ideas, or thought processes
Social perceptiveness	Being aware of the way others react to things and understanding the reasons behind people's reactions
Training and teaching	Identifying other people's educational needs, developing formal training programs or classes, and teaching or instructing others
Working directly with the public	Dealing with civilians on a regular basis

TABLE A-3 **Technical and Other Skills**

Term	Meaning
Complex problem-solving	Identifying difficult or complex problems, reviewing related information, evaluating and developing options, and implementing solutions
Equipment maintenance	Performing routine maintenance on equipment
Equipment selection	Choosing which tools are appropriate to get the job done
Judgement and decision-making	Considering the costs and benefits of an action to decide what's most appropriate
Operation and control	Controlling equipment or systems
Operation monitoring	Watching machines to ensure they're operating correctly
Operations analysis	Analyzing product requirements to create designs
Performing administrative duties	Performing admin tasks, such as keeping files and processing paperwork
Quality control analysis	Conducting tests and inspections of products, processes, or services to evaluate quality and performance
Systems analysis	Determining the best way for a system to work and considering all your options
Systems evaluation	Identifying measures of system performance and determining how to improve or correct a system's performance
Technology design	Generating or adapting equipment or technology to make either more user-friendly

TABLE A-4 **Resource Management Skills**

Term	Meaning
Management of financial resources	Determining how to spend money to accomplish a task, as well as accounting for the money you spent
Management of material resources	Obtaining and overseeing the appropriate use of equipment, materials, and facilities to accomplish a task
Management of personnel resources	Developing, directing, and motivating people at work, as well as identifying the best people to perform a certain job
Monitoring and controlling resources	Keeping tabs on resources and maintaining control of who uses them (and how they're used), including equipment and building locations
Time management	Managing your own time and others' time

Work Output Skills

Term	Meaning
Controlling machines and processes	Using direct physical activity or other types of control mechanisms to operate machines or processes
Documenting and recording information	Entering, maintaining, transcribing, recording, or storing information
Drafting and specifying technical devices, parts, and equipment	Providing documentation, detailed instructions, or specifications to tell others about how equipment, structures, parts, or devices should be made, assembled, modified, used, and maintained
Repairing and maintaining electronic equipment	Adjusting, calibrating, repairing, servicing, or testing electrical or electronic equipment or machines
Repairing and maintaining mechanical equipment	Adjusting, calibrating, repairing, servicing, or testing mechanical equipment or machines

Translating Military Experience to Civilian Terms

The way you're used to describing your work experience to other military members doesn't cut it in the civilian world, so when you're writing your resume or participating in an interview, switch up your vocabulary. Table A-6 helps you come up with new words to describe military terms civilians may draw a blank on (or that may make them uncomfortable). It doesn't cover acronyms; don't use those at all on your resume or in conversation with a civilian. Simply say what the acronym stands for and explain if necessary. For example, CONUS and OCONUS don't need extra explanation, but PCS, ETS, SHARP, and EFMP definitely do. Use your best judgment.

TABLE A-6 **General Terms**

Military Term	Civilian Term
Barracks or other buildings	Facilities
Casualty	Injured party
COB, COP, or FOB	Base, outpost, or headquarters
Combat	Hazardous conditions
Company	Company (business), department, or section

Military Term	Civilian Term
Counseling statement	Evaluation
Medal	Award
Mission	Task, function, initiative, project, or objective
Military occupational specialty or classification	Career specialty
Noncommissioned officer or NCO	Supervisor, manager
Officer or warrant officer	Supervisor, manager
Permanent change of station or PCS	Relocation
Pro gear or pro mask	Personal protective equipment
SITREP	Situation report, activity report, or data
Squad or platoon	Team or section
Subordinates	Staff, employees, or coworkers
Reconnaissance	Data collection and analysis
Rank	Pay grade, supervisory position, or position within the organization
Regulations	Policies, guidelines, or instructions
TAD or TDY	Business trip
Wire (inside or outside)	On or off the military installation, base, or outpost

Index

C

G

H

jobs *(continued)*
　market
　　considering when job searching, 146–147
　　statistics for civilian employment, 166–167
　personal preferences towards, 365
　placement opportunities, 303–304
　unrealistic vs. realistic, 146–150
　untraditional types of, 368
Joint Services Transcript (JST), 45
Judge Advocate General (JAG), 78–79
justice-involved veterans, 356–357

K

keywords, 366

L

labor union, 167–168
lawful interview questions, 239–241
leased employees, 153
Legal Assistance, 78–79
lenders, 322
lending closet, 77
loans, 274–275, 299, 330–331
loneliness, 354–355

M

Marine Corps
　joining, 215–216
　Transition Program (TRP), 30
　tuition assistance (TA), 54
　Wounded Warrior Regiment, 335
meal breaks, 267
Medicaid, 321
medical records, 60, 70–71
Medicare, 321
mental healthcare
　accepting need for, 345–346
　for homeless veterans, 360
　options for, 61–62
　prioritizing, 71–75

resources for, 39–41
suicide prevention and crisis intervention,
　346–348
mentorship, 271
MGIB (Montgomery GI Bill), 292–294
MGIB-AD (Montgomery GI Bill Active Duty),
　292–293
MGIB-SR (Montgomery GI Bill Selected Reserve),
　293–294
MHA (monthly housing allowance), 289–290
microloans, 274
mid-level jobs, 157–158
military
　associations, 212–216
　civilian employment vs., 150–152
　civilian life vs., 11–13
　humor, avoiding, 257
　investigation, transitioning while under, 26–27
　organizations, 213–215
　records, 44–45
　rejoining, 361
　salary
　　commission pay, 163–164
　　overtime rules, 160–163
　　overview, 159
　　salary and hourly pay, 159–160
　　tax brackets, 165–166
　　for tipped employees, 164–165
　skills on resumes, 122–123
　terminology, 377–381
　translating experience into civilian terms,
　　125–126
Military and Family Life Counseling, 39
Military OneSource, 40, 332
military sexual trauma (MST), 95, 342–343
Military-to-Civilian (MOS) Job Skills Crosswalk, 32
mini-interviews, 230–231
money
　affording rent without BAH, 311–313
　being careful with credit, 321–322
　budgeting, 323
　housing discrimination based on, 313–314
　methods of saving, 46

SE (Supported Employment) program, 107
seasonal employees, 153
security clearances, 196–198
security deposits, 312
SEd (Supported Education) program, 107
Selective Placement Program Coordinator
    (SPPC), 108
self-funding, 273
semi-structured interviews, 223
Senior Executive Service (SES) levels, 194
seniority levels
    entry-level jobs, 156–157
    mid-level jobs, 157–158
    overview, 154
    senior-level jobs, 158–159
separation leave, 22–23
serial interviews, 223–224
service dogs, 339
service organizations, 212–213
Service-Disabled Veterans Life Insurance
    (S-DVI), 339
SES (Senior Executive Service) levels, 194
7(a) loans, 274
severance pay, 19–22
sexual harassment, 262–263
SFL-TAP (Soldier For Life Transition Assistance
    Program), 30
sheltering in place, 65
show cause. See involuntary separation
situation, task, action, result (STAR) method,
    236–237
SkillBridge, 51, 111–112
sliding scale, 73
Small Business Administration (SBA), 36–37,
    273–275
Small Business Innovation Research (SBIR), 274
Small Business Investment Companies (SBIC), 274
small business loans, 273
Small Business Technology Transfer (STTR), 275
SMC (Special Monthly Compensation), 337
SNAP (Supplemental Nutrition Assistance
    Program), 350
social anxiety disorder (SAD), 203

social cues, 201–202
social media, 210–212
Social Security Disability Insurance (SSDI), 341
soft networking event, 209
soft skills, 257
Soldier For Life Transition Assistance Program
    (SFL-TAP), 30
special court-martial, 27
Special Monthly Compensation (SMC), 337
spouses, 41
SPPC (Selective Placement Program
    Coordinator), 108
SSDI (Social Security Disability Insurance), 341, 349
SSE (Supported Self-Employment) program, 107
SSI (Supplemental Security Income), 349
SSVF (Supportive Services for Veteran
    Families), 359
staffing services, 175–176
standard operating procedures, 69
standardized test scores, 285
standing at attention, 234
STAR (situation, task, action, result) method,
    236–237
state laws, 259–260
Statement in Support of Claim form (VA Form
    21-4138), 375
structured interviews, 223
STTR (Small Business Technology Transfer), 275
student loans, 299
Subsidized Stafford Direct loans, 299
substance abuse, 73–74, 357–358, 360
Substance Abuse and Mental Health Services
    (SAMHSA) Administration, 62
summary court-martial, 26
Supplemental Nutrition Assistance Program
    (SNAP), 350
Supplemental Security Disability Insurance
    (SSDI), 349
Supplemental Security Income (SSI), 349
supply stipend, 291
Supported Education (SEd) program, 107
Supported Employment (SE) program, 107
Supported Self-Employment (SSE) program, 107

About the Author

Angie Papple Johnston joined the U.S. Army in 2006. During her second deployment, Angie became her battalion's public affairs representative, covering breaking news from Tikrit to Kirkuk. She has earned a Combat Action Badge, several Army Commendation medals and Army Achievement medals, and numerous accolades for her work in Iraq. Angie also served as the Lead Cadre for the Texas Army National Guard's Recruit Sustainment Program (RSP) before becoming the CBRN noncommissioned officer-in-charge in an aviation battalion in Washington, D.C. She currently resides in South Korea with her husband (a soon-to-retire noncommissioned officer in the U.S. Army); their awesome son, David; and two dogs, Cujo and Achilles (who's named that only so she can say, "Achilles, heel," while he ignores her).

Dedication

In memory of Jon Thompson and all those for whom the war never ended.

Author's Acknowledgments

Thank you, Lindsay Lefevere, for making this possible. You're awesome, and I couldn't imagine anyone putting together better teams and juggling as much as you do. Also, the GG mask gets David into so many great conversations!

Chrissy Guthrie, you're a rockstar, and I'm totally not being dramatic. You are always one step ahead, and I really think you're amazing. Thank you for making everything so easy. I'm watching the Indy 500 next year!

Megan Knoll, thank you for looking at every angle of everything, ever, and making this a better resource for veterans. From pronouns to adding $0.80 to math problems because you know math is my problem, you never miss anything, and I am so grateful for all your help.

Sgt. 1st Class Sherry Dreese, Ret., thank you for your tremendously valuable contributions every step of the way. There's nobody I'd rather have egg-free bibimbap with, either. But for the love of all that's holy, close your drapes.

Mom, Dad, Darl, Tina, and Jesse: I love and miss you guys tremendously, and Mom, I love our Tuesday morning/Monday night calls and making Earth sandwiches with you. Knock, knock, Jesse! (Who's there?) Mom's favorite.

Kathleen Bienenstein and Bonnie Swadling, I love you so much. Thank you for always supporting me and being so smart (and letting it rub off on me).

Publisher's Acknowledgments

Executive Editor: Lindsay Sandman Lefevere

Managing Editor: Michelle Hacker

Editorial Project Manager and Development Editor: Christina N. Guthrie

Copy Editor: Megan Knoll

Technical Editor: SFC(R) Sherry D. Dreese

Proofreader: Debbye Butler

Production Editor: Mohammed Zafar Ali

Cover Image: © AE Pictures Inc./ DigitalVision/ GettyImages.com